THEY ALL DISCOVERED AMERICA

Charles Michael Boland

THEY ALL DISCOVERED AMERICA

Maps and drawings by the author

Garden City, New York
DOUBLEDAY & COMPANY, INC.

Selection from *Up from the Ape* by Earnest Albert Hooton. Revised edition copyright 1946 by the Macmillan Company and used with their permission.

Library of Congress Catalog Card Number 61–12494

Printed in the United States of America

to

JEANNE ELIZABETH

CONTENTS

several hundred years. His son, Snorri, is born here, but the Icelander's proposed colony is dissolved by the Indians and sex problems.

13 FREYDIS [A.D. 1014] 237

In which Leif Ericsson's bastard half-sister visits Vinland with the brothers Helgi and Finnbogi, bringing death on the grand scale to Plymouth.

14 BISHOP ERIC GNUPSSON [A.D. 1121] 247

In which a bishop is sent to Vinland. Nothing is heard of him after his departure from Greenland, but there remains a strong possibility that he left a lasting, though puzzling, memorial to himself in the city of Newport, Rhode Island.

15 QUETZALCOATL [A.D. C. 1010] 265

In which a god comes to the Aztecs, later to the Mayas and Inca. He leaves with each a prophecy of doom.

16 PRINCE MADOC OF WALES [A.D. 1171] 281

In which a peaceable prince, wishing to avoid family unpleasantness, sails to America to find a new home. Pleased with what he finds here, he returns to Wales and solicits colonists. In ten ships, his followers come back to America with him and profoundly influence a certain tribe of Indians.

17 PAUL KNUTSON [A.D. 1355] 301

In which a mission to save Vinland from heathen influences is sent to America. The vast search for the "lost" colony takes the missionaries to Minnesota where they leave a remarkable document recording their presence. The document later becomes the center of a 60-year, still-unended controversy.

18 PRINCE HENRY SINCLAIR AND THE BROTHERS ZENO [A.D. C. 1395] 325

In which a Faroese fisherman makes an unplanned voyage to America. He is given the first guided tour of the eastern

LIST OF ILLUSTRATIONS

Following page 126

Following page 246

PREFACE

THIS BOOK is about the numberless people who discovered and rediscovered America in the 2000 years before Columbus. While there are doubtless more than the 19 groups whose adventures are related here, I have chosen to dwell only upon those whose explorations have been documented in histories other than our own, or whose penetrations of North and South America provided tangible, archaeological evidence of their visits. The reasons why our own historians choose not to include these narratives in histories of the Western Hemisphere, and why archaeologists are reluctant even to comment upon the evidence will be examined in detail in the chapters to follow.

My own interest in this subject goes back to schoolboy days and is marked with the usual peak-and-valley progression normal to such interests, the ultimate peak being reached in the writing of this volume. I first became aware of pre-Columbian exploration of America when I encountered the twelfth-century Welshman, Prince Madoc, in the writings of George Catlin, the famed nineteenth-century artist-explorer. I wondered why Madoc was not included in our American histories. In later years I wondered about other equally fascinating pre-Columbians, and began to learn some of the answers to their seeming unacceptability by historians. As an art student in Philadelphia during the thirties, I spent many hours in the University Museum, where I practiced my own brand of diffusionism. I was intrigued with similarities between Asiatic and Middle American art, and wondered how these remarkable resemblances came to be. I also learned that there existed a branch of archaeology which thought as I did, but which, oddly enough, limited its speculations to comparisons between Asia and America. This branch held that contacts between Asia and America took place long before Columbus, but for some obscure reason, would not admit to contacts between pre-Columbian *Europe* and the Americas.

My interest was brought to its highest peak when, in 1953, I chanced upon a book by Frederick Pohl, who had spent many years trying to solve the riddle of the vikings and their voyages to New England. I began to search for traces of the Northmen myself, and later to search for traces of many of the others whose adventures are recounted here. It was, at best, a part-time effort because of the necessity of earning a living in television, a demanding field, but in 1959 I settled down to the task of producing this book, devoting all of my time to it.

As I brought my manuscript to completion, a most agreeable development occurred in the field of archaeology, and one which may augur well for the heroes of my book. In January 1961, news was announced of the authentication of a Roman head found in Calixahuac, Mexico, under three sealed and undisturbed floors. The head was pronounced that of a well-known type of the second century A.D. The report on this find was read by Dr. Robert Heine-Geldern, a German who has accomplished much in the field of Middle American archaeology. The magazine *Archaeology* called the report sensational, and indeed it is. It marks the first acknowledgment by a recognized authority of pre-Columbian contacts with the Americas by European peoples other than the vikings. In addition to Dr. Heine-Geldern, the head was studied and pronounced genuine by two other distinguished European scientists, Boehringer of Berlin and Kenner of Vienna. Dr. Heine-Geldern has informed me that there is no question of the head's genuineness. He also informed me that while the announcement of the find was read in his report at a meeting of the International Congress of Americanists in Vienna in July 1960, the head itself was actually found, by Mexican archaeologist Garcia Payon, twenty years ago!

Clearly, we can't accuse the Europeans of hasty conclusions. But, importantly, the Roman head, second century A.D., creates a breakthrough which may spur recognition of the other pre-Columbian artifacts abounding in North and South America.

With some optimism, then, I shall proceed to document the adventures of 19 discoverers of America who arrived here well ahead of Columbus. Unfortunately, they have been largely considered—by historians—to be myths and legends. I assure you that they are not, and, with your kind permission, I shall endeavor to remove them from the shadowy recesses they occupy in the file under "L" for "legend," and place them properly in the long procession of discoverers who came to America from Bronze Age times to 1492.

All of these fascinating fellows existed. All visited America before Columbus. All were adventurers, all had great courage. I hope to give most of them names and assist them in gaining a recognition that is rightfully theirs.

There will be no chapter on Columbus other than to mention him in summary. Anything more about the Genoese navigator could only consist of anticlimax. There are still a few people battling out the details of his voyages to the Indies, and I do not propose to complicate it further. Suffice it to say here that Columbus was the last of the true discoverers of America, and it was he who opened the door to its exploration and colonization. Because communications were better in Europe at the time of Columbus's journey, news of his discovery spread like spilled mercury through the courts of the Continent, and the surge was on. Because of the number of people who visited America before Columbus, and because of the records they passed on, it is naïve to believe that the seagoing Italian did not know whither he was bound, and approximately how long it would take him. Those who claim he simply struck out for "India" vastly underrate his shrewdness in plotting his trip across the Atlantic. He knew there was land here . . . and he knew it wasn't India. But he was curious, and desirous of building his fortunes through the fame he reasoned would accompany such a feat. And that's why he came.

The pre-Columbians who visited America fell into four categories: those who came to settle, those who came only to look, those who came by accident, and those who came as missionaries—including a Chinese.

Some told of their adventures personally, some had them documented by others. Some left evidence of their visit, some did not. All were romantics to a degree.

As luck would have it, we don't know the name of the very first discoverer of this, our fair land. But we know where he came from. And we know where he went, and what he did when he arrived. I hope you'll enjoy meeting him . . . and his "legendary" successors.

THEY ALL DISCOVERED AMERICA

CHAPTER 1

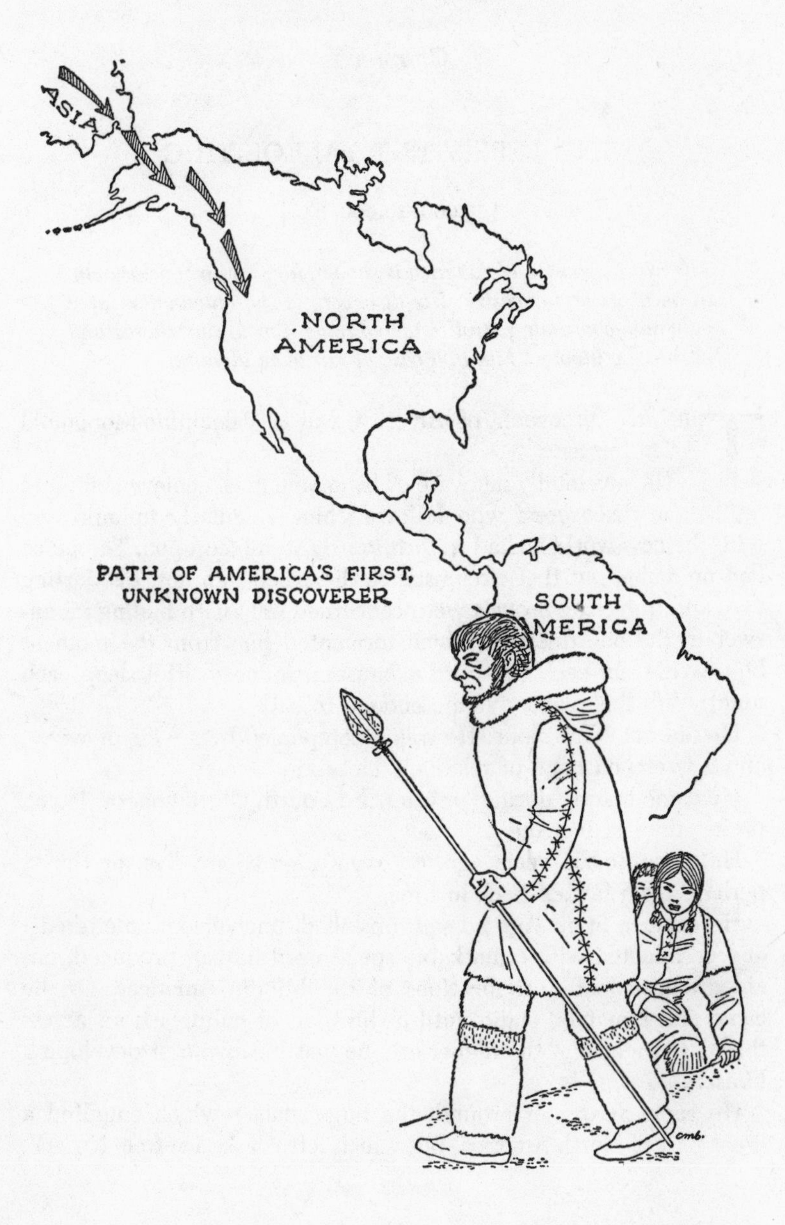
ASIA
NORTH AMERICA
PATH OF AMERICA'S FIRST, UNKNOWN DISCOVERER
SOUTH AMERICA
cmb.

Chapter 1

THE PERSISTENT PALEOLITHIC

[35,000–18,000 B.C.]

The first discoverer of America is shown, however inconclusively, to be of Asiatic ancestry. His discovery is the culmination of a millennia-consuming stroll which brings him to our shores and eventually involves him in a case of mistaken identity.

THE first discoverer of America was a Paleolithic-Mongoloid Asian hunter.

He was totally unaware of his momentous achievement, and unlike the discoverers who followed him, singularly unimpressed with the new world he had so fortuitously stumbled upon. The place had no name, but that circumstance disturbed him not; his darting eyes and quivering nostrils were concerned only with finding an answer to the one question which tormented him from the moment he saw the sun each day until exhaustion induced fitful sleep each night: Will this place give me enough to eat?

He did not come alone. He was accompanied by a wife, or wives, and a wretched band of relatively close kin.

He came before, during, or after the Fourth Glaciation, or, if you prefer, the last Ice Age.

He came 10,000 years ago, or twenty, or twenty-five, or thirty; perhaps even farther back in time.

He came, a Stone Age nomad, unskilled, uncivilized, unlettered—and germinated with remarkable speed until he had produced, unaided, the splendid civilizations of the Middle Americas. Or, he came and remained static until a diffusion of cultures from across the seas taught him the higher arts he was incapable of developing himself.

He came across—or around—the huge glacier which engulfed a great part of North America, but which left Alaska ice-free. No one, at this writing, has suggested that he came *under* it. He might, however, have come *between* two enormous fields of the glacier, since geological evidence indicates that the Mackenzie Valley, stretching down through Canada, was clear during the last glaciation.

Seemingly, the only authoritative statement that can be made about him is that he *did* arrive.

He was unacquainted with the principle of the wheel and he knew not the luxury of animals for draft; his method of transportation, therefore, is self-evident.

The route he traveled bears some reflection, and, in this light, I shall present an extremely brief summary of the discovery of America by the anonymous Paleolithic Hunter, much as it is postulated by modern instructors in the social sciences. I shall dip but briefly into the complex ecology which precipitated this discovery, dwelling primarily on the discovery itself.

Almost from the moment of his first dim awakening to the world about him, man began to wander. (The awakening may have been to the diffused light of an African jungle. The oldest finds of fossil man were discovered in East Africa, in 1932, by Dr. Lewis Leakey. He pried loose, from a 500,000-year-old geologic context, a skull fragment now known as Kanam Man.) Africa, Asia, and Europe fell in his path, and he even reached the isolated continent of Australia, where, intellectually, he came to a dead end.

In one sense, the life he lead was beautifully simple. His energies were devoted to obtaining food, procreating, and rearing his young. In another, his life was extremely difficult, being dedicated primarily to survival. The battle for survival frequently dictates movement of peoples from one place to another for many reasons, and so man took naturally to wandering. In his intellectual evolution, he was developing a peculiar sense that helped set him apart from other animals. Curiosity. He wanted to find out what lay across the next ridge. More importantly, he wanted to know whether what lay across the ridge was good to eat. Sometimes he crossed several ridges without finding anything to eat. Or, he found edibles in the forms of animals larger and more powerful than he, and, unable to subdue them long enough to dine upon them, simply crossed another ridge. If he traversed too many ridges without producing sustenance, we have evidence which shows that he was not above dining on his friends. Fortunately for mankind in general, the earth and its fauna managed to feed him adequately and he didn't cannibalize himself out of existence. As he grew in intelligence and intellect, he acquired the artfulness to make better weapons and create more effective ways to use them. This advancement, coupled with the discovery that he could obtain food from seeds which grew into edible plants led some of him into a primitive agricultural society, more or less permanently based in one area.

But even his new "settlements" had no real permanency. When he found a fertile valley that could sustain himself and his family, he would settle in it until he literally ate himself out of it. In short, the population would grow too big for the valley to sustain, and some, at least, would have to move on. Such a cycle might take three or four hundred years. In this pattern of settle and travel . . . settle and travel . . . one particular branch of man—after thousands of years—reached a point of no return which led to the discovery of America.

In Europe and Asia, some of him went north, for rather obscure reasons, although it is held by some that early man may have produced an "arctic-prone" type who was apparently drawn in hypnotic fashion to the forbidding, barren, unfriendly arctic wastes.

It should be noted that man had thrust north three times in his history, only to be driven back by the glaciers which produced the Ice Ages. It was only at about the time of the fourth Ice Age that he succeeded in maintaining his ground in the arctic regions.

And now we have our discoverer pinpointed.

This northerly oriented Paleolithic pioneer, after a tribal trek that had lasted many thousands of years, ultimately reached the frigid rim of Siberia. Beyond it lay the tortured corrugations of the ice-choked East Siberian Sea. He might have turned west; instead he walked toward the rising sun, inevitably, ineluctably arriving at a geographic point known today as East Cape, situated on the east shore of Siberia on Cape Chukotsk. Between East Cape and the Seward Peninsula, in Alaska, lies the Bering Strait. Its 66-mile breadth is all that separates Asia and North America. But the nomad Paleolithic did not know that he was standing on the shore of Bering Strait, for there was none. What had once been, and was later to be a strait was now a land bridge joining Siberia and Alaska, created by the incredible glacier, which, in forming, had lowered the waters of the earth's oceans enough to expose the sea bottom which lies between the tips of the two continents.

At the split second in history when man stood, shivering, on the edge of East Cape, he became the discoverer of the New World. From that point he negotiated the relatively narrow strip which accomplished the prodigious task of joining two mighty continents. (It was here that the twain met, perhaps in gleeful effort to negate the observation of a latter-day philosopher.) The first Paleolithic Hunter had come to America.

More of his kind, together with their families, followed in successive migrations and systematically began the inhabitation of North and South America.

This means of access to the new world lasted only a few thousand years. Mother Earth, perhaps weary of straining to weld the two continents, heaved a little sigh, and down went the land bridge, allowing the waters of the Arctic and Pacific Oceans to merge with a mighty roar in the resulting strait. It can be argued that the land bridge never went down; that the melting ice of the last glacier simply raised the level of the waters until they submerged the ridge between Asia and America. Perhaps. But I have encountered a suspicion that the strait could have become such in a rather quick, and violent, submersion of the land itself.

Now, North America and its sister to the south sat alone, cut off from the rest of the world in splendid isolation. But the divorcement from Asia did not prevent more waves of immigrants from pouring in. Indeed, it is thought by some that these immigrants continued to come until well into the thirteenth century A.D. They came by crossing the ice which dominates the Bering landscape through a good part of the year, or, having progressed into seagoing peoples, chanced the trip in their flimsy boats. Of the two methods, the ice-crossing is the more logical. Northern man, unlike his southern counterpart, never advanced much beyond a kayak-type of watercraft, and it is reasonable to assume that in waterborne immigrations only a small percentage of those participating made it. The Bering Sea is no place for a tyro tar to be caught in an open, undependable boat. The seas of the Bering can be mountainous; its currents are treacherous.

Crossing the ice would be relatively simple. The first leg of such a journey would take the adventurers to Big Diomede Island, the second leg to Little Diomede. These two rocky islets thrust themselves up to break the icy waters of the Bering Strait from the top of what was once the old land bridge. From Little Diomede, it's only a hop, skip and a slip or two on the ice to Alaska.

The waves of migrants which came into America spread themselves across the two continents in definable bands. The first ones presumably kept traveling south, and later arrivals stopped at the fringes of the earlier settlers' territories. Each band of Asiatics coming in, therefore, was forced to stop a little more northerly than their immediate predecessors. Whatever cultures they developed were brought to their apogees independently. They either expanded the cultures they brought with them, or had them implemented by later arrivals from the common point of departure in Asia. It would appear, then, that the Americas were filled from bottom to top, much as sand fills an urn when shoveled in periodically. Some of the migrants, the Eskimo types, never did penetrate to southerly climes, remaining forever icebound and developing separate and distinct cultures.

In summary, North and South America were invested by Paleolithic-Mongoloid-Asians who came here via a land bridge between Siberia and Alaska. They settled the two continents over a great period of time and did so in recognizably different cultures.

They were mistakenly called "Indians" by the Europeans who came to America in the fifteenth century, but are known as "Amerinds" to anthropology.

That is the theory accepted by the majority of anthropologists today, and that which is taught in our colleges and universities.

But what of the minority?

There exists, heretically, within the hallowed confines of the temple of anthropology, a small, though expanding, group of recalcitrants who disincline from the accepted doctrine. They tolerate the idea of migrations across a land bridge, but hold that the Amerind could only have developed his cultures through the influences of external forces, that is to say contacts with other peoples who came to the Americas with full-blown cultures and ceded them to the Amerind. For some inexplicable reason, they insist on confining all of these pre-Columbian contacts to peoples from across the Pacific. They acknowledge no European influences on the Indians of Middle and South America. This anomalous reasoning, which permits diffusion from the Pacific, but not from the Atlantic, is difficult to accept, particularly in the face of startling similarities to the Egyptian found in frescoes at Bonampak, a remarkable Mayan archaeological site in Chiapas, Mexico. It's even more difficult to accept when one considers the proximity of Europe to North and South America as opposed to the vast distance between Asia and the Americas. The rules of reasoning, as applied here, however, allow only for Pacific crossings.

But impatience is a cardinal sin.

It is enough, for the moment, that the formidably single-tracked theory which bars *all* transoceanic contacts is being shaken even mildly. That I cannot accept the apparent denial of Atlantic crossings in pre-Columbian times will be evident in the chapters to come. Of the many discoverers who reached here before 1492, all but one in my chronicle hail from Europe.

The reluctance to recognize the possibility of Atlantic voyages to America prior to the fifteenth century may stem from a fear of guilt by association. Some of the "wildest" theories extended on the origins of the American Indian emanated from those who gave him roots in Europe, Egypt, or Palestine. In the sixteenth century, for example, a benign old Spanish bishop, Bartolomeo de las Casas, horror-stricken at the treatment of the Aztecs, et al, by the Conquistadores, dedicated his life to saving the Indians from bondage and extermination. In so doing, he virtually became one with them and was given frequently to speculating on their beginnings. He finally came to the conclusion that they were descendants of the Ten Lost Tribes of Israel. His belief found many adherents. It was so intriguing to Viscount Edward King, an intense Britisher known more widely as Lord Kingsborough, that he devoted several years, and all of his money to substantiate Bishop de las Casas' theory. The task literally killed him. The multitudinous volumes which comprised his work were published at a frightful cost and so prohibitive was the price of the finished work that virtually no one could afford to buy it. The exhausted Kingsborough, whose work—apart from the untenable theory—is considered a masterpiece of Middle American history, died in a debtor's prison in 1837.

Other Spanish clergymen decided that the Toltec god, Quetzalcoatl, whom you will meet in chapter 15, was St. Thomas Aquinas, come to preach to the Indians, while others thought him actually to be the Messiah. A latter-day postulator declared him to be none other than Noah, and yet another reasoned that he was a shipwrecked viking.

G. Elliot Smith insisted that all Middle American culture came out of Egypt, and a missionary, Pedro Font, held loosely to the same idea. The Greeks came in for their share of speculation, as did the Phoenicians.

But there were insurgents even among these theoreticians. The Spaniards Ameghino and Galindo went off on another tack. Man originated in Argentina, Ameghino insisted, and it was from there that the world was populated. Galindo, according to Prescott, took the same view, but placed the cradle of humanity in Mexico, whence it spread to China and later to Europe.

I hesitate to dismiss Ameghino and Galindo abruptly. There is something vaguely disturbing about their idea. There are quite a number of bugs in the doctrine which categorically states that the American Indian originated in Asia. The greatest, and the only one I shall treat on here, is the language enigma. Try as they might, no anthropologist and no philologist has yet been able to tie the more than 1500 dialects of the American Indian into any Old World language. Oddly enough, the only similarities between speech in the New World and any other area on earth exist between the Amerinds and the Polynesians. In 1947, Thor Heyerdahl, an imaginative, but scientific Norwegian, proved that migrations from South America to the Pacific islands could, and very likely did, take place in remote times. He sailed the famous raft, Kon-Tiki, across the Pacific, from east to west, to demonstrate that such voyages were entirely possible. For power, he depended solely on the winds and the Humboldt Current. Despite the importance of his contributions, he has received nothing but bitter attacks from most anthropologists. His findings are derided and to illustrate by how much, the Peabody Institute is now readying an expedition to go to Indochina and sail from there to Polynesia, to prove that the colonization of the Pacific islands was from the *other* direction.

Such is the plight of the imaginative anthropologist. Heyerdahl's voyage was partially precipitated by the word similarities noted above. But, instead of speculating on them from his desk, he went forth and demonstrated that the islands could have been populated by Americans from the south. For his pains, derision.

And the battle rages.

The latest scholar to enter the fray is Louis A. Brennan, who, in *No Stone Unturned,* claims American origins for the Solutrean Culture in Europe. The Solutreans, it seems, appeared suddenly from nowhere about 9000 years ago. They had no bone implements, they had no art; they flourished for about 3000 years and disappeared as suddenly as they had come. Mr. Brennan wonders whether or not a land bridge may have existed across the Atlantic in remote times, and, beyond that heresy, wonders whether it could be in any way related to the "mythical" lost Atlantis. To make matters worse, he cites a report written for the Swedish geographical magazine *Ymer,* written by a Dr. Rene Malaise, of the Riksmuseum in Stockholm. The report, picked up by the *New York Times* on September 22, 1956, treats on the work of oceanographer P. W. Kolbe. Dr. Kolbe, it seems, while taking sediment cores in the Atlantic, at a depth of 12,000 feet, brought up some diatom shells of a fresh-water type. The surprising diatoms, according to the *Times,* could only be explained by assuming the presence of a mid-Atlantic ridge, once thrust up above the surface, and containing a fresh-water lake, from which the diatoms were obtained. This ridge, existing only ten to twelve thousand years ago, wedded Europe to Greenland.

Not content with scientific substantiation for a land bridge idea, Mr. Brennan then proceeds to wallop archaeologists in general for their unaccountable loathing of transatlantic contacts with the Americas. With great glee, Brennan chortles that a "mid-Atlantic ridge, if proved, would reorient American archaeology by 180 degrees." A terrifying thought, even to the most liberal of archaeologists.

The origins of the Amerind, it would appear, have been given a great deal of thought, providing many interesting, though inconclusive, theories explaining his presence in the Western Hemisphere.

Since it is difficult to shape a definitive statement clearly setting forth the origins of our Amerind, let us examine available data which might tell us when he arrived.

For many years prior to, and for several decades after the turn of the century, anthropologists taught their students that the Amerind had come to North America somewhere between 3000 and 3500 years ago. This doctrine was wholly accepted by all but the few doubters who normally dwell within any scientific camp. Foremost proponent of this theory was Dr. Ales Hrdlicka, then of the American Museum of Natural History in New York. He was interested in skulls, and had amassed large quantities of skulls (and bones) and knowledge about them. From 1929 to 1939 he made periodic expeditions to Alaska and the Aleutian Islands, digging out more skulls and bones. He found two distinct types of skulls in the prehistoric graves he was excavating: long heads and round heads. From these types, and collateral information accompanying them, he reasoned that man had come to America in two great waves, coinciding with the 3000 to 3500 year age attributed to the Amerind in the Western Hemisphere. His finds corroborated the existing theory. And Dr. Hrdlicka's opinion became the final, and often fatal, pronouncement on any new evidence. Finds were made from time to time which pointed toward a greater antiquity for the Amerind than the allowable 3500 years. But the luckless paleontologist who proffered an old bone which suggested a more remote birthday was drummed out of camp, and naught but woe could descend upon the brash anthropologist who authored a paper which even hinted that the established boundary might be conservative.

Then, in 1927, catastrophe struck.

A wicked old man who had once lived in Folsom, New Mexico, entered the picture. The old man had long since disappeared, for none of his bones were found, but his weapons were, and there was no mistake about it—they were ancient. The old man, it was proved, lived ten thousand years ago! Here's how Dr. William Howells, one of America's foremost anthropologists, tells of the find in *Mankind So Far:*

The Colorado Museum of Natural History had been digging out Pleistocene mammals at a place near Folsom, New Mexico, in 1926, when an arrow or dart point was found in place near the ribs of a fossil bison. *Announcement of the find was greeted with the then-habitual scorn and disbelief of the archaeologists.* But the same group turned up more points in the same place the following year, one of them actually between two bison ribs, and this time they sent for Dr. Frank Roberts of the Smithsonian Institution and Dr. Alfred Kidder of the Carnegie Institution, who came at once and were convinced. In 1928 Dr. Barnum Brown, of the American Museum of Natural History, went to the site at Folsom and found more points, together with the skeletons of twenty-three bison—strong evidence that the animals had been skinned by the hunters, the tails having been removed with the hide. That year there was a regular parade of experts across the site, and conversion was wholesale.

But conversion was not *total.*

The sentence above, which I have taken the liberty to italicize, not only describes, clearly, one of the major obstacles to validating pre-Columbian voyages of exploration in America ("then-habitual" should read "habitual") but also indicates, equally as clearly, that the "parade of experts" included many die-hards who returned to their laboratories and classrooms unconvinced. Certainly the ranks of the unconvinced included Dr. Hrdlicka. He was unable to bring down censure on the Folsom find, however, so he simply smiled and pronounced it an error. (It is intriguing to note, in passing, that Dr. Hrdlicka's most active period of excavation, "proving" the 3500 year theory, was actually undertaken *after* the Folsom find.)

Now the conflicts were worse than ever.

The inevitable dichotomy which had divided the social scientists on the development of the Amerind's culture, now reappeared as a force to split them into two more camps rallying for and against the Folsom Man. Of those who rallied *for*, the more progressive sought further methods of establishing the age of archaeological sites and finds. Dendrochronologists, for instance, came into being in great numbers. These men attempted to correlate known climatic variations with tree rings. A table existed which delineated dry, hot, and cold climate patterns over a period of several hundred years. Since it is known that the rings of a tree are, in themselves, a kind of climate record, it was possible to match tree rings with corresponding climate changes in the table. By using a piece of wood of known date, as a "check," and working backward to match the table and the piece to be dated, a reasonably accurate origin in time could be ascertained for the wood in question.

Through the years that followed the Folsom find, however, views were gradually changed, or, at least liberalized. Students began learning that the Amerind appeared in North America at least ten, and possibly as much as 13,000 years ago. The new belief provided margin for reshuffling, if something new should turn up.

It did, of course, but not within the emergency margin.

While Dr. Hrdlicka was still smiling and blowing large holes in the Folsom Man idea, a beguiling young lady intruded upon the scene in Minnesota. She was a skeleton, and, despite her sex and estimated age of fifteen, is put down in the annals of anthropology as "Minnesota Man." The girl's bones were found by a crew of roadworkers, industriously scraping away at a trench being readied to carry a roadbed across an ancient glacial lake, long since gone. Dr. A. E. Jenks of the University of Minnesota was called to inspect the remains, and was pleased at the good condition in which he found the skeleton. Complimenting the foreman of the roadworkers who was, as Dr. Jenks put it, "as intelligent as any college professor," the latter then appropriated the skeleton for study. The results of his findings were published in a paper titled: "Pleistocene Man in Minnesota," in 1936, and immediately precipitated a great brouhaha. Unhappily, the roadscraper had disposed of the earth covering the bones, and therefore, according to the critics, it was impossible to tell whether the girl actually lay in a deep grave, or in undisturbed gravels. If study proved that she was actually in a dug grave, then her body could have been placed there at any time in history, including recently. If she were shown to be embedded in ancient, undisturbed gravel, a stratigraphic reading would establish her age incontrovertibly. But the scraper had done its work well. There was no way of telling how the ancient lass had arrived at her final resting place.

Academic blood flowed freely in the scrimmages that followed. The question of Minnesota Man's age is not yet resolved. Dr. Howells relates that the renowned Dr. Hrdlicka, true to form, smiled and said the bones were like those of a Sioux Indian. Dr. Jenks replied that being *like* a Sioux didn't *make* it a Sioux. Analogies were drawn and a drowned sailor was drawn into the fray to prove that the skeleton could have lain on the bottom of a glacial lake without disintegrating. Other authorities drifted in and out of the debate, and the only principal involved who offered no opinion was the dead sailor. The Minnesota affair reached a white hot fury, and, in recognition of the valiant struggle of Dr. Jenks to prove his theory, some of his undergraduates, behaving in the manner of undergraduates, immortalized the conflict in a ballad. Earnest Albert Hooton, in *Up from the Ape*, first brought this gem to light. It was designed to be sung to the air of "Clementine":

THRENODY FOR THE FIRST LADY OF THE LAND

On the lakeshore, near a glacier,
In a Minnesota clime
Dwelt a Pleistocene Old-Timer
And his daughter, Clementine.

CHORUS

O my darling, O my darling,
Minnesota Clementine,
Parts of you are lost forever,
Dreadful sorry, Clementine.

O, her teeth were big as tomb-stones
And her nose was platyrrhine,
Mighty spacious and prognathous
Were the jaws of Clementine.

[*repeat chorus*]

Drove she mammoths to the water,
Every morning, just at nine,
Stubbed her toe upon an esker,
Fell into the freezing brine.

[*repeat chorus*]

Blubber lips among the cracked ice
Blowing steam and spouting brine,
But alas, she was no whale-cow,
So subsided Clementine.

[*repeat chorus*]

On a highway, with a scraper,
Planing bumps raised by the rime,
Up they brought her, Asia's daughter,
Pleistocinic Clementine.

[*repeat chorus*]

Counting varves and sifting gravel,
Bones and beads, one at a time,
Papa Jenks got her together,
Fossil flapper, Clementine.

[*repeat chorus*]

Thus the impudency of Dr. Jenks's loyal student body immortalized the little lass who had apparently fallen into a glacial lake, only to be retrieved thousands of years later in time to set off an argument still undecided. Dr. Jenks dated his Minnesota Man at

20,000 years. According to Dr. William Howells, opinion is about evenly divided on Minnesota Man's age.

Folsom Man and his distant relative, Minnesota Man, didn't hold the spotlight exclusively for very long, however.

In the 1940s, in a remote cave in the Sandia Mountains in New Mexico, not at all far from the former home of Folsom Man, a geologist from Harvard named Kirk Bryan made a spectacular analysis of the cave's floor, and came up with a report of an even older man in America. Evidence read in the strata showed human habitation during the last Ice Age, giving the Sandia Man an age of 25,000 years or so. Dr. Bryan, was, of course, subjected to the usual academic hooting and scoffing, administered in relative doses, according to the importance of the hooter or scoffer. Undisturbed by the storm, Dr. Bryan simply rested his case. Sandia Man is 25,000 years old, said Dr. Bryan, and that is that.

There were other finds, of course, all of them ancient in varying degree, each setting off a new fracas as it appeared. A find was made in Tepexpan, Mexico, where, in 1947, Dr. Helmut de Terra produced an articulated male skeleton of late Pleistocene origin. For his efforts, Dr. de Terra was soundly berated. Attacks were directed at de Terra, the innocent fossil, de Terra's method of excavation, and a host of other circumstances surrounding the dig. Dr. de Terra, shocked by the attitudes of his colleagues, retreated, badly wounded.

But in 1952, another find close by that of de Terra's, and from the same geological horizon, proved to be about ten thousand years old, and corroborated de Terra's fossil man. The paleontologists who were working at the site brought the dig to a screeching halt when it became apparent that they had stumbled onto something valuable. Anthropologists, geologists, archaeologists, and other paleontologists were called in to examine the site and witness the progress of the dig.

Obviously, a lesson had been learned by the de Terra vilification. With the experts on hand, the new find, at Iztapan, would bear no criticism, since the artifacts could be seen in situ, before removal.

In South America, further corroboration of the presence of truly ancient Amerinds was produced by Dr. Junius Bird of the American Museum of Natural History in New York. Digging in a Patagonian cave, Dr. Bird sifted through nine feet of earth and ashes, eventually bringing to light a magnificent display of human and animal bones in contemporary association. Dated at eight thousand years, the find establishes the occupation of the southernmost tip of the Americas at a surprisingly early period.

Evidence continued to accumulate, and the great majority of anthropologists had swung into the camp which was open-minded enough to accept an age of 25,000 years or so for the Amerind. Dr. Hrdlicka had passed from the scene, but now a new breed had sprung up, determined to keep the structure of existing theory strong and unchangeable. Their presence was not obvious, because the years went by with no opportunity to question any skeleton or artifact thought to be older than Sandia Man.

Until 1955, when lightning struck for the second time.

Some innocent charcoal samples from an ancient hearth excavated at a site in Tule Springs, Nevada, were sent to a laboratory to be put through a Carbon-14 test. This exciting new testing device, barely five years old, had become extremely valuable in dating organic material found at archaeological sites. Its inventor, Dr. Willard F. Libby, had perfected it as a result of his research in nuclear physics (he received a Nobel prize for it in 1960). It is an intricate and costly method of dating, but had proved accurate with an eerie consistency, dating objects as old as 25,000 years with an error margin of only 250 years. The test is possible because of the presence of an unstable isotope of carbon, called Carbon-14, in all living matter. This isotope is produced in the atmosphere when the nuclei of nitrogen atoms are struck by cosmic rays. The resultant Carbon-14 is then absorbed by plants, and by man, who lives, directly or indirectly, on plants. Dr. Libby discovered that the death of a plant or animal started a disintegration of its Carbon-14 content at a fixed rate. This could be measured in comparison with C-14 in living plants or animals, and the death date of the test matter determined. Dating charcoal from an old hearth, therefore, would reveal the approximate time the wood was used, since it had lost its life, or "died," when it was thrust into the fire to roast a mammoth steak. Archaeologists accepted the test almost universally; it was the first testing method which seemed foolproof. Huzzahs were sent up, papers were written, plaudits and paeans scattered like leaves in the wind.

This, then, was the miraculous, accurate, long-awaited test to which the Tule Springs charcoal was subjected. The results of the test were the beginnings of a death blow dealt to those who were unwilling to accept stratigraphic dating, or dendrochronology, or whatever, and who could discount those methods by pointing to the many bugs in them. The Tule Springs site was dated at about 22,000 years.

Here was Armageddon.

Here was incontrovertible proof of the existence of Ice-Age man in North America. The reactionaries were manifestly unsettled at the news. Perhaps the C-14 method itself wasn't as foolproof as supposed. It didn't seem possible that a site could prove out—unquestionably—to more than 20,000 years. The case for Sandia Man was still arguable; one couldn't, however, argue with C-14—at least not until now.

Whatever preparations may have been in work to challenge the authority of C-14 were almost totally discarded in 1956, when a new thunderbolt struck.

An amateur archaeologist in Texas came up with a new man. He was called Lewisville Man, and he staggered into the anthropological arena bearing the burden of 37,000 years of age.

The staggering ancient produced a sobering reaction.

The world of archaeology was stunned. The hoary man of Lewisville blithely tossed all existing concepts out the window. What's more, he demonstrated the absurdity of attempting to put bounds on man's residence on our two continents. Attacks, in print, have been relatively few, although I have heard two doubters question the validity of the testing orally. Archaeology is coming of age. Lewisville Man emerges victorious from Armageddon.

The Lewisville tests were made by the Houston, Texas, laboratories of the Humble Oil & Refining Company. Because of the importance of the dating, I asked Humble for a direct report on it. It was obtained for me by Humble's New York office. I reproduce it here, almost in its entirety:

We ran into some clearance delays in regard to the information on Humble's work on the Lewisville charcoal samples. We hope that the following information can be used by Mr. Charles Boland . . .

In March, 1956, we were asked by Mr. Wilson W. Crook, Jr., an amateur archaeologist of Dallas, to determine the age of charcoal from the Lewisville (Denton County, Texas) site. Inasmuch as it is our custom to make radiocarbon age determinations for outsiders only on samples submitted by museums, universities, and other nonprofit institutions, we asked Dr. E. H. Sellards, then Director of the Texas Memorial Museum, Austin, whether or not the date would be of archaeological significance, and at the same time asked Mr. Crook if he would submit the samples in the name of a sponsoring institution. It was Dr. Sellard's opinion that the site from which these samples came was of sufficient interest to justify the making of radiocarbon determinations, and Mr. Crook agreed to submit the samples in the name of the Dallas Archaeological Society.

A radiocarbon determination was made in the summer of 1956 on a sample which we received from Mr. Crook. The sample was carbonaceous material associated with much red clay. Unfortunately, the carbonaceous material was very finely divided, and its nature could not easily be ascertained. The age of the sample, as indicated by the radiocarbon assay, was greater than 37,000 years.

Inasmuch as the age of more than 37,000 years for the sample which Mr. Crook submitted was completely unexpected, we requested Mr. Crook to submit a better sample, preferably one which consisted of particles of materials large enough to be identified. Since Professor Elso Barghoorn, Curator of Paleobotany at Harvard, happened to be in town, we asked him if, in returning to Boston, he would stop off in Dallas and select a suitable sample. Professor Barghoorn, who has worked with us on numerous occasions on matters pertaining to radiocarbon dating, was happy to comply, and in company with Weldon Whitaker of Humble, who made the actual radiocarbon determinations, visited the site and selected two samples. One sample consisted of hackberry seeds which had been found in a hearth, and the other was the charred remains of three small logs which had been found in another hearth.

Unfortunately, the hackberry seeds turned out to be mostly intrusive calcium carbonate; the organic carbon content was so low that a sample of the requisite size could not be obtained. The charcoal sample, however, furnished a sufficient amount of carbon for radiocarbon assay. The age of the charcoal sample, as indicated by the assay, was again greater than 37,000 years.

With regard to the authenticity of the samples and the reliability of the radiocarbon ages, we are satisfied that the radiocarbon assays are completely correct . . . Until this sample was run, there was no known source of charcoal which contained virtually no radiocarbon. If one were tempted to "salt" an archaeological site with very old charcoal, how would one go about obtaining such charcoal—particularly charcoal of a wood which is and apparently has been indigenous to the site? The answer is, of course, that the procuring of such material would be virtually impossible.

The above material was contained in a letter from Humble's Public Relations Department and was based on information provided by Milton Williams of Humble's Research Center. It's a perfectly simple story. Two tests. Two datings, corroborative. The letter adds that Humble knows of only one attack, in print: it was made by a Britisher who believed that Humble had "washed the radiocarbon out of the sample."

There will always be a critic, so that the battle may still be considered in progress. It's a battle between theory and fact. Theory says that Lewisville Man doesn't exist, fact says he does. Fact appears to be winning.

The Ancient Texan may have innocently played the role of psychiatrist to social scientists inclined to be accident-prone. Some have seemed inordinately eager to set up doctrinal structures deliberately designed to collapse upon them. Perhaps the day of rigid inflexibility in theory is past, although there are still a few around which could collapse momentarily.

At the moment, for instance, it is declared that paleontologists will never find a primate in the Americas. Such a find would be indicative that a branch, or species of Homo sapiens originated here, and, by that token, Lewisville Man would be a mere infant. (Kanam Man, you will recall, appears to be about 500,000 years old, and that age will doubtless be pushed back by future finds.) But current doctrine says that "conditions are not right" for the finding of a primate in the Western Hemisphere (just as they "weren't right" for the finding of the Folsom Man?). I do wish they weren't given to such arbitrary pronouncements. Suppose a primate *should* turn up in North or South America? Suppose the scorned Ameghino and Galindo were right in declaring that man originated here?

I shudder.

But enough.

It is clear that the first discoverer and his origins need further study. And I'm sure that such study will be eagerly pursued.

In the manner of a political candidate seeking "equal time," I respectfully request that a proportionate amount of "further study" be applied by our social scientists to the almost totally shunned discoverers I am about to introduce.

They all came to America before Columbus.

Let us go, then, to meet the first—he came in a ship from the Mediterranean nearly 500 years before the birth of Christ.

CHAPTER 2

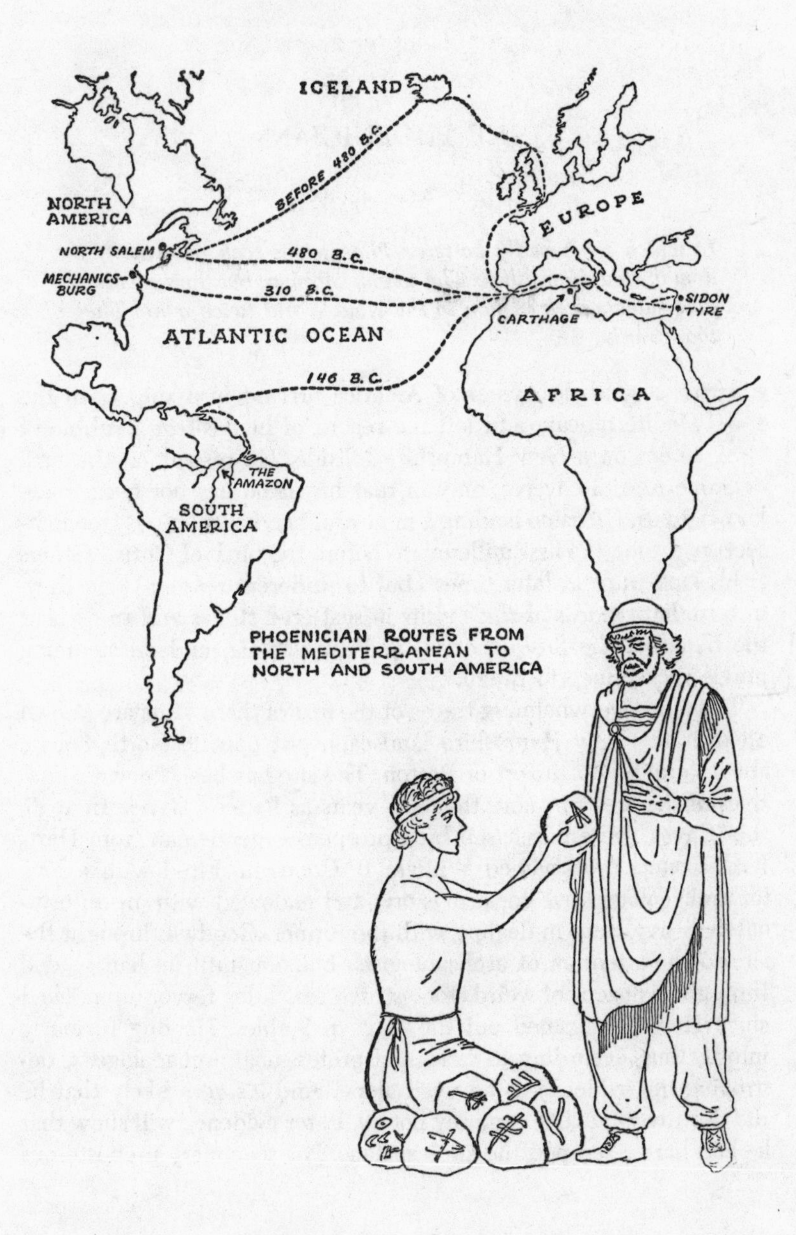

PHOENICIAN ROUTES FROM THE MEDITERRANEAN TO NORTH AND SOUTH AMERICA

Chapter 2

THE PHOENICIANS

[480 B.C.–146 B.C.]

In which some badly battered Phoenicians seek religious freedom in New Hampshire. The colony vanishes, but their collateral descendants seek asylum in the New World twice more. They, too, vanish.

THE second discoverer of America arrived in a ship from the Mediterranean, and left the record of his visit in a rubble of stones on a New Hampshire hillside. He resembled the first, or Stone Age discoverer, only in that his name has not been made known to us. He came leading a mournful band of religious freedom-seekers during the first millennium before the birth of Christ. Others of his kind came at later times (but for different reasons) and they, in turn, left records of *their* visits in scattered stones and ruins near the banks of the Susquehanna, in Pennsylvania, and on steaming jungle rocks, deep in Brazil.

The most overwhelming traces of the first of these visits are strewn all over the New Hampshire landscape just outside North Salem, about 50 miles northwest of Boston. The site has been known to natives of the area for more than 100 years as Pattee's Caves. In 1936, the "Caves" were purchased by a prosperous gentleman from Hartford, Connecticut, named William B. Goodwin. Fired with a love for archaeology, love for a mystery, and endowed with an unfortunately heavy hand in dealing with the former, Goodwin brought the site to the attention of archaeologists, but not until he had waded through its dozens of weird stone structures with a fervor unmatched since Hercules cleaned out the Augean Stables. He dug furiously into it, thus, according to saddened professional archaeologists, destroying the evidence as he went along. And it's very likely that he did destroy *some*, but certainly not *all*. Later evidence will show that he had barely scraped the site's surface. His seemingly preposterous theory about the site made him an object of ridicule for the remainder of his life. At risk of drawing the same ridicule, I propose to endorse Goodwin's theory. I think that Goodwin was on the right trail, but I think the people he places at the site were the *second* occupants of it, and their occupancy gave rise to a fascinating legend that has puzzled historians for four centuries.

We will dwell, now, on the *first* occupants.

In the Mediterranean, as the Neolithic, or New Stone Age, imperceptibly blended with the Bronze Age, the Egyptians were already adept at writing, taxation, and conquering, and had begun to investigate the idea of marine travel on a large scale. About 3200 B.C., they recorded their first sea voyage. They sent a fleet of forty ships over to Phoenicia to get cedar wood and may have used it to build their first *real* seagoing vessels. In 1500 B.C., Queen Hatshepsut dispatched some ships down the Nile from Thebes, and possibly by canal to the Red Sea. After a voyage of two months the fleet arrived at Punt. This was the first in a series of voyages to Punt by the Egyptians. Recent findings indicate that they were after antimony, an ingredient used in the manufacture of cosmetics. Entirely logical, since the expeditionary patron was a queen. Shortly after these Punt voyages, the Egyptians began to lose interest in sailing, even though they had advanced their own art of shipbuilding remarkably. The Cretans gradually took over the sea-rule of the Mediterranean, and very likely would have become a great world power had it not been for a disaster that wiped out Crete around 1250 B.C. An earthquake leveled the island, and the Cretan civilization was buried beneath tons of rubble, its fabulous cities eradicated, its population decimated.

Control of the Mediterranean now fell jointly to the Greeks and Phoenicians. Of the two inheritors, the Phoenicians were by far the more aggressive and inquisitive, and from their home ports of Tyre and Sidon, they roamed the Mediterranean, poking into all its shores with great enthusiasm. By 1200 or so B.C. they had reached the Pillars of Hercules, or Straits of Gibraltar, thus duplicating a feat the Cretans had performed several hundred years earlier. Considering the fact that the Egyptians deemed the Phoenicians rank barbarians and ill-fitted for coping with the sea, the latter took to the water quite expertly. They developed the keel, streamlined their ships, covered their decks, and improved the function of the sail. They sailed merchant ships and ships of war, both designs being borrowed from the Cretans. The vessels were probably anywhere from 80 to 100 feet long and employed a single, square sail. In addition they used oar-power when necessary. Some used a single bank of oars, others, as seen in early carvings, were biremes. On the merchant ships, the prows frequently featured carved horses' heads, and the sterns turned upward, rising high above the water. The warships were squatter and usually bireme and the equine decoration was eliminated. Below the water line they bore sharp rams, designed to stave in the hull of a ship engaged in battle. Both types of ships could average about 100 miles in a day's sail, meaning a full 24 hours. The most distinctive mark of the Phoenician ship, however, was its brilliant purple sail, dyed by the secret process known only to the Phoenicians. They may have employed this highly visible color in order to use the sails for signaling purposes, according to some marine archaeologists. They were busy traders, and it was commerce, rather than war, which hastened the development of their ships. They gave us our alphabet, but didn't bother to use it for anything as trifling as literature; it served them only as a means of recording business transactions. The Greeks, on the other hand, were addicted to writing things down, and it is only through *their* literature that we know anything at all of the Phoenicians.

The Phoenicians were extremely secretive about their trading sources, and employed devious methods to guard against revealing them. Indeed so secretive were they that they have come down to us as the "Silent People." But their contemporaries did not label them with such a mild euphemism. To the Greeks, and other Mediterranean peoples, they were simply liars. But the lies were told for commercial purposes only. It was very likely the Phoenicians who invented and nurtured the tales of sea monsters, boiling seas, and other horrors that so effectively kept competing fleets from probing the waters beyond the Pillars of Hercules. What better way to discourage competition than to play on the natural superstitions of sailors? Their determination to keep secret their trade routes sometimes transcended mere secrecy and resulted in physical calamity, self-inflicted. It is known that their ships were sometimes followed by avid Romans or Greeks, bent on discovering the Phoenician trading posts. In cases where the pursuers could not be shaken, the Phoenician captains employed a very simple device to end the chase.

They wrecked their ships on the handiest rocks or closest beach. Such grim methods certainly illustrate that the Phoenicians indeed made earnest effort to maintain their position as the number one Mediterranean traders.

They also hired themselves out whenever opportunity presented itself. When King Solomon built his fabulous temple, the story of which is related in the Bible (Kings: IX), he employed the ships of Tarshish to journey to Ophir (India) in order that he might obtain gold and silver, ivory, apes, and peacocks. The reason for hiring the Phoenicians was simple: The Jews knew where Ophir was, but, being poor sailors, had no guarantee that they could ever reach that fabled country if forced to rely on their own ships and seamanship. So Solomon hired King Hiram of Sidon, in Phoenicia, to fetch the precious articles that were designed to aid in the former's sybaritic pursuits—through which he eventually turned to idolatry and found disfavor in the eyes of the Lord. The men of Sidon, once arrived in Ophir, were duly impressed with the wealth so evident about them. Procuring their cargo, they returned to Israel and immediately set up voyages of their own to Ophir. They thus made repeated voyages to Solomon's treasure source, trading for its riches without so much as a by-your-leave from the Jews. That the Israelites were disturbed about this turn of affairs is apparent, though 100 years passed before they attempted to do anything about it. When they did, it was Jehoshaphat who made the plans. He built a fleet of ships modeled on the ships of Tarshish, and announced his intention of sailing to Ophir to enrich Israel. Unfortunately, Jehoshaphat's naval architects seem to have been preoccupied with things unmarine during the design phases of this venture, for the entire fleet fell apart at Ezion-geber.

But it must not be considered that the Phoenicians were confined to the intrigues of commerce. As noted earlier, they were good sailors, and, more than that, courageous and inquisitive. In the sixth century B.C., they circumnavigated Africa, thus anticipating Vasco da Gama by a good 2000 years. At first, the news of this heroic voyage was greeted with scoffs, and the Greeks, being firmly convinced that all Phoenicians were liars, pointed out that these tellers of untruths had boldly stated that they saw the sun shining from the north at one point in their cruise. Such an occurrence was impossible! But a more thoughtful Greek, Herodotus, pointed out that a northerly beamed sun would certainly be in order when one sailed to the south of the equator.

Later, in the fifth century, a Carthaginian, Hanno, sailed out beyond the Pillars of Hercules and established many African colonies along the western coast. Hanno returned with vivid descriptions of the continent, and his story was believed.

The most important Phoenician colonies, next to Carthage, however, were those on the Spanish coast. The oldest of these was called Gades, and stands today as Cádiz. From these Spanish colonies, the Phoenicians and Carthaginians made their way to Britain, where they did a brisk business in tin and amber. It is unthinkable that they failed to circumnavigate Britain as early as possible, perhaps as early as 1000 B.C., and we know that they discovered the Atlantic Islands soon after they probed Britain. In 1749, a pot full of Phoenician coins was found on the island of Corvo, the westernmost island of the Azores. They were dated in the decade from 330 to 320 B.C. Of extreme significance is the fact that Corvo lies only 1000 miles off the American mainland. Equally significant is the presence of an ancient ruin on that island, which, to my knowledge, has never been excavated. The coins were found near the ruin.

At the end of the fourth century B.C., a Greek named Pytheas, who dwelled in the western Greek colony of Massilia (Marseilles) was commissioned by his country to make a voyage into the waters beyond the Pillars of Hercules in order to find the sources of the Phoenicians' tin and amber. He reached Britain, after running the blockade set up at the Pillars by the Phoenicians, and made a tour of the island. He described at some length the inhabitants, their resources, and methods of mining. Being an extremely brilliant man, he also noted other things not concomitant with the purpose of his trip. He observed, for instance, that the tides of the ocean coincided with the phases of the moon. The Greeks, accustomed to the tideless Mediterranean, disgustedly wrote *him* off as a liar too, and presumably someone's head rolled for having entrusted such an important voyage to such an untrustworthy person. But Pytheas did make the voyage to Britain, and from there he sailed to an island called Ultima Thule. The voyage was fully described in two books produced by the scholar: *The Ocean* and *The Circuit of the Earth.* Unfortunately, the original volumes have been lost to us, but accounts of them by other writers have been handed down carefully.

Pytheas' voyage is of importance to us, particularly his voyage to Thule, because it has a specific bearing on Pattee's Caves in New Hampshire. When the learned Greek reached the Shetland Islands, he learned about the mysterious Ultima Thule from the natives. According to the information he noted about its location in respect to the Shetlands, the island of Thule was six days' sail to the north. A starchy debate has raged, off and on, among those who claim Thule to be Iceland, and those who insist it is Norway. Fridtjof Nansen, the Norwegian arctic explorer, held that it had to be Trondheim, in Norway. In his book, *Great Adventures and Explorations,* Vilhjalmur Stefansson, states five positive arguments for Thule being Iceland. All are predicated on logical interpretations of Pytheas' writings in re the northernmost island. I offer but one argument. I think it boils down to a case of mileage, and mileage alone. When the speed of a ship of Pytheas' day is considered, we find that the sailing vessels of the early Greeks and Phoenicians were capable of about 100 miles in a day's sail. It must be noted that a "day's sail" includes day *and* night sailing, or a complete period of twenty-four hours. Simple multiplication now places Thule at 600 miles from the Shetlands. Iceland is six hundred miles from those islands, while Norway lies a scant two hundred miles to the *east,* and not to the north, as the Greek states.

All of which brings us a step closer to New Hampshire and the Caves of Pattee. Having established the fact that Pytheas learned of Ultima Thule from the inhabitants of Britain's northernmost islands, common logic tells us that the Phoenicians learned of the same island from the same source, and at a much earlier date. Remember, the Phoenicians established the colony of Cádiz about 1100 B.C., and were probably exploring northern waters, and discovering and circumnavigating Britain not long afterward. Be it not forgotten, also, that we are dealing with the "Silent People" . . . a people who just wouldn't tell the rest of the world about their discoveries lest the information permit encroachment of their commercial centers. That the Phoenicians had long and significant contact with the Scandinavian countries is suggested most powerfully by the startling similarity in ship design of the vikings and the Mediterranean mariners. Each was a double-ended craft, each could be propelled by sail or rower. In one the figurehead is equine—in the other, serpentine. To me, these ships were too close in design not to have sprung one from the other. I think the Scandinavians and Phoenicians came to know each other extremely well.

Now we pick up the clues which trace the watery track of the Phoenicians to America, north and south. I think the Phoenicians made many trips to Iceland and the North Countries. And I think that during the course of these trips more than one of their ships was blown off course and sent scudding down to New England. In a later chapter I shall present documentary evidence that just such an occurrence brought one of the first vikings to America by accident, seventeen years before the arrival of Leif Ericsson. From the North Atlantic come mighty cyclonic wind families that blow in series down from the northeast. When storms of this type strike, they blow continuously for days, pushing any hapless vessel caught in their paths across the Atlantic from northeast to southwest with ease.

I think more than one Phoenician ship came to America that way.

And some of them went back.

And when the reports were studied, they paved the way for a large-scale migration to America that took place in three stages, beginning in 480 B.C. Some of these migrants came to New England, and stayed. Some strayed from the plotted course and came to the Chesapeake, whence they sailed north, up the Susquehanna River, to settle in what is now Pennsylvania. Others strayed even more and sailed to the coast of South America. And all of these migrations from the Mediterranean occurred before the birth of Christ.

All of which immediately poses three questions: 1. What could cause a large-scale migration of a people from an area in which they were so powerful a force? 2. What evidence indicates that the terminal point of the migration was America? 3. Why America?

To gain the answers, we must start with the first of the wars between Carthage and Greece. These wars were fought in the Mediterranean, off and on, from 480 B.C. to 275 B.C., ultimately became the Punic Wars and ended in the total destruction of Carthage in 146 B.C. When the Carthaginians were defeated in 480 by the Greek, Gelon, in the first of these wars, the peace terms he imposed on them were rather stiff.

He made them vow that they would cease the practice of human sacrifice in their religious ritual.

I think a number of them, objecting to so unreasonable a demand, elected to leave Carthage for a place where they could pursue their religious beliefs unhampered by the whims of tyrants. (Some 2100 years later, a band of Pilgrims came to America for the same reason.)

I think they came here for religious freedom. Human sacrifice, while not practiced with great frequency, was too fundamental a part of their religion to give up.

Evidence? At Pattee's Caves in New Hampshire there is, among the various stone buildings under study, a nearly rectangular sacrificial stone, just big enough to contain an outstretched human form. Around its edge is carved a two-inch run-off channel which drains from the top of the stone at its widest end. It rather resembles a gravy drain board. I know it is just big enough to hold a human body. I have lain upon it myself, flesh creeping, my wife pointing out that my head just touched one end of the drain channel, my feet stopping just short of the opposite end.

I was told by an archaeologist who dug at the site in 1955 that it was probably a leaching stone made by colonials for manufacturing soap. There was, he indicated, nothing unusual about it. Another, just like it, he informed me, was lying in the woods at Leominster, Massachusetts, about 50 miles away! Two stones, identical in shape and character, 50 miles apart, unlike any other stones ever found in New England. The catalogues which I possess illustrating colonial functional tools contain nothing even remotely resembling them. And I have since learned that another one has been reported atop Mount Shaw, in the Ossipee Mountains in New Hampshire.

I think they're sacrificial stones.

And I think they were hewn by expatriate Phoenicians-Carthaginians come to America for religious freedom. Freedom that permitted the sacrifice of humans when the ritual demanded. Ritual that demanded a medium for the execution. A stone table. Not quite the same method used in the Mediterranean. Or was it?

So much for the mass migration and parts one and two of the evidence indicating their presence.

Why America? Because they knew it was here.

In about the year 335 B.C., the Greek Philosopher, Aristotle, proffered a list of 178 Marvels, which treated on all manner of subjects fascinating to him in history, science, and general knowledge. In Marvel Number 84, he writes:

In the Ocean outside the Pillars of Hercules, they say that a desert island was found by the Carthaginians having woods of all kinds, and navigable rivers, remarkable for all kinds of fruit, and many days' journey away. As the Carthaginians frequented it often, owing to its prosperity, and some even lived there, the chief of the Carthaginians announced that they would punish with death any who proposed to sail there, and that they massacred all the inhabitants, that they might not tell the story, and that a crowd might not resort to the island and get possession of it and take away the prosperity of the Carthaginians.

The classical archaeologist dismisses this passage by indicating that the land referred to was England, if indeed, Aristotle ever wrote such stuff.

I don't think Aristotle was referring to England.

I think he was referring to America.

Aristotle was a painstaking fellow, given to detail. Had he been referring to England, I think he would have referred to the "desert island" as being the place where the Carthaginians obtained their tin and amber. I think, also, that he would have placed it more correctly in its geographic location. He simply states that it was "many days' journey away." He does not say it lies to the north. He gives no direction at all. He must have known all that was available about England at the time, as did Pytheas when he sailed to Britain a few years after Aristotle's death. Pytheas seemed to know where he was going, for he wasted no time in setting his course north from the Pillars to find the land he was sent to find. But Aristotle merely says it was many days' journey away, and gives no direction, which seems to imply that he meant a land other than that which gave up its tin to the Carthaginians. The descriptive, it must be admitted, could fit either England or America, for both have broad rivers, fruit-bearing trees and woods. But—and I must repeat—I think Aristotle would have been clearer in his directions had he been writing of England. In passing, the designation "island" for Aristotle's mysterious land of plenty is of no consequence. Even the largest bodies of land were frequently charted as islands by early explorers who had not fully explored the new lands they reported.

But we need more evidence. The efforts of the Phoenicians at stone manipulation did not stop with the grooved table. Pattee's Caves consists of more than twenty stone structures, the most dominant of which is a "Y" cavern or edifice, startlingly similar to structures found on the Island of Malta and in Western Ireland. There are 15 small dolmens each big enough to hold a person in a sitting posture, or lying down. There are huge megaliths, ramps, walks, an apparent plaza or processional area, and a system of underground drains for keeping the site free of rain water. The "Y" structure contains a fireplace, what seems to be an altar niche and a speaking tube. For an oracle? The tube still works. Bear in mind that all of these structures are built of huge slabs of stone. The sacrificial stone, for instance, weighs four and a half tons. Some of the larger megaliths probably weigh up to twenty tons, and all of them were placed in their positions by men. By men who were not Indians. Nor were they colonials. They were men from a culture difficult to relate to anything American.

In 1955, the Early Sites Foundation of New England, authorized and financed an expedition to dig at Pattee's Caves in an effort to date the site once and for all time. The archaeologists were led by Gary Viscelius, who was familiar with the site, having probed it some years before. His expedition concluded, after six weeks of digging, that the one-acre site was undoubtedly colonial, and had probably been built by Jonathan Pattee, who was an eccentric, a mail robber, an Underground Railroad operator in slavery days, or a number of other things. Depending on who was imparting the information. Legend had it that old Jonathan had built these tortured structures in company with his five hulking sons. The foundation established that Jonathan had one son who died in infancy—and five *daughters*, who, though of hardy stock could scarcely have helped their sire move those twenty-ton megaliths about the landscape. Jonathan had another son, who survived, but he still didn't provide enough manpower to account for the raising of the dolmens and megaliths.

After the Viscelius expedition packed up its tents and left, Frank Glynn of Clinton, Connecticut, decided that he wasn't satisfied with the findings. Glynn, a free soul who turned his back on a promising Madison Avenue career to work for the U. S. Post Office in Clinton, is an amateur archaeologist of excellent reputation. He has contributed profoundly to knowledge of the Indians in New England, and has been president of the Connecticut Archaeological Society.

Glynn's dissatisfaction with the "colonial" dating of the Caves was based on knowledge of a pine tree stump antedating the birth of Jonathan Pattee, which had been found growing in the middle of one of the stone structures. The disturbing stump had not been mentioned in the expedition's report, read at New Haven in late fall, 1956, and Glynn—probing about the place after the expedition had left—found yet another.

Then a curious thing happened. Glynn, still puzzling over the mystery of the Caves, took some samples of "colonial brick" found at the site to Dr. Irving Rouse of Yale University's Anthropological Department. Glynn suspected that the brick had been classified improperly, and, if anyone in archaeology could tell him whether his suspicions were correct, it would be Dr. Rouse.

Rouse examined the "brick" and confirmed Glynn's suspicions. It wasn't colonial brick at all. What's more, it appeared to be an ancient type of Indian pottery not indigenous to New England! The Early Sites dating had been partially based on finding this "colonial brick" under the foundations of some of the stone structures. Now the mystery was deeper than ever. How did the alien pottery get there—and when? How old was the pottery? And—of course—the question seemingly answered by the Early Sites Expedition now reappeared, looming larger than ever: *Who built the stone structures?*

Glynn tackled the Caves on his own.

He is certain the site is ancient; just how ancient he won't hazard. But further discoveries of pottery shards seem to point more and more to a Bronze Age or early Iron Age culture (3000 B.C. to perhaps 500 B.C.). He has produced much more evidence working quietly—and alone—than did the expedition. And I suspect he is going to turn up a good deal more. While he does not subscribe to my thinking on the "Phoenician-Carthaginian" theory, it merely demonstrates that he is exercising the accustomed caution of the detective on the trail of something hot. In other words, "no comment at the moment." He himself uses the phrase "Bronze Age" when describing his finds. More than finding pottery shards, he has determined that the original site was much larger than the acre it was thought to be. Here's how he describes the dig in an abstract he read before the Eastern States Archaeological Federation on November 7, 1959:

The hill site lies 25 miles west of the Atlantic Ocean. The south running Spicket River forms the local drainage. Colonial pioneers moved up its valley against at times bloody Indian opposition 1730–50. A road and farmhouses were built on the western side of the valley. On this valley world, the hill site looks down from the vantage point of the valley's high eastern rim.

From the rim the site runs eastward 1,500 feet. The north-south dimension is over 800 feet. The plateau-like hill seems to have been scoured by glacial action that left a few erratics. No Colonial road touched the area. The post-glacial soil is an apparently wind-deposited silt, fine-grained and shallow. Sub-marginal for an iron age agriculturist, such a soil offers attractions to the more primitive farmer. It is easy to clear and keep clear. On it even primitive hand tools can maintain a moisture-conserving mulch that will grow a small grain crop. Today the hill site supports a sparse, mixed forest.

Two human occupations have left evidence in the soil. A brief sheep-farming episode, 1828–48, has left widespread charcoal in the humus horizon. It probably reflects slash-and-burn clearing. An equally widespread charcoal horizon in the lower half of the soil's B zone may infer an ancient land clearing.

At many points the low-lying charcoal is associated with the debris of the horizontal quarrying of granite slabs. A fire-setting technique seems to have been employed. The quarried stone was erected into a *30 acre network of walls and structures*. At all points tested these walls rest on bedrock, often via bedding trenches cut from the old land surface in the lower B zone.

Note the italicized phrase: "a 30 acre network of walls and structures." Apparently the Early Sites expedition worked under some restriction which prevented its going beyond the surface evidence. In a recent conversation with Glynn, he told me that there is seemingly an even greater acreage involved, and he is in the process of seeking these new and larger boundaries at the moment. His report continues:

Settlement plan elements include– 1. A possible cliff cemetery. A steep cliff drops beneath the site's western wall. Numerous skulls are reported to have been recovered from its crevices. 2. A 30 acre system of "Celtic Field" type enclosures. The enclosed areas are short and broad and often subdivided. The overall arrangement is highly irregular. The resulting pattern differs radically from local, long rectangular Colonial land division. 3. A possible village site of closely grouped circular (hut?) hollows near the site's center and high point. 4. From it an almost 900 foot long interior road leads first to an apparently elliptical court. 5. East of the court lie the ruins of an elaborate three-quarter acre structural complex with many features of Megalithic temples. It includes a domestic section, remodelled 1828–33 by the sheep-farmer. In the last century the complex has been as thoroughly vandalized as publicized. The interior road continues easterly to a small stone structure, formerly sealed. It was broken into and rifled, evidently 1750–1850 A.D. A small drainage work lies south of the interior road. A 50 foot long channel cut through granite ledge once drained a hollow area upwards of an acre in size. As the drain has silted up, a bed of fresh water peat has grown up in the hollow over evidence of human occupation.

Megalithic temples, it must be noted, are strewn all over the Middle East, as are menhirs and dolmens, both of which are in great evidence at Pattee's Caves. Glynn's report continues for another two paragraphs of summation and states that resources have not permitted radiocarbon dating. Other artifacts have been found, but are under study, and cannot be commented on at this time.

In Plates 1, 2, 3, 4 and 5, I offer photographs of Pattee's Caves together with photographs of beehives and dolmens from Britain and Western Ireland.

I think we have a pattern. A pattern that traces a single culture. A culture that sprang from the Mediterranean and took root in England, Ireland and the Americas.

Pattee's Caves are not the only evidences of this culture in New England. In addition to the stone structures there are two more mysterious "signs" that indicate the presence of Mediterranean people in New England. Look at the rock carving in Plate 6. Is it a ship? A viking ship? Or a Phoenician ship? I say it's a Phoenician ship, carved on the rock by some nameless, awe-filled Indian who saw the ship more than two thousand years ago and was moved to record its presence so that others might see the evidence of his strange vision. I say it's Phoenician because it shows a yard at the top of the mast. Viking ships lowered their sails, yard and all, when at anchor. The Phoenicians used a furling method similar to that used on later sailing ships: the sail was furled by being drawn up and fastened to the yard. When the ship was at rest, its silhouette presented a "T" shape as opposed to a single stick of mast thrust up into the sky. The ship carving is on a stone in Assawompsett Pond in Massachusetts. And quite frankly, it has no business being there. Normally, the rock on which it was carved is under water, and was only revealed, along with other rocks bearing Indian pictographs, during a severe drought in 1957. The rock and its carving has no business being there because its underwater position proves that it had to be carved more than 2000 years ago, when the waters of the oceans of the world were much lower than they are today. The Indian who carved it stood on dry ground, gravely incising the image of the ship he had seen floating on the lake. The carved ship helps jar the tightly welded framework of archaeological pronouncement. It shouldn't be there any more than Pattee's Caves should be there.

Or the beautiful rosettes and the unfinished Doric column hewn in the living rock at Guilford, Connecticut. Who carved them? Indians? Hardly. Colonials? I don't think so. They were too busy wresting a living from the land to carve useless decoration in woodland rocks. Experts who have seen them say they're Mediterranean in origin. But, unfortunately, they can't be explained, so, theoretically, they don't exist to the archaeological world. But I've seen them. They're striking—and beautiful. Could they be the work of the same people from the ship carved in the rock at Assawompsett? Possibly. I can visualize the ship slowly probing the coast, perhaps putting into Leete's Island, near Guilford, to repair a sail or damaged hull. Time was not important. The artisans aboard the ship whiled away their time by chiseling familiar figures in the rock. One of the more ambitious tried his hand at carving the base of a Doric column. Another scooped the rock out of a rectangular rock to make a kind of drinking trough. The repairs, finished, they left, their leisurely incisions in the rock silent evidence of their fleeting presence. One day, perhaps, all of these structures and "signs" will be studied by competent archaeologists in an effort to document the pattern conclusively, whether it be negative or positive.

Unfortunately, the site at North Salem was drained of most of its rock in order to build sewers and other necessary stoneworks in the city of Lawrence, Massachusetts, during the 1920s. As an old resident puts it: "All day long . . . wagon after wagon came out of the woods loaded with stone from the Caves."

Wagon after wagon . . . possibly carting off the most valuable archaeological evidence in North America. It will never be known how much rock was taken from the site, or whether any of the rocks were exterior rocks bearing inscriptions to extend a clue to their original manipulators. Since the stone buildings at Pattee's Caves bear a closer resemblance to Neolithic structures than Bronze Age structures, it would be necessary to know whether what is visible was simply the basic structure, and whether the buildings could have been covered with some kind of mortar or cement to give them a more finished appearance. This would not necessarily apply to the smaller dolmens, since they were probably added at a later date by the second occupants of the site.

In conjunction with the finds at North Salem, other artifacts found in the general area must be noted. All have been recorded, none are in evidence today. Artifacts left by a Bronze Age people logically should be of bronze. Willoughby's *Antiques* shows a photo of a bronze dagger found at Merrimackport, in Massachusetts. The dagger has disappeared. Mr. William Goodwin once possessed a bronze spear dug up near Brentwood, north of the North Salem site; it, too, has disappeared. A bronze shield is said to have been dug from the ground near Windham, New Hampshire, a few miles west of North Salem. Goodwin himself dug many metal objects out of the North Salem site, but only a few, of iron, are in existence, and they belong to Mr. Malcolm Pearson, present owner of Pattee's Caves. A tiny fragment dug from the site at North Salem was catalogued as ceramic by the Early Sites Expedition, but careful removal of surface grime by Frank Glynn proved it to be of bronze. It is too small, however, to give evidence of its original form, or of the weapon or container it was once a part of. How many artifacts were destroyed by Goodwin in his enthusiasm will never be known either, nor will the number he gave away to any who were interested in his work. The attics of America doubtless contain much archaeological treasure, put there by bewildered inheritors who are completely puzzled by their purposes, saved only because they "belonged to Grandfather or Uncle Fred."

How long the Phoenician colony at North Salem existed is impossible to tell. But there is apparent evidence that two other Phoenician expeditions settled here for indefinite periods in Pennsylvania and in South America.

In 310 B.C., the Carthaginians suffered another calamitous defeat at the hands of the Greeks, this time being ingloriously beaten by a truculent Greek named Agathocles. That worthy had reason to desire a thorough trouncing of the Carthaginians, for they had routed *his* armies a short time before. I think that even more Carthaginians fled to America after that engagement, to join their own colonials at North Salem. Remember those coins found at Corvo? They were dated in the decade from 330 to 320 B.C. The battle in which Agathocles bested them took place in 310. I think they were left on the island by a ship that was wrecked there while en route to America. And I think that while some of the refugees reached North Salem and found haven there, other ships in the retreating fleet lost their courses and went to Pennsylvania.

Making landfall at the mouth of the Chesapeake Bay, they sailed into it and came to the Susquehanna, which ends its 250 mile course at the Bay. They continued up the river until they were stopped near Harrisburg, by a great falls. There they disembarked and went inland.

They left evidence of their visit. I have seen it, and have, in fact, some of it here in my home in New Canaan. It was uncovered because of a man named Philip Beistline, a resident of Mechanicsburg, Pennsylvania.

On Monday, April 17, 1948, the *Mechanicsburg News* carried the story of a strange stone found by Mr. Beistline, a former teacher who was, at the time of the find, eighty-five years old. Mr. Beistline was intensely interested in the Indians of the area in which he lived, and had amassed a collection of about 2000 Indian points, as well as other artifacts gathered in the beautiful woodlands of the Cumberland Valley. The stone bore strange markings which its finder knew were not Indian. He sent the stone to Cornell University, which apparently verified Beistline's suspicion that the markings might consist of Phoenician characters.

It was several years before he made the find public, and his announcement was largely precipitated by similar finds made by his close friend, Dr. William W. Strong, a physical scientist in Mechanicsburg. Dr. Strong, who had once been director of the Agricultural Research Institute at Mechanicsburg, was internationally known for his contributions to the study of chemical-physical selection methods of plant food production and preservation. He was also as avid an amateur archaeologist as Mr. Beistline, and on learning of the latter's find, Dr. Strong scoured the woods in York and Cumberland Counties, eventually collecting nearly a thousand additional stones, all with seeming Phoenician characters on them. All were indigenous sandstone, heavily coated with iron oxide.

More important, perhaps, was the finding of queerly grooved stones, of the same composition as the inscribed sandstones, but cut into many different shapes; some were obelisk in form, others were irregularly shaped and contained a variety of groovings, none of which were readily explained. The grooves were certainly made by human agency, but could not be dismissed as abrasions made by Indians in the course of sharpening points. One incredulous beholder of these stones, who sought to provide an explanation of the grooves, thoughtfully suggested "rock worms" as the engravers. The stones are unlike the product of any known Amerind culture, and the suspicion inevitably directs itself at an alien culture.

Phoenician culture, perhaps.

On many of his field trips, Strong was accompanied by Mr. George W. Nailor, also of Mechanicsburg, who drove the scientist's car, and also assisted in hauling the stones back to the Strong farm for study. I asked Nailor about these grooved stones, specifically requesting the location of the site where all were found. Nailor sent me this reply:

About the year 1938 or 1940, Dr. Strong and I were together in the area in York County that you visited this summer. [He is referring to an earlier trip I made to Mechanicsburg to see the stones.] We found a pile of flat stones (approx. 75) about 2½ feet long and 18 in. wide. Each stone having V shaped grooves cut across the flat sides exactly 6" apart.

He placed two of the stones one on top of the other with the grooves matching. He then put a wedge shaped stone in the groove and showed me that this would take the place of the mortar that we use in this type of building today. He said the ancient pyramids were built in this fashion, and he believed this was the ruins of an ancient temple.

Mr. Nailor then comments on Dr. Strong's pursuit of the study of things Phoenician, and adds that a geologist friend of the doctor's had estimated the corrosion on the stone to be about 2000 years old. More inscribed stones, he stated, were found near the grooved stones. In answer to my query on the location of the "temple" site, Nailor had to admit defeat:

Many of the people in this area have died or moved away and I could only find one couple that knew what I was searching for. They agreed to lead me to these stones but after two hours search they gave up. They believed someone had hauled them away for building purposes.

He adds that such a circumstance was entirely possible, because there were people in the area who saw the stones after Dr. Strong found them, and could recognize their value for building purposes.

And so we have a sorry repetition of the fate of the stones at

Pattee's Caves: *hauled away for building purposes.* Fortunately, enough of them were recovered by Strong and Nailor to permit continuing study. One of the grooved stones has recently undergone petrographic tests at Johns Hopkins, under the able direction of Edward Clifton, presently engaged in advanced research at the university. The stone was brought to Clifton by Charles H. A. Seitz, a geographer who had been interested in the Mechanicsburg stones for many years. He had visited Dr. Strong several times, and accompanied him on field trips. After Dr. Strong's death, in 1955, Seitz shelved his interest, but revived it again in 1959, when he determined to find out as much as possible about the grooved stones. The report from Clifton verifies that the stones were cut by humans, but the geologist makes no attempt to date them. Seitz believes they might be of an unknown Amerind culture, and does not think them to be of Phoenician origin. He dismisses the alphabet stones entirely. But Seitz is important to the Mechanicsburg stones. He is open-minded enough to want to know more of their origins—his archaeological colleagues seem determined to ignore them.

And now we have a fascinating conjunction of two apparently related pieces of evidence pointing to an occupation of southern Pennsylvania by Phoenicians: Flat, grooved stones seemingly adaptable for construction, and strange, inscribed stones bearing marks strikingly like the characters in the Phoenician alphabet.

Dr. Charles H. Hapgood, a geologist and instructor at Keene Teachers College, in Keene, New Hampshire, has made three trips to the area and plans to begin a dig next year at a site thought by the late Dr. Strong to be one worthy of investigation. Dr. Hapgood's enthusiasm for the project stems from his first visit to Mechanicsburg, made with some skepticism about three years ago. He obtained some of the alphabet stones from Mrs. Strong and brought them to Father Lucian Malouf, pastor of the Church of Our Lady of Cedars, in Manchester, New Hampshire. Father Malouf, a scholar deeply interested in ancient Mediterranean languages, was puzzled but felt that they could be Phoenician. He sent the stones to Phoenician language experts at the University of Strasbourg, in France, where a further study was made. In a recent letter, Dr. Hapgood informed me that the French experts see a resemblance to Carthaginian script in the marks on the stones, but are continuing their study, with additional material supplied by Hapgood, and will, at some time in the future, issue a formal report.

I first encountered Dr. Strong and his stones in 1959, when, in the course of research on the Phoenicians, I came upon a short tract written by Joseph Ayoob of Aliquippa, Pennsylvania, in the New York Public Library. It told of Dr. Strong and his odd, inscribed rocks. I was not too convinced of the validity of these rocks after reading Mr. Ayoob's report, but felt, in spite of the fact that the paper stated the case a bit too strongly, that it was worth investigating.

A month later, in company with my good and patient friend, John Drake, I made the trip to Mechanicsburg to see the stones. I was amazed at the number of these inscribed rocks jamming the old barn behind the late Dr. Strong's house. I was further amazed at the inordinate amount of historical material the scientist had amassed—all bearing on the Phoenicians. I photographed many of the stones and succeeded in borrowing some of the literature from Mrs. Strong.

The more I browsed through it, the more I was convinced that the evidence might be authentic. I asked Dr. George Radan, a classical archaeologist then living in the neighboring town of Darien, to drop by for a drink and a look at some photographs. Dr. Radan had just terminated a long association with the Haifa Museum, and possesses a good knowledge of early Semitic alphabets. I showed him photographs of the stones, and he jolted me somewhat by translating them. Most were single characters, but a few bore words. He was puzzled by the monotonous recurrence of single letters on the rocks; there is a preponderance of stones bearing the first few characters of the alphabet: "Aleph," "Beth," "Gimel," and "Daleth." The same recurrence had puzzled me, too, until I considered the nature of the pursuits that may have occupied the Carthaginians while they were here.

The pursuits, were, to my belief, carried on but briefly. I think that York and Cumberland Counties mark the sites of a second attempted settlement here which was extremely short-lived. The nature of the evidence indicates that the displaced Carthaginians were killed off by Indians shortly after their arrival.

First, consider the pile of flat stones found in the woods by Dr. Strong and George Nailor. That they were hewn by human agency has been confirmed by the first stages of the analysis performed at Johns Hopkins. I think they were being hewn and stacked for building purposes. Dr. Strong thought they might be the ruin of an old temple. I think he had it reversed. It was evidence of a temple to be built. That there were only 75 stones in the pile, and that there were no crumbling walls or hint of a foundation indicates that the "temple" died a-borning. Its construction was prevented by the advent of Indians with blood in their hearts. Whether the stones were intended for foundations or as decorative exterior stones may never be known. It is entirely possible that similar grooved stones were among those carted away at North Salem to build sewers for Lawrence. They would have been first to be pilfered, since they were uniform and provided ready-made foundation or wall stones. The inscription, or alphabet stones, were, I feel, ledger or grading stones. The more observant of the Carthaginians noticed immediately the preponderance of "rusty-looking" stones in the area, and deduced, rightly, that there was iron to be found thereabouts. The entire band probably went to work to dig it out; the trading instinct of the Carthaginians couldn't be eradicated by a mere naval defeat. Quite possibly, while the diggers were busy removing the ore, the more practical were speculating on markets for it. We can assume, then, a vignette of excavating Carthaginians, happily mining iron ore in the Susquehanna Valley, (one of the three major iron-producing areas in Pennsylvania) and placing it in piles as it is removed. Samples are taken, and the mineral experts determine the quality of the ore. It is then placed in other piles, according to its quality. At the base of each pile, a stone with a Phoenician character is placed, to label its worth. It is known that the Phoenicians used their alphabet for counting as well as writing.

I think it happened that way.

The stones are scattered about at this writing. Some have found haven in the State Museum at Harrisburg, just eight miles from Mechanicsburg, some have voyaged to France, one is at Johns Hopkins University in Baltimore, others are in Keene, New Hampshire, and there are five in New Canaan, Connecticut.

Dr. Radan says they could be Phoenician, but would prefer to hold further comment until he has studied them more comprehensively and submitted them to his former colleagues at the Haifa Museum. Mr. Seitz just doesn't believe that the alphabet stones are "worked" stones at all. He regards the markings as those of a natural erosive process in stones coated with oxide of iron. He has hope, however, for the grooved stones, but doesn't believe them to be of Phoenician origin.

Dr. Hapgood thinks they're Phoenician, and his opinion is bolstered to some degree by the early report of the ancient language experts at Strasbourg.

John Witthoft, State Archaeologist for Pennsylvania, attributes them to erosion.

Dr. Paul Stux, a research chemist from Ohio who possesses an impressive knowledge of Canaanite inscriptions, is skeptical. He wants to see related evidence.

It is revealing to note that all the active interest in the finds at Mechanicsburg come from individuals outside the state. There is, in Pennsylvania, a State Historical and Museum Commission in Harrisburg, as well as a State Archaeological Society with 12 chapters. No individual or group in the Keystone State has expressed the slightest desire to investigate the suspect sites further. It would appear that the Pennsylvania consensus considers the whole idea of Phoenicians to be utterly ridiculous.

The brightest aspect of the Mechanicsburg affair is that it is being kept alive, largely through the efforts of Dr. W. Albert Strong, son of the late Dr. William. Dr. Albert, a research chemist who now lives and works in Akron, Ohio, would like to see the question settled. He feels his father's work should at least be appraised by as many authoritative observers as possible, in hope of reaching a conclusion. Dr. Albert's interest in the stones was not always as intense as it has been in the last few years. He told me that he developed a profound hatred of stones in any shape or size in his childhood. This melancholy condition was brought about by Dr. Strong, senior's, habit of commandeering young Albert to assist in hauling new finds of stones. This operation consisted of two steps; hauling them from their distant resting places to the Strong automobile, then hauling them from that vehicle to the barn, there to be numbered and filed. The stone complex disappeared as he grew to manhood, and he is now able to handle and photograph the stones without so much as a tic. He maintains an active list of people who have shown interest in the stones and keeps them informed, periodically, on new developments or new opinions regarding the inscriptions and grooves. In October 1960, he invited those interested to a weekend seminar on the subject. More than 30 people attended, believers and scoffers alike. Such attention to a "wild" idea based on Phoenician penetration of America is intriguing; it may provide courage for scholars to extend positive theories.

(Joseph Ayoob, whose tract first brought me to Mechanicsburg, approaches the matter from a slightly different perspective. He has organized a Phoenician Historical Society, dedicated to substantiating the presence of the ancient mariners in America. The climate being what it is, he may have to meet the D.A.R. at thirty paces with drawn geneologies to maintain his footing.)

I'm sure Dr. Albert Strong's persistence will bring more active interest by qualified archaeologists.

The grooved stones show promise; I have hope, also for the alphabet stones. Had these stones been found in Lebanon, or in Crete, or on Malta, they would now be reposing in some museum, importantly labeled "Phoenician or Carthaginian ledger stones, or grading stones." But, having had the misfortune to turn up in America, their presence must not for a moment jar existing archaeological and historical concepts. If the pronouncement states that there were no Europeans here prior to the arrival of Columbus, then it must be ever thus. And let me assure you that the pronouncement exists; there is actually no "if" about it. It is alive, but difficult, at times, to produce as stated fact by any authority because it is an unspoken, unwritten dictum enjoined by those who subscribe vigorously to what we will refer to in succeeding chapters as the NEBC Principle, *No Europeans Before Columbus* in America. This Principle, I must dolefully admit, will be seen in active application throughout this volume. Until one day an archaeologist who hasn't read the pronouncement, or is suffering from a lapse of memory has the courage, or is foolish enough to draw, and utter, conclusions on these and other strange findings in America. But while we await his coming, we must be content with our "fables" and romantic phantasies.

Meanwhile, pretend not to be an authority, lest ye be hooted at. As they hooted at the gentlemen in Brazil.

The gentlemen in Brazil were several. They found inscriptions on rocks, at different places in Brazil, at different times. Two were scientists, one an engineer, and the third a retired industrialist. All have been attacked and their finds discredited. Their inscriptions were thought to be Phoenician, and the discoveries covered a period of more than 50 years. To discredit them is to imply fraud, or plain stupidity. Is it possible that two scientists, an engineer, and a retired industrialist all attempted frauds of a similar nature over a 50-year period, or were victims to incredible stupidity concerning inscriptions on rocks? Each, on finding the inscriptions, entered into research to determine, if possible, their natures. Each came, independently, to the conclusion that they looked Phoenician.

But the archaeologists and historians of Brazil deny that these inscriptions exist. That establishes a glorious bond between the social scientists of America, North and South: active adherence to the NEBC Principle.

But let us return to the four inscription finders.

The first, an engineer named Francisco Pinto, discovered more than twenty caves deep in the Brazilian jungle, each containing inscribed rocks. Before he was through, he recorded about two hundred and fifty inscriptions. An examination of one of the rocks by Brazil's Director of History and Geography brought forth corroboration of Pinto's suspicion that the markings were Phoenician. Pinto made his discoveries in 1872. In 1911, the Brazilian Government invited Ludwig Schoenhagen, a German language instructor and philologist, to visit Brazil and study the inscriptions. Schoenhagen, enraptured with what he saw, remained 15 years, lecturing and writing on what he considered genuine inscriptions.

The second Brazilian discovery of markings thought to be Phoenician occurred in the 1880s through the efforts of Ernest Ronan, a French scientist, who, with a team of interested Brazilians, combed the jungles for more inscriptions. They produced several, one of which, according to James V. Howe, translated into this message:

> I arrived with my companions and thirty workers in four boats after a long and dangerous journey to a safe port. After walking a few days inland we arrived at this mountain where we found many ores and mines. We worked here for sixteen years and we acquired much gold, copper and valuable jewels. Signed by Eklton, commander of this group and by his secretary, Nada.

In 1874, Professor Ladislaus Netto, then director of the National Museum in Brazil, discovered the famous "Parahyba Inscription," which recorded a message of despair, apparently carved by miserable Phoenicians deploring the unhappy fate that had brought them to a land of intolerable heat and omnipresent fevers. It received little attention among Brazilian archaeologists, but was investigated intently by German philologists, who thought it genuine. The scholar Schlottman published a commentary on it in *Janare Literaturzeitung*, No. 30, 1874, in which he discussed the inscription at some length. In 1953, Richard Hennig devoted two pages to it in his *Terra Incognitae*, but was forced to treat it negatively since another German philologist had appeared on the scene and pronounced it a forgery.

The most impressive study of Mediterranean inscriptions ever made in Brazil was by a scholar named Bernardo da Silva Ramos, a retired industrialist who, despite a late start, succeeded in obtaining 2800 inscriptions up along the Amazon. Hearing of mysterious rocks with strange scratchings upon them, he went in search of them, found them and laboriously copied them. Then he took them to a rabbi in Manaos. The old Jewish scholar scanned the scratchings thoughtfully, then proceeded to translate. He told Ramos that these writings were Phoenician, and could only mean that at some time in the dim past, Phoenicians had hacked their ways through the steaming Amazon jungle. Fired by this intelligence, Ramos continued his hunt for inscriptions until his death. He reported most of his finds in a book published in the 1920s. Needless to say, Brazilian archaeologists greeted the book with unbridled apathy.

At this moment, all supposed Phoenician inscriptions in Brazil are branded forgeries by the archaeologists and historians of that country. I can present no statement concerning them at all, for the simple reason that I could persuade no authority in Brazil even to comment upon them.

I think the inscriptions are genuine, and that they were left by pre-Christian travelers from the Mediterranean. It must be recognized that the Carthaginians knew Africa well. They had planted colonies along its western coast many years before. They must have learned of the trade winds and equatorial current, predisposed toward South America, which caressed Africa's western coast. The Spaniards learned to use these twin forces soon after the discovery of America by Columbus. In *History under the Sea*, Mendel Peterson of the department of history at the Smithsonian Institution opens the little book with this paragraph:

> Very soon after the voyages of exploration of Columbus and the early settlements in the West Indies the Spanish had learned that the sea and air

currents of the North Atlantic Basin could be well utilized to carry them from Spain to the New World and back again. Leaving Spain, ships bound for the Caribbean would normally drop down to the vicinity of the Cape Verde Islands and sail westward on the southerly winds, which came to be known as the Southeast Trades because of this fact. The ships would make a landfall around Trinidad, enter the Caribbean, and sail to the port of their destination, Cartagena, Veracruz or Havana, Cuba.

Peterson then describes the return voyage, plotted through the Florida Straits. The Spaniards knew how to get to South America, or its coastal islands, shortly after 1492. Is it reasonable to assume that the Carthaginians performed the same voyages? I think so. They have been shown to be inquisitive sailors, and earnest seekers after new trading posts. I don't doubt for a moment that they found their way to South America. In 146 B.C. the knowledge of the route to South America became a useful piece of information.

In that year, Carthage was destroyed by the Romans in the ultimate act of the Punic Wars. Carthage was no more, the sea power of the Phoenicians-Carthaginians was reduced to a mere memory. The shattered remnants of the Carthaginian fleet raced for the Pillars of Hercules and sped south, falling in with the trades and the current. They were steering for South America. And it is more than probable that they were pursued by ships from the fleet of Scipio Aemilianus, proud commander of the victorious Roman-African expeditionary force. Paul Hermann voices the belief that Scipio may have pursued the shaken Carthaginians to ascertain that they had indeed been driven into the far reaches of the Atlantic, whence they would never return. I think there's more to the story than that. I think that one (or more) of the Roman ships actually followed the South American-bound Carthaginians, and chased them all the way to Venezuela. There the Romans were shipwrecked. The Carthaginians continued on their flight and attempted no landing until they reached the mouth of the Amazon, where they paused, perhaps on Caviana Island, there to recover and take stock. From there they pushed up the Amazon to the region where da Silva Ramos found the mysterious inscriptions.

I think the stones from the Amazon and the stone from Rio de Janeiro are documents left by the Carthaginians. I think they came to Brazil to escape the Romans who conquered them in battle and pursued them across the Atlantic.

I have already expressed the belief that these unhappy Carthaginians were chased by a Roman ship which foundered on the Venezuelan shore. If not, how does one account for a find of Roman coins on that shore in the late nineteenth century? Were the coins all that remained of the unfortunate Roman ship? Or were they simply lost by one of the ship's complement as he left the wrecked vessel? And may we speculate on the possibility of more than one ship? I have often wondered about the origins of the "White Indians" of Venezuela. They were noted by the Spaniards in the sixteenth century. "White Indian" legends are smilingly dismissed by anthropologists and historians alike.

But I wonder. They invariably seem to turn up where there is suspicion of pre-Columbian settlement. New England, as you will see, was the locale of many such settlements. And I smile, too, as I read an observation by Dr. William Howells, writing of Indian types in *Mankind So Far:* "The Indians of New England seem to have been the least Mongoloid and most European-looking of any in appearance, and are fairly well-represented by the head on the Buffalo nickel."

Perhaps the Phoenicians-Carthaginians never set foot on our shores at all. Or perhaps they did. Let's examine the evidence once more:

Stone ruins in New Hampshire thought to be of Bronze Age vintage.

A sacrificial table in the above ruins.

Carthaginian coins on an island in mid-Atlantic.

Inscriptions on rocks in Pennsylvania thought to be Phoenician.

Mysterious grooved stones unlike the product of any known Amerind culture—from the same neighborhood.

Inscriptions collected from rocks in Brazil.

Roman coins in Venezuela.

Rumors of bronze shields, daggers, and swords.

A "Phoenician" ship carved in a Massachusetts stone.

An unfinished Doric pedestal and rosettes carved in the Guilford rocks.

There are doubtless more signs and artifacts, if we could but find them. Look at the map at the beginning of this chapter. From the Mediterranean, they came out in their ships to New Hampshire. (The Pilgrims sailed by accident to New England at a much later date.) Some went off course and landed in Virginia, sailing upstream some 50 miles to the Harrisburg, Pennsylvania, area. Their landfall was at the Chesapeake. (Raleigh and his colonists also made a landfall near the Chesapeake, later settled Jamestown and Roanoke Island.) Still others fled the destruction of Carthage and went to South America. (In 1952, Dr. Louis Alain Bombard put to sea in a rubber raft. Leaving North Africa in August, he arrived in Barbados, a few hundred miles from Venezuela, in December. His motive power: the southeastern trade winds and the equatorial current. The Spaniards had used the same natural forces 400 years earlier.)

I think the Phoenicians-Carthaginians were the second discoverers of America. Or, for the purists, the first *recorded* discoverers. Recorded? Yes, in the rocks of Pennsylvania, Brazil, and Connecticut. In the scattered glacial rocks of New Hampshire painfully turned into megalithic buildings.

And I also think that the New Hampshire site was the scene of another occupation by Europeans, those Mr. William Goodwin was concerned with. But they didn't come for another thousand years. And when they did, the Phoenicians were gone. Killed off by Indians, or assimilated into the area's tribes. But Mr. Goodwin's people did arrive, and created unknowingly, a legend that was to puzzle historians for centuries. Unable to trace its sources, they eventually put the legend down to a map maker with a too-active imagination. I say the fellow who started it was not expressing any imaginative quality at all. He was simply transcribing the facts.

But I must keep the proper progression.

You'll meet Mr. Goodwin's people in Chapter 6.

CHAPTER 3

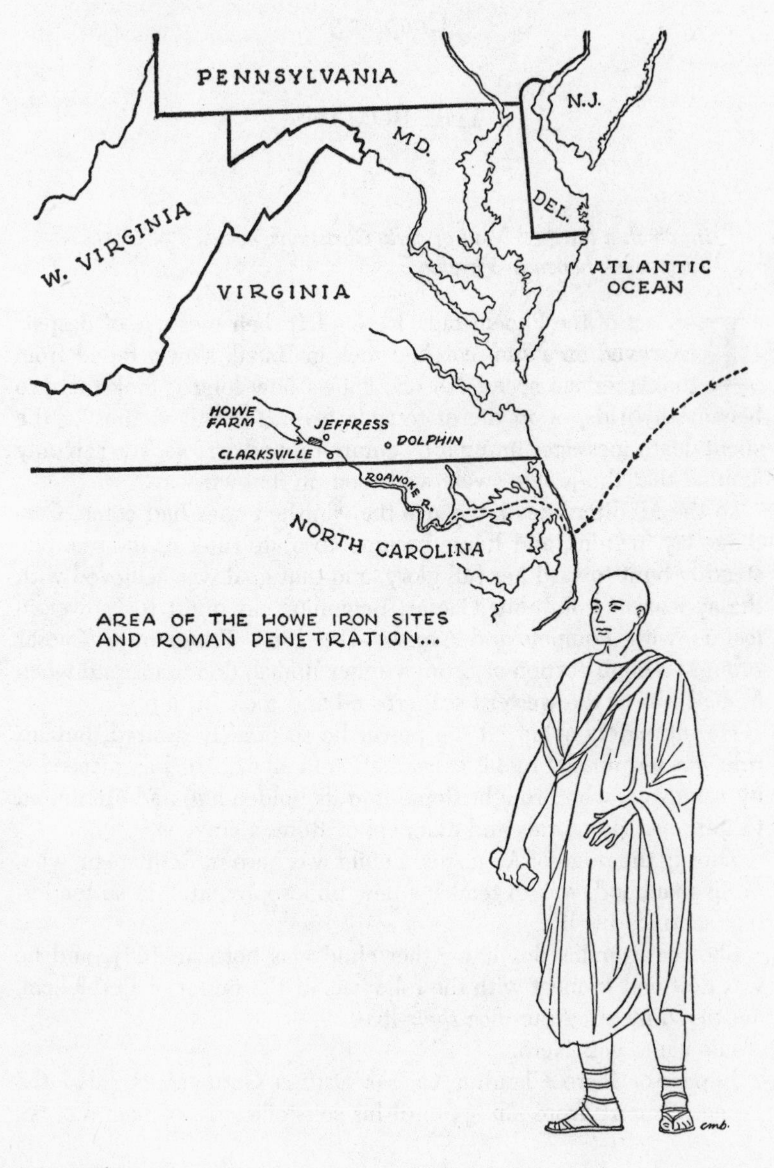
PENNSYLVANIA
N.J.
MD.
DEL.
W. VIRGINIA
VIRGINIA
ATLANTIC
OCEAN
HOWE
FARM
JEFFRESS
DOLPHIN
CLARKSVILLE
ROANOKE R.
NORTH CAROLINA
AREA OF THE HOWE IRON SITES
AND ROMAN PENETRATION...
cmb.

Chapter 3

THE ROMANS

[A.D. 64]

In which a terrified band of early Christians, accused of incendiarism, seek haven in Virginia.

THE last of the Phoenicians, having left their message of despair engraved on a sun-scorched rock in Brazil, slowly faded from the American scene. No one knows how long it took them to become hybrids, or to die of terrible fevers, or fall victims to the silent death messages brought by curare-dipped arrows. We can only assume that the jungle swallowed them in its own way.

In the Mediterranean, whence the vanished ones had come, Carthage lay in ruins, and Rome became absolute ruler of the sea. She steadily built toward her full glory, and that goal was achieved with the appearance of Julius Caesar. Beginning his quest for power in league with Pompey and Crassus—the First Triumvirate—Caesar brought a huge portion of Europe under Roman dominion, and when he had run to the western sea, crossed and took Britain.

He ultimately achieved the power he so fiercely desired, but his rule was terminated by his assassination in 44 B.C. He was succeeded by Augustus, who brought Rome into its golden age and attempted to improve the morals and manners of Rome's citizens.

During the reign of Augustus, a child was born in Bethlehem, who, in his manhood, was to tender a new philosophy, and, in so tendering, sacrifice his life.

Shortly after his death, another child was born, in Italy, and he was destined to meet with the followers of the infant of Bethlehem, and in so meeting sacrifice *their* lives.

His name was Nero.

Imperator Nero Claudius Caesar Drusus Germanicus ruled the Roman Empire from A.D. 55 until his self-inflicted death in A.D. 68.

Only seventeen when he succeeded the Emperor Claudius to power, Nero began his reign well, and showed promise that he would be a wise and good ruler. This admirable state of affairs lasted for but a short time. Nero was not truly equipped to handle wisely the power he had achieved, being unable to concentrate fully on matters of state. His inability stemmed partially from his desire to be an actor and musician, and partially from his love of excesses of all kinds. With these intrusive forces distracting him, he bolstered and maintained his power through various crimes which included the disposal of his wives and his own mother. He was inordinately fond of exhibiting himself at his circuses—displays in which all manner of vice was ritual—and he sometimes disguised these affairs as religious ceremonies in order to employ the services of the Vestal Virgins.

The Roman historian, Tacitus, in writing of Nero's Principate, disgustedly recounts one illustration of his excesses, "that I may not have again and again to narrate similar extravagance." Nero, asserts Tacitus, reached a peak in his profligacy when he ultimately took to using the entire city of Rome "as his private house." He prepared banquets in public places and provided extravaganzas unequaled in vice and general debauchery for public consumption. It is notable that Tacitus, deploring the fantastic behavior of Nero, describes the nature of his revels, but fails to record the reaction of the populace, for whom the revels were created. Unfortunately, the people enjoyed these spectacles rather thoroughly; and Tacitus, manifesting a total abhorrence of the emperor, could not bring himself to record any reaction which might have indicated approval of Nero's antics.

The illustration given by Tacitus is wondrous to consider. A raft was constructed and towed about Agrippa's Lake by other vessels whose crews consisted of the more depraved male population of the city. The vessels "glittered with gold and ivory," and they glided over waters filled with sea monsters from the ocean. Birds and beasts were obtained from foreign countries, but Tacitus dwelleth not on their purpose. On one side of the lake, brothels filled with noble ladies were set up, while on the other naked prostitutes were placed for atmosphere; they performed a choreography consisting of obscene gestures and movements. The saturnalia apparently continued for several days, doubtless fatiguing the undulating ladies of ill fame, for Tacitus notes that "a few days afterwards," Nero climaxed the orgy by marrying himself to one Pythagoras, a member of the depraved set. Tacitus, plainly revolted by his own chronicle, relates it thusly: "The bridal veil was put over the emperor; people saw the witness of the ceremony, the wedding dower, the couch and the nuptial torches; everything in a word was plainly visible, which, even when a woman weds darkness hides."

Having established, however roughly, the character of the man who was to be responsible for the next discovery of America, we will now establish how it happened to come about.

In the year A.D. 64, Nero's devotion to debauchery and murder-for-expediency was interrupted by a great fire which swept through Rome for six days and seven nights, according to most historians, though Tacitus himself allows it but five days. The fire apparently burst forth in the Great Circus, immediately consuming many small shops located there and quickly thereafter destroyed the Circus itself. Blazing furiously, the fire was carried on a high wind to the Palatine, Velia and Esquiline, residential areas near the Circus.

Tacitus paints a grim picture of the conflagration, and includes an intriguing passage which presages the suspicions and rumors concerning the cause of the fire which were to spread through Rome as rapidly as did the flames themselves, and force Nero to secure a scapegoat to satisfy the people.

Here is the way Tacitus tells it, in the Church-Brodribb translations:

> The blaze in its fury ran first through the level portions of the city, then rising to the hills, where it again devastated every place below them, it outstripped all preventive measures; so rapid was the mischief, and so completely at its mercy the city, with those narrow, winding passages and irregular streets, which characterized old Rome. Added to this were the wailings of terror-stricken women, the feebleness of age, the helpless inexperience of childhood, the crowds who sought to save themselves or others, dragging out the infirm or waiting for them, and by their hurry in the one case, by their delay in the other, aggravating the confusion. Often, while they looked behind them, they were intercepted by flames on their side or in their face. Or if they reached a refuge close at hand, when this too was seized by the fire, they found that, even places, which they had imagined to be remote, were involved in the same calamity. At last, doubting what they should avoid, or whither betake themselves, they crowded the streets or flung themselves down in the fields, while some who had lost their all, even their daily bread, and others out of love for their kinsfolk, whom they had been unable to rescue, perished, though escape was open

to them, and no one dared to stop the mischief, because of incessant menaces from a number of persons who forbade the extinguishing of the flames, because again others openly hurled brands, and kept shouting that there was one who gave them authority, either seeking to plunder more freely, or obeying orders.

The last sentence in Tacitus' description is extremely significant. Quite obviously, someone wanted the fire kept alive. When, at last, the flames were quieted, the people wanted to know who was so desirous of consuming Rome—taking the lives of so many of its citizens in the process. There was little time to ask these questions when the fire was brought under control, for it broke out in another section of the city almost immediately. Now it raged through less heavily populated neighborhoods and the loss of life was consequently not as great as it had been initially. When, for the second time, the flames were halted, Rome was indeed a charred ruin. Out of its fourteen districts, three were leveled to the ground, seven contained but a few shells of houses and public buildings and only four were relatively uninjured. Temples, monuments, art treasures of Rome and Greece, altars, shrines, private mansions, and blocks of dismal tenements all fell victims to the flames.

And the questions were asked again: Who was apparently so anxious to keep the flames fed? Why did the fire break out a second time, and in other, previously untouched sections of the city?

The first suspicions were directed at Nero himself, despite his sudden appearance in the city at the fire's height, during which time he made every human effort to accommodate the homeless by throwing open undamaged public buildings, erecting temporary shelters and lowering the price of wheat to feed the destitute. His actions, however humane and sympathetic, were viewed dimly. Rumor had it that while the flames were raging, he had appeared on a stage at a private gathering and sung of the destruction of Troy, presumably accompanying himself on the guitar or harp, both of which he played well. The popular misconception of his "fiddling" while Rome burned was thus derived from this rumor (and possibly with some foundation).

But other and more damning rumors began to circulate. The most widespread was that Nero set the fire in order that he might outlive the great city. In destroying it, he could then rebuild it in greater glory, and name it for himself. In truth, it is difficult to imagine that

Nero would have destroyed Rome at that time. The Roman treasury was in horrendous shape; the inflationary devices inaugurated by Nero himself led, in fact, to the total bankruptcy which shattered Rome in the third century. The rebuilding would be an inconceivably costly project and one not likely to do other than further damage to the already wounded treasury. Nero's ego, however, was such that could easily have dictated the destruction of Rome in order that he might have the greatest monument a man could achieve: a city designed and built by himself and named in his honor.

Nero was naturally disturbed at the persistence of this rumor which seemed to increase, rather than diminish as the fire became a memory. It was clear that he must find someone upon whom to affix the blame for the fire; the people were convinced that it was incendiary in origin, and he seemed to be the likeliest suspect. So a scapegoat was found, and in finding his victim, Nero unknowingly launched the next expedition across the seas to America.

He declared that the Christians had set the fire, and proceeded to punish them for their "crime."

The occurrence of the great fire of Rome, and the reference to the strange new sect found guilty of setting it marks the first appearance of Christians in secular history. Tacitus, in describing the circumstances which led to affixing blame for the fire on this odd sect, notes that they are called "Christians" and hastens to explain, for the uninitiated, that they derive their name from *Christus,* who had been executed many years in the past by the procurator, Pontius Pilate, under the Emperor Tiberius. The execution, according to Tacitus, thus checked the "most mischievous superstition" of Christianity, but only temporarily; it broke out again, he ruefully declares, not only in Judea, where it originated, but even in Rome "where all things hideous and shameful from every part of the world find their center and become popular."

The Christians in Rome in the year A.D. 64 were a curious admixture of many peoples. Their ranks included Jew and gentile alike, and they came from many countries about the Mediterranean. They were despised by the Romans because they openly professed a loathing for the old religion and the old beliefs, and by that token were considered to be haters of mankind, since mankind largely adhered to the objects of the Christians' wrath. That they were nonconformists and fanatic in their own beliefs was evident. They met in secret assemblies and it was whispered that cannibalism and incest were among the vile rituals of their terrible ceremonies. They were pacifists to a man, and firmly believed that Christ's second coming was but a short time off.

They provided the supreme solution for Nero.

He seized a number of Christians who had allegedly confessed to the crime of firing the city of Rome. From these, and later prisoners, he obtained the names of even more Christians, those who for reasons politic had not openly admitted their alliance with the new sect. Trials were held, and even though the charges were impossible to prove, sentences of torture and death were pronounced. Once the punishments were inaugurated, hundreds of Christians were arrested and sentenced to death simply for being Christians. The setting of the fire had been avenged by the early arrests and executions, now it was thought wise to eradicate the entire sect while the opportunity was at hand.

Death sentences were carried out in ways designed to amuse the populace as well as fulfill the penalty. Some were dressed in wild animal skins and herded into the amphitheatre. To the applause of the throng, they darted about, seeking escape until it was deemed time to bring about the executions. At the proper moment, packs of starved dogs were turned loose in the arena, and the crowd was treated to the charming spectacle of humans torn to pieces by canine fangs. The women were subjected to the most unthinkable indecencies as they were slowly put to death—their dirges provided only by the raucous cheers and obscenities of the spectators.

Burning was prescribed for some, and Nero himself brought this latter method to perfection when he drove his chariot about his own gardens at night, illumination being provided by the flaming bodies of crucified Christians placed at reasonable distances about the grounds.

In reality, the people of Rome weren't fully convinced of the Christians' guilt, and Nero's fiendish punishments came eventually to nauseate the Romans, perhaps because they were protracted for such a long period. This surprising reaction by people accustomed to watching bloody gladiatorial combats in the arena much as we today watch various sporting events had an unanticipated result. It created a sympathy for the hitherto despised followers of Christus which fortuitously aided in strengthening their cause.

Gradually the killing of Christians ceased, prompted partly by public disapproval of Nero's cruelty, and partly because Nero eventually had to concentrate on affairs of state.

The Christian population of Rome was decimated, their greatest leaders, St. Peter and St. Paul, were dead—victims of the persecution. Those remaining were forced to flee or go into hiding. Even though public opinion had helped stem the destruction of the queer sect, it appeared that an atmosphere had been created in which it was criminal simply to be a Christian. In such an atmosphere it is not strange that some of the persecuted sect should seek new places to worship their God and practice the teachings of Christus, who had shown them light in a dark world.

I think that a band of these beleagured nonconformists resolved to leave Rome and seek the lands to the west which were rumored to have been visited by the Phoenicians. Their composition was Jew and gentile; the Jews (and possibly even Phoenicians) among them may have had traditional information of these lands, obtained indirectly from their neighbors in Tyre and Sidon. The Romans and Greeks among them could have been acquainted with the sources from which Diodorus Siculus drew in compiling his 40-volume history of the world.

I think they knew about America.

And they came in a ship, or ships, sailing out through the towering Pillars of Hercules and across the unknown Atlantic, until they made landfall off Bodie, or Pea, or Hatteras Island. They coasted these islands until they found Oregon Inlet; from there they sailed up and into Croatan Sound, and from there into Albemarle Sound. They found the Roanoke River, and sailed up its winding course until they reached Clarksville, in Virginia. They moored their ships in the river and set out to explore the countryside. The Amerinds who first saw these strange craft from another world doubtless thought they were huge, man-carrying birds.

The ships obtained by the Romans were probably merchantmen. It would have been easier for them to pirate a merchant ship or two, rather than attempt to commandeer a man-of-war. Circumstance indicates that they obtained their ships in manner illegal; they had neither the funds nor the time to build ships of their own. Be assured, though, that the craft they appropriated were the best the Mediterranean had ever seen.

The Romans, by the year 64, had attained a superb craftsmanship in building cargo vessels as well as men-of-war. Lionel Casson, expert on ancient shipping, reminds us in *The Ancient Mariners* that the merchant navy of the Romans was enormous, in physical and numerical size. The government cargo carriers ordinarily ran to about 340 tons burden, but the grain fleet had ships of 1200 tons. In A.D. 40, when Caligula removed from Egypt the obelisk which now stands in Nero's Circus, he built a vessel designed to carry 1300 tons, long enough to transport the 130 foot obelisk. In A.D. 64, the Jewish historian, Flavius Josephus, sailed from Alexandria to Rome in a ship carrying six hundred passengers. The Greek, Lucian, in his *Navigium,* describes a Roman grain ship which was storm-driven into Athens. Awed by the huge ship, Lucian wrote an account of it. The vessel was 180 feet long with a beam of about 45 feet, and the depth of her hold was 44 feet. St. Paul's famous voyage from Egypt to Rome, during the course of which he was shipwrecked, took place in A.D. 62. Accompanying the Apostle were 267 others, a light passenger list, according to Casson. The ships were built of pine, fir, or cedar, while interiors were shaped with whatever was in best supply. The stern post rode high and carried a figure of a goose or swan's head, the stem fashioned squarishly, and blunt. Frequently the hulls were covered with sheet lead below the water line, a layer of tarred fabric being placed between it and the wood. Sails were of linen, and lines of flax, hemp, twisted papyrus or even leather. The square sail of the Phoenicians drove the ship, and, like the earlier ships, they could not sail well to windward, but could gather up to 6 or 7 knots with a good forward wind. A cabin for the master was placed aft, and her rudder was actually two steering oars at the stern. There was no real provision for passengers—they slept on deck, usually; some carried little tents which they could erect, viking-like, to get out of the weather. The ship's captain was equipped with a few aids to navigation, such as sounding lines and cups for sampling the bottom. He had no compass, but learned to navigate using landmarks by day, the stars by night.

Compared to the flimsy craft used by Columbus, these were sturdy, seaworthy ships capable of crossing any ocean in comparative safety. It is more than reasonable to assume that at least some of the crew were actual seamen; the others were taught to assist, or keep out of the way, as the voyage progressed.

And that is how I think it was with these persecuted Christians, forced to flee their city because of their individualism and open contempt for the Roman gods—and of the Romans themselves who were not Christians. They stole a ship—or ships—and sailed to Virginia.

In 1943, an engineer named James V. Howe bought a 223-acre farm along the banks of the beautiful Roanoke River, near the town of Jeffress, in Virginia. Interested in raising beef cattle, Mr. Howe reasoned that the quantity of land was sufficient, the climate temperate and the surroundings as pleasant as a man could wish. Since the cattle venture was to be a retirement pursuit, he did not plan to devote his full time to it. Mr. Howe possessed a formidable knowledge of firearms and had already written a massive, two-volume work on the subject, and planned to continue writing about the field he knew best.

Once having gotten the beef problem under control, and plotted a writing schedule hopefully designed to be productive—a monumental task for any man who would put words on paper—Mr. Howe took to wandering about his newly acquired estate to see just what he had bought. He found, among other things, that his land contained an abundance of bog iron, a type of iron which is found on or close to the surface, and is easily worked because of its low melting temperature. Because of its ease of acquiring and working, it was used extensively by colonials in North America from the seventeenth century.

Mr. Howe recognized the presence of bog iron when he began finding pieces of slag, which, he reasoned, had resulted from Indian campfires burning long and hot—hot enough to fuse some of the surface iron. Then he began finding pieces of iron, and, struggling for an explanation of their odd, jagged shapes, decided that he had also acquired the remains of an ancient meteor along with his property. He was intrigued with his "meteor," and saved the many pieces that he stumbled upon. He was even more intrigued when he began picking up pieces of obviously *worked* iron, that is, fashioned by human hands.

Worked iron meant people, and Howe concluded that he had found the site of an old forge, presumably worked by colonials. He knew that the fragments could not have been produced by Indians, since the aboriginals never worked that metal. He delved into the history of the area and discovered that only one attempt had been made to process Virginia's bog iron within historical times, and that effort came to an abrupt and violent conclusion, before production could be started, when a band of intemperate Indians massacred the crew. No other ventures were made after that. The land, he knew, was once part of a huge 4000-acre estate granted to an Army officer of the Revolutionary War, Major John Nelson, in appreciation for his services. Major Nelson, who received the property in 1782, subdivided it in 1815, giving 1000 acres of it to his son. A parcel of the son's land eventually became Mr. Howe's. The segment purchased by Mr. Howe was still as wild as it had been during the Revolution; no attempt was made to utilize the land. It was virgin. And it was determined that there was absolutely no record of iron being worked anywhere on the property from the time of the Nelson occupation.

With this knowledge, Howe was forced to conclude that his iron was not forged by colonials. Now he concentrated on the search for more of the puzzling iron, and in a relatively short time acquired four hundred pounds of it, all manifestly worked. Howe told me that he eventually uncovered sixteen sites, five of which were on his own property, the remaining eleven scattered through Mecklenburg County and in Brunswick County, some 60 miles to the east of the Howe farm. He also located a natural draft furnace which had evidently been used by the mysterious ironworkers. Iron turned up at old Indian campsites, indicating that the Indians had either picked it up from the areas where it had been worked, or traded for it. Apparently they weren't quite sure what to do with it, for the iron at these sites shows no further working, or even hints of any utilitarian purpose to which it might have been put.

The Howe finds were not confined to the surface. Realizing that the ground beneath might reveal the identity of the workers, he began to excavate the land carefully. Iron was found to a depth of 34 inches. Then he struck gold, or, more properly, bronze. One afternoon, as he was digging at what he terms site no. 4, which lay on his own place, he spotted the glint of something he knew wasn't the dull, darkish iron he had been finding. Carefully spooning out the dirt encrusting the object, he slowly revealed a bronze cup, a large jagged piece missing from it, but in relatively good condition. It was recovered from 18 inches below the surface. An analysis of the cup's metal showed that it contained silver in the amount of from one to two per cent. Six cups of similar type and content have been recovered from the ruins of Pompeii and all are on display at the Naples Museum. Three more finds of bronze followed rapidly; two were fragmentary and the third was a bronze spindle whorl.

The isolated finds of bronze amid the debris of what had been an ancient ironworks hinted that they had been brought in from abroad by the ironworkers and not made on the spot. No traces of copper or tin, the metals used in bronze, were found at any of the sites.

Still another revelation was due to stimulate Howe. On May 28, 1950, the Richmond (Virginia) *Times-Dispatch* carried a story of two strangely marked rocks found about a mile apart in Brunswick County, Virginia, near Dolphin. On June 11, the Durham (North Carolina) *Herald* carried the same story. The rocks, according to the newspapers, were thought to be of Phoenician or Chaldean origin, or of some Semitic civilization. He hurried to the sites and examined the inscriptions carefully. He photographed both rocks by the "chalking" method, to insure better reproduction, and also unretouched. Archaeology is quick to strike at any who chalks in rock inscriptions for photographic purposes. No matter how innocent the soul who performs such an act, condemnation and intimation of fraud ensues, the implication being that the basic design has been augmented to suit the finder's whim.

James Howe realized that he had a three-piece jigsaw puzzle, and he was determined to make the pieces fit properly. He had iron, which included a short, thrusting-type sword, a curved sword with the end broken off, small knives, small chisels for cutting metal or stone, ancient nails, headers for making nails and other iron fragments which had been worked. He also had a bronze cup in reasonably good condition and three other fragments of that metal, including a spindle whorl. To round out the baffling picture, he had two rocks with ancient, unrecognizable carvings on them.

In an effort to maintain a scientific approach to his digs and finds, Mr. Howe enlisted the aid of various experts in the fields most nearly concerned with each of the puzzle fragments. One entered the picture unsolicited. He was R. W. Breckenridge, professor of Metallurgy and Mechanical Engineering at Iowa State College, in Ames, Iowa. Breckenridge became interested in the Howe iron after reading newspaper accounts of it. He obtained a representative number of slag and iron specimens from Mr. Howe and proceeded to study them. When he had completed his study, he wrote to the Virginian, telling him of his conclusions. This is his opinion of the iron, as quoted from Howe's report on the iron sites, read at the Eastern States Archaeological Federation Meeting held at the American Museum of Natural History in New York, on October 13, 1949:

> Several of the microstructures of the ancient Greek iron which Prof. W. C. Howe of Columbia University had made an extensive study of about twenty years ago are duplicated in the specimens I polished, etched and examined from your collection. Certainly the material is not cast iron from a cupola, wrought iron from a puddling furnace, or steel from a convertor.

Mr. Howe then points out that Professor Breckenridge had made only metalographic comparison tests on the iron, using microphotographs of ancient Greek iron. It had not been possible to make chemical analyses on the iron to determine its actual composition. That in no way minimized the importance of Breckenridge's conclusion; he had used the prototype method of establishing period, an accepted one in archaeology.

The Breckenridge report encouraged Mr. Howe. Now, for the first time, a clue had appeared, pointing specifically toward the ancient origin of the iron that Mr. Howe had suspected. Further encouragement came from a completely unanticipated source. Mr. Emil Wagner, whose specialty in life was not archaeology or anthropology, but who created and edited company house organs to earn his keep, became interested in the Howe sites and went to see the iron hunter. Although Wagner dealt in matters industrial, he sometimes used editorial material that was highly *un*-industrial in his publications—giving them a touch seldom encountered in periodicals dedicated to the dissemination of news about machinery, etc. The Howe story appealed to him and, after seeing Howe, and inspecting his collection, Wagner became quite excited. He not only wrote a two-part story about the mystery, but he sent samples of the metal off to the A. M. Byers Company in Pittsburgh, Pennsylvania. He requested that they examine the samples in an effort to determine their age. Byers assigned E. P. Best, a metallurgist of 30-odd years experience, to the task. Best went to work immediately, and gave the strange metal a thorough going-over. When he ended his tests, he had determined the chemical structure of the iron, microphotographed it and decided it was old, having been made by the "Direct Process" of ironworking used by the ancients. He then sent a report to Wagner, who published it together with an explanation of the Direct Process:

> Wrought iron used to be made by what is now known as the Direct Process in which there was no step between the first reduction of the ore in the furnace and the shaping under the smith's hammer. Fuel and ore were put into a trough . . . and raked forward into the furnace as reduction took place. Draft was supplied by bellows . . . worked by foot, the bellows being reopened by cords attached to the ends of bent poles. At the end of a heat, there was a spongy mass, mostly iron, at the bottom of the furnace. This was then removed and hammered and heated again and again to remove impurities. Extreme variation in product was the rule. Practice of late years includes a process or two between the original reduction of ore and the forging. There's close control and good uniformity.

Continuing in the article written for the house organ of the Gisholt Machine Company, Wagner presents Best's report:

> Those samples you sent us and which you say come from Virginia look to me as though someone must have made them from the nearest iron ore that was easy to dig. The samples lack uniformity, are variable in structure and chemical composition—earmarks of iron made many years ago. They were almost certainly made with the Direct Process. Yes, they're old, probably a couple of hundred years or more. No, I can't say they're ancient. But I can say this—if I had a piece of iron I knew to be ancient I'd expect to find it, on examination, to be about like those pieces of yours. What they show is altogether consistent with primitive manufacture.

One could hardly expect to encounter a more conservative report. Still, Mr. Best has made his point. He asserted that the samples were "almost certainly" made by the direct method, noting their variability in structure and chemical composition. Mr. Best is an expert. His position was that of an expert with a company which is the nation's biggest producer of wrought iron. He says the samples are old, but, in the conservative manner of the scientist, says they're possibly a couple of hundred years old. A positive contribution, but not enough. Wagner adds, in his own article, that even the admission of an age of a couple of hundred years is significant; that loose dating puts the iron back far enough in time to preclude its being colonial. An age of only 200 years would predate the first colonial occupation of the sites where the iron was found.

With two promising metallurgical reports to bolster him, Howe then attempted to obtain expert opinion on the bronze cup, along with the other bronze fragments. He took them to the Smithsonian Institution, along with many fragments of iron. The men of the Smithsonian examined all the evidence, put them on display in clean cases, smiled and shook their heads. They had no opinions. They didn't know what they were. The cup resembled similar cups in the Naples Museum, but, "realistically" the cup and the fragments were found in America. How could they possibly be older than the last decade of the fifteenth century?

And there rests the case of the bronze cup. And the fragments.

Slightly dejected, but by no means discouraged, Mr. Howe tackled next the problem of the inscriptions on the rocks. The rocks, you will recall, were found near Dolphin, Virginia, about ten miles north of Lawrenceville, the county seat for Brunswick County. Nearby the rocks were two other iron sites, and the short, thrusting sword was found twenty miles southeast of the rocks. Letters were sent to Professor George G. Camerion of the University of Michigan, Dr. Nelson Glueck of the Hebrew Union College in Cincinnati, Ohio, and Dr. Michael I. Rostovtzeff at Yale University. Photographs of the inscriptions were enclosed, and Howe asked for translations or opinions.

Dr. Glueck replied: "I assure you that the various signs and letters found have absolutely nothing to do with any Semitic language whatsoever. They are very interesting and obviously very important."

Professor Camerion replied: "There is not much possibility of interpreting the signs on your photographs so that we can explain these words as Sumerian; rather, they look like rude scratchings such as may be found on public or private monuments all over the world from all periods of time. This is, of course, one man's opinion."

Mr. Howe's report to the Eastern States Archaeological Federation, from which the above quotes were extracted, does not quote Dr. Rostovtzeff.

The replies received are extremely significant. One of two conditions is evident: Either the men who study ancient languages in universities and museums throughout the world actually possess scanty knowledge of archaic communications or fear of ridicule restricts formulating a positive conclusion. I suspect the latter condition is closer to the truth. Once again we witness the thought paralysis which seizes scholars when artifacts, monuments, or inscriptions of an alien culture are found in America. They simply shouldn't be here, and if one ventures to document them as specific relics of a specific culture, censure, ridicule, and loss of reputation could result.

By now Mr. Howe was exactly nowhere. The agonizing frustration of inconclusiveness left him in a daze, but a ray of hope broke through from the Smithsonian. They notified him that they would engage in a dig at Clarksville, about 10 miles from his home.

The dig was precipitated by the threat of a government dam (Buggs Island) being built on the Roanoke below Clarksville. On its completion, in 1952, many of the Howe sites would be covered with the dam's backwater forever. Time was of the essence. Accordingly, the Smithsonian's Carl F. Miller began excavating along the river, near Clarksville, in the summer of 1951. The dig produced 78 human skeletons and quantities of slag and iron, together with Indian artifacts. The site was identified as an ancient Indian campsite and cemetery. The iron was of the same structure as that found in other iron sites locally.

Quantities of charcoal were found in hearths that were uncovered.

No Carbon-14 tests have ever been made on this charcoal. Mr. Howe has quietly repeated his requests for C-14 tests on the Clarksville charcoal several times. He has been unable to obtain tests.

A most disturbing thought occurs here.

First, why has no C-14 test been run on organic material from one of the most baffling sites in the United States? C-14 tests are now made almost as a matter of routine, even on sites where the age can be closely approximated without it. At Clarksville, the charcoal was found in situ with fragments of iron thought to be of the same structure as early Greek iron. Opinions on the iron's structure were offered not by amateurs, but by two men respected in their fields. In order to settle the question of the age of the site, and thereby obtain further clues to the age of the iron, a C-14 test would necessarily be the first item on the agenda. But no C-14 tests have been made.

Perhaps it is better phrased conversely: An expedition, digging at a site where supposedly ancient fragments of iron have been found, obtains organic material suitable for C-14 tests, but fails to have these tests performed. Can a complete report be made on the site? Apparently it can. The report is in. All except for C-14 tests.

Perhaps the Smithsonian plans to make these tests. When? Eight years have elapsed (at this writing) since the expedition dug.

A more profoundly disturbing thought occurs now.

Suppose that Clarksville site wasn't Indian at all. Suppose it was a site occupied by Romans. Suppose these Romans lived at the site, trading with the Indians, and in that manner obtained pottery, and points, and other Indian utensils and tools and weapons. Is the possibility too remote? Or could the site represent an assimilative period marking a time when the Romans and the Indians were becoming one? Could that account for an admixture of Indian and Iron artifacts and fragments?

Why not?

But . . .

The site was excavated in Clarksville, Virginia, a commonwealth located in the United States of America. The location alone stipulates that it must be Indian. The ground rules for archaeology state specifically (although they are unwritten) that any site uncovered in the United States must be Indian, or colonial, and cannot have been occupied by humans other than Indian prior to 1492.

Such are the apparent ground rules.

Skeletons exhumed from a suspected Indian site are automatically tagged "Indian" and filed. (Because they were found in America.) Indian artifacts are unmistakable. They, too, are tagged and filed. The iron presents a slightly different problem. But it must be colonial. The Indians found it and took it to their campsite, thinking it could be worked into points or tools. Finding their skills not enough to accomplish same, the iron is thrown away at the site.

Clear?

All but the explanation dealing with who made the iron—and when.

It can only be colonial. (Every schoolboy and archaeologist knows that no Europeans could have been in America in the first century A.D.: NEBC Principle.)

But there is one way of getting some sense out of the puzzle. Charcoal was found. Put it through a Carbon-14 test, immediately.

I cannot provide a happy ending for this story. I cannot tell you that the charcoal was tested and found to be 2000 years old, and having come from the same horizon as the iron, indicates, stratigraphically, that the iron and the charcoal were contemporary. I cannot furnish a report from the Smithsonian stating all of this. There is none.

There was no C-14 test.

Do I sound too harsh?

Let us recall, with heads bowed, the "colonial brick" at North Salem which, oddly enough, proved to be pottery not indigenous to the area.

There is more.

Mr. Howe, now fighting a losing battle, has tried to obtain C-14 tests from the University of Arizona. It refused on the grounds that the university could only test material found in Arizona.

He attempted to interest Dr. Libby in the charcoal, through the good offices of Professor Breckenridge. Results: zero.

Meantime, of course, the dam has been built, and many of the 16 sites are gone forever; engulfed by millions of tons of water from the Buggs Island Dam. All of the sites first discovered by Mr. Howe are lost.

He appealed to the Smithsonian to dig out some of the original sites on his property ere the flood waters inundated them for all time.

The Smithsonian said "no."

They said the sites were "too mysterious."

I don't think they're mysterious at all. I think they're Roman. And I think the sites were occupied sometime during and after A.D. 64, by persecuted Christians: Romans, Greeks, and Jews; possibly even some Phoenicians or other Mediterranean peoples. I think they came to America, driven by Nero's revolting indecencies—committed on their persons in the guise of death sentences—and lived happily in Virginia, trading with, and later assimilating with the Indians. I also think that the Clarksville site might be the last real trace of them.

Except for the inscriptions.

The rocks containing what seem to be only letters I will not presume to theorize upon. I think the clues lie in the rock (Plate 9) which contains symbols and "letters" alike.

Below are the five symbols, or signs, which appear on that rock; below these, in turn, are comparable symbols known as "Chrismons" (signatures or monograms of Christ) and letters which appear to be Greek:

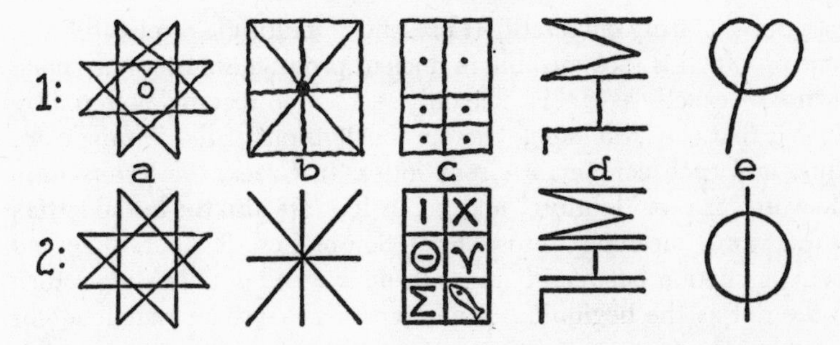

Figure *a* in line two, according to Rudolph Koch, a German who has compiled *The Book of Signs,* is an octogram, prevalent in pre-Christian times, meaning unknown, and later used as a Chrismon by the earliest followers of Christ. In this instance, it is considered to be the intersection of four "x's" and represents a concealed monogram. The figure in line 1, found at Dolphin, is, as can be seen, almost identical. A dot in the center, with a minute triangle above it has been added by the engraver, perhaps as further confirmation that this indeed was the monogram of Christus, and not the ancient octogram used by pagans. The triangle, in pre-Christian times, symbolized creative intellect, and was originally an ancient Egyptian symbol for the Godhead, as well as Pythagorean symbol for wisdom. The Christians borrowed it and displayed it as the sign of the triple personality of God. The circle, or dot, I cannot explain. The dot is the beginning of all signs; it is the mark from which all signs spring. The unknown carver may have felt it best represented the beginnings of life—the new life being led in the Virginia wilderness by former citizens of Rome.

Figure *b,* in line 2, is Koch's illustration of another Chrismon, a double cross consisting of the Greek "x" and the cross itself. Its counterpart in line 1 is absolutely identical, with another small addition graved by the inscriber. To finish it off, the cutter carefully enclosed the sign within a square. This form had a number of meanings to early peoples. It was an emblem of worldliness, it signified the number four in a variety of manifestations: the four elements, the four corners of the Heavens, the four Evangelists and the four rivers of Paradise. In his mystic way, the carver was creating a sign readily recognizable to his contemporaries but appearing to us, 2000 years later, only as an interesting design, its meaning long since forgotten.

Figure *c* is truly enigmatic. It presents a multitude of possibilities, none of which is recognizable in ancient prototypes. There are none portrayed exactly as is this. The only segmented rectangle offered by Koch is that of a "fish" sign, wherein the divisions of the rectangle are equal and each contains a Greek letter. In Greek, the letters form the word "fish" or "Ichthys," and, rebus-like, are also the initial letters of five words meaning "Jesus Christ, Son of God, Saviour." I see no real conjunction between figure *c* in lines 1 and 2, unless we return to the dot as the beginning of all signs, and consider that it might possibly represent a repetitive pattern of "seeds" within rectangular symbols, welded together, representing world and nature.

Figure *d*, as it appears on line 1, seems to be a monogram, most probably that of the engraver. It is meaningless until the probable letters are separated and we see it as it would appear in single letter fashion in line 2. The three suggested letters on the lower line are the Greek Σ, or "S," the Ꞁ, or retrograde "C," and the ⌶, which resembles an "H" turned 90 degrees, and has no counterpart in the Latin or English alphabet, although its incidence falls about where the English letter "G" would. Koch admonishes that care be exercised, however, in attempting to determine the exact structure of ancient monograms. These designs were sometimes disguised; letters would sometimes be drawn in reverse, or only partially inscribed. By this reasoning, the retrograde "C" noted above would be the standard "C", drawn in reverse. The letters that I think were used all date from the Eastern Greek alphabet which came into general use about 460 B.C., and maintained its character for many centuries. It is at once apparent that interpreting such a monogram remains largely a matter of conjecture to any but the most knowledgeable philologist.

Figure *e* can be interpreted in two ways. Its form is used in at least 5 Greek alphabets, beginning with its use as an equivalent to the letter "Q" in an alphabet derived from inscriptions at Thera which date back to the ninth century B.C. It gradually changed its appearance, dropping the vertical center line to approximate the tail of our modern "q" but has disappeared altogether in modern Greek. It can be traced to the ninth century B.C. as a letter. In the fifth century B.C., however, it took on a new meaning in the Eastern Greek, at which time it was used as an aspirate, symbolizing the "ch" sound, and its shape underwent a slight metamorphosis. The tail was shortened, and a vertical riser was added above the circle: Φ.

On the Virginia rock its meaning is not decipherable with any satisfaction. It could be another monogram, or, if one were to strain for a meaning, it is conceivable that it was set down as the first two letters of Christ's name by someone using Greek shorthand to transmit a Latin name. Even I reel slightly at this thought, so I think it best that the symbol be put down as an imponderable until such time as a courageous scholar comes forth with a solution to its meaning.

Ancient iron, ancient bronze, ancient inscriptions.

Found in America and apparently, at this writing, of interest to no one but Mr. Howe.

Bronze cups in the Naples Museum are dated at 2000 years or more. They were found in Pompeii.

A nearly identical bronze cup in the Smithsonian carries a question mark. It was found in America.

A nail header found in an old Roman site at Saalfeld Fort in Germany is dated at A.D. 200. It was found in Europe.

A nearly identical nail header in the Smithsonian carries a question mark. It was found in America.

Threaded nuts found near Neuwied, Germany, in an ancient Roman site, are dated at A.D. 200. They were found in Europe.

Nearly identical threaded nuts in the Smithsonian carry a question mark. They were found in America.

Inscriptions on rocks fail to produce even speculation from ancient language experts.

Charcoal is removed from a site containing iron thought to be ancient. No C-14 test is made.

The case is apparently closed.

Many of the sites are under water.

No one is interested enough to reopen the remaining sites or perform C-14 tests. The Romans, if they were Romans, are dead.

Requiescant in pace.

But I mustn't be too critical of the professional archaeologists. I must dedicate a paragraph to the amateurs of Virginia, as well. Eager to learn what investigations of the Howe sites had been made by the Archaeological Society of Virginia (a group, like its counterparts over the country, composed of a few guiding professionals and a great many amateurs), I wrote to the society's secretary and inquired.

In reply I was told that the writer believed that Mr. Howe had had the materials from his site examined and they were "determined to be colonial." The letter closed with this declaration:

"Howe never revealed the location of the site to our society."

An odd declaration. I have before me a report read by James V. Howe, at the E.S.A.F. Meeting held at the Valentine Museum in Richmond, Virginia. The paper was read sometime between 2:30 and 5:00 P.M., on Friday, November 11, 1949. In attendance at that meeting were Dr. C. G. Holland, then president of the Archaeological Society of Virginia, and Mrs. Robert W. Claiborne, director of the Valentine Museum, plus many members of the Virginia State Society. Two papers on the archaeology of Virginia were read by members of the Virginia Society, during the same afternoon session participated in by Mr. Howe.

In his paper, Mr. Howe described the sites and locations.

Perhaps the Virginia Society deals only in matters colonial.

It may not be considered discreet to communicate with, or listen to, one who talks of alleged pre-Columbian sites.

That is the only manner in which I can explain the declaration that Mr. Howe never revealed the location of his site to the members of the Archaeological Society of Virginia.

Requiescant in pace.

CHAPTER 4

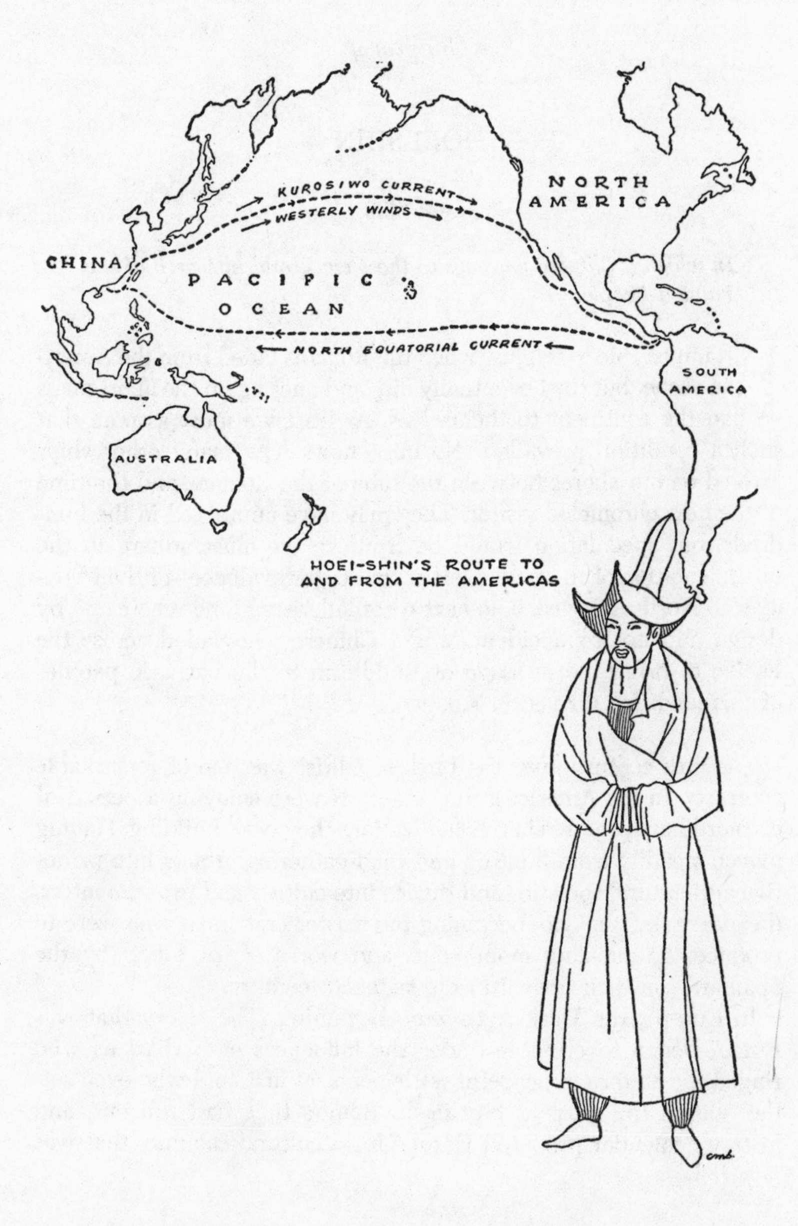
KUROSIWO CURRENT
WESTERLY WINDS
NORTH AMERICA
CHINA
PACIFIC
OCEAN
NORTH EQUATORIAL CURRENT
SOUTH AMERICA
AUSTRALIA
HOEI-SHIN'S ROUTE TO AND FROM THE AMERICAS

Chapter 4

HOEI-SHIN

[A.D. 499]

In which a Chinese journeys to the New World in search of the Painted People.

IT IS impossible to tell just when the Romans faded from the American scene, but they eventually did, and once again the aboriginals had the continent to themselves. At least we must assume that such a condition prevailed. No one knows how many other ships arrived on our shores between the time of the Romans and the time of the next chronicled visitor. They may have numbered in the hundreds, but speculation would be fruitless; we must adhere to the documentation of those who left accounts—or evidence—of their voyages to North America. The next recorded visitor, one who came by design and not by accident, was a Chinese who sailed across the Pacific to bring the message of Buddhism to the barbaric peoples of this land. He arrived in A.D. 499.

The fifth century after the birth of Christ was one of remarkable contrasts. In the Americas, the Amerinds were enjoying a period of extraordinary progress in the civilizations they were building. Having moved steadily from hunting and food-gathering groups into primitive agricultural societies and thence into cultists and experimenters, they were, by A.D. 400, becoming the master craftsmen who were to produce the amazing monuments and works of art found by the Spaniards on their arrival in the sixteenth century.

In Europe, the Dark Ages were beginning. The "glory that was Rome" began to crumble under the influences of barbarians who ringed the empire in peaceful settlements, at first, and who even settled within the glorious city itself. Rome's time had run out, and history's calendar prepared Europe for a cultural calamity that was to last for nearly a thousand years. Beginning in A.D. 375 the Roman Empire was inundated for two bloody centuries by hordes of barbarians who swept in from the north and east. The first of these rapacious hordes were those of the Huns, who came from some mysterious place along the frontiers of China. These fiercest of nomadic invaders routed out other barbarians in their paths, bottling up a good many of them close to and within the borders of the Roman Empire. Eventually all of the barbarians tested the strength of the Romans and the Romans were found decidedly wanting. But then it must be considered that the attackers of Rome were many, and barbarian in the bargain. Hordes of Visigoths, Ostrogoths, Vandals, Franks, Lombards, Burgundians and Anglo-Saxons scurried over the Empire, leaving decimation where they touched. The fall of Rome was documented in A.D. 476 by Odoacer, who simply affixed a terminal date to what had been a fact for many years.

And the Dark Ages descended upon Europe.

And people lived in fear.

China, however, was experiencing a renascence in its own Oriental way; there was no darkness, and no fear. The fifth century, for the Chinese, brought the Celestial Kingdom to a new peak of industrial and cultural development. More importantly, it brought about a breakdown of the aloofness that was China in context with other nations. China suddenly became outgoing and curious about other peoples. And, paradoxically, while its frontiers were producing the Tartary Huns whose goal was total destruction, the nation itself was producing a new breed of men, men who were missionaries and sought to bring the word of Buddha to all who would listen.

In A.D. 499, a zealous Buddhist monk named Hoei-Shin stood on the edge of the China Sea and stroked his chin thoughtfully. Hoei-Shin lived in the enlightened age which Buddhism had brought to China, and the good monk was mentally blocking out a missionary journey across the sea he gazed upon. Fired with the desire to "extend the joyful mission of salvation to all nations of the earth," Hoei sought new worlds to bless with his message. He had heard tales that a land called "Tahan," or "Great China," lay across the boundless waters of the China Sea and knew that it was populated with the "Painted People" who were indeed barbarians. The land was thought to be about 5000 Chinese miles to the east, in the land of the rising sun. Freely translated, that comes to about 1500 English miles.

Hoei was fortunate. *His* China was a burgeoning, outgoing nation. Prior to the first century A.D., China had withdrawn from the world, neither welcoming foreign visitors, nor showing any desire to visit other lands for any purpose whatever. The Chinese had attained a high degree of civilization, but enjoyed it rather smugly, rejecting the idea of intercourse with other peoples. China, to its own people, was depicted as the "Flower of the Center" of the universe, with all other peoples maintaining fringe positions and looked upon as swine, dogs, or vermin of one sort or another. So barbaric were these fringe people considered that it was unthinkable to impart to them any of the culture so beautifully flourishing in the Celestial Empire.

It was written that the precept of the empire was: "To retain laws and customs according to the traditionary manner, and to extend these laws and customs to other lands. But this extension is not to be affected by the oratorical powers of single messengers, nor through the forces of armed hordes. This renovation, as in every other sound organic growth which forces itself from within can only take place when the Outer Barbarians, irresistibly compelled by the virtue and majesty of the Son of Heaven, blush for their barbarism, voluntarily obey the Image of the Heavenly Father, and become men."

According to Charles G. Leland, who investigated the adventures of Hoei-Shin, such a race holding the opinions expressed above could undertake no voyage of discovery, and attempt no conquests. In fact, Leland adds, in the entire 4000-year-recorded history of China up to the first century A.D., there is not one single instance of an individual traveling to foreign lands for the purposes of adding to his own information, or that of others.

In Hoei-Shin's time, however, the Oriental mood had changed; traveling abroad was encouraged and it became virtually mandatory that monks and missionaries spread the word of Buddhism in every quarter. And so Hoei, being perhaps a bit more imaginative and adventuresome than his colleagues, looked to the unseen land across the sea as his target. In a land where dwelled a people so barbarous as to paint their bodies, he presumably reasoned, there would be vast opportunities to de-heathenize them.

Hoei was actually speculating, at that point, about the Indians in Alaska and the Aleutian Islands. Britisher Sir Charles Raymond

Beazley in his *Dawn of Modern Geography* points out that this place was known as the Land of Marked Bodies, and clearly refers to the Alaska Eskimos, who were devotees of tattooing: thus, "Painted People."

The original information concerning Hoei-Shin was culled from the labors of a German Sinologist named Karl Friedrich Neumann, and offered in translation to America by the above noted Charles G. Leland, a historian who was largely preoccupied with the American Indian. Since our American Indian is thought to be of Oriental descent, it was natural for Leland to become interested in Chinese latter-day exploration. He published the story of Hoei in 1875, titled *Fusang*. The name "Fusang" was another name for America, and derives from the Fusang tree, which was known to grow there in great quantities. Since the Fusang tree has been identified as the aloe, it appears that Hoei traveled as far south as Mexico, and possibly to South America.

In 1875, another historian, Edward P. Vining, also an American, set down a fat volume dwelling on the subject and called it *An Inglorious Columbus*. He generally agrees with Leland that Hoei-Shin must have reached Mexico at least, but adds nothing more pertinent or revealing than Leland. Vilhjalmur Stefansson, writing in his *Great Adventures and Explorations*, notes that it was probably the legend of Hoei-Shin which prompted Peter the Great of Russia to send the Danish navigator Vitus Bering off to search for land east of Kamchatka. Bering succeeded, of course, and had a sea and a strait named for him, but in 1741 died an untimely death on a desolate island, which also bears his name.

The complete story of Hoei-Shin, as told by Neumann through Leland, is this:

During the reign of the dynasty of Tsi, in the first year of the year-naming, "Everlasting Origin" (A.D. 499), came a Buddhist priest from this kingdom, who bore the cloister name of Hoei-"Shin"—that is, Universal Compassion—to the present district of Hukuang, and those surrounding it, who narrated that Fusang is about 20,000 Chinese miles in an easterly direction from Tahan, and east of the Middle Kingdom.

Many Fusang trees grow there, whose leaves resemble the Dryanda cordifolia; the sprouts, on the contrary, resemble those of the bamboo tree, and are eaten by the inhabitants of the land. The fruit is like a pear in form, but is red. From the bark they prepare a sort of linen which they use for clothing, and also a sort of ornamented stuff. The houses are built of wooden beams. Fortified and walled places are there unknown.

They have written characters in this land, and prepare paper from the bark of the Fusang. The people have no weapons, and make no wars, but in the arrangements for the kingdom they have a northern and a southern prison. Trifling offenders were lodged in the southern prison, but those confined for greater offenses in the northern, so that those who were about to receive grace could be placed in the southern prison, and those who were not, in the northern.

Those men and women who were imprisoned for life were allowed to marry. The boys resulting from these marriages were, at the age of eight years, sold as slaves, the girls not until their ninth year. If a man of any note was found guilty of crimes, an assembly was held; it must be in an excavated place. There they strewed ashes over him and bade him farewell.

If the offender was one of a lower class, he alone was punished, but when of rank, the degradation was extended to his children and grandchildren. With those of the highest rank it attained to the seventh generation.

The name of the king is pronounced Ichi. The nobles of the first class are termed Tuilu; of the second, Little Tuilu; and of the third, Na-to-scha. When the prince goes forth, he is accompanied by horns and trumpets. The color of his clothes changes with the different years. In the two first of the ten-year cyclus they are blue; in the two next, red; in the two following, yellow; in the two next, red; and in the last two black.

The horns of the oxen are so large that they hold ten bushels. They use them to contain all manner of things. Horses, oxen and stags are harnessed to their wagons. Stags are used here as cattle are used in the Middle Kingdom and from the milk of the hind they make butter. The red pears of the Fusang tree keep good throughout the year. Moreover, they have apples and reeds. From the latter they prepare mats. No iron is found in this land, but copper, gold, and silver are not prized, and do not serve as a medium of exchange in the market.

Marriage is determined upon in the following manner: The suitor builds himself a hut before the door of the house where the one longed-for dwells, and waters and cleans the ground every morning and evening. When a year has passed by, if the maiden is not inclined to marry him, he departs; should she be willing, it is completed.

When the parents die, they fast seven days. For the death of the paternal or maternal grandfather they lament five days, at the death of elder or younger sisters or brothers, uncles or aunts, three days. They then sit from morning to evening before an image of the ghost absorbed in prayer, but wear no mourning clothes. When the king dies, the son who succeeds him does not busy himself for three years with state affairs.

In earlier times these people lived not according to the laws of Buddha. But it happened that in the second year-naming, "Great Light," of Song (A.D. 458), five beggar monks from the Kingdom of Kipin went to this land, extended over it the religion of Buddha, and with it his holy writings and images. They instructed the people in the principles of monastic life, and so changed their manners.

A fascinating document. If, however, we are to consider it contextually with what we now know of pre-Columbian American history, it is at once accurate and contradictory.

The first problem in unraveling the chronicle of Hoei-Shin is to determine where he arrived in America. There are five clues which point to Central America and the land of the Mayas:

1. The reference to the Fusang tree, which bears a startling resemblance to the aloe or century plant found throughout Mexico.
2. The reference to the name of the king. Hoei states that the king's name was "Ichi." The tribe which wielded the most pronounced influences in the art and architecture of the Mayas was the "Itza."
3. The precious metals. Hoei indicates that gold, silver, and copper are not prized. This was true of all the Indian civilizations.
4. Mention of writing. The Mayas had a glyph language.
5. Notation of the absence of warfare. The Mayas were a peaceful people, largely occupied with the building of their cities until shortly before the arrival of the Spaniards in 1519.

The Fusang tree, so closely resembling the aloe, is a versatile tree. According to Hoei, the natives of the land ate its sprouts and its red fruit. From the bark they prepared linen for clothing, and some kind of ornamental stuff which, unfortunately, is not described. They also made paper from the Fusang's bark.

Now consider this account of the properties of the aloe from a booklet published by the Pan-American Union on Mexican Indians. "The agave or maguey plant [aloe] was known as the 'friend of the poor.' Its leaves furnished thatch for roofing houses. From its tough fibers, much like hemp, a strong thread was made which was used even more than cotton for weaving cloth. The thorns at the ends of the leaves were used for pins and needles and to draw blood in religious ceremonies. Its roots were cooked into a nourishing food. Finally, its juice was fermented into an alcoholic beverage, *pulque*, then as now the national drink of Mexico."

In fact, so beneficial were the properties of the aloe that the Mexican government, in a moment of soul-searching, actually once considered exterminating the plant . . . "lest the people be retarded."

In the process of narrowing down the exact location of Hoei's stay in America, it must be pointed out that the aloe was used by the Aztecs in Central Mexico, the Mayas in Yucatán and neighboring states and by the Inca in Peru. But we have other clues to examine.

The Chinese tells us that the name of the king was pronounced "Ichi." Leland suggests that the name "Ichi" is similar to "Inca." I feel a closer sound structure between "Ichi" and "Itza," the name of the Maya tribe which roamed Central America for many centuries and eventually settled in Yucatán. Their largest city was called Chichén Itzá, which means "mouth of the wells of the Itzas." In the time of Hoei-Shin, the Itzas are thought to have lived on the southern coast of Central America, perhaps in Guatemala, Chiapas, or El Salvador. I think that they did, and that they came first in contact with Hoei on that coast: the Itzas introduced many Asiatic features into the art and architecture of Chichén Itzá.

The next clue lies in the reference to the precious metals of Hoei's Fusang. "Copper, gold and silver," he says, "are not prized." Again it must be pointed out that none of our pre-Columbian Indian civilizations used these metals as exchange, but we have two more clues to follow.

"They have written characters in this land," Hoei noted, and in this clue we move slightly closer to the Maya. Had Hoei been referring to Peru, he could not have made the above statement, for an obvious reason: the Inca had no written language. The Aztecs, who did, must be ruled out simply because their empire was built 600 years after Hoei-Shin. (The Inca did not come into being—as Inca—until the eleventh century; I include them in this process of elimination in deference to the thoughts offered by Mr. Leland and others who felt that the Buddhist missionary landed in Peru.)

Now that we have ruled out the Aztecs and the Inca on the basis of time, we will note briefly the reference to "absence of warfare."

The Maya of the period were apparently builders, not warmakers, and this speculation is corroborated by the absence of scenes of warfare from their murals and other art forms dating from that time.

It appears, then, that we have five clues which indicate that Hoei-Shin probably spent his time in America among the Maya. Unfortunately, we can neither confirm nor deny the descriptions of prisons, marriage, criminal offenses, mourning, noble succession, etc., but we must ponder three sentences which might appear to make Hoei's document a product of a rich imagination.

"The horns of the oxen," Hoei wrote, "are so large that they hold ten bushels. They use them to contain all manner of things. Horses, oxen and stags are harnessed to their wagons."

Seemingly a harmless description, but disturbing when one considers that the Maya had no dray animals. And they did not use the wheel. We must therefore conclude that the reference to the oxen, stags, horses, and wagons are elements introduced either by a transcriber of the legend to give it a more wondrous quality, or that Hoei touched Japan in his voyage. The incidence of oxen, horses, and wagons becomes easier to accept if an extraneous reference to Japan had been inserted into the account without naming the country. If such were the case, then Hoei accomplished his voyage to America by island-hopping, the feasibility of which will be demonstrated later. I don't feel, however, that that method was used by the missionary. Speculating further, he may even have reached Peru, where the predecessors of the Inca had domesticated the llama. The method of loading a llama as a pack animal consists of slinging a basket on either side of the animal. The capacities of the baskets were great, and could easily have become great "horns" capable of holding ten bushels. The llama itself, in the evolution of the writing, had become oxen.

The infusion of alien matter into a legend is common. In ages when miracles and marvelous things were recorded with complete gravity, it frequently caused writers of factual stories to insert monsters, incredible happenings and fantastic sights, perhaps, as indicated above, to "spice up" the story, or to relieve the boredom suffered by the transcriber in his task. The Homeric poems are good examples of the facts being virtually inundated by fantastic occurrences and incredible events. In a later chapter you will encounter the legend of Brendan, perhaps the most "loaded" legend in literature. As it traveled from country to country, in translation and retranslation, it acquired enormous quantities of material not present in its original form.

It would appear then, that there is no real explanation for the contradictory paragraph. I don't, as noted, subscribe completely to the island-hopping method of getting to America, and I will demonstrate also that I don't believe Hoei ever reached Peru. So we must accept the account of draft animals and wheels as an imponderable, but one which in no way negates the facts so evident in the travels of Hoei-Shin. But let us examine the mode of the good Buddhist's actual voyage.

In both the Leland and Vining accounts of the voyage of Hoei-Shin, as well as the comments by Dr. Stefansson, I miss a full explanation—or even speculation—concerning the method by which the missionary crossed the Pacific. Throughout the Leland and Vining accounts it is apparent that the most widely held theory was that of island-hopping. If you look at the globe, it's easy to trace a relatively smooth path from China to Alaska without ever getting too far from land. Sailing from Shanghai, for instance, with Alaska as its goal, would bring a ship first to Japan, at Kyushu. From Kyushu, coastal sailing through the Japan Sea, keeping Honshu on the starboard side, would bring the ship to Hokkaido, the northernmost Japanese island. From Hokkaido, the Kurile Islands reach northeasterly to the peninsula of Kamchatka. From there the Komandorskie Islands offer the first landfall to the east. It was on the westernmost of these islands that Vitus Bering died, the island's name remaining as his memorial. Changing course to southeast, the ship would arrive quickly at the Aleutian Island of Attu, and the home of the Hairy Ainus, first of the Painted People to be encountered. Now, hopscotching the Aleutians, the ship could make its way—seldom out of sight of land—to Alaska. Once there, it would be purely a matter of time to sail down the coast of the American mainland to any point in Mexico or South America.

The above method is certainly one by which Hoei-Shin could have arrived safely in America. I agree that he could have come by this route, but I also feel that he could, and probably did, come by a direct west-to-east course across the Pacific, making his first landfall somewhere in Mexico. And I think he came in a ship as fabulous as the journey itself.

Hoei's voyage took place during the Six Dynasties, which flourished in the Celestial Kingdom from A.D. 265 to 589. That period in China's history was marked by great cultural advances which served to stimulate material progress. Among the crafts that were brought to a high degree of refinement was that of shipbuilding. The humble junk, which provided transportation and shelter on rivers and lakes, suddenly burgeoned into an oceangoing monster. Giant junks, incredible to behold, began making the run between Canton and India with regular stops at Java, Sumatra, and the Malay Archipelago. China, in its new role as an "outgoing" nation, became a traveling nation.

In order to gain a clearer picture of travel in China during the fifth century, it would be well to examine the journal of one Fa-Hsein, a shaman of the Liu Sung Dynasty. In the year 399, Fa-Hsein, in company with 12 other Buddhist monks, undertook a journey to India, overland. He walked from Central China across the Desert of Gobi, over the Hindu Kush and through India down to the mouth of the Hooghly River, which enters the Bay of Bengal just south of the city of Calcutta. H. A. Giles, professor of Chinese at the University of Cambridge, in commenting on this journey perilous says it was "a supremely dangerous expedition, in the glow of which the journeys of St. Paul melt into insignificance." But Fa-Hsein's exhausting stroll across Asia was only the first half of his journey, and it is the second in which we are interested. The Buddhist took ship on the Hooghly and sailed to Ceylon, where he lived for two years. These years were largely spent in obtaining books of the Buddhist canon and images of the Buddhist deities. He had already collected some, and was now in process of completing his collection. The gathering of these sacred writings and objects had precipitated his journey; when he had amassed all he could safely transport, he was ready to return to China.

In 414, he sailed from Ceylon, alone, since he had lost all of his original company along the way. According to the journal which he kept faithfully during the course of his travels, he "took passage on board a large merchant vessel, on which there were over two hundred souls, and astern of which there was a smaller vessel in tow, in case of accident at sea and destruction of the big vessel. Catching a fair wind, they sailed eastward for two days; then they encountered a heavy gale, and the vessel sprang a leak. The merchants wished to get aboard the smaller vessel; but the men on the latter, fearing they would be swamped by numbers, quickly cut the tow-rope in two."

Fa-Hsein became extremely disturbed when he found that the crew was busily engaged in throwing all bulky objects overboard. He feared the loss of his books and images, a precious cargo, since China had none of these. The Buddhist then took his pitcher and ewer, and whatever else he could gather and concentrated his thoughts on Kuan Yin, the hearer of prayers. Fa-Hsein prayed only for the safe arrival in China of his books and deities.

Fa's prayers were answered. The gale blew for 13 days and 13 nights, after which the ship drifted helplessly for ninety days, eventually reaching Java.

The most remarkable aspect of the diary of Fa-Hsein is the reference to the ship on which he sailed. Mindful that his journey took place in the fifth century, it is impressive to realize that his ship carried two hundred others, and was able to stay afloat in a gale which blew for 13 days and nights, despite a leak in the hull. Fa-Hsein's ship was indeed a great, oceangoing ship. And it was only one of many.

The missionary left Java after a five months' stay and sailed now for Canton on a ship of the same size. Again there were two hundred others aboard. The ship was provisioned for 50 days since that was the normal time for the Java-Canton run up through the South China Sea. Trouble again beset Fa-Hsein, and the voyage, marked by severe gales, took 82 days. The merchants on board threatened to cast the missionary away, describing him as a "religious mendicant," but one of the passengers stated that he would tell the Chinese king, who was a Buddhist, if they dared commit such an atrocity. The merchants wavered, and Fa-Hsein, his books and his images were saved.

A later traveler, one Ibn-Batuta, who roamed the world as a sort of Oriental Marco Polo, describes a voyage he made in the year 1330 aboard a Chinese junk out of Calcutta. Ibn was unhappy because he could not get a first-class cabin and was therefore forced to travel in a cabin without lavatory or bathroom. Since he was traveling with his wives and slave girls, the quarters must have been a trifle cramped. According to Paul Herrmann, in his *Conquest by Man*, these junks not only had private baths and class cabins, but they carried as many as 1200 people, including a crew of about 600, plus perhaps 400 marines to defend the passengers and crew against pirates.

Clearly, the Chinese junk had outgrown its river character. I discussed the probable size of such a ship with marine architect L. Francis Herreshoff, an editorial colleague of mine at *The Rudder*. He assured me that a ship big enough to carry the two hundred passengers mentioned by Fa-Hsein need not have been more than 150 feet long. Since Fa only noted the number of passengers, we have no way of knowing what the ship's complement was. If it compared in any way with the later ship of Ibn-Batuta, it could have been several hundred feet long. It probably bore a close resemblance to contemporary junks; it was simply built on a greater scale. In Ibn-Batuta's account, large Chinese ships had up to a dozen sails and carried oars "as big as ships' masts." The manipulation of the oars was accomplished by two groups of men standing facing each other. The groups, of ten to fifteen men, moved the ponderous sweeps by alternately pulling on ropes attached to the oar. The vessels themselves were probably built of camphor wood, the sails made of cane or bamboo. Flat-bottomed and square-prowed, they were full-sterned and featured prominent stems. Eyes were very likely painted on either side of the prow, enabling the vessels to "see."

The evolution of the junk shows that these craft became ocean-going at an early period in the first millennium and kept right on growing. It is, therefore, not unreasonable to assume that Hoei-Shin, the first recorded Asiatic visitor to America, might have had such a ship at his disposal.

It is also not unreasonable to assume that many others might have been here before him. And returned. And told others of their experiences. How did Hoei know that he would find land to the east? Did he learn of it from some luckless voyager, who, in the manner of Fa-Hsein, had been caught in a storm which blew him out past the Philippine Islands? Could more than one ship have been blown across the Pacific that way? I think they could have. And I think they were. And they brought the message of Buddha to the Indians of Mexico, Central and South America, and left evidence of their visits indelibly engraved in the art and architecture, customs and beliefs of our Indians. What about those five beggar monks mentioned in the last paragraph of Hoei's document? They had been here in 458. That's 41 years prior to Hoei's visit. Where did they learn about Fusang . . . or whatever name they called it by? From others who had visited here even earlier? Why not? Since the Chinese probably had the compass some 2000 years before Christ, it is not inconceivable that they undertook long journeys into the unknown waters of the Pacific, secure in the knowledge that they could return.

Acceptance of a direct voyage across the Pacific by Hoei-Shin is not difficult. Assuming that he had a big ship, and a compass, and knowing that the prevailing wind in the Pacific is northwesterly, he was risking very little. The Spanish Franciscan monk and historian, Juan de Torquemada, mentions "foreign merchants" who had landed in California, and even asserts that Spanish travelers saw the remains of a Chinese vessel on the beach. There is a report of a Japanese vessel wrecked in California at about the time of Torquemada (early 1600s), but the exact date is unknown. Hawaii reports a Japanese shipwreck in 1832. Another occurred in the Queen Charlotte Islands in 1833. The battered crew was received somewhat unenthusiastically by the natives, who murdered all but two. The two survivors then became "men without a country." They were shipped to England, thence, in a highly roundabout way, to Japan. But the emperor would not permit them to re-enter the country, presumably because they had been contaminated by contact with the outside world.

Reports of Asiatic vessels shipwrecked on American shores certainly serve to corroborate the planned voyage of Hoei-Shin, but I must admit that such thin evidence cannot sustain the argument. More evidence is needed.

And it exists.

It is scattered through the jungle ruins of Middle America, in the country of the Mayas, and reveals itself with pleasant frequency in the Southwestern United States and in the highland country of the Inca to the south. It is evidence which documents the occurrence of not one, but many trans-Pacific voyages engaged in by Oriental peoples and clearly demonstrates that the account of Hoei-Shin, as related in the Chinese Annals, fifth century A.D., was the authentic report of a journey to America, and not the imaginative figment of a Buddhist fiction writer.

All of which brings us to Dr. Gordon Ekholm, distinguished Associate Curator of Anthropology at the American Museum of Natural

History in New York. One of America's foremost mexicologists, Dr. Ekholm, through that ineluctable dichotomy which springs into being in the wake of every scientific postulation, can best be described as a "diffusionist," although he carefully suggested that I refer to him as a "controlled diffusionist."

In the ceaseless study of American Indian cultures, there are two distinct camps, quietly at war, each dedicated to the proposition that the other is wrong. Dr. Ekholm described these separate groups clearly in an article written for *Natural History,* in October 1950:

> The problem of whether or not the American Indian cultures were influenced by those of the Old World has been argued since the time when Europeans first came to know the American Indian in the 15th and 16th centuries. As we shall see later, it is a problem difficult to prove definitely one way or the other. It is a field in which quite opposite opinions are sometimes held by persons equally well informed.
>
> On the one hand, there are those who have been labelled "independent inventionists," those who believe the American Indian civilizations evolved by themselves in the New World without benefit of cultural promptings from the Old. This side of the argument has been upheld for the last three decades or more by a majority of the anthropologists working in the American field. The possibility that significant transpacific contacts may have occurred has been almost totally discounted, *and those who study anthropology in the United States are strongly indoctrinated with this point of view.* [My italics]
>
> In contrast to those who would view the American civilizations as an independent growth are the so-called "diffusionists". These would minimize the likelihood that the same things could have been invented more than once and would explain the cultural parallels in the Western and Eastern Hemispheres as a result of historical contact.

These, then, in Dr. Ekholm's own words, are the two opposed camps. And they are at war. Of the two, the diffusionists manage to maintain their dignity more successfully, quietly presenting the evidence which does the shouting for them. The independent inventionists, in contradistinction, do more than a moite of shouting, possibly because their cause will inevitably go the way of Hrdlicka's long heads and round heads, and because the diffusionist evidence cannot be ignored.

But I must tell you about this evidence.

In the thirties, Gordon Ekholm became intrigued with cultural cross-pollenization as he probed the ancient artifacts of the Indians of the Southwest. He had made a study of outside influences on the indigenous culture of the Indians he was pursuing academically, and had already noted a few mysterious forces which seemed not to come from within the borders of the United States. It was not, however, until he began digging in Middle America that he was able to begin compiling occurrences of alien influences on American cultures on a grand scale.

And his evidence was impressive.

From California, he had obtained a stone fishhook, almost identical with another . . . from Easter Island. The bark books of Mexico proved eerily like those of Sumatra. War clubs from Melanesia, in the Southwest Pacific, in unusual shapes, became twins with similar weapons from Peru and Mexico. He noted the remarkable resemblance between the Panpipes of Brazil and the Panpipes of the Solomon Islands. And the resemblance here was not merely in design . . . the pitches of the instruments were alike!

A two-bar, back-strap loom from the Philippines, he found, was nearly identical with the looms of Mexico, and so was the product which they manufactured. Implements and manufacturing methods in the working of bark cloth were found in Mexico; they could have come from the Celebes.

There were other indications that a diffusion of cultures had occurred not once, but many times in the ancient past. Ekholm kept amassing the evidence. But such evidence was not forceful enough to convince the independent inventionists. Implements and weapons, they stated, could easily have been invented and reinvented by many societies simultaneously or at different times. That is true. Many modern inventions have been arrived at independently by two people in opposite parts of the world.

But there was one area of similarities which was a bit harder to explain.

It lay in the art forms of Asia and Middle America.

Ekholm offered a comparison of sculptured panels from Asia and Middle America. Both were based on the lotus plant as the prime design element, both contained decorative fish, and both utilized the "rhizome" or underwater, rootlike stalk of the plant in the design (Plate 12). In a paper published by the International Congress of Americanists in 1951, Ekholm observed:

It is certainly remarkable that in India, as well as in Middle America, the rhizome, a part of the plant not normally visible, because it is submerged and deeply buried in mud, should have been made the basic element of a whole motif, and, moreover, be stylized in the same unrealistic manner as an undulating creeper.

And it *is* remarkable.

But still the evidence piled up. And more in the direction of Hoei-Shin. Design similarities between the styles of the Late Chou of China and the so-called Tajin style, normally found in and near Veracruz, were noted. Both styles utilized a "mask and dragon wing" theme (Plate 13). A bronze vessel from ancient China and a stone known as the "palmate" stone of Mexico were found to share the same interlaced pattern, somewhat modified in the Mexican design. A Brazilian jar featured the same stylized grotesqueries as did a bronze drum from the Shang period in China.

A recurring theme in Middle American art is one employing a decorative device of discs or props between the elbows and knees of human or animal figures. This theme is found in America from New Mexico down into Bolivia. In Asia, it is found from Borneo to New Guinea (Plate 14).

One of the most startling parallels offered was a pair of wheeled toys. Each was fashioned as an animal, each could be rolled about on four little wheels. One came from Mexico, one from India. There is nothing truly remarkable about the toy from India, but how can the wheeled toy from ancient Mexico be explained . . . when the Amerinds didn't use the wheel?

Ekholm, working sometimes alone, sometimes in collaboration with Robert Heine-Geldern, a German who has contributed greatly to our knowledge of Middle American culture, continued digging and studying through the forties. Then, in 1950, he dropped a bomb.

An exhibit of the parallels he and Heine-Geldern had collected was displayed at the American Museum in New York. The exhibit was timed to coincide with a meeting of the International Congress of Americanists, and thus was exposed to an inordinate number of American anthropologists simultaneously.

With remarkable understatement, Ekholm comments on the exhibit in *Natural History:*

> It [the exhibit] was especially prepared for a meeting of the International Congress of Americanists . . . and was thus seen by an unusually

large number of specialists concerned with the problems of American Indian origins. The interest shown by these experts and the lively debates that ensued were sufficient proof that our exhibit was dealing with an important problem.

Lively debates. Only those who have ever witnessed "discussions" between opposing schools of thought in the sciences can appreciate the "liveliness" of said debates. In the museum exhibit, 18 displays were shown, including all of those mentioned above, plus tooth inlays, blowguns, comparisons of betel-nut chewing and coca-chewing, nose flutes, and other parallels. But the comparisons do not stop at such artifacts and customs.

In the I.C.A. paper mentioned above, which was written in collaboration with Robert Heine-Geldern, (he of the Roman-Mexican) Ekholm comments on the similarities between the Aztec fire serpent theme and its Hindu-Buddhist counterpart, the mythical sea monster called the "makara."

He writes of the Atlantean figures (Atlas-like figures which bear great objects on their shoulders) which occur in India and at Chichén Itzá, capital city of the last great Mayan empire. Architectural similarities from both sides of the Pacific are noted, with one intriguing, mysterious occurrence.

The Mercado, at Chichén Itzá and the temple pyramid of Cambodia are virtually from the same architectural drawing board. Yet the Mercado dates from *before* the Cambodian temple! Could there have been traffic of Amerinds to Asia, as well as influxes of people from the Far East? I see no reason why not.

Continuing with the seemingly endless list of parallels, Ekholm comments on the resemblances between the structures of the Aztec court and the courts of Burma, Siam, and Cambodia. He reflects upon the use of the parasol as a symbol of royalty and rank. In use since the third millennium B.C. in Asia, it is portrayed in the magnificent frescoes at Bonampak. (In this latter instance I suspect a strong *transatlantic* influence. The Bonampak frescoes are as Egyptian as they are Asiatic.)

Ekholm, in the same paper, feels that trans-Pacific contacts were made in volume between the second and seventh centuries, and may have continued until a much later date. Hoei, it will be recalled, came to America in the fifth century. I have already asked the question: "Where did he hear of America, the land to the east?" I think we have the answer in the many trans-Pacific voyages that are silently documented in the parallels shown by Ekholm and Heine-Geldern.

In commenting on the convincing evidence of Asian-American intercourse, Ekholm states: "We must bow to the evidence of facts, even though this may mean a completely new start in our appraisal of the origin and development of the American Indian higher civilizations."

Agreed.

But it might be asked: "If there was so much traffic from Buddhist cultures into America, why wasn't there a profound and lasting influence on the religion of the Mayas?"

Apparently it suffered the same fate here as it did in certain sections of Asia itself.

"We know," Ekholm writes, "from the history of Southeast Asia how easily [Hinduism-Buddhism] may disappear or be submerged in local paganism. Among the Cham of Annam, Hinduism and Buddhism had been firmly established from the second to the fifteenth century, thus through almost a millennium and a half. Yet, Buddhism disappeared completely after the fall of the Cham kingdom in A.D. 1471, and Hinduism degenerated so rapidly that its remnants are at present hardly recognizable."

I think the evidence and the arguments are substantial.

I think Hoei-Shin came here in A.D. 499, and *did* bring the message of Buddhism; not, perhaps, to the people he originally intended it for, the savage "Painted People" to the north, but to the civilized people to the south. One day, perhaps, the account of Hoei-Shin will be incorporated into our histories of the Americas as a matter of course, as will the Phoenician colonizations. But we must be patient. The spectre which hovers above nearly all of these pre-Columbians, evidence destroyed or unobtainable, prevails here, also.

The terrible calamity of the burning of the Aztec and Maya books by the fanatic Spanish bishops, the Bishop de Landas, the Bishop of Meridas, the Don Juan de Zummarragas, blindly led by the belief that the art and literature of the Indians was inspired by the devil have forever stilled the hope of gaining a thorough knowledge of the history of Middle America and South America.

Or has it? Relatively little work has been done in these areas when the vastness of these civilizations is considered. Some day, a Gordon

Ekholm or one like him may uncover books that were overlooked by the Spaniards. Perhaps then we will know—conclusively—the identities of the ancient travelers who plied the seas between the Americas and Asia in the distant past.

Hoei-Shin was one of many. The evidence that he—and many other Asiatics—visited America exists.

I offer but one further proof that he was here. I offer merely a single photograph, and place no parallel beside it. It is one of the famous "laughing heads" of Totonac, near Veracruz (Plate 16). In Totonac dwelled a number of extremely fine artists. Their work is different from other Indian art expressions. And I think they specialized in portraits. I also think this laughing head is a portrait of a visiting Chinese.

It may even be old Hoei-Shin himself.

CHAPTER 5

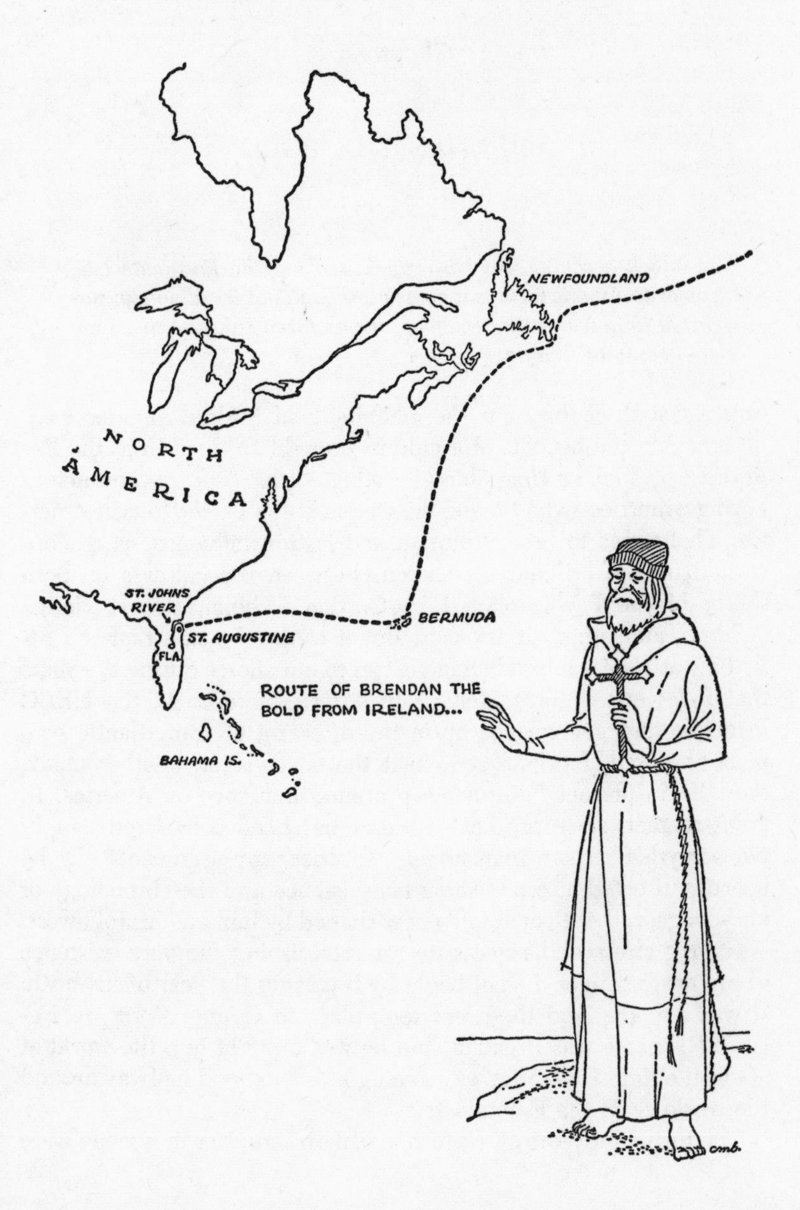
NEWFOUNDLAND
NORTH AMERICA
ST. JOHNS RIVER
BERMUDA
ST. AUGUSTINE
FLA.
ROUTE OF BRENDAN THE BOLD FROM IRELAND...
BAHAMA IS.
cmb.

Chapter 5

BRENDAN THE BOLD

[A.D. 551]

In which a courageous Irish monk, seeking the Fortunate Isle, comes to America. He is somewhat, though not inordinately, surprised to find an entire colony of his brethren enjoying the tropical beauty of Florida.

IN THE sixth century A.D. the inhabitants of Middle America were enjoying the benefits of a culture brought to them from the Far East by such as Hoei-Shin and others of his country—and neighboring countries—who braved the waters of the Pacific to visit America. Theirs was to be a profound and lasting influence, as demonstrated by the brilliant correlations between the cultures on both shores of the Pacific offered by Gordon Ekholm, Robert Heine-Geldern, and other diffusionists. But it cannot be said that the Atlantic was remiss in producing visitors to our shores during the years that followed. Unfortunately, with strict adherence to the NEBC Principle and general apathy in the direction of transatlantic contacts observed, I cannot state that the next visitor, another monk, though of different faith, left a profound influence on America. In point of fact, since my next explorer has been considered naught but a myth for more than fifteen centuries, any arguments will be heartily directed at establishing his existence and the chronology of his voyage, rather than at influences shaped by him and his followers.

Having stressed the necessity for establishing the very existence of my next voyager, I shall begin by reporting the year of his birth. It was A.D. 484, and the event took place in County Kerry, in Ireland. His name was Brendan, and he was brought into the world at about the time Hoei-Shin was coming into manhood halfway around the world from the Emerald Isle.

The turbulent years of the fifth and sixth centuries in Europe were marked by vast movements of men. The Dark Ages were already a fact, and of the men who were routed from their normal places of habitation, some were scholars who sought to flee the unsympathetic natures of the barbarians now strongly entrenched in positions of power throughout the continent. These scholars undertook a mass movement of their own, designed to bring them to unclouded areas where the thirst for knowledge could be satisfied—and knowledge already gained jealously preserved against the day when light would again come to Europe.

One of the principal sanctuaries known to the men of learning was Ireland. Its physical location was such that it had not appealed to the Romans as a conquest, and it was consequently not a target for the barbarians who presumably had quite enough to do in plundering the continent itself. Add to the immunity of physical location the presence of great universities and other temples of learning scattered through Ireland and it offered the ideal refuge for those of scholarly bent. And so it was that Ireland became heir to the knowledge that was Europe's during the Dark Ages, and held it and cherished it and carefully nurtured it until such times as it could be re-endowed upon Europa's benighted children.

Curiously, while the influx of scholars and savants from Europe was in progress, an outgoing movement was occurring among certain groups of the Irish themselves. It was a holy movement of hermits and of some who, while not purely ascetic, went out from the island for various periods and reasons, and it was one of these latter with whom we are concerned.

The provenance of this seemingly strange movement was the hot, dry deserts of Egypt and from a local Irish custom which appealed to the monks. Communications between Egypt, with its Coptic Monks, and Ireland, with its new-born ascetics, were surprisingly good. The Egyptian brethren were given to staying in the desert for long periods of fasting and meditation; the Irish borrowed the idea, but sought *their* refuges on the bleak offshore rocks of Ireland. Being a creative people, they added a fillip of their own: one of the punishments meted out for major and minor infractions of the law in Erin was the custom of casting the offender adrift in a boat. Presumably, if the offending party were innocent, he would be thrown safely ashore at some indeterminate point. If he were truly guilty, then the sea would swallow him and his crime expiated.

The mystery and adventure of the "adrift-in-an-open-boat" idea appealed to the sixth-century Irish monks, and consequently they took to flinging themselves into open boats and being cast adrift by their friends with alarming frequency. Most of them either arrived at a strange landing place on the shore, or reached some of the inhospitable crags mentioned above. In the latter case, they settled down to lives of prayer and meditation, living off the fish they could catch and the eggs of sea birds conveniently provided by the gulls and other feathered creatures which lived upon the rocks.

Thus it was that when Brendan the Bold took to his curragh, in company with fourteen other monks, to seek the Fortunate Isle—or the Blessed Isles, or the Isles of Paradise, call them what you will—he was performing according to custom. He did find a place which strongly resembled his Fortunate Isle, and, having spent a reasonable time there, returned to Ireland and resumed the monastic life.

Brendan the Bold, Brenaind Moccu Alti, St. Brendan of Ciarraige Luachra, Brendan the Navigator, or the Monk of Clonfert, was born in Ireland, as already noted, in County Kerry, in A.D. 484. Kerry is sea country in Ireland. Through it the River Shannon flows down from the green, wet hills to spill into the deep, mysterious waters of the Atlantic on the west shore of the island. In the fifth century, the call of the sea was born into the men of Kerry; they cheerfully gave up their feeble attempts to wrest their livings from the land, preferring to devote their toiling hours to the construction of Ireland's finest curraghs, or open boats, and to the pursuit of such foods provided by the sea.

Brendan, therefore, had as his birthright the mystic appeal of the sea from the day he saw light in the sod house of his parents, Finnlugh and Cara, who were Christians. Ireland was not all Christian in those remote days, and Brendan's heritage is mentioned only to demonstrate that he was a born Christian, and not a convert, as were some of Ireland's saints.

Following custom, Brendan remained but a year with his parents, at the end of which time he was sent to the convent school of St. Ita, in what is now Killeady, in Limerick. Ita reared Brendan in his formative years, and was to exert a profound influence on his later life.

In his seventh year, Brendan returned to the place of his birth, in Kerry, and began his formal education under the guidance of one Erc, Bishop of Altraighe Caille, who maintained an ecclesiastical school for such boys as were deemed material for the Church. In Brendan's case, his future was foreordained, for, according to the *Seanchus Mor*, a thesaurus of requirements of the Church, "every first born of human couple, the mother being a lawful wife, belongs to the church."

According to Dr. George Little, in his *Brendan the Navigator*, the saint-to-be learned Latin, and probably Hebrew and Greek. History was studied, and the literary forms of Gaelic. Since his instructor, Bishop Erc, was a Druid, it can safely be assumed that mathematics and astronomy were required, and, in fact, may have given Brendan the knowledge of navigation which was so useful to him in later years. At the school, Brendan had already begun the pattern which was evident in the lives of the men who served God in Ireland: the renunciation of home and parents in the mission of disseminating Christianity. When he had finished his period of formal education, Brendan undertook a walking journey about Ireland, pausing now and again to study, but mostly traveling, afoot, to discover the Ireland he knew not.

In his twenty-sixth year he returned to Bishop Erc's side, and the old prelate ordained him a priest. Having achieved that station, Brendan proceeded to form the nucleus of a monastic group, some of whose members were later to join him in his great voyages. They dwelled on Diadche, a mountain west of the Bay of Tralee, and which loomed up above the bay that is called Brendan. In later times, the mountain also took Brendan's name, and can be found as such on today's maps. It was from this peak that Brendan and his men departed, to go down to the sea and embark on their several voyages of discovery.

St. Brendan was impelled to undertake his wanderings across the sea because he had heard a strange tale of a "Delicious Isle" which had been visited by one Fionn-Barr, a kinsman of Brendan. It appears that Fionn-Barr had, at some vague time in the past, sailed in a curragh to find a monk named Mernoc, an insubordinate fellow who had taken leave of the monastery where he had lived with Fionn-Barr and other monks. Fionn-Barr eventually found Mernoc on the above noted Delicious Isle, and, after spending some time in his company, was prevailed upon by Mernoc to sail to a place he called the Island of the Saints.

Sailing in a well-stocked curragh, the two ultimately came to a fabulous country—a land of sun and spice and fragrance. Unfortunately, a sign was given them that precluded their staying in this wonderful land. They returned to Ireland. Impressed with the story, Brendan determined to seek the beautiful country visited by Fionn-Barr. And so he and his monks set about the building of a curragh strong enough to take them across the wild sea.

When the curragh was ready, Brendan sailed from Ireland on one of the most controversial voyages, or series of voyages, ever undertaken by a sailor. Because the story of the voyages did not appear in written form until the eleventh century, the tale is largely dismissed as pure legend, if not myth, by historians. Dismissed, that is, whenever a historian condescends to dignify the story of Brendan by referring to it at all in any historical context.

The Bollandist Monks, in whose collection of the *Acta Sanctorum* can be found the life of Brendan, consider the story incredible, and do not include any account of the voyage in the Brendan *Life*. It might be noted here that Jean de Bolland, whose name the monks bear, obtained a great deal of his material from the files of a Flemish Jesuit, whose Continental point of view may well have caused elimination of the tale as just another wild fantasy of the "impossible" Irish. Such is the weary pattern of history when set down by individuals whose tastes, digestion, or biased conclusions become the basis for recounting historical events.

Despite the Flemish Jesuit friar, the tale of Brendan and his explorations spread rapidly through the civilized world from the sixth century on, first by oral presentation, later in many written forms. As literature, it became a best-seller in French, Italian, German, Portuguese, and other languages. As a matter of philological study it attracted scholars from many countries who attempted to dissect it. As a matter of controversy it has emerged periodically to occupy the thoughts of scholars all over the world. It has been attacked on probable and improbable grounds, ranging from expression of disbelief that it is even Irish in origin, based in part on the fact that the most widely known version, *Navigatio Sancti Brendani*, is in Latin —and presumably, therefore, Continental in origin. It has been compared to the story of Sinbad the Sailor, unfavorably and favorably.

Some say Brendan derives from Sinbad; the truth is that the Sinbad story postdates the voyage of Brendan, and it is intriguing to note that there is much evidence of contact between Ireland and the Arab countries even in those remote times.

Centuries after it was first written, it still held a sway on explorers, cartographers, and literati. Martin Behaim, who presented his famous globe to the world at Nuremburg in 1492, placed Brendan's island at a spot west of the Canaries. Of Brendan and his voyage, Behaim states simply: "In the year 565, (sic) after Christ's Birth, St. Brendan, with his ship, came to this island. He saw there many wonders, and after seven years he came again to his own land."

In passing, it is well to recall that the globe was made in 1492, while Behaim was in the service of the King of Portugal. Speculation on whether Columbus was interested in Brendan's Isle has caused many lively debates also, with most scholars opining that if Columbus *did* know of Brendan's Fortunate Isle, he gave no credence to it. I wonder. It is also curious to note that the original name of Brendan's Isle, *Hi Brasil* emerged in later centuries as the name of a country in South America.

It is known that the Spaniards and Portuguese accepted the Legend of Brendan, and, as late as the sixteenth century, both sent expeditions to find Brendan's Isle. According to the distinguished Thomas Wright, who presented—and commented upon—the Brendan story for the Percy Society in London, in 1894, "a king of Portugal is said to have made a conditional cession of it (Brendan's Isle) to another person when it should be found"; and when the Crown of Portugal ceded its right to the Canaries over to the Castilians, the treaty included the Island of St. Brendan, as the *island which had not yet been found.*

He also adds that many believed that the ill-fated Don Rodrigo, who fled Spain at the Arab invasion, found a retreat on Brendan's Isle.

It is evident, then, that the voyage of Brendan has had its fair share of believers, as well as scoffers, and has prompted countless speculations and controversies through the centuries since it took place. It is extremely difficult to determine just how much has been written on it; according to E. G. R. Waters, the British philologist, there are more than 80 manuscripts dealing with Brendan extant in Europe today. The New York Public Library lists more than 30 titles, in five languages. Since the overwhelming quantity of versions of this manuscript, each differing from the other in many respects, precludes one *absolute* version, I will not attempt to reproduce the legend here. Rather, I will rely on the dissection of the legend into three separate voyages, as performed by Dr. Little, recapitulating the first and third voyages and dwelling precisely only upon the second, or American voyage.

The dissection noted above has been Dr. Little's greatest contribution to the hitherto confusing story of Brendan. Through the hundreds of years since its first appearance in written form, it has been embellished by countless transcribers apparently unable to refrain from "enhancing" the tales with touches of their own and ultimately weaving the three separate voyages into one fantastic chronicle. As the hagiographical writers became attracted to it, the wondrous, incredible additions to the story gradually buried the original beneath tons of fanciful debris. Dr. Little painstakingly weeded out the facts in the story and determined that Brendan had made not one, but three distinctly separate voyages, the second of which took him to North America. Dr. Little is no dilettante in the sciences. A historian and archaeologist of international repute, he is president of the Old Dublin Society, a member of the Maritime Institute of Ireland, the Royal Society of Antiquaries, and other scientific bodies.

The first voyage of Brendan the Bold began in A.D. 545, and lasted for seven long and exhausting years. Embarking from Kerry in a curragh lovingly constructed by the monks of Brendan's band, the Saint put bravely into the sea, knowing not where he was going, but trusting that Divine Providence would lead him to the Fortunate Isle. His craft was small, but exceedingly seaworthy and served him well during his fruitless search for his earthly Paradise. Dr. Little provides an excellent description of the questing craft:

Gunwales of willow, the interstices filled in with wicker, formed the framework. Over this hull were placed three layers of hides, oak-tanned, possibly designed so that twin air chambers were formed to improve the flotation of the craft. Holly resin sealed the hide-joints, and tar was used as the caulking. Butter was used in waterproofing the covering, and two additional sets of hides were stowed in the event repairs were needed. The curragh carried a mast and sail, though the mast was probably carried unshipped, then set into place when the wind was proper. Otherwise, oars furnished the main source of power. The sail itself was probably of the lug-type, the kind still used in Ireland today. Triangular in shape, it, too, was made of hides.

For cooking, the curragh most likely carried a brazier similar to the kind used today in the curraghs of Aran. It consists of a shallow metal dish in which turf or charcoal is fired. The dish itself is suspended between the gunwales on a metal rod, keeping it safely away from the hides. Water was carried in skins; dried fish and grains, together with roots and edible sea moss filled the larder. Sweeps of bool and thole pin design were shipped, and the curragh's draft was very slight; probably not more than a few inches.

When it had been provisioned, the sail was hoisted and, on a good breeze aft, the frail craft was steered to the north. More than a month later, half of which was spent in drifting, the now-starved monks made their first landing at St. Kilda Island in the Hebrides. In weakened condition, the monks rested long enough to regain strength and revictual the ship. Then they left the bleak, uninhabited isle and went next to an island densely populated with sheep. In the Faeroes, it was possibly the Island of Storms. Evidence of the good monk's visit and later veneration on that island remains in a place named *Brendansvik*, and in a round tower on the nearby island of Stremoe. Tarrying but briefly, they added one of the fatter sheep to their larder and departed.

Next the monks found themselves in the improbable situation of observing Eastertide on the back of a whale. Mistaking it for an islet, they landed, all save Brendan, and celebrated Mass. Then they lighted the brazier to assist in preparing the Paschal Feast. The whale, tolerant of the tramping feet of men upon his back, demonstrated his objection to the brazier's heat by sounding. In a medieval version recorded by Thomas Wright, the incident is thus recounted:

"And when the fyre was right hote, and the meet nygh sodden, then this yslond began to move; whereov the monks were afeered, and fledded anone to the shippe, and ledt the fyre and meet behind them, and mervayled sore of the moving."

A harrowing experience, but with a happy ending. Brendan, who had remained in the ship, threw staves to his disenfranchised brothers and all were saved. Dr. Little doesn't truly dismiss this episode as fable; he cites a recorded instance, identical, of a similar happening in Kerry in the 1920s. The adventure befell four fishermen of

Kerry who, on finding an apparently dead whale, covered with weed and crustaceans, took possession of it. Two of the fishermen elected to stay aboard the whale until the others could return for help to assist in towing the mammoth ashore. To ameliorate the bite of wind and damp of spray while waiting, the two on the whale took a brazier from the curragh and set about making tea. The whale of Kerry behaved in the same disgraceful fashion as had the whale of Brendan. Feeling the brazier's heat, and being not dead but merely sleeping, and concerned not a whit for the safety of the Kerry fishermen, the blubbery monster dived. Fortunately, the curragh had proceeded not far to shore and the luckless sailors were saved, poorer by one brazier.

The whale story in the Brendan legend was so widely accepted as fact in the Middle Ages that the maps of Olaus Magnus, in 1557, and Gastaldi, in 1564, actually chart the whale's position. In answer to those who would cite the recurrence of whale stories in legends of other cultures to discredit the Brendan story, Richard Hakluyt, the sixteenth-century English geographer, states that the Brendan whale was the foundation of all later whale fables, employing the Norse historian Angrim as his authority.

Leaving the scene of the whale's impertinence, Brendan and his fourteen monks now drifted for a time, eventually sighting the Island of Noss, in the Shetlands. Here they landed, staying eight days, until the feast of Pentecost. This was the *Island of the Birds*, which figures in every version of the story and which apparently contained some remarkable creatures.

The feathered ones, it would seem, entertained the monks by singing canons for them, and the monks in turn, sang canons to which the winged choir listened, rapt.

Returning to fact, the monks then sailed for three months, eventually reaching Mainland Isle of the Shetlands. Here they encountered an aged monk, Albiu, who prepared a feast for them. Leaving the old monk and his monastic community, they then drifted aimlessly about the North Atlantic, again falling victim to dwindling rations. After a long period they came to another island where all became ill. No fatalities resulted, although the period of recuperation was lengthy. They were then able to reprovision and sail once again. Now they sailed back to the Shetlands, first to Mainland, then to Noss. Next they visited a rocky crag in the bleak North Atlantic, possibly Rockall, an unfriendly uninhabited stone sitting alone and uninviting, its peak covered with sea birds, its steep sides forbidding any landing. From there they went to Iceland where one of their number left the ship against orders and perished in the onrush of a lava stream. Hastily leaving the hostile island, they sailed south and found a skerry inhabited by Judas Iscariot, briefly enjoying a respite from Hell. They interceded with the devils of Hell for him, gaining him additional time from Hades. (He was, it seemed, let out for short periods by Satan, always being returned to his damnation by fiends sent to fetch him.)

Having done their best for Judas, they eventually sailed to an island where dwelled the hermit Paul, a resident of the island for sixty years. Paul convinced Brendan that he should return to Ireland and the Saint forthwith sailed for the Emerald Isle, thus concluding his first voyage, thought to have been of seven years' duration.

I have not included the countless miraculous details accompanying the recording of each landing and sailing period, save for the incident of the whale, the arrival at the Isle of Birds, and the discovery of Judas Iscariot.

I include them only because they serve as pertinent examples of fact being inundated by fancy. All three, I think, have basis in fact, and were embellished greatly by later writers.

I think it highly possible that the sailing monks could have mistaken a dormant whale for a small islet. It may have been their intent to anchor beside it for a brief respite. The whale dived and they sailed away. That's all. But it offered an excellent opportunity for further exposition, and so some nameless monk, transcribing the legend, and sensing the opportunity to add color, thoughtfully added the celebration of Mass, a brazier, and a highly dramatic ending.

The Island of Birds was doubtless the island noted in the legend. Brendan's original report of the voyage probably included a lengthy comment on the birds and their constant singing. Again, an obliging transcriber, pleased with Brendan's happy reaction to the warbling avians, thought it only fitting that Brendan return the compliment.

The incident of Judas Iscariot upon a rock is, I think, the most credible of all, when the fiends from Hell are removed from the story structure. Brendan and his band came to a rocky islet where they found a lone monk. Perhaps temperamentally unfit for the recluse life, the poor fellow had gone quite out of his mind and notified Brendan that he was, indeed, Judas. He then described the terrible circumstance he was in, what with traveling back and forth to Hell. This incident also was reported as it occurred. This time the transcriber simply took the agonized ravings of the demented "Judas" and made them descriptives uttered by Brendan.

But we are not truly concerned with the fanciful aspects of the Brendan legend at the moment. The third voyage, his last, took place when Brendan was well advanced in years. It was undertaken because he had killed a man, and became a penance for him. According to Dr. Little, it is the most difficult of the three voyages to trace accurately. His mode of travel is not revealed, but it is evident that his last odyssey consumed ten years of his life and took him all through the British Isles and into the far corners of the Mediterranean; it is known that he visited Palestine, Egypt, and Greece. Beyond the elapsed time of the voyage and knowledge of some of the places he touched upon, little can be told.

Having established the occurrence of three great voyages undertaken by St. Brendan during his long life as a monk, we turn now to the second voyage, his most important to my chronicle, for it was the voyage which took him to America, and earned him the title *Brendan the Navigator*.

On returning from the first of his wanderings, Brendan was restless because his seven-year quest had not taken him to the Fortunate Isle, or *Hi Brasil*, as it is noted on many medieval maps. Recognizing that he would not be content until he had found this wondrous place, he sought the advice of the childhood foster mother to whom he invariably turned for counsel in time of stress.

Ita advised Brendan to put to sea once more, but warned him that he must not use a curragh. Apparently she felt that a craft derived from animal sources (skins) could not enter the Land of Promise of Saints. She therefore suggested that he construct a new ship, one built of wood, and also suggested that he use a *rutter*, or sailing guide, to aid him in his search. Apparently she took a dim view of his predisposition toward permitting wind and tide to take him about the sea at will. The *rutter* could be obtained, perhaps, from Fionn-Barr, whose story of the Delicious Isle had inspired Brendan's first voyage. Brendan agreed to follow her advice, and so set about building a new ship.

Again, Dr. Little's superb research provides an excellent description of a ship of the type probably constructed by the Saint. Built of oak, she was presumably clinker style, her strakes fastened by rivets. Half-decked, she carried a single pine mast and her sail was of strips of wool stitched together in the manner of viking sails. Seams caulked with pitch, she carried cordage of nettle fibre and an anchor, and possibly a chain hawser of iron. A large, biconcave paddle served as steering apparatus and she carried no oars. She was of sufficient size to carry a crew of sixty.

Provisioning was designed more thoughtfully on this voyage, the good monk having had bitter experience with short rations and illnesses on his first journey. Now he put aboard seeds—and possibly grain—and "useful plants." Blue sea holly was carried as protection against scurvy, and live swine and dried fish were stowed. It is evident that he also shipped a quantity of iron and the means of working it; the legend notes that he had to cast a new anchor on this voyage. Additional sail material was stowed, as well as spare dowels, and of course, a plentiful supply of water in casks and water skins.

Three trained ravens were taken aboard, possibly as aids in determining the presence of land, since he had no compass. The raven has since become a symbol for Brendan, and paintings of the Saint almost invariably show a raven somewhere in the portrait. The ship was built and launched, according to the tradition, in Westport, in County Mayo. From there it was sailed to Aran Mor, to remain a month before the actual departure for the Fortunate Isle.

At last the day came when Brendan and his sixty followers were ready to sail on a second quest for the Fortunate Isle. They again turned north from Ireland, but soon shifted course to the west. After forty days of sailing they entered into an ocean region of gloom and fog; a dark, forbidding place. Then, the air clearing, they encountered an iceberg, the sight of which held them fascinated for three days. Never had they observed such simple beauty as that resplendent within the huge ice cake: "color of silver, harder than marble, of substance of the clearest crystal." The meeting with the iceberg is employed as the first clue concerning Brendan's whereabouts in the North Atlantic by Dr. Little. He points out that they were somewhere off the coast of Newfoundland, in the Grand Banks region. His conclusion is proper; anyone who has sailed the lanes to Europe knows of the great occurrence of icebergs in spring in those waters. Greenland's calving glaciers spill their unwanted children into the waters of Davis Strait in huge quantities when the first warmth of spring touches upon them. Brendan put out from Aran Mor on March 22, in the year 551. He had sailed forty days when he came upon the berg which means that it was sighted early in May, just right for the first of the ice vanguard about to fill the waters off Newfoundland throughout the spring. Little also points out that the berg was arched, in itself a sign of the first stage of collapse and indicative that the ice mass was in waters warmer than the Arctic waters where it had been spawned.

When the monk's ship was at last turned away from the iceberg, the course was still to the west, for they made landfall shortly thereafter. Drawing close to the shore to inspect the strange new land they had chanced upon, they were given to wonder at a congress of peculiar animals sprawled along its beaches. The beasts were possessed of "catlike heads, eyes of the color of a bronze cauldron, fuzzy pelts, boars' tusks, and heavy, spotted bellies." Strange monsters, indeed, until Dr. Little identifies them as walrus, common to eastern North America as far south as Nova Scotia until the end of the seventeenth century. In sum, Little states, the clues given thus far, a "dark zone," or the foggy seas off the Grand Banks, the number of days' sail from Ireland, the notation of a course to the west, the iceberg and the presence of walrus all serve to bring Brendan to an American landfall at Newfoundland.

Wary, perhaps, of the spotted-bellied creatures on the beach, St. Brendan decided against landing, choosing instead to continue "coasting" along the shore to the southwest.

Not too many days passed, with the rugged coast of Newfoundland still to starboard, when death visited the little ship of Mayo. Aboard the ship was one Crosan, the king's jester, though it is never made clear to which king Crosan performed his jests, and how it was he elected to leave the favored life of a court clown for the austere life of a sailor into unknown seas. Somewhere off Newfoundland's bleak shore, Crosan breathed his last. The ship anchored, services were read o'er his lifeless form, and he was taken ashore and buried "in some sequestered bay."

The saddened company then departed and apparently set a course southward, leaving the land behind. With grief for their departed friend not yet stilled, death struck the vessel again, this time coming to the company's smith. Again a morose atmosphere pervaded the ship as services were read and now the smith's body was consigned to the deep. Little remarks that this is "the first recorded of Christian burials at sea discoverable in the histories of Northern Europe."

Continuing on course, Brendan's ship sailed without incident, other than sighting a water spout, for many days. Little expresses the thought that they set their course south by east and made their next landfall in the Bahamas. It is at this juncture that I must offer some disagreement, considering sailing time given after their departure from the islands he calls the Bahamas.

I feel strongly that Brendan's next landfall was in the Bermudas, with his first anchorage there in the harbor of what is now St. George, on St. George's Island. A landing there was not prudent; hordes of black, naked pygmies massed on the shore and threatened them with their weapons. Despite this disturbing presence, the ship remained at anchor for seven days in St. George's, presumably with a heavy, wide-awake guard through each tropic night. When they were ready to leave, the anchor fouled and they could not weigh it. With the smith long since buried at sea, Brendan was in a dilemma until he prevailed upon one of his monks to try at forging a new anchor. The willing monk succeeded, and they left St. George with an adequate replacement.

Setting a course west (or southwest) they quickly sighted Bermuda Island itself, and put in to investigate the waters of Great Sound. It is reasonable to assume that they found the best harbor, that of the present town of Hamilton, and dropped anchor there. No sooner had they performed this act than they were startled to see an aged monk, who had emerged from a small oratory on the island. Ragged of dress and bent of back, he greeted them and bade them welcome. He told Brendan that he had dwelled upon the island "almost beyond the memory of man." Originally, he had come there in company with twelve others, but illness and time itself had taken them until he alone remained. The old one, for some reason, was unduly anxious that they tarry not, but leave the island quickly. Brendan, as Little notes, agreed to leave, though with some puzzlement. It was hard to fathom why this old anchorite would be so anxious to rid the island of them so soon after their arrival.

Preparing to depart, their ship was threatened by a "monster" which rose from the deep and menacingly circled the craft. Dr. Little identifies the monster as a basking shark. While the crew eyed this formidable beast with apprehension, another "monster"—a manta ray—rose from the deep to give battle to the shark. Finally after a furious combat, the two, locked in mortal struggle, sank from sight and once again the waters were still. Preparations were again resumed to take departure, but Brendan, watching the old monk on shore, perceived that he seemed weakened and unsteady. Hurriedly landing, Brendan quickly administered last rites to the dying monk and stayed until death was a fact. Now Brendan perceived, Little opines, that the old monk had hastened them away in order that they would not witness his last moments and so cast a pall on their joyful quest. The monk was buried and all returned to the ship, now to depart again on a westerly course.

For eight days they sailed on "summer seas," with spiced breezes hinting at fragrant lands to come. The eight days consumed here would be the time needed to sail from Bermuda to Florida, their next apparent landfall. Dr. Little has them sailing eight days from the Bahamas to the neighborhood of Miami, a geographical premise not easily accepted. I think they sailed from Bermuda, west and south, for eight days, and arrived at or near the present city of St. Augustine. Later events will help justify this reasoning.

On arrival at St. Augustine, they found a "land odorous, flower-smooth, blessed. A land many melodied, musical, shouting for joy, unmournful." They anchored their ship and made haste to go ashore in this magnificent new land—this Paradise. It could only be the Fortunate Isle. How fortunate were they, to find their goal with so little grief!

Now they experienced a repetition of the Bermuda incident. Another old monk appeared, and bade them welcome. He told them that his name was Festivus, and he had been in America thirty years, apparently with many other monks of Erin. Brendan may have been surprised at encountering Festivus here in Florida, as Dr. Little suspects, but I am inclined to believe that by now he was taking such meetings in stride. He had, after all, met with monks in other strange places during the course of his first voyage and any shock he may have felt at meeting others of his kind must long since have been dissipated after his unhappy meeting with the old monk of Bermuda.

We know not how long the newly arrived monks rested and recounted news of Ireland to the residents, but it is evident that Brendan wished to explore the new land as soon as possible. At the earliest convenience, then, an expedition was prepared. Once again we are faced with a paucity of detail in description of the area covered by Brendan except that the presence of a river too wide to cross is recorded. The length of the exploratory party's travel is given as forty days. They camped on the bank of the wide river, where they were joined by a young man. The legend is not clear on whether it was an Indian or a younger monk from the Irish settlement. The young man wrought a profound influence upon Brendan, however, for after conversing with him (for how long we do not know) the Saint decided to return to Ireland.

The party then returned to the eastern coast and the settlement at St. Augustine and made ready to depart. Presumably Brendan returned to Erin by the simple device of reversing his course. It is to be suspected that he had kept a strict log of the voyage west, to aid in returning. That much Ita had impressed upon him when she spoke of the wisdom in using a *rutter*.

That is the story of Brendan and how he came to be in America in the sixth century after the birth of Christ.

The remarkable piece of literary detection performed by Dr. Little in demonstrating the probable course of St. Brendan from Ireland to America is a valuable move toward bringing the legend into its proper perspective. Until now, the legend has remained just that—a legend, smiled at by historians, eagerly probed by philologists and entirely dismissed by archaeologists. The lack of interest by archaeologists is, in this case, perfectly understandable—up to now. If the tale has been looked upon as a fable, archaeologists—who are not historians—could hardly be expected to probe for traces of a mythical person, particularly since there has been no reasonably accurate argument delineating the place in America where Brendan might have sojourned.

I think that Dr. Little now provides a basis, however thin, for interest from archaeologists.

Although I have expressed disagreement with Dr. Little on two phases of his theory, my oppositeness does not detract from his findings. I feel, rather, that it implements them in helping pinpoint the areas in need of investigation if we are to produce evidence of Brendan's stay in America, or evidence of the monks who preceded him here.

Dr. Little would have Brendan sail from Ireland to Newfoundland, then to the Bahamas, and ultimately to the Miami, Florida, region. I agree that Brendan went first to Newfoundland, but, considering the factual details of the legend, I would place him first in the Bermudas, then in the region of St. Augustine. The distance from Bermuda to St. Augustine is about 900 miles. Brendan's curragh was probably capable of slightly more than 100 miles sailing in the course of a 24-hour day. The legend states that he sailed west for eight days after leaving the last island on which he landed. The distance from Bermuda to St. Augustine fits the sailing time, the distance from Miami to Great Bahama, about 90 miles, does not.

In placing the settlement of monks where Brendan landed at St. Augustine, I reason as did the Spaniards of the sixteenth century. They selected that place as a habitation for the same reason the monks did earlier. It is sheltered, it provides a good harbor, and it offers the most appealing anchorage along the many miles of Florida beach stretching from the mouth of the St. Johns River to the harbor at Ponce Park. It appealed to monk and Spaniard alike, but I think the Spaniards had an advantage not open to the monks. When the *conquistadores* found the entrance to the harbor of St. Augustine, they went in and discovered old foundations—all that was left of the Irish settlement. Being practical, and noting that others before them had considered the place attractive, they simply moved in and threw new structures over the old foundations. I suspect that some of the old Spanish buildings still standing in St. Augustine, those built in 1565 and after, are built on stones patiently put in place by a band of forgotten Irish monks.

The next argument in favor of St. Augustine as the site is mention of the wide river the monks of Brendan's band were unable to cross. Some of the less perceptive dissectors of the legend who place Brendan in Florida suggest that the river might be the Mississippi. Physically, it would be impossible for Brendan to have reached the Mississippi in 40 days from Florida. The distance across the shortest possible route between the two is close to 600 miles. The monks were not trained wilderness marchers and would have been doing extremely well had they been able to average even as much as 15 miles a day. That speed would give them 600 miles but the crossing of rivers must be considered. In Florida alone, a minimum of a dozen rivers would have had to be crossed, and such crossings would necessitate raft construction at each waterway. Losing a half day per river would easily discount the possibility of traveling 600 miles in 40 days.

Dr. Little surmises that the river in question might have been the St. Johns, and in this I agree. That river is nearly seven miles wide near its mouth, to the north of St. Augustine, and is more than a mile wide as far inland as 150 miles. I think the monks of Brendan wandered the region between the coast and the St. Johns River during their 40-day exploration, eventually reaching the formidable river where they pitched their camp.

It is futile to speculate on the identity of the young man whose conversation caused Brendan to return to the island of his birth. It is entirely possible that he was of the monkish colony in residence, and that colony itself presents an intriguing speculation. It is known to students of folklore that the Indians of Florida had a tradition among them of white men who lived in their land, and who were users of iron.

Traditions, however valuable, will not serve to substantiate the visit of Brendan or the colony of monks. But there is a dim hope that a new brand of archaeology now being pursued in Florida might assist. Dr. John M. Goggin of the University of Florida has, for the last few years, been using underwater archaeology in his home state in probing four types of underwater sites. They are, as he lists them in *American Antiquity* for January 1960, those containing discarded refuse and "lost" material, submerged sites of former human occupation, shrines or places of offerings and, of course, shipwrecks.

Of the types listed, it is conceivable that the "refuse" sites would logically produce evidence, if any, of pre-Columbian European occupation in Florida. The refuse sites are, according to Dr. Goggin, the most common, and the most productive of these have been springs. He notes that several thousand Indian and Spanish artifacts, along with such refuse as peach pits and corncobs have been removed from a single spring at Fig Springs, on the Ichtucknee River in Florida. I have already expressed the thought that hopes for recovery of unmistakable Irish artifacts are dim, and for good reason. First, like the monks at Pattee's Caves, the monks of Florida would have been blessed with few personal possessions to be worn out and discarded. Iron implements used by them might be produced from the wells and springs of Florida, as pottery might. But in these cases we cannot discount the human factor present in recovering such artifacts. In sites where Indian or Spanish artifacts are expected to be found, all such material would logically carry labels classifying them as one or the other. In the absence of complete metallographic tests or thorough examination of pottery, any piece of metal or shard of pottery would have to carry these labels, simply because the products of other, earlier cultures are not anticipated. The "colonial brick" at North Salem was partially due to human factors of this influence. Colonial artifacts were anticipated, therefore all artifacts were labeled colonial. A sylogistic method, but one which is understandable because of the existence of the NEBC Principle.

I have asked Dr. Goggin about the artifacts withdrawn from various underwater sites he has probed in Florida, and he assures me that all material produced thus far has been identifiable. I'm sure he is correct in his evaluations; I will, however, express the hope that "unidentifiable" objects, which every dig produces to some degree, be considered from a pre-Columbian point of view before being relegated to the "X" drawer in the laboratory.

There is one other area which might produce evidence of sixth-century occupation. In observing that some of the old Spanish structures erected in St. Augustine in 1565—and later—might have been built upon existing foundations, I again express hope that indications of earlier occupations might emerge in this area. In a report on Southeastern Archaeology in *American Antiquity* for October 1959, Charles H. Fairbanks notes that continuing excavations had, at that writing, been in progress in St. Augustine. The digs were conducted by Hale G. Smith and Robert Steinback, working under the auspices of the St. Augustine Historical Society. Thus far, the work had been carried out on known eighteenth-century buildings. Perhaps, if a dig is ever executed at an older site, the uncovering of substructures might deserve more than cursory inspection. A natural, human tendency in finding substructures is to declare them earlier foundations of the same period, possibly resulting from buildings destroyed by fire, later rebuilt with new foundations placed in the original cellar excavation.

We can but hope.

That Brendan and earlier monks were here, is, I think, established. That the tale is one of fact and not fancy has been demonstrated by Dr. Little. Those who attack its authenticity can, I would venture to say, be classified loosely as those possessed of lethargy.

It is infinitely easier to dismiss it as phantasy than to scrape away the encrustation of centuries of fanciful embellishment to produce the true skeleton of the chronicle.

The attacks on the legend of St. Brendan have been many and varied, and, in one case at least, unconsciously amusing. On March 14, 1892, Dr. Robert D. Benedict, a student of literature, presented a lecture before the American Geographical Society in New York. In it he sought to demonstrate that the Brendan legend could be nothing more than pure myth. He used a guilt-by-association technique: the famous Hereford map was employed as the basis for argument. This ancient chart, a map of the known world by a monk named Richard de Haldingham, was made between 1275 and 1320. Limned on parchment five feet five inches in length and four feet five inches wide, the map is shown as a full circle and rendered in several colors.

In erudite manner, he points out the obvious errors on the part of the map maker; Italy, for instance, runs in the wrong direction, the British Isles are "remarkably inaccurate," the north and east of Asia are totally absent. Dr. Benedict then dwells at great length on the fabulous beasts and other marvels which adorn the body and the margins of the map. He points out depictions of *Gangines,* a remarkable animal like the camel which lived on perfume and apples; if it smelled a bad smell, it died. He introduces his audience to the Gryphon and the Aramspian, the Avalerions, the Monoceros (before the Monoceros is placed a virgin, who, as he comes, bares her breast to him, on which he, abandoning all ferocity, lays his head, so that, having gone to sleep, he is taken as defenceless) the Satirii, the Ambari (a race without ears) the Himantopodes, the Psylii, and other equally magnificent and fabulous creatures and races.

He introduces, briefly, other maps containing as much balderdash as the Hereford map to strengthen his cause. Now, having set up his target, he drives the shaft home. Returning to the Hereford map, he indicates a group of islands which are labeled "The Fortunate Islands." The islands of St. Brendan. (There are six.)

Having thus established the mythical quality of St. Brendan's Islands, he proceeds to disintegrate the entire legend. His basis for the attack on the Brendan legend seems to derive from his impression that Brendan steals some of Columbus's thunder, a ridiculous premise, but one the lecturer is most positive about, and at which he takes offense. He goes into great detail concerning the wondrous things which happened to Brendan and remarks on the fabulous creatures encountered by the good monk and his stalwart band.

Having thus discredited Brendan by demonstrating that the entire tale is pure myth, he delivers his *coup de grace:* ". . . the legend of St. Brendan is a very good sample of monkish fiction pure and simple—an *imaginary voyage* [his italics] to be ranked with Robinson Crusoe and Gulliver's Travels and Peter Wilkins. . . ."

He then refers to the Greek satirist, Lucian, and his tale of sailing across the Atlantic until he reached the moon. The story, called *The Veracious History,* is patently a fabrication, and so stated in the preface by the imaginative Greek. But, in the preface, he comments on Homer: "The great leader and master of all this rhodomontade is Homer's Ulysses, who tells to Alkinous about the winds pent up in bags, minotaurs and one-eyed cyclops, wild men, creatures with many heads, several of his companions turned into wild beasts by this enchantment, and a thousand things of this kind which he related to the ignorant and credulous Phoenicians."

Dr. Benedict then regrets that the author of St. Brendan affixed no such preface to the tale of the monk.

Obviously, Dr. Benedict was not aware of events in his own time. He apparently did not know that Heinrich Schliemann, the German archaeologist, who, in the 1870s, began the work which led to his discovery of the cities of Troy, determined their location by reading Homer's *Iliad,* a "fiction full of monsters and wondrous beasts," by the same "unreliable" author.

Brendan's visit to America was not the first by monks from Erin's shore. Nor was it the last.

I'd like to introduce you now to a multitudinous band of them who came to America by circuitous routes in the year 982.

CHAPTER 6

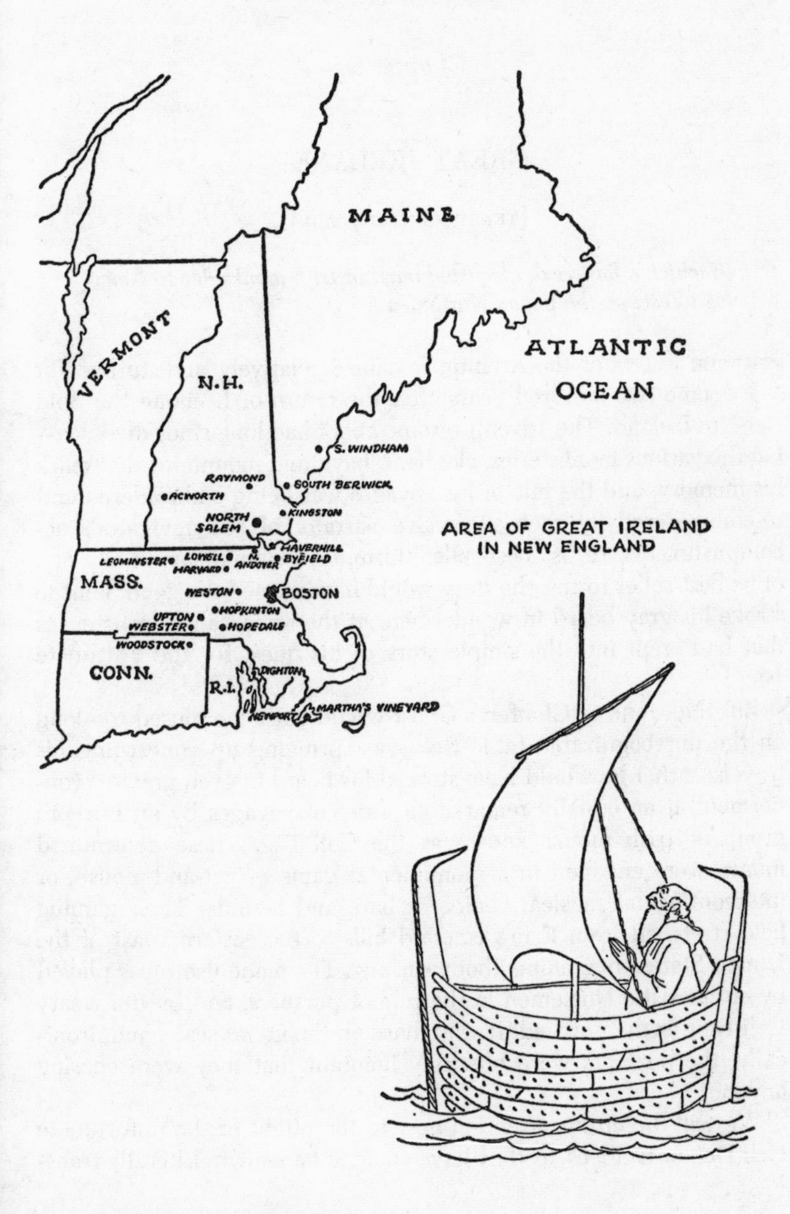

MAINE
ATLANTIC
OCEAN
VERMONT
N.H.
MASS.
CONN.
R.I.
S. WINDHAM
RAYMOND
SOUTH BERWICK
ACWORTH
KINGSTON
NORTH
SALEM
HAVERHILL
BYFIELD
LEOMINSTER
LOWELL
HARVARD
N.
ANDOVER
WESTON
BOSTON
HOPKINTON
UPTON
WEBSTER
HOPEDALE
WOODSTOCK
DIGHTON
NEWPORT
MARTHA'S VINEYARD
AREA OF GREAT IRELAND
IN NEW ENGLAND

Chapter 6

GREAT IRELAND

[TENTH CENTURY A.D.]

In which a harassed, disgusted band of Irish monks flee to America to escape the pagan Northmen.

THE waters of the Atlantic remained relatively undisturbed for some two hundred years after the return of Brendan the Bold to Ireland. The adventuresome abbot had long since died, leaving the various monasteries, claghans, bays, and mountains that mark his memory, and the tale of his voyages was being embroidered and re-embroidered by each successive narrator of the navigator's accomplishments. In its "best-seller" form, or, I should say, in any one of its best-seller forms, the story would have caused the good Saint to stroke his gray beard in wonderment at the remarkable occurrences that had crept into the simple story of his quest for the Fortunate Isle.

But the Monk of Clonfert's Ghost would not have mused too long on the unrecognizable fable that was springing up concerning his travels; rather he would have stroked his beard in even greater wonderment at an equally remarkable series of voyages by an intrepid group of Irish monks known as the Celi Dei. These determined monks were engaged in a monumental game of cat-and-mouse, or intercontinental musical chairs, or hare and hounds. Their gaming field stretched from Erin's emerald hills to the eastern coast of the United States—beginning about A.D. 795. The game itself was played by enthusiastic Norsemen in the role of pursuers, and by the weary Celi Deis as the pursued. It was chase on the grand scale, and, ironically, the pursuers were blissfully ignorant that they were chasing anyone.

We will direct our attention now to the plight of the unfortunate Celi Dei, or Culdees, as they have come to be known. Literally translated, "Celi Dei" means "Servants of God," and the Celi Dei truly illustrated the aptness of their name by living a most spiritual, ascetic life. While we examine the attitudes and persons of the Celi Dei, we will also make note of the later confluence which brought together the long dead monks and the wealthy gentleman from Hartford, William B. Goodwin. This chapter, then, will be concerned first with the Celi Dei and their unhappy flight to America—to colonize "Great Ireland"—which flight was spread over nearly two hundred years—and of the innocent (if such a word can be used) Northmen who precipitated it.

We will then observe the frustrations of Mr. Goodwin as he attempted to prove the existence of the Celi Dei on our shores, his battles with those who denied it, and the remarkable, and puzzling, inflexibility of the latter.

The Celi Dei were the Christians of Ireland even before St. Patrick arrived on the scene, but their Christianity was an admixture of old Celtic rites and the new ideas of the European Catholic Church. The Celi Dei, however, exhibiting a strong maverick streak, did not take too kindly to ideas on the new faith emanating from the Continent, and in their fiercely individualistic, Irish way, became "problem children" to the church.

Archibald B. Scott, in his *History of the Pictish Nation, Its People and Its Church,* describes them well.

"The Celi Dei," Scott wrote, "possessed no affection for ecclesiastical organization or machinery. He was God's man and needed no earthly master to whip him up. To know the will of God was meat and drink; to do it was life. The appetites were subordinated to the longings of the soul, and the Celi Dei had disciplined their bodies to endure the severest hardships. They possessed no personal property except the clothes they wore, a scanty store of food and the area of ground covered by their hut or cave. They lived on the simplest fare, and often procured and prepared it. No woman was permitted near their dwellings. [This was to change later. Their gradual but steady absorption into the Church made it necessary to acquire and protect property. They took wives so that they could guarantee inheritors of their own beliefs.] They had not fled from mankind with the selfish motive of winning their own personal salvation; but to testify, in their open examples, to the blessedness of the simple, righteous, divinely guided life."

These were the Celi Dei.

The European Church viewed these rugged individualists dimly. Monks were sent into Ireland to bring about the absorption of the Celi Dei, but invariably retired in confusion, bringing tales back to the Continent of the "impossible" Irish and of the complete decadence of the Church there. The Celi Dei ignored these foreign emissaries for nearly two hundred years, but ultimately, reluctantly, became part of the European Church.

During the period with which we are concerned, however, the Celi Dei were happily pursuing their ascetic lives in hermitage and cave, *disirt* and mountain top, usually in disconnected bands. They were scattered all about Ireland, and had moved out of the country into the northern islands, settling first in the Orkneys, then gradually ascending to the Shetlands and Faeroes. They are recorded in the Faeroes as early as 725, and during the years that followed the founding of their colony on these islands, they acquired a rugged cross to bear.

The "cross" took shape in the form of Northmen.

Periodic raids on the northern islands instilled in the monks a dread fear and hatred of the Norse pirates. They refused to remain where any Northman might appear. It is quite possible that some of the monks may have fled to Iceland during the eighth century as a result of these raids. We do know that they were settled in Iceland in the year 874, as later evidence will show. It was not, however, until the closing years of the eighth century that the great hegiras from Ireland began, sad voyages which were eventually to lead to an Irish colony in the New World—the "Great Ireland" of the Icelandic sagas.

The Celi Dei apparently maintained communication lines between their isolated settlements, and news of the raids in the northern islands must certainly have been broadcast. The monks in Ireland, therefore, would have acquired a sympathetic dislike for the Norse raiders at first, and then an active loathing based on what they, themselves, observed of the viking depredations. Dr. D. D. C. Pochin Mould, writing in her *Ireland of the Saints,* offers a clue to the origins of the Celi Dei's hostility to the Norsemen.

"The Norse inroads" she writes, "meant a terrible upheaval and drain on Irish life. They began with raids on islands and coasts in 795, but about 832 developed into permanent settlements. The Norse sailed up the Irish rivers and placed their fleets on the inland lakes, floating fortresses from which they could descend on all the country around. They founded a series of coastal towns, Dublin, Wexford, Waterford, Limerick, the first cities that Ireland had had and through which much of her trade began to pass. The Celtic monasteries, placed on the waterways and on the coast for access to the main communication lines, were sacked again and again: Clonmacnoise ten times, Kildare sixteen, Armagh nine times."

There is little wonder that the Celi Dei, possessed of a profound love for their fellow men, found it extremely difficult to extend that love to the pillaging vikings. But they were men of peace, and chose to turn the other cheek to the Norsemen by the simple device of leaving any area where the Scandinavians penetrated.

It is reasonable to assume, then, that the documented colony of Irish monks in Iceland came about because the holy men fled the northern islands to escape the vikings. Their presence on the island of fire and ice is unquestionable; it is recorded in the Icelandic sagas. It is also evident that their first colonization of Iceland coincided with the beginning of the Norse raids on Ireland. Dicuil, the Irish monk who wrote a voluminous history of the world in the year 830, relates that the Irish colony in Iceland was existent in 795.

The little colony flourished, conceivably being expanded by its own procreation and by the addition of other monks who had heard of it. For three quarters of a century the ascetics practiced their Christianity unmolested, free from the onslaughts of the northern pagans. But in 874, fate dictated that they must move again.

In that year, Ingolfr Ardnason, a Norwegian noble, in rebellion against Harald the Fairhaired, King of Norway, decided to emigrate to Iceland with a band of equally rebellious followers. Some came from Norway, some came from Scotland, and a great number came from Ireland. This circumstance produced the relatively high percentage of Irish blood in the Icelanders since those Norwegians coming from Erin had, in many cases, taken Irish wives or brought other Irish with them as slaves.

Ingolfr was aware of Iceland and its location because of one Floki, who had lived on the island for about a year in 860–861. Arriving there with intent to settle, Floki turned his cattle and sheep loose, but imprudently neglected to provide feed for the coming winter. He and his crew spent the summer fishing, and so delightful were the hours thus spent that he completely forgot to go a-haying. Winter descended and the cattle and sheep starved to death. The following spring, hurt by this hostile act on the part of the animals, Floki was forced to return to Norway. To rationalize his ill fortune, he called the country Iceland, implying that the severe cold had killed his cattle. The name was justified in his mind by the pack ice which he had seen floating down from polar regions. So it was that Iceland received its bad name. In truth, Iceland's climate is very like that of southern Canada or the northern parts of the United States, its mean temperature in the south being about 30 degrees in winter and 52 degrees in summer. In the northern parts, the average is two to four degrees lower.

Despite the misnomer applied by Floki, Ingolfr chose Iceland as his refuge from the tyrannical Harald the Fairhaired, largely because he thought the island to be unoccupied. Accordingly, he sailed to Thule and founded the city of Reykjavik, the Bay of Smokes. He did indeed find the island unoccupied, but soon discovered unmistakable evidence that the Irish had been there before him. The mysterious communications system maintained by the Celi Dei had obviously brought word of the coming of the terrible Northmen even before they arrived, and the Irish wasted not a moment; they fled once again to avoid contact with the pagan. The *Flateyjarbok,* a collection of Icelandic sagas written in the thirteenth century, records the presence of the Irish:

> . . . before Iceland was settled by the Northmen, there were those people whom the Northmen call Papas. They were Christian men, and people think they must have been from the West of the Sea [Ireland] because there were found after them Irish books and bells and croziers, and yet more things by which it might be perceived that they were Westmen [the Norse term for Irishmen]. These things were found in East Papey and Papyli. It is also spoken of in the English books that at that time men went between the lands.

According to William B. Goodwin's book, *The Ruins of Great Ireland in New England,* they also left stone ruins which can still be seen on the island of Papey, off the east coast of Iceland. They were of "beehive," or round, stone construction, and later we will examine similar structures in America.

The flight from Iceland marked the third exodus of the harassed monks; they had vacated Ireland, they had fled in panic from the bleak and stormy northern islands. Now they must again take to their curraghs and leave the Ultimate Island. Their colonies had, in all likelihood, grown during the eighty years of Icelandic occupation and were doubtless large by 874. (They may have been large to begin with, since many writers have suggested that the Irish had been visiting Iceland and America for many centuries prior to 874. The evidence presented in the chapter on Brendan certainly substantiates such speculation. The Icelandic colony itself may have been in existence for a long time, and expanded by the great influx in 795.) It is not difficult to imagine, then, a procession of curraghs, similar to the one Brendan first sailed in, hastily provisioned and launched into the uninviting waters of the North Atlantic, hopefully steered toward yet another promised land.

Logic indicates that they would steer to the north or west to seek haven. To the north, however, lay ice fields with which they were doubtless familiar; even had they elected to brave the perils of a land both unknown and icebound, they would have had to consider the frailty of the skin curraghs against the hazards of sailing through ice fields. Since the vikings were still active to the south, return to the Faeroes, Shetlands, Orkneys, or the motherland was out of the question, and to the east lay Norway itself, the mountainous land which spawned these evil, plaguing pagans.

To the west they must go, and to the west lay Greenland.

They went there because it was in the west, and very possibly because they knew it was there. It must be considered that these Irish were a wandering people, and even those who were induced to stay in one of the "organized" colonies for a time must inevitably have gone off on individual excursions to remoter places. And they returned to the colonies. Thus the existence of Greenland was probably known; they hadn't gone there in great numbers earlier, simply because it hadn't been necessary.

And so they effected a mass migration to Greenland.

And it was to last for 108 years. It is documented in the Icelandic sagas. Barren as it is, they found peace in Greenland during the century of their residence. While capped with a gigantic mass of ice 10,000 feet thick, Greenland's coastal areas are fertile and tillable, creating a thin, green fringe surrounding the huge glacier that is the country itself. Trees are few, but the summers, which are surprisingly hot, produce myriad flowers and grasses, the latter providing forage for cattle. Crop seasons are short, but farming can be accomplished with some effort expended. I would think that the monks probably liked Greenland, its barrenness appealing to the ascetic side, the brief punctuation of summer growth providing respite from the bleak, needed by even the strictest adherent to the simple life. It was the perfect background for those subscribing to the philosophy of the Celi Dei.

Until another viking serpent ship, with billowing sail of red and white, appeared off the west coast of Greenland in 982.

It was the dragon ship of Eric the Red, Eric Raudi, truculent exile from Iceland, himself seeking a place of refuge from the annoyances of his fellow man. Expelled from Iceland for homicide in 982, Eric was forced into a three-year exile imposed on him by Icelandic law. His patience with his countrymen and their foolish laws exhausted, Eric now went in search of his own "Fortunate Isle," a land wherein *he* could be the law, and apply it in his own fashion. He chose Greenland as his paradise, going there according to a pattern so familiar in all pre-Columbian voyaging: he knew it was there, because another Icelander, one Gunnbjorn, had been there earlier in the tenth century and reported its location.

Eric did not simply find a place to settle immediately; he spent the first several months of his voyage to Greenland in exploring the country. Not until winter's icy presence forced him to snug down did he select a site for his proposed colony. When he did, it was on the west coast of Greenland, at a place which he called Brattahlid, to the north of what is now Julianehaab. The ruins of the structures which housed Eric's colony can still be seen there, and are, in fact, in process of continued study by the National Museum of Denmark.

Re-creating the voyage of Eric and its effect upon the Irish monks in residence is comparatively easy. As Eric coasted Greenland, noting each bay and cove and headland, the terrible sight of the ominous striped sail was beheld by the monks. It could only mean one thing; another raid. Eric's continued voyaging, fortunately, gave the Irishmen ample time to gather themselves and their progeny into another flotilla of curraghs and hurriedly abandon their century-old colony.

Again they fled west, the same prohibitions on easterly, southerly, or northerly sailings prevailing as they had a century before. And this time their westward course took them straight to North America. But again, as in Iceland, the monks left evidences of their colony to puzzle old Eric. *The Libellus Islandorum*, a work of Icelandic historian Ari the Wise (1067–1148), states:

They [Eric and his crew] found these men's habitations both east and west in the land, both broken hide boats and stone smithery, whereby it may be seen that the same kind of folk had been there as inhabit Wineland, and whom the men of Greenland call Scraelings.

The passage, with its reference to "broken hide boats" and "stone smithery" clearly indicates the presence of Irishmen. In no case can it be construed to mean Eskimo, and for excellent reason: the Eskimos had not reached that part of Greenland in the year 986. Use of the term "Scraeling" is a logical one. It is a name found frequently throughout the sagas, and its true meaning has never been determined, but it is always applied to the natives of Wineland, or Vinland the Good. Some scholars suggest that it means "men who are savages," others think it might mean "men who use skin boats." I was told by a very pleasant Icelander, Dr. Eric Ericsson, as we sat over a scotch-and-soda in The Naust in Reykjavik, that it meant "men who dressed in skins." I think Dr. Ericsson's definition is as sensible as those of the philologists, since it seems to be a description that a Northman would apply to the Indians he encountered in Vinland. As the years passed by, the term came to include the Irish and Icelanders who were known by later vikings to live in New England.

But while Eric was furrowing his brow over the strange boats and smithery, the curraghs of the fleeing Irishmen were already hull down on the horizon. Eric did not see the Irish, nor did he witness the hectic embarkation. Doubtless, he thought no more of the strange remains, once having noted them, and devoted himself to the more realistic task of providing quarters for his crew and family.

The Irishmen, meanwhile, devoted themselves to an equally realistic task. Where, next? A relatively short voyage of four or more days' duration gave them the answer. Their course—already noted as due west or perhaps west by south—brought them to a point somewhere between Button Island and Belle Isle Strait, on the bleak coast of Labrador. It would seem that the Labrador coast would be unappealing even to the most dedicated of ascetics, and apparently that condition held for most of the monks. Some of them did stop off to found a colony of unknown duration on Sculpin Island, for, according to Goodwin, there are stone ruins on that island not indigenous to an Eskimo culture. But most of the monks continued coasting Labrador, going slowly but steadily east and south. Perhaps they had had enough of extremes in climate and hopefully sought a land with more temperate inclinations. Perhaps now, they were ready to forsake the ice of the north in favor of a land that would bear a closer resemblance to Ireland.

It is conceivable that the entire flotilla put into Sculpin for a time, and a vote was taken. Some elected to remain on the rocky islet, the others chose to push on. So we can imagine a scene of farewells and Godspeeds as the curraghs silently glided away from Sculpin, leaving there the few who considered Sculpin a sound choice.

With a good wind and fresh provisions of birds' eggs, fish and whatever game they could snare, the homeless monks and their families continued their odyssey. Down they sailed to the Strait of Belle Isle and across to Newfoundland. They coasted this land and crossed Cabot Strait to reach Cape Breton Island. Rounding the island to the east, they reached Canso in Nova Scotia. Again they coasted the land to Cape Sable. At that point, one of two courses lay open: they could continue to coast Nova Scotia, painfully nosing the coast up into the Bay of Fundy, where, forced by the land to turn west and south, they would continue to New England. Or, they could have decided to risk the open water that lay ahead, hopefully trusting that they would find land beyond the horizon. I'm inclined to think that they chose the land-hugging course which eventually brought them to the beautiful country at the mouth of the Merrimack in Massachusetts. I think the terminal point of their voyage was decided by reason of fatigue rather than any other factor. They had surely passed many places along Maine's coast which would have been suitable for a colony site. But the Merrimack country is beautiful, and beauty of surroundings need not be an obstacle to the pursuit of godly things, but rather an asset in illustrating the wonders of God and nature.

Thus they came to the Merrimack. And sailed into it.

And when they had reached what is now Haverhill, they were stopped by a natural barrier, a falls, and found an Indian trail nearby. And they went up the trail to find a wondrous pile of rocks in various stages of collapse—and they knew they had found another haven. This one might be yet the best of all. It was far enough inland to offer a reasonable guarantee of freedom from the ravaging Northmen, and it presented a number of structures which could be easily cleaned out, or dug out, and used immediately for shelter and ritual.

In short, they had arrived at Pattee's Caves—the site of the Phoenician occupation more than a thousand years before.

We have no way of knowing whether the peregrinating Irishmen found Pattee's Caves by accident, or whatever they learned about it from the Indians. It is more than reasonable to conclude that their first contacts with the red men were friendly, and that some effort was made at communication. That pattern holds true for nearly every subsequent recorded meeting of white men and Indians for the first time. Their relationships are nearly always cordial at the outset, and only deteriorate when the acquisitive character of the white man begins to emerge fully. The pattern is seen in later visits of the Northmen and the Pilgrims and the Puritans and all the Europeans who came here to seek religious freedom or land or gold or adventure, and incidentally, decimated the Indian in the process.

Since we cannot deduce the manner in which the monks and their flocks arrived at Pattee's Caves, we might attempt to reconstruct their attitudes at finding the Caves, and observe that the initial pleasure at finding such a haven soon turned to blackest gloom.

Unbounded joy must surely have prevailed when the new country had been evaluated. For the first time they were provided with ample candidates for conversion. The woods abounded with simple heathens who were friendly and would listen to these strange white men. The woods themselves were enormous, as were the cleared places and the beach areas stretching north and south from the Merrimack. Here indeed was a place where a man could get off by himself if he chose, or bring the message of Christianity to the heathen as the opportunity arose. Pattee's Caves, at North Salem, also called Cowbell Corners in modern times, was a ready-made heaven. With little trouble, the Y-cavern was cleared, its efficient drains discovered, its speaking tube wondered at, its useful niches for altar and image purposes viewed with approval. (Or, did they add these themselves?) Quickly, it was turned into a chapel. Its smallish size was no liability whatever. Many such microscopic churches served their communities well in Ireland, and the buildings they had constructed in Iceland and Greenland and Sculpin were as small, or smaller. It was architecture by the angels.

The original plaza leading out from the Y-cavern was freed from debris and the fifteen little dolmens added. Someone carved the figure of a running deer on a stone within the Y-cavern. Other structures were added and soon the woods at North Salem were alive with the activities of the new colony. I will not attempt to describe the physical nature of the structures at North Salem beyond the description given in Chapter 2 and the brief delineation here. Goodwin described them most comprehensively in his *The Ruins of Great Ireland in New England*, Frederick Pohl devotes a chapter to them in his *The Lost Discovery*, papers have been written in many publications concerning them, and they are treated upon in books as recent as late 1959. To present them fairly would occupy disproportionate space in this volume; I refer you once again to the photographs in Plates 1, 2 and 3.

As the monks settled down into the routine life at North Salem, their emotions could have betrayed naught but joy. The woods were filled with game, large and small, the Spicket River and the Merrimack swarmed with fish, the Indians could supply them with knowledge concerning the cultivation of maize. It was grape country, too. Goodwin suggests that they may have used the sacrificial stone as a wine press, but, unless they had some method of shoring up the sides, it seems that such an application would have been highly inefficient.

North Salem and Pattee's Caves were truly an Eden.

But not for long.

They were to have their peaceful retreat shattered twice more by the incubus from the north. The first calamity was to descend even before they had completed a year of residence in New England, and the second four years later. But the seriocomic details of these events remain for later chapters.

Leaving the saintly monks to enjoy the peace and solitude of their New Hampshire asylum, we will now take up the circumstances which caused the raising of their ghosts, in manner most stormy, by William B. Goodwin, whom you have already met, briefly, in Chapter 2.

Mr. Goodwin, a man of many interests, was a dedicated student of history, and fortunately possessed of enough money to indulge himself thoroughly in this most unprofitable of pursuits. He had, while recuperating from an illness in Jamaica, become interested in the Columbus story, and had initiated a dig in an effort to locate a city thought to have been founded by Diego, brother of the Genoese

Navigator. He spent enough time in the Caribbean to satisfy his curiosity, if not fully accomplish his purpose, and also to begin a long war with distinguished historian Samuel Eliot Morison, author of many books on Christopher Columbus. Here in the states, he had several other wars, major and minor, in various degrees of intensity, chiefly with archaeologists, anthropologists, and historians who disagreed with his theories.

Lest the above statement prompt the reader to conclude that Mr. Goodwin was what archaeologists, anthropologists, and historians are quick to label "crackpot," I must point out, delicately, that some, at least, of Mr. Goodwin's wars were justified. I'm inclined to believe that, rather than being a "crackpot," he simply vented his temper, with remarkable directness, on those who wouldn't, or couldn't, bring themselves to believe that any penetration of North America before Columbus had ever happened. He couldn't tolerate the creeping Anglophilia that seems to grip American historians whenever the subject of pre-Columbian exploration of America by Europeans is even hinted at. He simply couldn't understand the NEBC Principle.

His methods of proffering his own beliefs in this highly speculative field, however, were slightly less than scientific, and, in many cases, these unorthodox methods shocked men of science into apoplexy whenever the name of Goodwin was whispered. He was, for instance, as apt to dig out an archaeological site with a tractor as with a spade. But he did bring more than one piece of evidence pointing toward pre-Columbian discovery of America to light; unfortunately, no accredited authority has ever accepted any of his findings. Which is why we are concerned with him.

I think he was more right than many of the experts.

Goodwin's pursuit of the off-beat took him all over the world, and while on a trip to Seattle, Washington, in 1921, he came in contact with Professor Olaf Strandwold, a one-time superintendent of schools in that state. Strandwold was interested in runes, and Goodwin was interested in vikings. Their meetings, therefore, were mainly concerned with the problem of the Northmen and their voyages to America. During the course of one of their conversations, as Goodwin tells it in *The Ruins of Great Ireland in New England*, Strandwold mentioned a curious stone ruin he knew about in Upton, Massachusetts. He thought it might be Norse, and suggested that Goodwin investigate it on his return east.

Goodwin did. On returning to his home at Hartford, Connecticut, he went immediately to see Mr. Henry A. Cheney of Hopkinton, Massachusetts, a mutual friend of Strandwold and Malcolm Pearson. Cheney introduced Goodwin to Pearson, on whose parents' property the mysterious ruin stood, and the two began a long friendship—a friendship of such enduring nature that Goodwin—on his death in 1945—willed the site at North Salem to Pearson.

Goodwin was enthusiastic over the strange, "beehive"-like structure at Upton, but was diverted from studying it immediately on learning of an even more mysterious site. Pearson and Cheney, it seemed, knew about a sprawling jumble of rock at a place called North Salem, in New Hampshire, and the two thought Goodwin should see it. They felt that it, too, might be Norse. Needing no prodding, Goodwin and his companions drove off to the tiny village of North Salem, specifically to Cowbell Corners, within the town. Parking the car at the foot of a sloping ridge, they climbed to its top, Goodwin staring incredibly at the vast panorama of monoliths, megaliths, dolmens, and other assorted rocks strewn about in quiet chaos. His eyes dilated. Here was pre-Columbian evidence by the ton!

The gentleman from Hartford wasted no time.

He bought the nearly thirty-acre site and lovingly enclosed it with a 6-foot cyclone fence. As quickly as possible, he engaged Mr. Roscoe J. Whitney of Leominster, Massachusetts, to set about clearing the woodland debris and begin the restoration of the stonework. A crew was brought in to dig and clear, and Pearson, a professional photographer, assigned to record the progress of the venture step by step. The restoration proceeded apace; walls were restored, dolmens put back in their original positions, tons of mulch removed and excavations begun. It is in the two latter areas that Goodwin has drawn the most vehement criticism. In removing earth and mulch, he is said to have destroyed the profile of the site to such a degree that no reading of it can ever be accomplished. That might be so, but subsequent excavations indicate that the "gold" which lies in the site has yet to be struck because it lies deep in lower strata.

As the digging progressed, Goodwin began to reject the "Norse" idea, and came gradually to the conviction that his site was one which had been built by no other than Irish monks. He dug furiously into the site, and into Irish history simultaneously, shouting in joy with each new revelation of similarities between the structures at North Salem and other, similar stone workings in Ireland, Scotland, England, and Spain, known to have been built by Irishmen in ancient times. Now he was obsessed with the theory, and would not rest until he had expert pronouncement upon it. He invited more than 1500 people to the site to examine it, pursuing them as they inspected the stones, machine-gunning them verbally with his postulation anent the monks of Erin.

In 1939, he managed to persuade Dr. Hugh Hencken, director of Prehistoric Studies at Harvard, to come to the site. Hencken consented, and examined the queer place minutely. He was plainly puzzled, but could not agree with Goodwin that the site was of Irish origin. He admitted to many similarities between it and Irish ecclesiastical architecture, but told Goodwin he believed it to be colonial.

Goodwin was enraged.

He immediately produced a typewriter and dashed off a lengthy piece on the Caves and his theory on its builders, and sent it to Samuel Eliot Morison, who was editor of the *New England Quarterly*. The *Quarterly* did not publish Goodwin's piece; instead, they published an article by Hencken, in which the historian repeated that which he had already conveyed to Goodwin. Hencken's report was, however, fair. In it, he stated that the corbeled vaulting found at North Salem certainly suggested comparable vaulting in Irish monasteries. He also pointed out the apparent "*soutterains*," or underground connecting passages in evidence at North Salem, likening them to similar passages present in most Irish medieval buildings. He did note, however, that the North Salem soutterains were too shallow to be considered true examples. He also noted the presence of a decayed pine stump which suggested that the site was older than Pattee's occupation of it, since the stump was growing through one of the foundations.

But he also proceeded to dispose of the Icelandic sagas which contained references to *Great Ireland* or *White Man's Land* as so many folk tales. He noted passages in the sagas which recount conversations with the dead. (What more natural, in an age of superstition and universal belief in ghosts than to include such matter? Will our own colonial history one day be dismissed as fable because of the Salem witch trials?)

Dr. Hencken refers also to a piece of stone, thought by Goodwin to be a stone mace. On finding it at the site, Goodwin sent it to Dr. V. Gordon Childe, an archaeologist who had made a careful study of a Bronze Age site in the Orkney Islands, known as Skara Brae. It was sent to the Britisher because Goodwin saw a resemblance in it to a mace found by Childe at Skara Brae. Hencken says "it does not appear to bear more than a generalized resemblance to anything found at Skara Brae. But even if it did, an object dating from many centuries before Christ could not be used as evidence of a Christian Monastery of the ninth or tenth century A.D."

True. But Dr. Hencken, through some curious oversight, neglects to mention that Childe was extremely enthusiastic over the mace, and so notified Goodwin. He felt it a valuable find and implied that perhaps Goodwin had stumbled onto a site similar to the one at Skara Brae. Instead of speculating in that direction, Dr. Hencken chose to date the site as colonial, although—again—in fairness, it must be noted that he also wrote: "the site deserves more than a merely negative conclusion."

I find difficulty in accepting the logic set forth in such papers as Dr. Hencken's. Throughout, it bears more than a mild suspicion that the site may be quite old. But it is pointed out to the reader that it can't possibly be. It must be colonial. Another tired old device is used in stating that "an object dating from many centuries before Christ could not be used as evidence of a Christian Monastery of the ninth or tenth century A.D." Of course it couldn't. But with the tenaciousness of the scientist grimly determined to discredit another's theory, the open mind becomes firmly closed; no examination of the intriguing possibility of Bronze Age occupation of the site is entered into by Dr. Hencken. Instead, he uses the comparison of the maces as an argument against Goodwin's theory. Here is a rigid inflexibility, a paralysis which prevents speculation in other avenues. The independent digging by Frank Glynn, recorded in Chapter 2, has already indicated a Bronze Age occupation of Pattee's Caves. Such a dating would not preclude the presence of Goodwin's Irish monks, or of the Phoenicians which I place at the site c. 480 B.C., or thereabouts. It would simply indicate that the site is even older than anyone suspects. In archaeology, the finding of many cultures on a single site, with great time lapses between them is common. I see no reason whatever to doubt that the structures at North Salem could have been built by an early Bronze Age people, later occupied by fleeing

.ATE 1. *(above)* One of the
)lmens in the Plaza at Pat-
e's Caves, North Salem,
ew Hampshire. The site is
)w a tourist attraction called
Mystery Hill."

.ATE 2. *(right)* General view
Pattee's Caves looking to-
ard "Y-Cavern." The many
ysterious stone structures
e scattered over a 30-acre
te.

PLATE 3. *(above)* The sacrificial stone at Pattee's Caves, intended for hun
sacrifice by the Phoenicians. Note run-off groove or drain. Two others have b
reported in the area.

PLATE 4. *(below)* The Lanyon Dolmen in Cornwall, England. Is it a protot
of the dolmens at North Salem? This one, used as a burial chamber for a neolit
chieftain, was originally covered with earth.

ATE 5. *(above)* A beehive structure in County Kerry, on Ireland's west coast. ıny of the strange stone buildings in New England bear a startling resemblance these Irish beehives.

ATE 6. *(below)* Ancient carving of Phoenician ship, revealed when waters of ke Assawompsett, Massachusetts, were lowered. Carving is now under water ain.

PLATE 7. *(left)* Some of
hundreds of stones found r
Mechanicsburg, Pennsylva
thought to bear Phoeni
characters. The incisions h
been whitened for ph
graphic purposes.

PLATE 8. *(right)* The author with one of the Phoenician character stones and a section of one of the strange grooved stones found near Mechanicsburg. The grooved stones may have been facing stones for a temple.

PLATE 9. *(left)* Myster
symbols carved on a roc
Brunswick County, Virg
thought by the author t
the work of Romans, c. 64,

ATE 10. *(right)* This
cient bronze cup was
ıg from the ground in
irginia. Six similar
ps, excavated at Pom-
ii, can be seen in the
aples Museum.

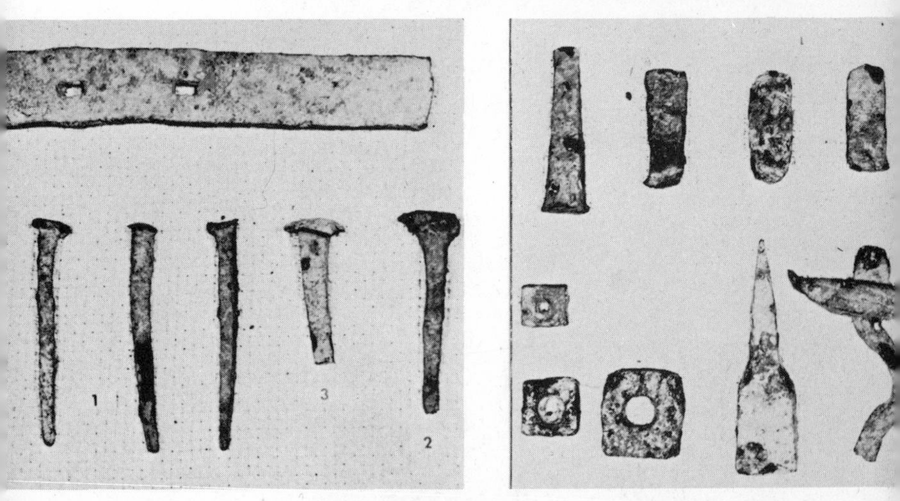

ATE 11. *(above)* Nail header, nails, threaded nuts and other artifacts of worked
n found at Jeffress, Virginia. They are startlingly similar to ancient Roman iron
ınd in Germany, dating from the second century, A.D.

PLATE 12. *(left)* Pre-Co bian contact between Asi Middle America is sugg by the designs at left. In the lotus and fish then used with similar arra ments of fish and plant. design at the top comes southern India, the lowe from Yucatán.

PLATE 13. *(right)* Transpacific contacts with the Americas is suggested by these "mask and dragon" designs. The figure at top is Chinese, Late Chou style, the modified figure below is Mexican.

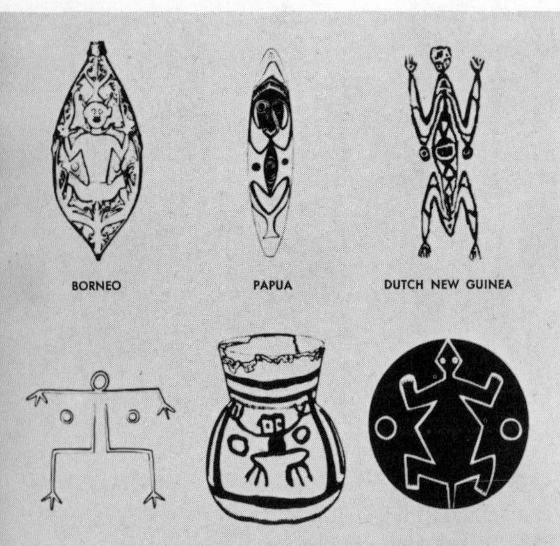

PLATE 14. *(left)* The ho disc theme. (Props bet elbows and knees were mon to the art created on sides of the Pacific in pre umbian times.)

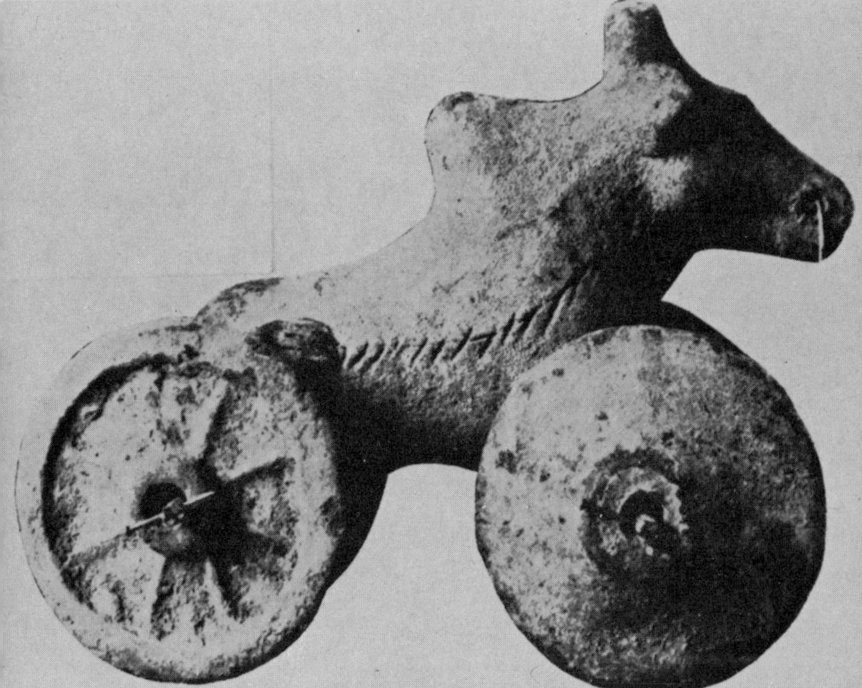

PLATE 15. The finding of wheeled toys in Middle America startled archaeologists, particularly since the wheel was not used in the New World. Was the Mexican toy *(above)* modeled after its older Asiatic counterpart? *(below)*

PLATE 16. This "laughing head" comes from the Vera Cruz district in Mexico a
was made centuries before Columbus's arrival. The features in the face are dec
edly oriental. Is it Hoei Shin, or one of his companions?

Phoenicians and, still later, occupied by Irish monks absquatulating from the vikings. The location of the Caves is favorable to all three, if we consider them in context with voyages from Europe by early mariners sailing largely at the mercy of wind and tide. Landfall at or near the Merrimack is highly acceptable; discovery of the site by voyagers entirely possible through conversation with Indians or by accidentally stumbling upon it on an inland exploration. The Indian trail which leaves the Merrimack near Haverhill and wends north would take them almost into its midst.

Such contradictory conclusions do not remain the sole province of Dr. Hencken, however. In a recent conversation with Dr. Junius Bird, who once dug at the site himself, and later selected the archaeologist who led the Early Sites expedition, I had these three thoroughly baffling statements in the course of a 20-minute telephone interview:

1. The Early Sites expedition concluded, and rightly so, that there was nothing more to be gleaned from the site.
2. There is more evidence at the site, provided a "competent person" be put in charge of the dig.
3. "I wouldn't recommend another dig" because "we have enough Indian stuff already."

I am confused. Dr. Bird seems determined that the site shall not be permitted to yield more evidence of its antiquity, yet he hints that there is more evidence there. He insists that "colonial brick" was uncovered beneath the foundations of some of the buildings, yet more of this same type of "colonial brick" has been identified as Indian pottery by a man thoroughly schooled on that subject. Apparently there was a lengthy occupation of the site by Amerinds, but the evidence of that occupation was entirely missed by the Early Sites expedition. And Dr. Bird attaches no importance to the finds of Frank Glynn, the amateur archaeologist from Chapter 2. But he generously acknowledges Glynn's freedom to continue digging at the site, if he must. This, in spite of the certainty that the expedition's erroneously labeled colonial brick apparently is Indian pottery. This, in spite of the fact that a piece of "ceramic" noted as such by the expedition mysteriously proved to be bronze.

Patently, it would be insane to label Dr. Bird and archaeologists such as Viscelius, who led the Early Sites expedition incompetent;

how then can their reasoning be explained? Would it be so embarrassing or awkward to have the North Salem site develop as a Bronze Age site? Or, what would happen if an Irish occupation suddenly became obviously evident? Suppose artifacts pointing to the Phoenicians should be obtained? Mathematically, I would guess that the number of red faces, multiplied by the number of artifacts found, divided by the numbers of cultures represented would be equal to the number of scholarly words issued in support of the theory that the site is colonial.

Now let it not be thought that I lack respect for Dr. Bird. He has had a long and distinguished career in his field, but is victim to the mechanically scientific procedures which dictate that everything must be proved negative, even in the face of positive evidence. The NEBC Principle is a reasonably safe credo—up to now—but could change momentarily. It is safe because of the Great Shadow that seems to hang over all apparent signs pointing to pre-Columbian discovery: seeming lack of substantial evidence, literary or actual.

The Irish ascetics, vowed to poverty, never carried enough material possessions to leave behind. Add to that the destruction of Irish records which might reveal the ramblings of the Celi Dei, plus the general reluctance of the European Church to acknowledge their existence—and the shadow grows deeper.

We must return to Goodwin. Naturally, he was enraged at Hencken's verbal pronouncement, and even more enraged when the *New England Quarterly* published a Hencken evaluation of his site in the negative, pointedly rejecting his own piece. When Goodwin ultimately published his own book on North Salem, he blasted away at Hencken with all his might. He also took time to fire broadsides at Samuel Eliot Morison, anthropologist Earnest Albert Hooton of Harvard, Edmund Burke Delabarre of Brown University, and others. His attacks on Hencken and Delabarre, who had written a book discrediting all runic inscriptions found in New England, were based on their seeming determination to date everything in America from 1492. Hooton received a resounding wallop for having failed to acknowledge, or return, a bone sent him for analysis by Goodwin. The Old Warrior then asserts that a bloc was formed to prevent him from obtaining funds to expand the digging at the site. The blood runs deep throughout the book.

Goodwin was prevented from further digging at the site, but for other reasons (or, perhaps, we might even be permitted to say "additional" reasons). The coming of war was a determining factor, but so was the finding of other sites. Goodwin began combing New England for similar sites to the rocky ruin at North Salem, and came up with more than a dozen.

The experts explain them away as "colonial root cellars." Goodwin has a much more intriguing, and I think, a more arresting theory. He reasoned that the monks began to spread out from North Salem, founding offshoot monastic centers all through New England. As the map at the beginning of this chapter demonstrates, the outposts spread from Maine to southern Massachusetts, and possibly into Connecticut. While no two of the structures at these sites are identical, all bear a naggingly reminiscent likeness to the "beehive" structures built by Irish monks in Ireland and Europe. No authentic beehives have been found at North Salem, but the possibility of their existence must not be ruled out. Remember the wagon loads of rock removed from the site to supply sewerage and drainage needs for the city of Lawrence.

The establishment of mission outposts would be a natural development. It is reasonable to assume that many of the monks at North Salem began yearning for isolated dells of their own, and moved accordingly. With so many potential converts roaming the woods it would be foolish to refrain from bringing them the message of Christianity, rather than wait for them to come to North Salem.

At Kingston and Raymond, New Hampshire, north of Pattee's Caves, are stone structures resembling those at North Salem. Both are on an old Indian trail, and would have been quite easy to reach. A site at Acworth, also in New Hampshire, could have been reached by one of two methods: the monks could have gone overland to Acworth, or they could have sailed down the coast, around Cape Cod, and into the Connecticut River. Ascending it into New Hampshire, they might have disembarked somewhere near Charlestown and proceeded from there to the hill at Acworth, there to build three beehives. They stand on an elevation of 1600 feet and are built of dry masonry. Since they stand near no human habitation, they present a real challenge to those who consider all of Goodwin's collateral structures "root cellars."

There is also more than a mild suspicion that the wandering monks may have gone into the Thames River at New London. Dr.

Frank Speck, one of America's foremost ethnologists and a long-time student of the American Indian, comments on a legend of "little people" among the Indians of that region. Since the Celi Dei were probably direct descendants of the "little, dark Celts" who settled in England and Ireland in the time before Christ, the Indians conceivably were describing a visiting band of monks. In the Thames River area lies another site, strikingly similar to the site at North Salem, but never recorded by Goodwin. It is now under study by Frank Glynn, and at this writing, no report on it can be issued, other than to indicate Glynn's belief that "the site is much older than local historians would have it."

A site at South Windham, Maine, contains nothing but a flight of stairs, carved in the living rock. The remarkable aspect of these stairs is that they start nowhere and go nowhere. At least, it would seem so. But someone carved them in the rock. The reasons for carving them have long since been lost to man's knowledge, but excavations at the head and foot of the stairs might well produce the evidence to provide the reasons.

The monks were busiest in Massachusetts. Structures at Lowell, Waterford, Leominster, Harvard, North Andover, Weston, Worcester, Hopkinton, Upton, Millis, Medway, Mendon, Hopedale, Webster, and on Martha's Vineyard all bear striking similarities in technique, if not in actual appearance, to the stone ruins at North Salem. In addition, there are apparent sites at South Berwick, Maine, West Shawsheen, Massachusetts, and another in New Hampshire, as yet unprobed. Woodstock, Connecticut, might have a site, but Goodwin never inspected it. The owner, according to Goodwin, discouraged visitors by brandishing a shotgun at strangers.

Of all the "outpost" mission sites, the one at Upton, on the Pearson property, is the best example of "beehive" construction, and the best preserved. It consists of a perfectly symmetrical beehive, with an entrance of stone, 14 feet long, approaching it. The entrance is low and is marked with a stone lintel four feet high. This pile of stones has been labeled "root cellar" by colonialists, but there is good evidence that it was part of a succession of other buildings. Stone foundations have been found in the Pearson garden at depths of from four to eight feet. Very little excavation has been done at Upton, and the elder Pearson now has the beehive boarded up to discourage sightseers. Perhaps one day it will be thoroughly excavated in an effort to determine its relationship, if any, with North Salem and the monks.

At Hopkinton, a short distance from Upton, stands another of the little buildings. Goodwin thought it might be an Indian sweat house, though not of Indian design.

The construction at Shawsheen Village, between Lawrence and Andover, in Massachusetts, is large, and suggests an animal effigy. Goodwin pondered the site, but never investigated it. His thoughts on it wavered between Irish and Algonquin origins.

The site at Raymond, New Hampshire, surprisingly revealed two circular, partially underground houses connected with a narrow passage-way.

At Harvard, Massachusetts, an underground building was found, with the possibility of another nearby.

The beehives at South Berwick, Maine, proved to be legendary. Goodwin was never able to find them, although he offered liberal rewards for information concerning their locations.

Little can be said of any of these sites other than that Goodwin recorded them. All but one are known to exist, all are built of stone and all are at least partially underground. Some show evidence of soutterains such as appear in authentic Irish stone structures. But the harassed Goodwin was the only one who found a pattern in them, the only one who thought it important to visit them and investigate them within the bounds of time.

It is easy to dismiss them as "root cellars." Presenting this explanation disproves them as pre-Columbian sites rather comfortably. I think they form a pattern, as Goodwin suspected, and I think it extremely unfortunate that no serious investigation of the collective sites has been made. I can only wonder, why? The finds at Pattee's Caves by amateur Frank Glynn would seem to point to an early Bronze Age culture, come from Europe to settle on our shores. In addition to the pottery finds, Ruth Galinat, secretary of the Connecticut Archaeological Society, found a circular mound in the woods at the edge of the site. Will it reveal the remains of a conical-roofed dwelling, circular in shape, similar to the Bronze Age hill cultures found in Europe? If it should, then it will help upset the existing doctrine of archaeology. The credo says that there were no migrations of peoples from Europe prior to the sixteenth century. To consider a migration by Bronze Age peoples, at a time when man wasn't supposed to know enough about navigation to cross the Atlantic would be most embarrassing. And so a school of thought which believes that all unusual phenomena in New England or anywhere, are colonial, must adhere rigidly to that manner of thinking. In spite of the evidence.

Ignoring Pattee's Caves will not cause them to evanesce. Branding Goodwin a "crackpot" will not make the sites any less important. The technique of name-calling has been applied to proponents of seemingly "wild" ideas in other times, with little credit to those who issued the opprobrium. George Catlin, the brilliant author-artist who devoted the greater part of his life to the study of the American Indian, particularly in the West, was unabashedly labeled a liar by those anthropologists and historians who *knew* that his masterful records of Indian life were false. These reckless men of science had never visited the regions and tribes described by Catlin, but they knew, incontrovertibly, that he was lying. Many years were to pass before other scholars, following Catlin's path, would discover that his erudite delineations of our Western Indians were beyond question.

And the pattern has not changed.

Goodwin is still looked upon with annoyance. By all but Frank Glynn, although Glynn doesn't subscribe to the Irish theory either. But he is astute enough to suspect that Goodwin's site is ancient. And to do something about it.

Which is why he is carefully excavating it—again.

In light of Glynn's finds, the Early Sites Foundation is, at this writing, pondering a new expedition to sift the mysteries of Pattee's Caves. They have approached Malcolm Pearson for permission to reopen the site to another archaeological group, presumably in charge of some "competent person," as indicated by Dr. Bird. Such a move would probably put Frank Glynn into eclipse, since he is but an amateur. But Glynn's "bigness," and open-mindedness is illustrated most illuminatingly in his reaction to this intelligence.

"I'd be glad to see it," he told me. "I'd be glad to see any effort directed toward finding the original builders of Pattee's Caves—whether or not it would include a contribution by me."

If another expedition should be inaugurated, I shall look forward eagerly to the sparks that will inevitably fly. The Early Sites Foundation has a board of directors. One of them is Junius Bird. Dr. Bird told me he would not recommend another dig at the site. Other members of the board apparently feel another dig is in order. It seemeth more blood is about to be spilled.

I sincerely hope there will be another dig. And I sincerely hope it will include Frank Glynn. Whatever happens, it is certain that Goodwin's ghost will be comfortably settled on a big megalith, in the shade, patiently watching and waiting for vindication. If no Irish evidence is turned up, it is conceivable that the spirit may cause an airy disturbance; I'm inclined to feel, however, that Goodwin already knows the answer, and will simply hang about to see how it comes out.

That such a place as Great Ireland existed is beyond doubt. It is a fact set down in the Icelandic sagas. And it is reported by Icelanders, not Irishmen. And their sojourn at the place where Goodwin puts them, and with which I heartily agree, was not the end of their wanderings. In the next chapter, I will show how the colony at North Salem accidentally turned into an international settlement, and how that surprising turn of events was duly recorded in the sagas.

Let us go now to meet Ari Marson, the Baptized Prisoner, and the incident of the Captive Castaways.

CHAPTER 7

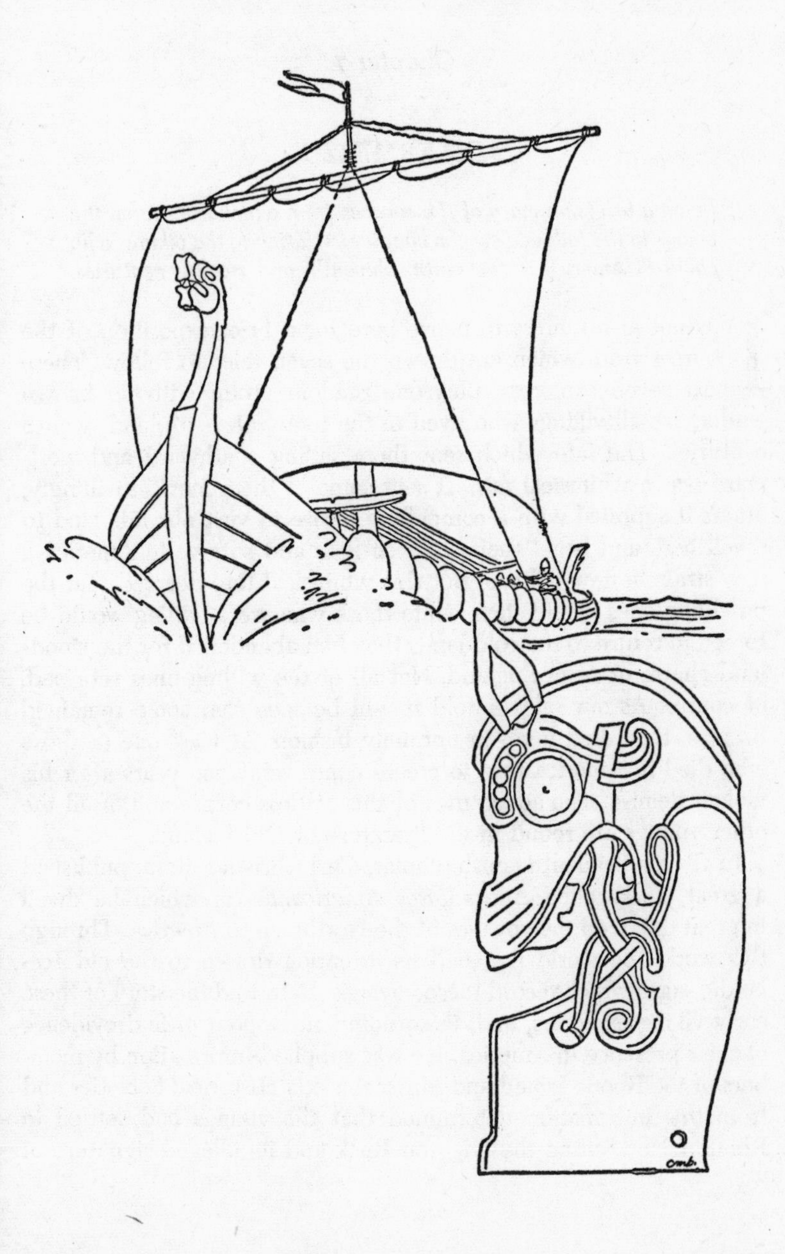

Chapter 7

INTERMEZZO

Being a brief summary of the sources from which are drawn the events in the following seven chapters, relating to the vikings who came to America in the tenth, eleventh, and twelfth centuries.

It is not at all amiss to pause here for a brief exposition of the sources from which are drawn the seven tales to follow. These next seven explorers, plus one random group with no known leader, are all vikings who lived in the tenth, eleventh, and twelfth centuries. The fate which sent them sailing southward and westward was a whimsical fate. It sent some of them most unwillingly; others it supplied with a compelling desire to visit our fair land to dwell here and beget their children here and so give to America a new strain, a new culture. But this whimsical fate decreed that the unwilling ones would stay—while those who were willing would be forced to return to the cold lands they had abandoned for the woodland charm of New England. Not all of the willing ones returned, of course. As our tales unfold it will be seen that some remained because they died here—in untimely fashion. At least one of those who died in America rose to create controversy 700 years after his violent demise. The adventures of this restless corpse and of all the other vikings are found in the literature of Old Iceland.

In 1837, a brilliant Danish scholar, Carl Christian Rafn, published a great work called *Antiquitates Americanae,* in which he dwelt in great detail on the voyages of the Northmen to America. Through this work, the world first had its attention drawn to the old Icelandic sagas which record these voyages. Rafn told the story of these early viking explorers, and, in so doing, attempted to find evidence of their presence in America. He was supplied information by members of the Rhode Island and Massachusetts Historical Societies and from this information determined that the vikings had settled in Rhode Island, citing the Dighton Rock and its alleged signature of

Thorfinn Karlsefni as evidence. Two years later, Rafn included the Newport Tower in his evidence of viking penetration, and these deductions led to a long period during which the Norse settlement of North America was accepted and much discussed. How Rafn was attacked and discredited will be told in the ensuing chapters. I mention him here to mark the beginning of the period of awareness of Northmen by Americans.

The sources which gave Rafn his theories are the same sources which have caused bitter debate in the 123 years since, and have had millions of words written concerning them, pro and con. They are, primarily, the old Icelandic sagas, although corroborative evidence of the existence of Vinland the Good is found in sources other than these wonderful tales.

The stories of Ari Marson and the castaway Icelanders, of Leif Ericsson, his brother Thorvald and his sister, Freydis, of Thorfinn Karlsefni and Bjarni Herjulfsson, and of Eric, Bishop of Greenland, are all to be found in the sagas.

Three manuscripts tell of these vikings and their voyages; *The Flateyjarbok,* (*Flateybook*) or *Flat Island Book,* so called because it was found on the island of that name, just off the west coast of Iceland, *Hauk's Book,* a history named for its co-author, Hauk Erlendsson, and an anonymous manuscript known as *AM* 557, 4to, and called *The Saga of Eric the Red.*

The *Flateybook* was written during the fourteenth century, being completed about 1390. Two priests, Magnus Thorhallson and Jon Thordarson, transcribed it, meticulously assembling the hitherto oral sagas that told the story of the Icelanders and Greenlanders and their various adventures. It contains two accounts of voyages by Greenlanders to America: *The Tale of Eric the Red,* and *The Tale of The Greenlanders.*

Hauk's Book, written by three people, of whom Hauk was one, contains the saga of Thorfinn Karlsefni, who sailed to America sometime around the end of the first decade of the eleventh century. This saga was written sometime between 1299 and 1334, the year of Hauk's death.

The Vellum *AM* 557, by an unknown author, contains *The Saga of Eric the Red,* and bears a marked similarity to that found in *Hauk's Book.* It was completed about 1400.

All of these sagas have been subjected to intense study by numerous scholars in an effort to clarify the errors, contradictions, and discrepancies they contain. It has been observed by many saga students that all are perhaps derived from one single source, predating the times attributed to the versions listed above. It is more than reasonable to assume that pertinent material appealing to the particular transcriber was drawn from this older, unidentifiable saga. Some, notably Gathorne-Hardy, an Englishman who wrote an erudite disquisition on the vikings and their American penetrations in 1921, have concluded that the writers of *Hauk's Book* inclined toward presenting the material in a manner designed to favor Icelanders, while the *Flateybook* was concerned more intently with recording the deeds of the Greenlanders. Thus, while all the sagas corroborate each other, they contain intermixed material and contradictory delineations. A precise analysis of them, however, clarifies many seeming contradictions within the stories, and enables the student to derive a sensible progression in the events recorded therein. I have taken these sagas apart and reconstructed them much in the manner of those who have preceded me in the field.

The sources I shall use are the *Flateybook* and *Hauk's Book*, placing them in the progressions I feel they should follow, and noting intermixed material as it occurs. It must be remembered, whenever a deletion of material from a particular story occurs, or whenever a sequence from another story is added to one under discussion, that all came from a common source. These apparent "liberties" are taken on the conviction that my own conclusions, as well as those of others who have accepted the challenge offered by these intriguing tales, are sound interpretations of the original progressions of the stories. This approach is simply a reversal of the method used by the first copyists of the sagas. In the *History of Icelandic Literature*, for example, Stefan Einarsson indicates that Hauk Erlendsson created his own version of two earlier works by Ari Thorgilsson (Ari the Wise) called the *Landnamabok* and *Islendingabok*. His assertion is based on Hauk's own statement that he used the books as sources. He closes this intelligence with this declaration:

"I took from each book whatever it had, more than the other, but to a great extent they contained the same matter."

So it evolves upon those who would study the sagas to "unscramble" what the writers of these classics "scrambled."

In addition to the sources noted, there are many other references to Vinland and its brief occupation by vikings. *Islendingabok* and *Landnamabok*, mentioned above, are actually the first histories of Iceland and Greenland, and were written by Ari the Wise about the third decade of the twelfth century. The various Icelandic *Annals* corroborate the existence of Vinland also. There are many collections of these and they are faithful documents of events occurring in Iceland and other countries.

A twelfth-century manuscript written by a Benedictine abbot named Nicholas Bergsson gives a geographical description of Vinland the Good.

The most notable reference to Vinland in a non-Icelandic work is found in the ponderous history written by Adam of Bremen, sometime before 1076. Adam obtained his information on the New World discovery directly from King Svend Estridsson, ruler of Norway and Denmark from 1047 until 1076.

Other references exist in and out of Iceland.

But I think I have made clear the point that the stories of the vikings you will presently meet, and their voyages to America are among the most well-documented journeys in history.

CHAPTER 8

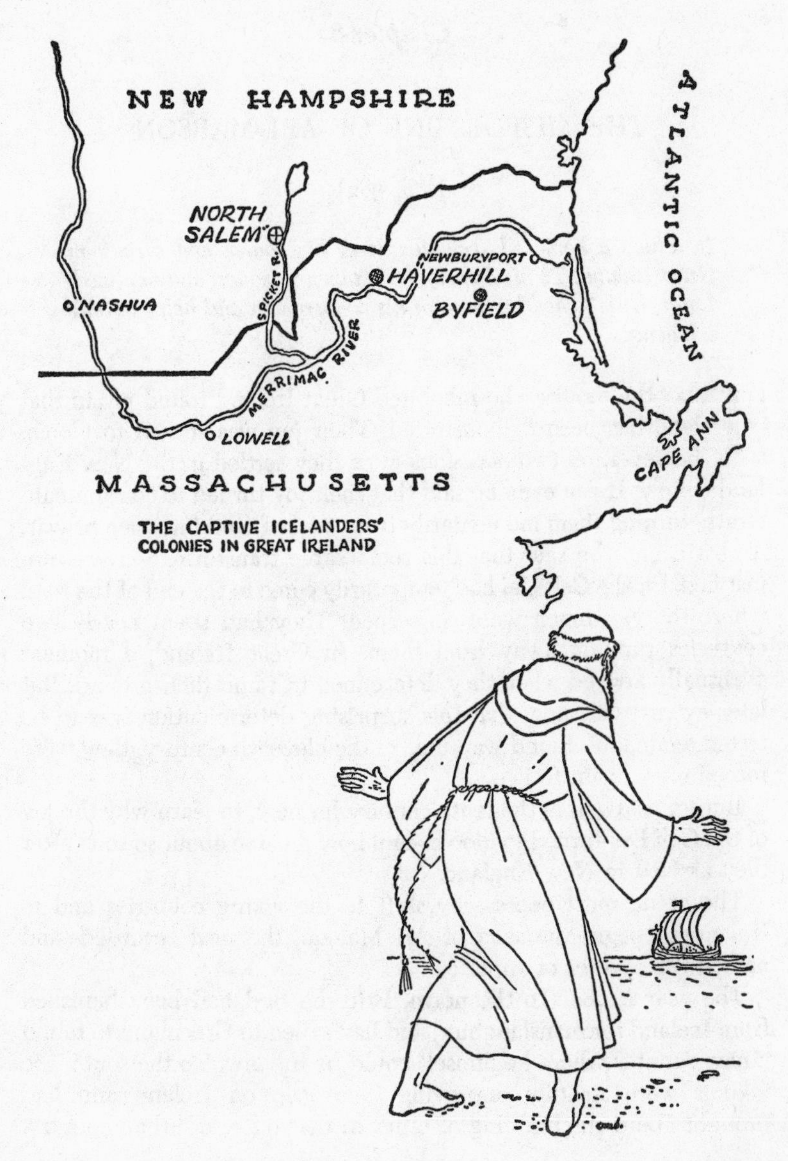
NEW HAMPSHIRE
NORTH SALEM
NASHUA
SPICKET R.
NEWBURYPORT
HAVERHILL
BYFIELD
MERRIMAC RIVER
LOWELL
ATLANTIC OCEAN
CAPE ANN
MASSACHUSETTS
THE CAPTIVE ICELANDERS' COLONIES IN GREAT IRELAND

Chapter 8

THE MISFORTUNE OF ARI MARSON

[A.D. 982]

In which a bemused Icelander loses his course and arrives in Great Ireland. To his dismay, he is taken prisoner, and baptized. Later, he is joined by more of his countrymen and helps initiate a legend.

THAT the monks who inhabited Great Ireland found joy in that land has been demonstrated. Their joy was turned to gloom, however, on two occasions after they settled in the New England colony. It can even be said that their joy turned to consummate wrath, turning them momentarily from men of God into men of war. And it cannot be said that this remarkable transformation was unjustified, for the Celi Dei had temporarily come to the end of the road where the Northmen were concerned. They had spent nearly two centuries running away from them. In Great Ireland, a moment eventually arrived when they determined to stand their ground. But later events will show that this surprising determination was to be tested again, and found wanting. In the eleventh century, they were forced once again to flee.

But let us dwell in the tenth century for now, to learn why the joy of the Celi Dei turned to gloom—and how it came about so soon after they arrived in New England.

The scene must necessarily shift to the viking countries and to Ireland to begin the saga of Ari Marson, the next recorded—and named—discoverer of America.

The year is 982. To the north, Eric the Red had been banished from Iceland for manslaughter, and had sailed to Greenland to found a new country where he himself could be the law. To the south, the vikings were steadily improving their grip on Ireland and had brought about the building of cities in that once un-urban country.

The towns of Dublin and Wexford were thriving, and Limerick, where the saga of Ari conceivably began, was becoming a great seaport, carrying on trade with many countries and providing berth for the countless viking ships which came to its harbor. The occupation by the vikings had, however, increased the emigration of monks from Erin greatly, and they spread themselves out over all of Europe, bringing with them the knowledge they had nurtured so carefully during the beginnings of the Dark Ages.

The vikings who had ravaged Ireland initially, and later helped to rebuild it, were largely Danes and Norwegians. The Icelanders who came to Ireland came only as traders, not being given to pillaging as were their cousins to the east. It was probably on a trading voyage to Ireland that Ari Marson lost his way, and came to dwell, most unwillingly, in Great Ireland. I suggest this train of thought because Ari's story was first made known by one Rafn, a merchant of Limerick, and who was probably a good friend to Ari. It is not unreasonable to assume that the news of Ari's disappearance, and later identification in Great Ireland, should have been relayed to Rafn, perhaps because Rafn had been the last to see Ari before he vanished.

We will assume, then, that Ari Marson, returning to Iceland from a trading voyage to Limerick in Ireland, was blown off course and pushed by fierce winds to New England. It is from the *Landnamabok* that we learn of Ari Marson's unplanned voyage to America. The reference is extremely brief, but demonstrates the actuality of Atlantic voyages in the tenth century, and also corroborates further the existence of Great Ireland, or Hvitramannaland. Here is the way it is set down by Ari the Wise:

Ulf the Squinter, son of Hogna the White, took all Reykjaness, between Thorkafjord and Hafnafell; he married Bjorg, daughter to Eyvind the Eastman, sister to Helge the lean; their son was Atli the Red, who married Throbjorg, sister to Steinolf the Humble; their son was Nar of Holum, who married Throkatla, daughter of Hergil Neprass; their son was Ari; he was driven by a tempest to White Man's Land, which some call Great Ireland; it lies to the west in the sea, near to Vinland the Good, and VI days' sailing west from Ireland. From thence could Ari not get away, and was there baptized. This story first told Rafn the Limerick Merchant, who had long lived at Limerick in Ireland. Thus said (also) Thorkell Gellersson, that Icelanders had stated, who had heard Throfinn, Jarl (earl) of the Orkneys relate, that Ari was recognized in White Man's Land, and could not get away from thence, but was there much respected.

There is more to the saga, a litany of Ari's family, whom he married and a reference to Leif Ericsson, a distant relative. The intriguing aspect of Ari's story as told in the saga is the matter-of-fact way in which it is presented. Clearly, the saga-teller knew of the existence of Great Ireland. It is not accompanied by lengthy descriptives. The saga merely states that it is called Great Ireland by some, White Man's Land by others. The one doubtful passage is that which indicates the sailing distance. *Six* days sail from Ireland, to the west, in a ship of that day would mean 900 miles of travel. Since there is nothing in the ocean 900 miles from Ireland, there is a possibility that the 6 should read 16, which would bring the mileage to 2400, or just about the correct distance. Next we note that Ari was forcibly detained by the inhabitants of White Man's Land, or Great Ireland, and, in due course, was baptized. Since Ari was a pagan, his baptism was a logical procedure in the eyes of the Celi Dei. (Christianity did not come to Iceland until the year 1000. The conversion of that island came with a directness typical of the methods of the Icelandic vikings. They simply called a meeting of the Althing, or Parliament, and voted themselves Christian.) But the question asked by every scholar who has read the saga is: Who could have baptized Ari if not a Christian living in the place where Ari was detained? The answer, of course, lies in another question: What Christian would have been living in America in the year 982 but an Irish monk?

Let us return, now, to North Salem, and look in upon the saintly monks in their woodland retreat. The time is during the first months of their residence in this wonderful new land, and all are engaged in the various pursuits necessary to restoring Pattee's Caves, providing sustenance for the monks and their women and children and reclaiming the savages. Some of the monks are at work at the Caves, others off in the woods seeking game. Still others are quartered with various heathens whom they hope to bring to conversion. Since fish play an important part in their lives, a group of Celi Dei are down at the foot of the Merrimack, coaxing finny denizens from the waters of the Atlantic, robes blowing in the wind, lines cast with happy anticipation, beards bleaching in the sun and patches of whitened faces becoming darker as they experience the novel phenomenon of "tanning." It is a beautiful day, and God looks down upon his flock with a smile. The land is truly a miracle.

Until a speck appears on the horizon.

It is a small speck, and grows larger until it materializes into a sail. And the awful truth is upon them.

It is a red and white striped sail. A terrible ululation sweeps through the quivering monks on the beach and they hurriedly tumble into their curraghs and frantically row back up the river to the landing near the Caves.

The Northmen have again come to shatter their peace.

We can easily imagine the hurried "town meeting" that was called to apprise everyone of the striped sail. This time, however, the Celi Dei, instead of quickly gathering meager possessions and scattered flocks and plunging into curraghs to flee, apparently experienced a change of philosophy. They elected to fight the intruding pagans.

And they gathered their forces and rowed down the Merrimack to meet the invaders.

The wretched, weary, exhausted vikings aboard Ari's trading ship doubtless shouted in exultation on sighting the sandy beaches flanking the mouth of the Merrimack. They headed straight for the river, there to sail in and seek temporary shelter ashore. It is conceivable that their ship may have been damaged—here they could repair and reprovision their vessel. Land was indeed a welcome sight.

The Icelanders were again filled with happiness when, on sailing into the Merrimack, they sighted the oncoming curraghs of the Celi Dei. Here were friends! And in a strange land! The vikings would have quickly recognized the flowing robes and luxuriant beards of the monks. They knew others like them in Ireland, and knew that they were men of peace. With sail now lowered, the vikings eagerly bent to oar in hurried stroke to meet the monks. They kneweth not that the monks had violence within their breasts.

It might be considered, in retrospect, that the monks acted too hastily. These approaching vikings were not quite of the same stripe as the earlier marauders who had wrought such destruction on the shores of Erin. These were Icelanders, and descendants of the followers of Ingolfr Ardnason. Their fathers had settled Iceland in a very unwarlike manner, and had sought to live lives of peace. They tried to follow a doctrine of brotherly love, and created the west's first democratic form of government. In the year 930, they created the Althing, by which they governed themselves, and which has been called the "Mother of Parliaments." It served as model for the British, and the British manner of governing became America's, with modifications. These new vikings would have been content to spend a brief time with the Celi Dei, obtain food and water for their ship and depart quietly in hope of finding Iceland.

But the Celi Dei were unaware of the character of this new breed of viking. They were afraid of the newcomers, and their thoughts could only re-create dim visions of sacked monasteries, screaming women and children, and chaos and death. Frightened as they were of the vikings, however, they were held firm in the grip of other emotions: they loved their new land—and they were tired of running away. That much seems certain. A new Celi Dei emerged; a Celi Dei who was determined to stand his ground. In a terrible moment of decision, the Celi Dei, forsaking their Christlike devotion to peace and love, became warriors. Or at least it would seem so.

Because they took the Icelanders prisoner.

To the Icelanders, the act came as a surprise. To the Celi Dei, it probably came as sheer amazement. But the deed was accomplished. It could only have been accomplished because of the weakened condition of the Icelanders after their journey perilous, and because these were not the old vikings. It is more than reasonable to assume that on seeing the approaching band of flowing-robed monks, the Icelanders' hearts lifted and they gave thanks to their heathen gods that they were in a friendly country.

And so they were taken by surprise, by a band of ridiculously inadequate aggressors, fighting with a fury born of fear. The very incongruity of the sight of the monkish legions waging war could have been the biggest single factor contributing to the submission and capture of the Icelanders.

In all probability, the monks were embarrassed about the whole affair, once the *coup* had been effected, but now it was *fait accompli*, and the Northmen were decommissioned. Whether any, or how many, of the monks and Northmen were killed is, of course, not known. Neither is it known, nor will it ever be, how many Northmen were taken prisoner.

But they were, and peace once more restored.

And when the Icelanders were disarmed, and their ship destroyed to prevent their escape, they were baptized, to a man, and to a woman, if Ari had any aboard. Since he had been on a trading voyage, the presence of women is doubtful; if he had shipped women, he would simply have been following a custom practiced by vikings, and other seagoing peoples, for untold centuries. Biological laws being what they are, women became part of a ship's complement in perfectly natural order.

The Catholicizing of the Icelanders in Great Ireland, however, did not provide a total guarantee that they would not cause awkwardness of some sort, or even attempt an escape, so the problem of what to do with them inevitably arose.

The Celi Dei, somewhat sheepish, I'm sure, on realizing that they had beat into submission a band of humans bearing them no malice, were still determined that they should not return to Iceland, thereby revealing the location of the monks' colony. It would follow then, that while they had to permit freedom of movement to the Icelanders, they could easily keep them in a relatively confined area under loose guard. The areas occupied by the vikings were undoubtedly those at the present towns of Byfield and Haverhill. Permitting the vikings to settle in these regions would keep them inland, and narrow the opportunity for clandestine shipbuilding should they entertain the thought of decamping without formally notifying the Celi Dei.

So it would appear that the colony at North Salem, begun by the Phoenicians, or even, as time may prove, an earlier people, possibly from Mycenae, and continued 1500 years later by the Irish, now had expanded into an international settlement. It also follows that intermarriage took place, and the Icelanders moved into governing positions in the colony. In addition to intermarriage between Icelander and Irish, there is also the probability of weddings with appealing Indian maidens from the Algonquin tribes which lived in the area. Such assimilation must surely have taken place among peoples living peacefully together.

And so it came to pass, in the year 982, that the colony in Great Ireland took on a new flavor. But the melting pot that is America, having been set to simmer 700 years before it is generally dated, was due to receive another lot of ingredients. Before four years had passed, another unwilling immigration of Icelanders occurred.

We must return briefly to the waters between Iceland and Greenland to witness the unfolding of a drama which was to swell the Irish-Icelandic colony even more.

After Eric the Red had established his tiny settlement in Greenland in 982, he made plans to entice more colonists to his new land. The original colony consisted of Eric, his wife, Thiodild, his young sons, Leif, Thorvald, and Thorstein, a bastard daughter, Freydis, and, of course, the crew of his ship. A good beginning, but too few people for Eric to rule. During the three years of his exile, he dreamed of the colony he would found and plotted it to the minutest detail. He knew what lands he would apportion to the newcomers, and what kind of laws he would impose upon them. But it was not until 985 that he could put his plan into operation.

At the conclusion of his exile, Eric lost no time in returning to Iceland to gather followers. He named his new country "Greenland" in order "that men might better be attracted to it if it had a good name." Thus was born the first public relations campaign in the Western Hemisphere. Eric was successful. In 986 he had recruited upward of a thousand colonists, ready to return with him to Greenland in 35 ships. All manner of provisions, clothing, sheep, cattle, and horses were also shipped, and on an unknown date in 986, Eric the Red led his fleet of peaceful adventurers from Iceland to Greenland.

Not all of them arrived.

Only fourteen ships made landfall in Greenland, their crews and passengers numbering not more than about 700, since the viking ship in use at that period carried only about 40-odd people comfortably and safely. Of the remaining 21 ships, *The Saga of Eric the Red* tells us that "some returned to Iceland, others were cast away." The teller of the saga knew that some ships had returned, possibly cured for all time of any desire to attempt the stormy waters between Iceland and Greenland. But the teller does not state how many, and so we have no knowledge of how many were "cast away." And it is these ships with which we are concerned.

I do not think *all* of the ships were lost.

Some, caught in the terrible storm which caused the others to turn back or founder, reached America. They were blown south and west, by the same capricious winds which had introducted Ari Marson to the North Salem monks.

In being blown to the south and to the west, the wretched Icelanders aboard the storm-trapped ships eventually came to New England. I think that some of the ships made landfall in the Cape Ann region, where they landed, wearily, and held council. They soon discovered the Merrimack, which offered better shelter from the sea, and sailed into it. At some unmarked point along the banks of that river, a shout went up, for the second time, when one or more of the Celi Dei saw this new intrusion of striped sails. Momentarily, the world again seemed to be tumbling about the shoulders of the Celi Dei—but only momentarily.

To those who sighted the ships, a quick glance revealed an inordinate amount of women, plus children and livestock. These ships would surely be easy to capture, along with their seemingly exhausted crews and passengers. Again the word went out; the monks were called to council of war. And again the cudgels were taken up and another grim procession thrust toward the battered ships of the would-be Greenlanders. The Icelanders from Ari's ship, if they knew about the approaching viking ships, were held under guard until this new group could be brought into captivity.

I would think that this second clash between Irish and Icelander was much briefer than the first. And the Icelanders were made prisoner. Ships were destroyed, and livestock temporarily penned until their dispersal could be accomplished fairly.

And I think that the baptism which took place this time was even more successful. The Greenland-bound colonists were comprised of wives and children to a great degree. It can safely be assumed that the women in these ships took to the baptisms eagerly. They knew about Catholicism, even though they had not yet experienced it. To the women, this new religion was a good one. It was most appealing because it eliminated veneration of many gods of various natures, and put before them one God, and a God of Peace, at that. Even though these women were married to vikings who were considerably more conservative than their forefathers, a religion which would not condone raiding trips and long voyages of conquest away from home (not to mention occasional fighting among themselves) was one to be embraced fully and quickly. Being women, they sought only security and happiness for themselves and their husbands and their children. Here, in this strange land, re-enforced by a strong religion based on peace, they might find it. I imagine these viking women came to like Great Ireland. When this second conquest had been achieved, the path of determination of the Celi Dei was quite simple. The new arrivals were merely added to the existing Icelandic colony, with perhaps only a slight increase in the necessary guard, or watch.

The colony was again expanded.

There remains but one reference which needs clarification in the paragraph from the *Landnamabok* which tells of Ari's sojourn in Great Ireland:

> . . . Ari was recognized in White Man's Land, and could not get away from thence, but was there much respected.

Who recognized him? And brought the information back for a saga-teller to recount?

Possibly one of the castaway ships from Greenland.

It could only have been a brief time before Ari and his colony learned of the capture of the Icelandic ships, and learned how they had come there. Reflecting on this information, it is conceivable that Ari stole away to the coast anticipating the arrival of other ships.

And one came, and Ari managed to warn it away to prevent its capture. Why didn't he return with the ship? Many reasons can be considered. He might well have married since his arrival in the colony at Great Ireland, and would have been loathe to desert his wife. Too, he might have felt a loyalty, and very likely did, to the remaining Icelanders who needed a leader in the event escape were made possible. Had I been Ari, I think I would have talked with the people aboard the ship and asked them to send help, had I wanted to escape with my wife and companions. Ari's disappearance, had he gone with the ship, would only have tightened the security measures taken by the monks, and made escape impossible. But Ari could have lived with the hope that the lone ship would reach Iceland and return with re-enforcements. The consideration that Ari was happy in his new home must not be overlooked, however. Having found peace, and a wife, and a pleasant life here, he might well have resigned himself to spending his life here, with the resignation later turned to acceptance and even happiness. That he might have acted as described above is not beyond question; he still had ties to Iceland, and would have considered it only proper to warn off any other unsuspecting castaways.

It would have been such a ship which brought news of Ari's detention in Great Ireland, his baptism, and the intelligence that he was "much esteemed" there.

If later attempts were made to find Ari, they are not recorded in the sagas.

When Ari had succeeded in warning away the distressed ship, he returned to his colony at Byfield, or Haverhill, to resume the quiet life with his spouse, and as leader of the colony.

Thus far, I have reconstructed those events which I think occurred in and around North Salem in the late years of the tenth century. Now I shall offer two apparent proofs of the actual existence of that colony in which those events took place.

The site at North Salem, with its international flavor, quite obviously gave rise to a legend which persisted into the sixteenth century, when it disappeared from the historian's writings, and no longer was recorded by the cartographer's pen.

The legend concerns the fabled stone city of Norumbega.

Norumbega was the name given by various explorers to many parts of the New England coast; in some cases it was generously applied to the *entire* eastern coast. It was also said to have been a river, and in one case, a mythical Indian city. In 1529, a map showing the extent of Giovanni da Verrazano's explorations was published and it placed Norumbega, or *Aranbega,* which was one of its several variations, in New England. In 1541 the Flemish cartographer Gerhardus Mercator placed *Anorumbega* near the Hudson River. A map by Gastaldi shows it to be near Cape Breton, and in this instance it is called Norumbega. In its description as a river it was said to have been an artery which was brackish at the mouth. In the case of the Indian city it is described as a thriving town with high towers and substantial buildings. In 1583, Sir Humphrey Gilbert, the English explorer, set out to find it. In 1582 a map was published showing the territory between the St. Lawrence and Penobscot Rivers. The territory is carefully labeled Norumbega.

Many books and papers have been written about Norumbega and its location, the writers differing in nearly all cases concerning its exact situation. One, a dedicated American industrial chemist named Eben Norton Horsford, convinced that he had found its former site, went so far as to erect in the late 1800s a stone tower on the Charles River near Watertown, outside Boston, as a memorial to the fabled city.

The mystery surrounding Norumbega has long been dwelled upon, but the difficulty in locating it has impelled latter-day historians to ascribe the whole thing to fable or folklore or fanciful imagination.

I don't think it's a mystery at all. I think that the early explorers who came here had heard about such a city from Norse contacts. The story was handed down and broadcast throughout Europe—by Norwegians—first as Great Ireland or Hvitramannaland or Albania or White Man's Land. The name is said to mean, in Norwegian, "something describing Norway" but this is pure conjecture. No one truly knows its actual meaning. I would not be surprised if it were shown to mean "the place the Norwegians talked about."

That such a place did exist I have no doubt. If it had not, I don't think Verrazano would have described it, nor Mercator placed it on his map. And I don't think Sir Humphrey Gilbert would have gone hunting it.

I think Norumbega was, simply, Great Ireland, or Hvitramannaland or Albania, or White Man's Land—call it what you will—and it contained a band of Irish monks whose stone buildings were impressive enough to warrant the description "city"—and "colonial" settlements peopled by Icelanders.

Physically and historically, the ruins at North Salem and the legend of Norumbega serve to substantiate the existence of a place called Great Ireland. There is one more accumulation of evidence which serves to document the existence of a collateral colony of Icelanders subject to the dominion of the monks of Cowbell Corners.

The towns of Byfield and Haverhill, in Massachusetts, are located a few miles south and east of North Salem and Pattee's Caves. The area about these towns probably marks the location of the Icelandic colony inaugurated by the Celi Dei.

To date, there have been found, in the Byfield-Haverhill region, seven rune stones identified and translated as such. Most are grave markers and bear references to the deity. One seems to be a marking stone to indicate a trail. In addition to the marking stones there are two others which may be related to the Icelandic colony in Massachusetts. One is a rune stone in the Aptuxcet Mission at Bourne, at the head of the Cape Cod Canal. It bears an inscription which says: "Jesus amply provides for us here and in heaven." The other was found at the head of the Parker River, where it enters the Merrimack near West Newbury. It is a rune stone describing a shipwreck. According to the translator, it tells of 34 men (the average crew of a viking ship) stranded on an island, amid turbulent waters in the dead of winter. The remarkable thing about this stone is that it has a counterpart in Ringerike, Norway. The Norwegian stone commemorates a shipwreck in Vinland: "They came out of the ocean and over vast areas, as they were in need of clothing to dry themselves, and of food. Away towards Vinland, they came upon the ice in the unsettled regions. Evil can take away luck, so one dies young."

Are they referring to the same shipwreck? Did the crew include one or more young men from Ringerike? Did word get back to the homeland of the shipwreck, and a memorial carved by grieving parents? It appears too strong for coincidence.

The runes on these stones were translated by Professor Olaf Strandwold, the scholar who started Goodwin on his journey to North Salem. Strandwold was born in 1871, in North Dakota, and obtained his higher schooling at Concordia College in Moorhead, Minnesota, and at the University of North Dakota. He was keenly interested in language, and particularly fascinated by old Norse and runic writing. Professionally, he spent 35 years teaching and supervising in North Dakota and Washington schools. I set forth these facts to demonstrate only that Strandwold was not a "professional Scandinavian." He was a scholar, and interested in the past history and language of his forbears.

Unfortunately for the Washington professor, his work was published by another Norwegian, industrialist Magnus Bjorndahl, of Weehawken, New Jersey. I say "unfortunately" because the joint effort of these two Scandinavians made them apt targets for those who saw in Strandwold's book a desperate attempt to prove the case of the vikings—by biased Norwegians. Erik Moltke, another Scandinavian who apparently considers himself the ultimate authority on runes and rune stones (and those who would translate them) says of Strandwold: ". . . this author lacks the most elementary knowledge of Scandinavian languages; he is able to find runes in any crevice or groove—and decipher them. He is lacking in all scientific qualifications for occupying himself with runological subjects."

A tasty bit, demonstrating the benignity of one scholar to another. In a later chapter you will learn more of Professor Moltke's acid opinions: he calls an eminent German philologist "Hitlerian" for daring to state that pre-Columbian exploration did take place. In two other instances, he uses out-of-context quotes to damn two more gentlemen of philological bent.

The petulant Moltke, however, may have been strongly influenced by what could be considered a huge practical joke played on the scholars of America by a psychologist named Edmund Burke Delabarre. In 1928, Professor Delabarre became interested in a chunk of graywacke standing just offshore in the Taunton River at Assonet, above Lousy Cove. It had a name, the Dighton Rock, and had been a subject of curiosity and speculation for more than 200 years because its riverside surface was covered with all manner of inscriptions, carvings, and peckings. Since the redoubtable Cotton Mather first copied the inscriptions in the seventeenth century, many theories had been extended concerning the inscriber, or inscribers of the rock. The theories included Egyptians, Phoenicians, Scythians, and others to the number of twenty-two. One inspired theorist considered some of the markings to be the signature of Christ, placed upon the rock during the period when he had traveled to unknown countries. Of the twenty-two theories, nineteen carried with them independent translations or interpretations, or interpolations of the cabalistic symbols on the rock.

In 1837, the rock came into international prominence when the distinguished Carl Christian Rafn, a Danish archaeologist and director of the National Museum of Denmark pronounced some of its markings viking, and offered them as evidence of pre-Columbian viking penetration of North America. Rafn published his findings in a voluminous work called *Antiquitates Americanae,* and its appearance caused enormous interest in things viking in New England and seemingly documented the Norse theory once and for all time. Rafn had found what he thought to be the signature of Thorfinn Karlsefni, the viking trader who came to this country in 1010. In addition, he stated that the Newport Tower had been built by Bishop Eric Gnupsson, who came here in 1121, as Bishop of Vinland. To clinch his argument, he added that the Skeleton in Armor, dug out at Fall River, Massachusetts, in 1831 was the remains of Leif Ericsson's brother, killed in America by Indians.

I think it can be safely assumed that Professor Delabarre was dedicated to the NEBC Principle, and that he was hopeful of discrediting the Rafn theory. He made little progress until it occurred to him that he ought to see the copy of the inscription made for Rafn by members of the Rhode Island Historical Society. (Rafn had never been to America.) Delabarre obtained a photostat of it from Denmark and compared it with the original still in this country. He struck gold. Rafn, it seemed, had added lines to the original inscription in order to produce the signature of Thorfinn. Rafn was a fraud! A fraud, that is, for Delabarre's purpose; he knew well that "reconstruction" of an inscription or artifact is, under certain conditions, perfectly acceptable in archaeological circles. The additions by Rafn had not been extensive; they simply filled in missing lines connecting what was already on the rock. But this knowledge gave Delabarre his ammunition.

Through endless pages of his book, he reiterates that the inscriptions on Dighton Rock are now so vague and overimpressed and worn and interlaced that it is virtually impossible to read anything into them at all. In this declaration he is entirely correct, and in this light, Rafn himself was, as a later scholar hints, made the butt of a practical joke by the members of the Rhode Island Historical Society. In short, since Rafn had never seen the rock and was not familiar with its state of decay, he was trapped into giving an interpretation of an interpretation. In scholarly manner, Delabarre shreds Rafn and damns him for his "fraud."

It is clear, however, that Delabarre, having gained the means of discrediting Rafn, became completely frustrated when he could offer no positive theory on the rock or any of its inscriptions. Patently, in order to give his book a garrison finish, he had to offer something tangible concerning all or any of the rock's inscriptions. But now his sense of humor came to the fore. The most striking evidence in favor of viking presence in America was the so-called signature of Karlsefni. He had succeeded in blasting it, but now it occurred that it might be interesting to use the same markings comprising the Karlsefni signature and show them to be somebody else's signature.

Now he apparently engaged in some lengthy historical research and emerged with the information that one Miguel Cortereal had embarked on an expedition to America in 1502, and was never heard from again. Miguel had gone in search of his brother Gaspar, who had disappeared the previous year on a similar expedition. This was the information Delabarre needed. He had a vanished Portuguese explorer whose name contained letters similar in appearance to the marks on Dighton Rock. With tongue in cheek (and fingers crossed, no doubt) he proceeded to show that the rock bore the signature of Miguel Cortereal, the presumed date, 1511, an inscription indicating that Cortereal had been leader of the Indians in the area, and, in all seeming sincerity, a coat of arms of Portugal.

Strengthened by his accidental fortune in replacing the alleged viking signature with one more acceptable, one which could be dated in post-Columbian times, Delabarre, heady with victory, proceeded to destroy *all* inscribed rocks in New England (and there are many) attributing them to anything and anybody other than Norse.

The nature of Delabarre's practical joke is manifest in nearly every page of his book. Stating over and over that the rock is "indecipherable," and that the observer brings away from the rock any impression he chooses, he then "finds" a signature, *using exactly the same method to produce it, and using the same characters, as Rafn had.* He solemnly adds lines and letters to reveal the Cortereal signature. Here is the passage in which he describes the nature of the Cortereal signature:

> . . . one may quickly convince himself that the letters M I G V . . . C O R T E R . . . are present beyond question. Some of them show most clearly in some photographs, others in others. The second E and the L of Cortereal are defaced by overlying Indian glyphs. The E L of Miguel, and the A below them *are probably almost worn away by attrition.* [My italics]

Nowhere does he state that the inscription is *there;* instead he says that its presence is "highly probable."

Warming to the task, he covers all avenues in defense of his little joke. He admits, with feigned puzzlement, that a Portuguese inscription in the Congo, dated from the same period, doesn't resemble that on Dighton Rock. He treats on the "coat of arms," noting that it is indeed highly condensed from the original Portuguese coat of arms, but explains that "exigencies of space" probably prevented the carving of the symbol correctly. He does not attempt to explain how the carver could have been hampered by space limitations on a rock eleven feet long by four feet deep.

And so on.

An unforeseen result of the book and its seeming documentation of the Cortereal signature was a decoration awarded Delabarre by the Portuguese Government for having established the presence of a Portuguese in New England long prior to British colonial occupation. This recognition eventually activated the Portuguese population of Rhode Island into a movement to have the rock and its surrounding woods ordained a shrine. It has been done. I don't think even Delabarre foresaw that his treatise on Dighton Rock would have such far-reaching effect. Lest the good Portuguese of Rhode Island and elsewhere heap censure upon me for questioning the validity of the Dighton Rock revelations and by that token cast reflection upon Miguel Cortereal, I plead the censure be stayed. In Chapter 19, I shall give them back a much more important Cortereal, João Vaz Cortereal, sire of Miguel and Gaspar. He came to America in 1474, eighteen years before the Genoese Navigator.

Ordinarily, Delabarre's book would be appreciated as a rare satire on scholarly archaeological works which strain to prove that which is unprovable, but it has done much damage to continuing study of inscribed rocks in New England. Delabarre has said they don't exist, and therefore, it is so. Scholars dedicated to the NEBC Principle have swallowed it whole, and apparently it is extremely useful when occasion demands damning the evidence of things Norse in New England (or elsewhere). It could well have influenced Moltke in making his unwarranted criticism of Professor Strandwold.

Strandwold was as much a scholar as any in the field who profess to be expert in runes and runic writing. I incline to feel so because, in his little book of translations of American runic inscriptions, he behaves rather oddly, compared to some of his colleagues. He treats only on the inscriptions and what he considers them to mean. Nowhere does he attack men, as such, for differing in theory.

Now I must momentarily speak of the cloud which hangs over so much pre-Columbian evidence, as if placed there by those who would fight grimly to support the NEBC Principle.

The site of the grave stones at Byfield is gone, the whereabouts of the stones unknown. Mrs. Lawrence M. Rogers, owner of the site, only recently sold it and it is, even now, being built upon. The stone telling of the shipwreck, found on the Parker River, has been missing for many years.

But I can supply a sort of happy ending. There is one stone still in existence, and which can be seen at almost any time. It is the Aptuxcet Stone, which lies on a wooden dais in the reconstructed

Aptuxcet Trading Post, in Bourne, Massachusetts. The post lies just off Route 6 on the south side of Cape Cod Canal. Visit the post, and see this rock. With the rate of disappearance increasing with each passing year, I hold little hope for the remaining viking rocks of New England.

Between Delabarre and building programs, they may soon be but dim memories—as are the grave stones of Byfield.

But I must depart from grimness. The vanished grave markers of Byfield are but seven; perhaps more will be revealed by archaeologists, amateur and professional, who might one day seek to help establish the presence in America of ancient peoples come from Europe—and its northern islands—at a time before there was a Columbus to bring to the Continent news of a vast, unexplored land to the west.

In the tenth century, Columbus was yet unborn, but the churning waters of the Atlantic continued to bring new visitors to America.

The next one, of the same calling as Ari Marson, came and saw but conquered not. He didn't even trouble to land. He came while the castaway Icelanders were still engaged in the initial struggle to acclimate themselves to their new homes—and he came because he was searching for his father.

CHAPTER 9

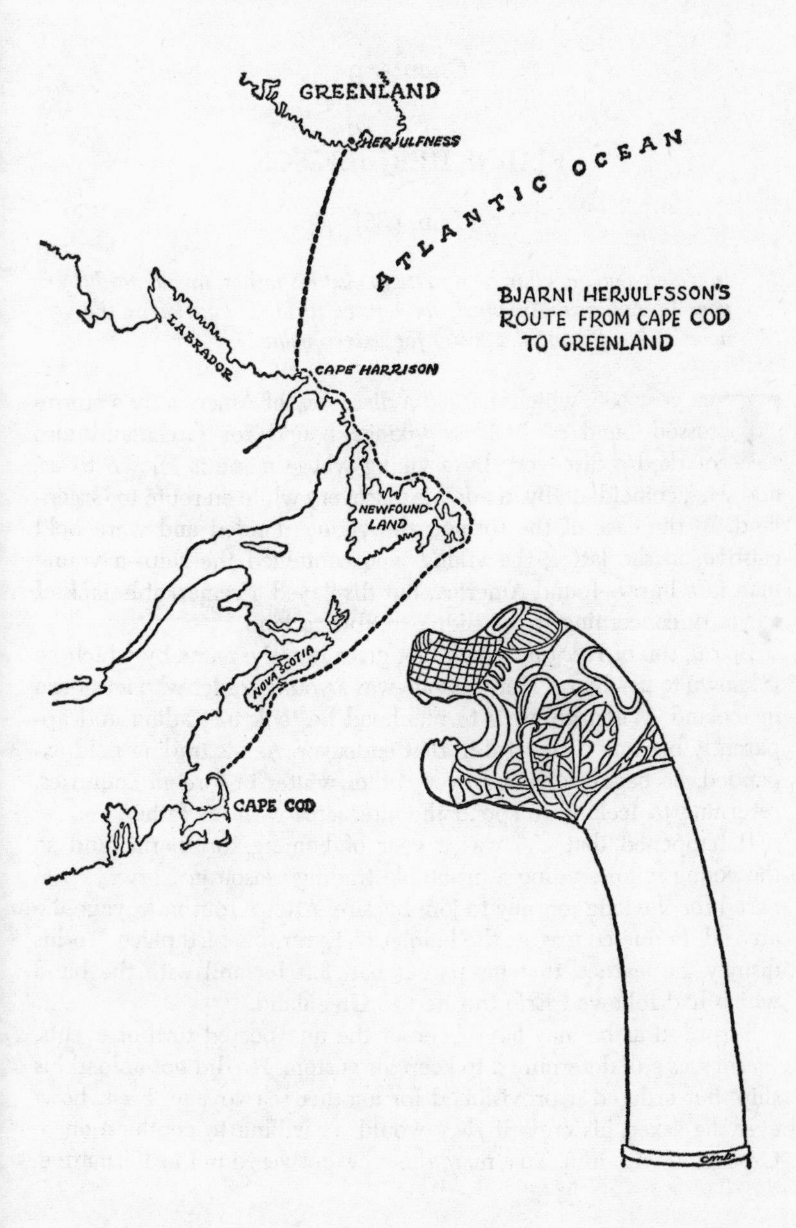
GREENLAND
HERJULFNESS
ATLANTIC OCEAN
LABRADOR
CAPE HARRISON
BJARNI HERJULFSSON'S
ROUTE FROM CAPE COD
TO GREENLAND
NEWFOUND-
LAND
NOVA SCOTIA
CAPE COD

Chapter 9

BJARNI HERJULFSSON

[A.D. 986]

In which a young viking, en route to visit his father, involuntarily goes to America. Annoyed, he refuses to land, and keeps the news of his discovery a secret for sixteen years.

THE year 986, which marked a discovery of America by a storm-tossed band of luckless vikings bound for Greenland also marked a discovery by a viking whose name is known to us, and who, coincidentally, made *his* discovery while en route to Greenland. In the case of the former, the vikings landed and were held captive; in the latter, the viking who captained the ship—a young man in a hurry—found America, but displayed a remarkable lack of curiosity concerning it: he didn't trouble to land.

Bjarni, son of Herjulf, which fact gives him the name by which he is known to us—Bjarni Herjulfsson—was a young trader who was born in Iceland. When he grew to manhood he took to trading and apparently became successful in that endeavor. As his trading field expanded, he began to spend every other winter in foreign countries, returning to Iceland to spend the alternates with his father.

It happened that 986 was a year of homing for Bjarni, and so the young sailor, ending a profitable trading season in Norway, prepared for the long journey to join his sire. After a routine voyage, he arrived, in due course, at the hamlet of Eyrar, his birthplace. To his dismay, he learned that his parent had left Iceland with the band which had followed Eric the Red to Greenland.

Surprised as he may have been at the unexpected turn of events, Bjarni was still determined to keep his custom. He did not unload his ship, but ordered it provisioned for another sea voyage. First, however, he asked his crew if they would be willing to continue on to Greenland with him. To a man, the crew answered in the affirmative.

Bjarni then presumably renewed old acquaintances in Eyrar while the crew made his ship ready.

Bjarni's vessel was a trading ship, and different in many respects from the colorful warships that are usually seen in illustrations depicting viking subjects. The warships, sometimes called *Dreki* (dragon ships) or *Langskip* (long ships) were painted in gaudy colors, their big woolen sails emblazoned with falcons or other symbols. The figureheads were carved dragons or serpents; from the stern rose a dragon's or serpent's tail. The brightly decorated shields of the warriors were slung over the gunwales, each shield overlapping the next, easily obtained in time of battle. The gunwales themselves were usually broad enough to walk upon, to make boarding an enemy ship easier.

By comparison, a tenth-century trading ship was drab. Although painted above the water line, Bjarni's craft was probably coated with seal tar or some other similar substance as protection against toredo worms. Of shallow draft, the ship was perhaps seventy feet long, with a beam of up to 18 feet. Clinker-built, she had a capacity of up to thirty tons and was constructed so that a minimum of water was shipped. Her single mast carried a square sail made of striped wool. Boomless, the sail limited the ship's performance to running only before a following or quartering wind. Steering was accomplished by a large steering oar in the stern on the starboard side. When the wind failed, the vessel could be propelled by oars manned by the crew. A ship of Bjarni's type probably had a crew of thirty and seats for 28 to row. According to data gathered by Professor Gustav Storm, Paul du Chaillu and others, her speed was about 6¼ knots maximum. Under favorable conditions, the Norse trader could sail 75 miles in a day, or 150 miles when sailing day and night continuously. But her prow displayed no dragon's head or serpent, nor did tails spring from the stern. Her gunwales carried no shields. Traders did not have to be fully armed; they benefited from a sort of gentleman's agreement that made them free from attack. It just wasn't considered manly for vikings to pirate trading ships.

When Bjarni was notified that his ship was ready to sail, he returned to his ship and made ready to get under way. But a dark thought crossed his mind. He hadn't the vaguest idea of where Greenland was, except that it lay somewhere to the west. There was obviously no one at Eyrar who could direct him, and, since he was a young man in a hurry, he didn't bother to seek out any who could elsewhere. Being a fair man, the dark thought prompted the youthful Norseman to issue a word of warning to his crew:

"Our voyage will be considered unwise," Bjarni told his men, "since none of us have been before in the Greenland sea."

But the warning didn't frighten off the vikings. They merely reaffirmed their willingness to go with him. In the words of the ancient saga, here is the story of the voyage, according to a translation from du Chaillu's *Viking Age:*

> . . . they set out to sea, and after three days' sailing, land was out of sight, and the fair winds ceased, and northern winds with fog blew continually, so that for many days they did not know in what direction they were sailing. Then the sun came into sight and they could distinguish the quarters of heaven. They hoisted sail and sailed all day before they saw land. They wondered what land this could be and Bjarni said he did not think it was Greenland. The men asked if he wished to sail towards it, and he answered that he wanted to go near it; this they did, and soon saw that it had no mountains but had low hills and was forest-clad. They kept the land on their left, but the corners of the sail were toward the land. Then they sailed for two days before they saw other land. They asked Bjarni if he did not think *this* was Greenland. He answered: 'No, it is very unlike, I thought, for very large glaciers are said to be in Greenland.' They soon approached the land and saw that it was flat and covered with woods. Then the fair wind fell, and the sailors said they thought it best to land as they lacked both wood and water, but Bjarni did not want to land, and said they had enough left. At this the men grumbled somewhat.

The sagas are full of delightful inconsistencies. Sometimes given to elaborate embellishment, they also lean occasionally to understatement. "The men grumbled somewhat" is a good case in point. The vikings were sailors, they were human, and they had been tossed about in their tiny craft for days in a series of fierce storms that had surely induced the Icelandic equivalent of "cabin fever." Wanting to land was a perfectly natural desire and Bjarni's seemingly arbitrary refusal very likely brought the crew to just a hair this side of mutiny. It is fitting testimony both to Bjarni's strength as captain of his ship, and to the iron-clad discipline prevalent on Norse ships that the trader had his way. It might be well to consider also that Bjarni could probably best any man in his crew with one hand still on the tiller. The saga continues:

He told them to set sail, which they did, and turned the prow seaward, and sailed in that direction with a southwesterly wind for three days, and then more land came in view which rose high with mountains and a glacier. They asked Bjarni if he would like to go ashore there, and he answered that he would not do so as the land had an inhospitable look. They did not furl their sail, but sailed along the shore and saw that it was an island.

Note the change in attitude above. This time the sailors returned to the polite form of inquiry they had employed when the first land was sighted. They *asked* Bjarni if he would *like* to land. Bjarni again said no, and this time there was no "grumbling." The saga resumes:

They once more turned the prow of the ship from the shore, and set to sea with the same fair wind, but the gale increased, and Bjarni told them to take in a reef, and not sail so fast, for the ship and its rigging could not stand it. They sailed four days, until they saw land for the fourth time. They asked Bjarni if he thought this was Greenland.

Here the crew had become even *more* polite. Clearly, resignation had set in. Now they asked Bjarni if he "thought this was Greenland." No mention of going ashore; simply a hopeful question. If this spectacularly one-track-minded captain they were burdened with elected to sail the seas for the duration of time, they were with him all the way. But all things come to them who wait, and the crew was rewarded with a positive reply from their leader. The saga relates that Bjarni answered:

This most resembles Greenland from what I have been told, and here we will land. They landed in the evening at a cape where a boat was lying. Herjulf, Bjarni's father, lived on the cape, and it is called Herjulfness, after him. Bjarni now stayed with his father, left off sea-journeys, and dwelled there during his father's lifetime, and after his death.

That's the story, as it is told in the *Flateyjarbok*. A later saga tells how news of the voyage first came to light. In 1001, Bjarni journeyed to the court of Earl Eric, successor to King Olav Tryggvason of Norway. He had been summoned to receive an appointment as "Earl's Man," which meant he would be a representative of the king on his return to Greenland. At the court, possibly fortified with some early viking version of gløgg, and mellowed by the passing years, Bjarni talked, describing the three lands he had seen, but not touched upon.

The reaction to Bjarni's story was swift and pointed. "On this account," the saga states, "Bjarni was somewhat slandered." Here again the classic understatement of the sagas becomes evident. Freely translated, "somewhat slandered" means that the vikings who learned of Bjarni's tale subjected him to torrents of verbal abuse, probably close to the point of no endurance. He may even have been threatened with physical violence.

By the code of the old vikings, Bjarni had committed an unpardonable sin. To a viking, the discovery of new country called for only one procedure: land and inspect. If possible, plunder. In no circumstance did a Norseman ever sight new land and ignore it. But Bjarni was an Icelander—a trader—not one of the "old" vikings. Even so, he probably felt an overwhelming guilt at his own lack of curiosity, and certainly did not want it broadcast that he committed this cardinal crime simply because he wanted to spend the winter with his father. And so just hadn't talked about it—until the fateful moment at Olaf's court. He may have even sworn his crew to secrecy concerning it. Being made of stern stuff, however, Bjarni withstood the abuse heaped upon him, succeeded in keeping his appointment as Earl's Man and returned to Greenland the following year.

Disputes over viking voyages to America have mainly been confined to scholarly brawls between adherents to the NEBC Principle and those who would strive to prove that such voyages had occurred *de facto*. The saga of Bjarni, however, has provided intramural strife between factions of the *pros*. For many years a handful of scholars regarded the Bjarni voyage as a complete fabrication—created, perhaps, by Bjarni in order to gain attention at the Earl's court in Norway. Some pointed out that its occurrence only in the *Flateybook* was proof of its falsification, insisting that the discovery of America was made by Leif Ericsson when *he* was blown off course on a voyage from Norway to Iceland.

Eventually the saga came to be accepted. It had been written by a scholar recording the history of Greenland and its people, and who certainly had no thought of discrediting the voyage of Leif. Then, too, if one were to accept the *Flateybook's* horrendous story of Freydis (whom you will meet in Chapter 13) it would be inconsistent to discard the story of Bjarni.

Part of the opposition to Bjarni's tale stemmed from the seemingly improbable detail in it. How could a ship be blown 2000 miles off course? Where, along the eastern coast of North America, could

Bjarni have sighted three separate lands between his first landfall and Greenland? The existence of three lands separated by four-, three-, and two-days' sailing time could not be shown. The tale, therefore, was unacceptable.

In the nineteenth century, several students of the sagas decided that the story had to be authentic; it was inextricably woven in with the saga of Leif Ericsson in that Leif reversed Bjarni's sailing directions to get to America. Now the problem took on a different aspect: granted that Bjarni could have been blown surprisingly far off course—a truth already bitterly known to the trader Ari and the castaway Icelanders—where were the three lands Bjarni sighted before he arrived in Greenland?

Early attempts to find Bjarni's three lands by reversing the chronicle of sailing times from Greenland usually culminated in locating the fourth land—or the land Bjarni had sighted *first*—much too northerly, i.e., in the region of Nova Scotia, Newfoundland, the St. Lawrence, or approximately in those latitudes. (Some scholars, through unintelligible deductions, located it as far south as the southern Atlantic states.) But the northerly regions were not satisfactory, because the first land sighted by Bjarni was also the fourth or last land sighted by Leif Ericsson—and Leif's land, Vinland—had been shown by several scholars, independently, to be in the latitude of Boston (as demonstrated in the next chapter). The big question, then, was: Where, exactly, was the first land sighted by Bjarni, the land that was to become part of Leif's Vinland the Good?

In 1921, a Britisher named G. M. Gathorne-Hardy wrote a book called *The Norse Discoverers of America.* It was the most penetrating treatise on the vikings yet published and approached the mystery of the sagas in an extremely intelligent and logical manner. Gathorne-Hardy was convinced that Cape Cod was Leif's Vinland, and, by that token, Bjarni's first land.

Gathorne-Hardy demonstrated that Bjarni probably emerged from the storm at some point off Cape Cod. He coasted to Provincetown and then set his course northeast, knowing, from the unaccustomed position of sun and pole star, that he was too far to the west and south of his goal. After two days he arrived at Nova Scotia, his second land.

From there he sailed northeast again, arriving after three-days' sail somewhere off the Avalon Peninsula in Newfoundland, the third land. Thus far his distances, correlated with the estimated speed for a viking ship (150 miles per day) corresponded loosely. The distance from Provincetown to Cape Sable, Nova Scotia, is about 250 miles, easily achieved by a viking ship of the speed noted in two-days' sail, and with time to spare. In discussing the second leg of the voyage, the Britisher is not quite so precise. He indicates no specific landfall, nor any specific point of departure from Nova Scotia, stating only that Bjarni left the land and sailed "about 500 miles" to reach the Avalon Peninsula. In using the 500-mile figure, he begins to stretch the capability of the ship's speed, but the "stretch" still falls within reason. Having brought Bjarni to the second and third lands, he now has him coast the eastern shore of Newfoundland to somewhere in the vicinity of Cape Freels. Now he is ready to speed Bjarni on the last leg of the voyage, but this time he is forced to stretch the speed of the ship to an even greater degree. Stating that the mileage from Cape Freels or Cape St. John—either one of which could have been Bjarni's point of departure—is "under 720 miles" (an incorrect estimate) he has Bjarni cover that mileage in four days' sail. The argument he advances is logical when applied only to Bjarni's voyage; it doesn't hold up when the same four-days' sailing time is considered in application to Leif's later voyage. Gathorne-Hardy notes that a strong southwesterly gale was in force, and that Bjarni had to reef in to remove strain from the ship's timbers and mast. Correct. He also notes that in such a forceful wind, the little viking ship could conceivably have covered the distance to Greenland in four days. Also correct, under extraordinary circumstances. Two details must be considered here, however. One: the mileage to Greenland from Cape Freels or Cape St. John is more properly stated as 800 to 850 miles, creating a much more substantial strain in accepting the time given to cover such a distance, even in a gale-force wind. Two: when Leif sailed to America by reversing Bjarni's sailing directions, he sailed to his "Helluland"—which was Bjarni's third land sighted—in the same four days. But he had no gale force wind to drive him. Comparison of the two sagas does not hold. In commenting on Leif's voyage, Gathorne-Hardy prudently avoids the comparison. Leif—after four-days' sail—would have landed at nearly the same spot that Bjarni had departed from on the last leg of *his* voyage. He doubtless had members of Bjarni's old crew with him to insure reaching the lands

Bjarni had seen. The British scholar's deductions, then, can be considered as *nearly*, but not quite, correct.

Frederick Pohl, who in 1952 published *The Lost Discovery*, and in it extended an equally brilliant argument for the case of the vikings, also attempted to reconstruct Bjarni's voyage. He agreed with Gathorne-Hardy that sailing times given in the saga meant open-water sailing times, and further strengthened the thought by determining, from mariner friends, that open-water sailing meant from point of land last seen to landfall. With this information, he set out to retrace Bjarni's voyage. His calculations on the first and third legs of the voyage were tenable, but, for some mysterious reason, he had Bjarni, in the second stage, start east and north, then turn abruptly west to sight Newfoundland on its western tip. Then he brought him up through the Strait of Belle Isle, but makes no mention of the fact that on such a course Bjarni would then have noted *five* lands altogether on his voyage: Cape Cod, Nova Scotia, Newfoundland, Labrador, and Greenland. In short, his premise fails at the second stage.

In order to determine Bjarni's route from the land he sighted first to Greenland, some pertinent facts must be considered:

1. The speed of a tenth-century viking ship: 150 miles a day.
2. The sailing times given are times spent on open water, i.e., from point of land last seen to landfall. Otherwise, the distance from Cape Cod to Greenland, 1700 miles, doesn't match the distance Bjarni's ship could have covered in the nine-days' sail indicated in the saga (1350 miles). Coasting times and distances must be added.
3. Labrador and Newfoundland are to be considered one land, as suggested by Gathorne-Hardy.
4. Bjarni's saga must be checked against the saga of Leif Ericsson and details of the two compare agreeably. Each is needed to prove the other out.

Next, the route should be worked backward from Greenland in order to reach the ultimate land, or the land first sighted by Bjarni. Starting, then, from Herjulfness, in Greenland, which was near the present settlement of Julienehaab, Bjarni's four-day sail would have brought him to Labrador-Newfoundland, counting these two countries as one, his three-day sail would have brought him from the southeast tip of Newfoundland to Nova Scotia and the two-day sail covers the distance between Nova Scotia and Provincetown on Cape Cod.

Now, in reversing these sailing distances and starting from Cape Cod—sailing in a northeasterly direction—it is possible to reconstruct Bjarni's voyage thusly:

When the *series* of storms (as noted by Pohl) which had blown Bjarni to America had cleared, the viking was within 150 miles of Cape Cod. The saga states that he sailed all day before sighting land. Presumably, he took his bearings at a point southwest of Martha's Vineyard, possibly due south of Newport. Judging his position by the sun's placement in the heavens, he knew he was too far south and west of his goal. He therefore turned his course northeast, sailing up between Martha's Vineyard and Nantucket before he sighted *land.* Bjarni did not include small islands in his report of the voyage. He encountered many islands along his route; he only considered the "lands" he had seen as being important to the narrative. (Later he thought that Newfoundland-Labrador was an island, but would still include it as a *land* because of its vast area.)

The first land that Bjarni saw was Cape Cod. He coasted it until he came to the Provincetown area. From there he could see the mainland, twenty-odd miles to the west, and, having already decided that this land was not Greenland, again set his course northeasterly. Since he had approached the cape from the south, he could see its extensive beaches snaking westward and correctly guessed that this cape was connected to the mainland he could see from Provincetown. The mainland, therefore, was included as part of the first land, but not approached because it was to the west, and did not resemble Greenland.

Leaving Cape Cod, he sailed for two days, covering from 250 to 300 miles before he sighted land. This course brought him to a point east of Cape Sable, in Nova Scotia. Exactly where he sighted Nova Scotia is difficult to determine, but it may have been, as Frederick Pohl suggests, some 30 miles off the island at a point where he could see the 370-foot hill just south of Liverpool. Assuming that it was, he was probably to the southeast of it when the landfall was made. He then turned his course toward the hill, and again shifted it to north as he discerned the low, wooded coast of Nova Scotia.

Recall, now, that Bjarni stated that this land was not like Greenland, either, and so decided not to land. "At this time the men grumbled somewhat." The grumbling is an important clue in the story. Under ordinary circumstances, Bjarni would have followed the coast as far as possible, or convenient, a standard viking procedure. But the grumbling crew caused him to decide against it, and he ordered the ship turned east again at the earliest opportunity. That opportunity did not present itself immediately, for the fair wind failed and it is reasonable that Bjarni coasted or drifted under slack sail, or had his crew row, in a northeasterly direction, until the wind freshened again. When it did, he turned east. His coasting, however, took him at least to about the region of Halifax, where the wind livened and he resumed his open-water sailing. He sailed due east until the land fell away. Then he shifted course to northeast. Taking the little ship northeasterly across open water would bring the vikings to a point southeast of Cape Race, on the Avalon Peninsula of Newfoundland. His landfall there occurred at the time when he sighted either Hawke Hill, an elevation of 1100 feet, or Butter Pot, which stands at 999 feet. Both are in the eastern Avalonian chain and would be visible up to about thirty miles at sea, in a southeasterly direction. The approximate distance covered in this segment of his sailing out of sight of land, from east of Halifax to the hills of the Avalon would be between 450 and 500 miles. The saga allows three days for this portion of the journey and the mileage is agreeable. It may, in fact, have been 450 miles or less; we don't know at what point Bjarni, disgusted with the crew's mutterings, decided he'd better head for the open sea on the theory that land out of sight was land out of mind—a healthier circumstance for the unhappy crew. He may have coasted as far north as Sheet Harbor before turning east.

At Newfoundland, he again decided not to land, but since the crew made no stirring over his decision, he elected to coast this, the third land he had sighted. He decided to coast, I suspect, for two reasons: While he had declared that the land looked inhospitable, the presence of mountains—which he knew to exist in Greenland—might have tempted him to stay close to this land; it might, after all, lead him to Greenland. Second, he was now at 55 to 50 degrees east, and he might be in the longitude of Greenland, since he had already sailed nearly 20° to the east.

Now he sailed Newfoundland's coast for more than three days, crossed the Strait of Belle Isle and coasted Labrador for nearly two more days before he again turned northeast.

His first day of coasting Newfoundland took him from the Cape Race region to somewhere southeast of Cape Bonavista. His second day brought him north and west into Notre Dame Bay, probably just above Twillingate. The third day saw him steering westward still to Cape St. John, then to Partridge Point, and then north along the land to Hare Bay. Dawn of the fifth day found him rounding Cape Bauld and across to Cape Norman. Now, in daylight, he could see the landfall away to the southwest, and he could also see the hills of Labrador across Belle Isle Strait. He crossed to Labrador and sailed north to somewhere east of Batteau. The fifth day brought him to Cape Harrison, and there two things became apparent to the bewildered trader. He was too far west again, and the land from Cape Harrison *continued* west. Only one course lay open. Leave the land astern and resume the northeast course.

Taking departure from Cape Harrison, Bjarni sailed four days to arrive in Greenland. The distance covered was about 600 miles, in keeping with the ship's speed. He not only reached Greenland, but made his landing virtually at his father's doorstep.

It can be seen in the map that Bjarni thought Newfoundland and Labrador to be one. He sailed directly across the Strait of Belle Isle, thinking it a bay, similar to the ones he had sailed across in Newfoundland. Again the circumstance of his voyage must be considered carefully. He was in a hurry to get to Greenland. He probed not into each bay he reached, but sailed into it only far enough to determine the next land in the direction he was steering. He *assumed*, for example, that White Bay was a bay; he could not see its head from where he crossed it, he was simply racing for the next land in sight to the north.

When he came to the Strait of Belle Isle, he had already sailed around Cape Bauld and arrived at Cape Norman. From there he satisfied himself that the land fell away to the southwest, which was of no appeal. He could also see the hills of Labrador across Belle Isle Strait and assumed them to be the other side of the "bay." As he sailed north and rounded Cape St. Charles, he again found himself turning west until he reached Cape Harrison. It was there that he could see the land turning abruptly south and west, and knew that pursuing such a course could only bring him to a more westerly point.

He assumed that he was coasting on an island, and, in some disgust—or annoyance, at least—turned north and east once again. At Cape Harrison, he was but 600 miles from Herjulfness, where his father lived. Gathorne-Hardy stated that Bjarni had covered nearly 800 miles because of the strong gale he had behind him. But the saga also states that they reefed in to spare the ship. The four days allowed in the saga for the last leg of the journey again agrees. Bjarni doubtless maintained his normal speed of five to six knots, despite the breeze, because he trimmed his sail to meet the situation.

These, then, were the lands sighted and sailed by: Cape Cod, Nova Scotia, Newfoundland-Labrador, and Greenland. From this reconstruction it can be seen that the mileage requirements are fulfilled through a combination of open water sailing times and time allowed for coasting . . . a route which allows for the logical error of assuming Newfoundland and Labrador to be one land is shown . . . and all of the distances covered during the specified sailing times could be easily duplicated by Leif on his subsequent voyage to America.

From this reconstruction, it is also possible to determine, with reasonable accuracy, the actual time consumed by Bjarni in his voyage from Cape Cod to Greenland. His open water sailing time was nine days, the time spent in coasting Newfoundland and Labrador added five more for a total of fourteen. But another day, at least, must be added to account for the time lost in drifting, rowing, or sailing at considerably less speed than usual when "the fair wind failed" at Nova Scotia.

It would seem, then, that Bjarni Herjulfsson's epic journey from America to find his migrating parent consumed at least fifteen days. There is no physical evidence of Bjarni's visit, nor will there ever be. Bjarni Herjulfsson was certainly history's most incurious voyager, but his unplanned excursion was of extreme importance in that it precipitated Leif Ericsson's discovery of America—and its resultant recognition.

We will go, now, to meet Leif.

CHAPTER 10

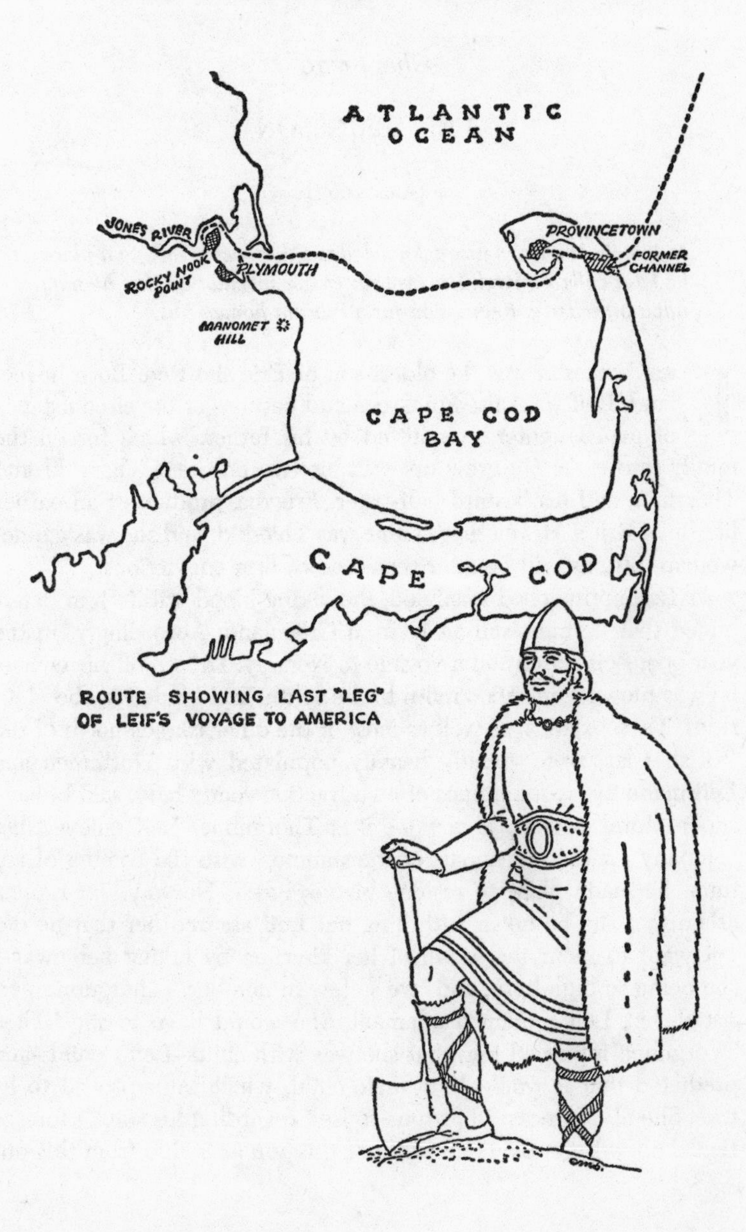

ROUTE SHOWING LAST "LEG" OF LEIF'S VOYAGE TO AMERICA

Chapter 10

LEIF ERICSSON

[A.D. 1003]

In which America's first acknowledged discoverer sails to a place he later calls Vinland. His visit raises the speculation that he may have provided a foundation for a Pilgrim homestead.

LEIF ERICSSON was the oldest son of Eric the Red. Born in Iceland, Leif was raised in Greenland because of the circumstance of manslaughter, committed by his father, which forced the family into exile. He grew up with his two brothers, Thorvald and Thorstein, and his bastard half-sister, Freydis, product of an earlier liaison of Eric's. His mother's name was Thiodild, and she was a quiet woman, but, as will be later seen, one of firm convictions.

As Leif approached manhood, the viking blood within him determined that he must sail away from Greenland. Accordingly, in the year 999, Leif set out on a voyage to Norway. Driven off his course, he was blown some 1600 miles to the south, and landed in the Hebrides. These islands, as well as most of the other islands north of the British Isles, were already heavily populated with Northmen and Leif made the acquaintance of an attractive young lady, said to have supernatural powers. Her name was Thorgunna. Leif enjoyed her company for the better part of the summer; with the coming of autumn he made plans to resume his voyage to Norway. Thorgunna asked that she be taken with him, but Leif assured her that he did not want to incur the wrath of her kinsmen by taking her away—she being so high-born, and "we so few in number." Thorgunna persisted, but Leif remained adamant. She would have to stay. Then Thorgunna informed him that she was with child—Leif's child—and predicted that it would be a male child, which later proved to be true. She also forecast ill fortune to Leif regarding his son. "I foresee that thou wilt get as much profit of this son as is due from this our parting." Then she told Leif that she would come to Greenland one day and bring the son with her.

Unstirred, Leif gave her a gold finger ring, a Greenland mantle, and a belt of walrus tusk. He then sailed for Norway. His son did come to Greenland eventually, and Thorgunna's dire prophecy held. It was said that the boy was mentally unbalanced, and he died quite young.

Leif was well received in Norway at the court of King Olav Tryggvason. The king, with remarkable perception, could see that Leif was a man of great accomplishments. When the two had become friends, the king asked Leif if he planned to return to Greenland during the next summer. When Leif assured the king that he would if Olaf wished him to, the king was delighted. He had a mission for Leif to accomplish.

Olaf was a Christian convert and had taken to the new religion with great enthusiasm. He had all of Norway Christianized by 1000, and Iceland, as noted in an earlier chapter, had become Christian the same year, by voting themselves so. Such a mundane transition from the old pagan ways to the new religion might seem bizarre, but then the Icelanders knew quick-tempered, easily riled, petulant Olaf. He wanted his subjects Christian, and they had better conform, or else.

The mission Olaf wished Leif to perform was that of bringing Christianity to Greenland. The saga sayeth not that Leif was happy about the request, but he did as he was asked. Thus Leif became the first missionary to Greenland, perhaps not altogether willingly. The young viking asked for Olaf's protection from Old Eric. Leif probably knew that his red-bearded sire would not be agreeable to accepting the tenets of this new—and to Eric's way of thinking, effete religion—religion which decreed turning the other cheek to an enemy assault. That sort of philosophy was completely unintelligible to Eric.

Bracing himself, Leif set sail for Iceland, bringing with him a priest selected by Olaf. The young Ericsson proclaimed Christianity throughout the land, and his mother, Thiodild, took to the new religion quickly. Perhaps exhausted from her years of marriage to the troublesome old red beard, and perhaps taking unfair advantage of the new credo, she caused a chapel to be built a few yards away from Eric's house, thus infuriating him. She not only became a sort of nun, but refused, thereafter, all marital intercourse with Eric. The saga which relates this unhappy state of affairs, and which makes clear the irascible, belligerent, bellicose, petulant nature of Eric, and as clearly defines his unpredictable and ungovernable temper, describes his reaction to the conversion and withdrawal of his wife in remarkably conservative language.

"This," the saga states, "vexed Eric."

That Eric was also displeased at his son's "treacherous" behavior is evident. Eric frequently referred to Leif's priest as the "juggler," or "trickster," and could not tolerate the humble man of the cloth. The tension built up between Leif and his father by the introduction of Christianity doubtless hastened Leif's decision to go to the New World. It would appear that he waited not long to make this decision after he heard of Bjarni Herjulfsson's voyage, on Bjarni's return to Greenland in 1002. When the story came to Leif's ears, the young viking saw in it a hope of carving a new world for himself, as his father had many years before. Accordingly, Leif went to see Bjarni and eventually bought his ship. Enlisting a crew of thirty-five, perhaps containing some of the men who had accompanied Bjarni on the earlier voyage, Leif prepared to sail to the new lands to the west.

He then paid his father the courtesy of asking him to lead the expedition, presumably reasoning that his father would find some way of getting out of it gracefully. Eric did. Consenting to accompany Leif as the expedition's leader, he rode a horse down to the ship. The horse stumbled and Eric immediately took this to be a bad omen.

Quoth Eric: "Not is for me fated to find more lands than this where we now dwell; we now no longer may follow together."

Eric returned to his home, and Leif and his men prepared to sail.

Reversing Bjarni's old sailing directions, Leif sailed out across the North Atlantic, below Davis Strait, toward Labrador, the third land Bjarni had sighted on his voyage in 986. It must be assumed that Leif sailed in the same direction whence Bjarni had come, and for the same number of days. Therefore, he was out four days before he sighted land. It is not reasonable to consider that Bjarni gave Leif a different course from the one he himself had sailed. Bjarni, could, conceivably, have told Leif to sail more directly south, knowing that Newfoundland extended far to the east. But there was always the possibility that the wind might have carried Leif too far to the east and he would have missed the land completely, sailing south to he knew not where. It is therefore logical to reason that Leif sailed almost to the same point of land from which Bjarni had departed for Greenland.

On arrival, "they sailed up to the land and cast anchor, and launched a boat and went ashore, and saw no grass there; great ice mountains lay inland back from the sea, and it was as a [tableland of] flat rock all the way from the sea to the ice mountains, and the country seemed to them to be entirely devoid of good qualities. Then said Leif, 'It has not come to pass with us in regard to this land as with Bjarni, that we have not gone upon it. To this country I will now give a name, and call it Helluland [Flat-rock Land].'"

They tarried in Labrador but briefly, then sailed southeast, crossing the Strait of Belle Isle and coasting to the tip of Newfoundland. From there they sailed until they came to another land, and we can assume that the open-water stage of this segment of the voyage consumed three days. "This was a level wooded land, and there were broad stretches of white sand, where they went, and the land was level by the sea. 'Then,' said Leif, 'this land shall have a name after its nature, and we will call it Markland [Woodland].'" Leif was now in Nova Scotia, Bjarni's second land.

Now comes the passage in the saga which holds the key to the location of Leif's camp in the New World—the place where he stayed for a winter, built houses, and planned to return to settle permanently—as told in the *Flateybook* (Reeves translation):

They returned to the ship forthwith, and sailed away upon the main with north-east winds, and were out two "doegr" before they sighted land. They sailed toward this land, and came to an island which lay to the northward off the land. There they went ashore and looked about them, the weather being fine, and they observed that there was dew upon the grass, and it so happened that they touched the dew with their hands, and touched their hands to their mouths, and it seemed to them that they had never before tasted anything so sweet as this. They went aboard their ship again and sailed into a certain sound, which lay between the island and a cape which jutted out from the land on the north, and they stood in westering past the cape. At ebb-tide there were broad reaches of shallow water there, and they ran their ship aground there, and it was a long distance from the ship to the ocean; yet were they so anxious to go ashore that they could not wait until the tide should rise under their ship, but hastened to the land, where a certain river flows out from a lake. As soon as the tide rose beneath their ship, however, they took the boat and rowed to the ship, which they conveyed up the river, and so into the lake, where they cast anchor and carried their hammocks ashore from the ship, and built themselves booths there. They afterwards determined to establish themselves there for the winter, and they accordingly built a large house. There was no lack of salmon there either in the river or in the lake, and larger salmon than they had ever seen before. The country thereabouts seemed to be possessed of such good qualities that cattle would need no fodder there during the winters. There was no frost there in the winters, and the grass withered but little. The days and nights there were of more nearly equal length than in Greenland or Iceland. On the shortest day of winter the sun was up between "eyktarstad" and "dagmalastad."

In the foregoing lies the key to the location of Leif Ericsson's camp in America. Students of the sagas have puzzled over it for centuries. More than fifty have offered theories on the route of the voyage and the location of Vinland. Thoughts on Vinland itself have placed it from Greenland to Florida, with nearly all the available topography in between covered at one time or another.

The most penetrating analyses of the saga placed Leif and his wine country somewhere in New England; many of these placed them specifically in the Cape Cod region. Boston has come in for its share of the speculation, since it lies loosely in the Cape Cod design, and, as a result of such thinking, bears two memorials to the vikings. One, the stone tower referred to in Chapter 8, was erected by Eben Horsford, who was convinced that the Hub marked the site of Leif's landing. The other memorial came about as a result of Horsford's Tower. The city fathers of Boston, reasoning that there might be something to "this viking theory" caused a statue of Leif to be raised on Commonwealth Avenue. It is surprisingly unviking-like, and carries the character of a ballet dancer rather than that of a rugged Icelander, tenth-century style. According to Philip A. Means, who tells of the circumstances surrounding the commissioning of the statue in *The Newport Tower,* the statue is literally the result of a practical joke by its sculptress. Miss Anne Whitney, the lady in question, was commissioned to create the statue and forthwith sculpted a model showing Leif as a typical viking. As Means puts it, she showed him as "the brawny bruiser he probably was." It was rejected, and "she made another in a spirit of raillery, pretty as any chorus girl who ever wore a fake chain in a ballet." To her horror, this one was accepted, cast and raised.

Of those scholars who placed Leif in the Cape Cod region, and there have been nearly twenty of them, the theorists who advanced the strongest cases were Hjalmar Holand, G. M. Gathorne-Hardy, and Frederick Pohl. I have already referred to the two latter, and Chapter 17 will acquaint you further with Mr. Holand.

Gathorne-Hardy wrote his book, *The Norse Discoverers of America,* in 1921, and in it he provided bases for Holand and Pohl to pursue further studies of the question. He stated the case for Bjarni Herjulfsson and suggested the manner in which his route might be determined. He also delved extensively into the question of *Eyktarstad* and *Dagmalastad,* the Icelandic time periods which offer clues to Leif's whereabouts. Collating his own research with the thinking of those who had preceded him, he established that Leif's camp could not have been above the 49th parallel, and was, presumably, much below it, probably on Cape Cod. The fact that the vikings noted daylight at *Eyktarstad* and *Dagmalastad,* time periods corresponding to 7:30 to 8:00 A.M. and 4:00 to 4:30 P.M. on winter's shortest day places them somewhere in the Cape Cod region. Other factors came into play, such as the known northern limits of the wild grape which, except for an area in the Annapolis Basin in Nova Scotia, stops at Maine. The grapes were found by Tyrker, a servant of Leif's who proceeded to make free-run wine, in secret, and, when it was ready, disappeared for a time. Leif sent a searching party for him, but he staggered into camp in an extreme state of exhilaration, announcing his discovery of grapes, although it is evident that he withheld the announcement until he had sampled the grapes' product. Leif ordered that the grapes should be gathered, and from the abundant harvest, named the country *Wineland,* or *Vinland.*

There is one item of borrowed material in this saga. It has been the bane of most scholars' attempts to make sense of it. It is in the reference to "no *frost,*" or *snow* in winter. Some of the explanations for this unusual occurrence in New England have been indeed ingenious, but none has considered that this passage is patently borrowed from the saga of Thorfinn Karlsefni, who spent a winter in North Carolina. The same phraseology occurs in Karlsefni's saga, and in light of his location, makes sense. It doesn't when used in context with Leif.

Even though Gathorne-Hardy had done a masterful job in removing some of the mystery from the saga, there were areas he entered into not at all. He didn't, for instance, compare the routes of Leif and Bjarni, which comparison would have greatly weakened his reasoning, nor did he attempt to find Leif's mysterious "island which lay to the northward off the land." He also avoided naming a specific location for Leif's shelters.

In the 1940s, Hjalmar Holand suggested that Frederick Pohl make a thorough investigation of the New England shore line in order to find, if possible, a place which fit the geography of the sagas: a cape, a river which flowed from or through a lake into the sea, and an island "which lay to the northward off the land." Pohl eventually decided that the Bass River, which flows into Nantucket Sound from Follins Pond—on Cape Cod—were the river and lake respectively. Then he determined that Leif's Island was a sandspit called "Great Point," extending northward from Nantucket Island. In order to show that it was *the* island, he demonstrated that Great Point—normally connected to Nantucket—is frequently cut off from the island after a northeaster.

In addition, Pohl found several "mooring holes" in the pond and along the river. These holes were sometimes used by the Northmen in anchoring their ships. They worked on an ingenious principle, and were employed primarily on rocky shores. The ship was anchored by a bow line just offshore, the stern coming up against the shore line. In a convenient rock, a hole of perhaps four or five inches was drilled, on the shore side, and at a slight angle, away from the ship. A mooring pin was then placed in it, to which the stern line was attached. In the event of a quick flight from the mooring, the bow line was drawn up, the crew pushed the ship out into the water and one of the crew simply flipped the hawser to which the pin was attached. The flipping action pulled the pin out, and the ship was free.

These, then, were the evidences that Pohl produced to extend his theory, arrived at in a most scholarly manner:

1. Cape Cod's Bass River and Follins Pond shown to be the "river and lake" of the saga.

2. Mooring holes found in rocks along the banks of the Bass River and in Follins Pond. The most important of these was one found in a rock skerry, 50 feet from shore, in Follins Pond. It seemed to indicate Leif's actual mooring at the campsite.

3. Evidence that showed Great Point, a sandspit jutting off the north-

ern tip of Nantucket to be an island after the high tides of a northeast storm.

There was more evidence, and Pohl listed it all in his "ten geographic requirements" which, he stated, had to be met for any theory to be acceptable. Gathorne-Hardy had listed seven cardinal points. I felt that each had missed—or misinterpreted—something along the way, though it was a long time before I was able to offer implementation to these well-delineated theories. Holand, I might add, had suspected Boston, Kingston, Massachusetts, and the Bass River as possible sites for Leif's debarkation. He ruled out the first two because they were not on an east-west shore, a condition which I shall demonstrate to be unnecessary in establishing Leif's campsite.

Having first accepted the Pohl theory, I probed the Cape Cod region for years, looking for further evidence. Unfortunately, no artifacts of any kind had been found to support the theory, nor the presence of old foundations which might be indicative of viking houses. I did some digging on the cape at sites which I thought might be fruitful but produced nothing. In 1957, I found a depression in the woods near Mill Pond—adjacent to Follins Pond—which I thought might be an old foundation. I sampled it with the assistance of my wife Jeanne and oldest son Barry; we produced colonial material but no Icelandic artifacts. Barry also discovered what seemed to be stones laid on the ground in the shapes of crosses. Excavation under these proved unrevealing.

Jeanne and I journeyed to Iceland to study eleventh-century weapons, utensils, etc., in order to improve my own knowledge of them. Dr. Kristjan Eldjarn, distinguished curator of the National Museum in Reykjavik, personally saw to my education in this respect. We flew north, and traveled east and west in the tiny island, observing particularly the ancient houses and the methods by which they were built. Iceland still has quite a number of sod-roofed houses in the deep country, and they are similar to the type Leif might have built here. When we left Iceland, we were exhausted, not so much by the pressured schedule we had kept, but by the extraordinary kindness and hospitality of the Icelanders. It's impossible to rent a car in Iceland, but we had one each day of our stay, with its owner to drive it. We were stuffed with Icelandic "snacks" (a euphemism for a staggering meal) and shown the historical treasures and places of Iceland until we were reeling. We survived.

On returning from Iceland, I told Pohl about the site I had probed on Mill Pond and suggested that he investigate it further. A tight time schedule indefinitely precluded additional digging on my part. Pohl requested a dig from the Massachusetts Archaeological Society and they eventually came to dig it over a weekend, in November of 1960, a surprisingly short time to devote to any sort of dig. (In 1950, they had dug at Follins Pond, also for a single weekend. I suspect a reluctance here to produce viking evidence. Manifestation, perhaps, of the NEBC Principle.) The Mill Pond dig has produced nothing.

Despite the precise theory extended by Pohl, and my own attempts to assist in bolstering it by the uncovering of artifactual evidence—there were aspects of his interpretation which disturbed me.

Pohl had shown that Leif had landed on an "island," Great Point, the sandspit at the northern tip of Nantucket. His reasoning was based on the knowledge that Great Point is sometimes cut off from Nantucket after a northeast storm, thus making it an island. Since Leif came down with a northeast wind, the chances are that the Great Point *was* an island at that moment due to the higher tides accompanying a northeast storm. But now I shall have to return one of Mr. Pohl's arguments to him. He had also stated that the vikings knew Cape Cod was a true cape by subsequent exploration. Therefore they called it a cape, which fact they did not know the day they landed. By the same token, I thought, subsequent exploration would have shown them that Great Point was only an island in the periods following storms. Therefore they would not have referred to it as an island, but rather as a sandspit, or an "island created by the tides."

Next, Pohl took them in a west by north direction to the Bass River. I couldn't agree with that direction, particularly since the saga said they "stood in westering past the cape." By no stretch of the imagination can "west" be translated as the direction from Great Point to the Bass River. The saga says they steered to the west of that cape. Pohl sails them below the cape. No viking would have said "west of the cape" when he meant "below." I was puzzled.

The saga next states that they sailed into a sound that lay between the island and that cape. That puzzled me, too. Nantucket Sound just didn't seem right. Could the Icelandic word "sund" which is used to convey the meaning of "sound" in the saga, have other meanings? It did, as I was to discover.

In his next interpretation, Pohl read the phrase "it was a long distance from the ship to the ocean" as meaning it was a good distance between the mouth of the Bass River and the open sea beyond Monomoy Point. I disagreed. From the mouth of the Bass River all one can see is open sea, in any direction. It didn't coincide.

The next condition fulfilled by Pohl seemed incontrovertible. "They hastened to the land, where a certain river flows out from a lake." (Or *through* a lake, as other translators have suggested.) The Bass River certainly began in Follins Pond. The two could well be the river and lake of the saga.

But it still didn't seem absolutely right.

I pursued the mystery.

The one clue which had driven others before me mad was "the island which lay to the north of the land." There is no such island on the New England coast, if that is to be the location of Leif's encampment. The New England shore falls away from east to west, and any island along its edge would properly be classified as lying to the south of a land, except in the case of an island which lay to the north of another island. And that couldn't truly be called to the north of the "land."

There is no island to the north.

Unless it be an island which no longer exists.

I began a systematic study of old maps relating to Cape Cod generally. There was no island, once in being, which could have fit the the description. The suspicious areas for such an island were limited. An island fitting the description could only lie to the north of Cape Cod or Cape Ann. And therein lay my first real inspiration. Cape Cod's shape is intriguing. It had the form of an extended arm, as though about to flex its muscles. The upper arm juts out from Buzzard's Bay and makes an abrupt turn at Chatham, becoming the forearm. At the tip of the forearm is the Provincetown area, frequently called the cape's "fist."

Could the fist have been an island once?

I found a weak spot in its topography.

Just below the fist of Cape Cod across Pilgrim Lake and Salt Meadow, the land lay extremely low. Could the lake and meadow once have been open water between the fist and the forearm of the cape?

I asked the question in a letter to L. W. Currier, then geologist-in-charge at the U. S. Geological Survey in Boston. He answered promptly:

"There are no data available to support the idea that within the history of man, the Provincetown area was an island to be connected later with land to the east, except that it appears *to have been temporarily cut off by high storm tides through Salt Meadow and Pilgrim Lake, so that some corrective measures were taken some years ago.*" (My italics)

I was moving in the right direction. The Follins Pond theory holds that Leif's island was Great Point, at the tip of Nantucket, which even today can be cut off from the main island after storms.

Now, it appeared, Provincetown, or the fist of the cape, formerly behaved as Great Point still does. And, because of its size, and its juxtaposition to the forearm of the cape, Provincetown could more reasonably be described as an *island* to the north of the land than could Great Point.

But the evidence still wasn't strong enough. If I could not recognize Great Point, which becomes an island *only* after high storm tides, then I could not accept Provincetown on that basis. No—the island of the saga had to be a permanent one, at least permanent during the times America was visited by the vikings. In exploring the cape area after settling for the winter, Leif and his men would surely have seen that Provincetown and the cape were one in good weather. They would therefore, as noted earlier, have called it "an island created by the tides" (or storm). The same reasoning applies to Great Point.

In theory, Provincetown could hold its own as the site of the first viking landing, but it still didn't fulfill completely the condition of the saga.

My letter to Mr. Currier was written in 1957. I had to wait nearly three years for the final evidence to turn up.

In the issue of April–July 1960, the Massachusetts Archaeological Society Bulletin published a paper by Dr. Rhodes W. Fairbridge, professor of Geology at Columbia University. In it, with an accompanying graph, he indicated that *the waters of the Atlantic were two to three feet higher 1000 years ago than they are today!*

I had the evidence.

I had found Leif's mysterious island.

If Provincetown's Salt Meadow and Pilgrim Lake were low enough in modern times to become one with the sea after high storm tides, then, with two to three feet of additional normal water in the ocean —1000 years ago—Provincetown *was* an island!

Add to the additional depth of water the abnormally high tides following a northeast storm, and the evidence is complete.

Provincetown, site of the Pilgrims' first landing in America, also appeared to have served as Leif Ericsson's point of arrival.

But I needed still more evidence.

The annoying word "sound" has to be explained.

"They went aboard their ship again and sailed into a certain sound, which lay between the island and a cape which jutted out from the land on the north—"

The only water to the west of Cape Cod is Cape Cod Bay, which under no circumstance can be construed to mean "sound." And the water between the forearm of the cape and Provincetown, through the meadow and the lake could only properly be called a channel. Where was I going to find the sound?

I found it when I realized that my next problem was not one of geography, but of semantics. In reading and rereading the sagas, and in probing the mysteries of Icelandic the better to understand them, I had fallen into the same trap as had all other translators of the Icelandic tales. The Icelandic word "sund" is used to describe the water the viking sailed into. Every translator who has attempted to unscramble the riddle of the vikings has taken the word to mean, literally, "sound," the word it so resembles in English.

Now I made a more thorough investigation of the meaning of the word. To my relief and delight, I discovered that it is also used to mean *channel,* or *passage,* and does not restrict its meaning to *"sound."* (It must be pointed out here that the Icelandic language has remained almost totally pure since its beginnings. The insular pride of the Icelander has prevented the intrusion of foreign words, and kept constant the meanings of many words in use a thousand years ago. The word *sund,* therefore, has the same meaning today as it did then: *sound,* or *passage,* or *channel.*) And the water between the fist and the forearm was a *channel.*

Thus far, my progress in interpreting the meaning of the saga was holding up. I had the island, I established the "sound." Now I had to find the river which "flowed down to the sea from [or through, or off] a lake."

But first, I had to determine why Leif sailed to the west of the cape. That was simple. Leif, coming into Provincetown in a northeaster, naturally steered around to the lee side of the island, presumably at the spot which is today the town's harbor. Behaving as any sailor would in strange country, he went up to the top of the highest elevation nearby, to reconnoiter. That would mean he ascended either 70-foot Telegraph Hill, just above the present harbor, or he may have gone over to the slightly higher ocean side dunes to look about. I favor Telegraph Hill. Its height has probably remained more constant than the height of the ever-changing dunes. From that vantage point he could easily see Manomet Hill, over on the mainland just below Plymouth. The saga states that the vikings went ashore in fine weather, meaning the day was clear following the storm. Their time of arrival can be fixed at early morning, perhaps shortly after dawn, because they tasted dew, sweeter than anything they had ever known.

Descending to the ship, Leif then "steered to the west of the cape," using Manomet Hill as his fix. His reasoning sent him west because the look of the land indicated mainland, and he knew that they were on an island, with possibly another island below them. He could not see the entire conformation of the cape on that first bright morning, so he steered to what he thought would be solid mainland.

But there was yet one more location to find. Where was his river which flowed into the sea from a lake? A study of topographic charts of the area west of Provincetown offers but one possible area.

Plymouth.

The place where the Pilgrims landed.

And it contains a river. And the river flows out of what was once a lake. The Pilgrims called it—their largest river—the Jones River. It empties into Duxbury Bay about two miles above Plymouth. Its bed is surrounded by marshland. One thousand years ago, according to the Fairbridge paper, these marshes, which even today are underwater after a storm, were not one, but a series of lakes!

Now I had the river and the lake.

But more research was necessary. The saga states that Leif left the island, sailed to the west and then went aground before he reached the river. Unable to contain themselves, the men took the afterboat and went up the river, found a secure anchorage, returned to the ship, and, when the tide had freed it, conveyed it up the river, anchored it, took their hammocks from the ship and built shelters.

That meant that Leif had to sail the 21 miles across Cape Cod Bay in a ship averaging four knots, go aground, perform an exploratory trip, return from it and get his ship upriver and to the anchorage, and build some sort of rude shelter for the night. He also had to see that a meal was prepared for the men. And all this had to be done in the course of about a 13-hour day. The time has been established by Pohl, in reckoning the approximate departure and arrival time of the vikings. The wild grapes found by the party were ripe, and that would indicate late September as his time of arrival, at which time day would last for about 13 hours.

Pohl proffered a timetable for Leif to sail from Great Point to the Bass River, up the river and back, etc., and managed to put it all into the confines of that day.

I could not agree, primarily because such a timetable left no time for exploring, a course which would have been mandatory.

I decided to re-enact the last leg of Leif's voyage according to my own conclusions—to get the "feel" of it, and to see what Leif's problems might have been from a point of actual happening.

My good friend, John Williams Streeter, then Historian of Science at Philadelphia's Franklin Institute, happened on the scene just as I decided I had to go over Leif's water route from Provincetown to Plymouth. I told him of my problem over a scotch-and-water at the Yale Club, in New York, in June. The fates were smiling. By August 6, 1960, we were aboard Streeter's magnificent sloop, the *Candida,* sailing out of Manchester, Massachusetts, headed for the open sea.

Also aboard as our third crewman, was Bernard Powell, a friend from Norwalk, Connecticut, who is an encyclopedia science editor and rabid part-time archaeologist. Our course from Manchester was due east, to a point 60 miles out on the ocean. From there we set our course at SSE, and I took the tiller of the *Candida,* steering from there by dead reckoning to Provincetown. We had timed our voyage so that we would arrive off Salt Meadow Beach around 3 A.M., leaving plenty of time to skirt the fist of the cape and take our departure from Race Point, west of Provincetown, just after dawn. These maneuvers were necessary since we couldn't sail through the "sound" which had once existed between Provincetown and the fist.

I steered through the night, with Vega at the tip of the mast, and later by running down the moon's track. We were on time. By 6 A.M. we were off Race Point, accompanied by three frivolous whales which accompanied us for about a half mile. Eventually, satisfied that we were not one of them, they sounded and disappeared.

Now Race Point fell away and I steered west, the clear bright morning showing me Manomet Hill, the same fix which Leif had used on his journey across Cape Cod Bay one thousand years before.

I could imagine the reactions of Leif as he steered his ship to the west in the quiet of the morning, his crew silent, waiting to see what this new land would bring. As he approached Manomet Point, he scanned the shore to the north and south of his fix, his appraisal quickly telling him he would find no shelter for his ship directly ahead, nor on the open, rocky shore to the south. To the north, however, he saw a break in the shore line limned out by the jutting finger of Gurnet point, thrust southward, not quite meeting the extended arm of Plymouth Beach which reaches north to within a mile of Gurnet, and its farther extension, Saquish Neck. On sighting Saquish and Gurnet, Leif altered his course to due west to sail between Saquish and Plymouth Beach.

At about the same point where Leif would have altered his course, I did the same aboard the *Candida*. Now we sailed toward Saquish and soon were entering the Cowyard. Somewhere beyond these two points—Saquish and Plymouth Beach—Leif ran into trouble. The saga says that "at ebb tide there were broad reaches of shallow water there, and they ran their ship aground there, and it was a long distance to the ship from the ocean . . ."

The location matched the saga. From the shallow waters in Plymouth Harbor, the distance across the partially enclosed waters of Cape Cod Bay to the open ocean beyond Cape Cod is about 21 nautical miles.

The purist in me demanded that I actually sail the course which I felt had been taken by Leif Ericsson on the last day of his voyage to America. The realist in me, however, reasoned that it was not necessary to run John Streeter's beautiful sloop, the *Candida*, into the mud and sand shallows off Plymouth. Accordingly, at 11:35 A.M., five and a half hours from Provincetown, we cast anchor in the channel opposite Cordage, about a mile and three quarters above Plymouth. We were now in the waters between Kingston Bay and Plymouth Harbor. Our journey from Race Point to Cordage channel had taken 5 hours and 33 minutes, averaging about 4 knots, or about the speed of Leif's ship. I chose the place to anchor as a possible place for Leif to go aground feeling that it would have been logical for the young viking to steer for the high ground now marked by Myles Standish's monument at Duxbury. It appeared to offer shelter. When Leif left his dragon ship to continue on that same direction, he found, to his surprise, a river flowing into Kingston Bay. Sailing into the river he saw that it widened into a lake, on the south bank of which he found a cove. He chose that cove in which to anchor after a comprehensive survey of the lake.

With the *Candida* securely moored, Powell and I rigged the boat's sailing dinghy, and, leaving Streeter aboard the big boat, sailed north to the Jones River. Like Leif, we first sailed toward the high ground, altering our course when we became aware of the river channel looming up on our port side.

The Jones River enters Kingston Bay to the east of a promontory called Rocky Nook Point. A few hundred yards south of the point, the river channel becomes surrounded by marshland and, as a boat proceeds upriver it is evident that the vast marsh was once under water. It has not lost its extremely clear perimeter at any point. About three quarters of a mile downstream the river channel turns abruptly to the west, the marsh edge narrows and then widens for another half mile to the northwest when the channel turns south, and continues in marshland for another half mile.

As the *Candida's* sailing dinghy slowly took Powell and me into the Jones River, around Rocky Nook Point, we could see the marsh spread out before us. At the moment, however, it was not the whole marsh I was interested in. I had spotted the cove mentioned above on the topographic charts I had studied. It was that cove I wanted to see.

An hour and twenty-five minutes after leaving the *Candida,* we lowered our sail opposite the tiny cove.

It was a perfect, sheltered anchorage for a shallow-draft ship.

Particularly a viking ship.

The marshes along the banks of the Jones River are as uninviting as any other marsh, and one sloshes, rather than walks through them. Powell and I accordingly sloshed across the boggy terrain to the cove. We examined the area thoroughly and spotted fresh water sources which were similar to those present a thousand years ago. We checked out all the rocks in the marsh, hoping against hope that one would produce a rune, or a symbol, or even the doubtful mooring hole in evidence on Follins Pond. Unhappily, we found nothing.

The cove is about two hundred yards wide and indents from the perimeter of the big marsh abruptly. The bank rises above it to a height of more than thirty feet, affording shelter from sea winds, particularly the southwest wind, which is the prevalent one of the area. It is nearly rectangular in shape.

In stating the case for the Jones River as the site of Leif Ericsson's first encampment in America, its advantages over Follins Pond must be examined. Had Leif gone up the Bass River into Follins Pond, he would have put himself in an awkward position strategically. A camp on the banks of an inland lake, five miles from open water, with only one exit would certainly not be advantageous to strangers in an alien and possibly hostile country. Such a camp would expose him to attack from 180 degrees by land, and a good-sized flotilla of enemy craft could easily have bottled him up in the lake. Even had he been able to escape such a flotilla and run down the river for the sea, he would have been vulnerable to continuing attack from the banks of the river as he fled to open water.

The Jones River site, however, would offer many advantages to a newly arrived viking band not yet educated to the nature of the country's inhabitants:

1. The cove was only a few hundred yards from the mouth of the river.
2. The promontory of Rocky Nook Point had, and has, fresh water sources.
3. The elevation above the cove provided shelter and a lookout station.
4. The promontory was then surrounded on three sides by water, making it easy to detect a waterborne attack party from a distance. That afforded plenty of time for the vikings to prepare a defense or run to the bay, where they could flee to the sea if outnumbered.

5. Rocky Nook Point was then connected to the mainland by a narrow strip of land. Attack from the land, therefore, could come from only one direction, making a viking defense infinitely easier.

Having inspected the viking cove, Powell and I returned to the dinghy and sailed back to the *Candida,* where Streeter had remained. We arrived at 3:58 P.M.

Now we had duplicated nearly all of the steps taken by the vikings on their last day out from Greenland. We had run to the land and entered a river which fell into the sea from a lake. Then we had spent an hour inspecting the cove site. The saga does not mention this facet of Leif's landing, but I hardly think it likely that less than an hour would have been spent in determining the advantages of the site.

The saga then relates that the vikings returned to their stranded ship, freed it and ". . . conveyed [it up] the river, and so into the lake, where they cast anchor . . ."

We did not attempt to take the *Candida* into the river. Tide was beginning to go out when we returned and, since *Candida* draws six feet of water, it seemed better not to risk it. But a simple timetable can establish the actions of the vikings for the balance of the day. It probably took them no more than an hour to get their ship back up to the river and anchor it. The remaining daylight hours were spent in removing gear from the ship, preparation of a meal and building temporary shelters.

The Follins Pond theorist established that Leif probably arrived here late in September when his length of day would have been about 13 hours. I think he is correct in that assumption. But in getting the vikings from Great Point, off Nantucket, to Follins Pond, nearly every minute of the day is accounted for, with little or no time for necessary exploration of the area to determine its desirability. My timetable was a bit easier for Leif:

6:02 A.M.	took departure from Race Point
11:35 A.M.	dropped anchor, Kingston Bay
12:01 P.M.	sailed, in dinghy, to Jones River
1:25 P.M.	arrived at Leif's cove
2:25 P.M.	departed cove
3:58 P.M.	arrived back at the *Candida*

Our "last leg" had consumed 9 hours and 56 minutes, *including* an hour's inspection of the cove. (Nearly an hour of that time should be subtracted because of the dinghy's slow pace.) Leif needed another hour to get his ship to the cove, leaving him two hours for shelter building, etc.

It was a slightly easier day for the vikings and gave them time to look about to some extent.

All the evidence pointed strongly toward the Jones River as the site of the first viking settlement in America.

But there was yet another point to be disposed of, in order to establish it fully. The thought of that mooring hole in Follins Pond kept gnawing at me. With water levels proved different 1000 years ago, could the hole have been cut at that time by a viking? Assuming, of course, that it was a genuine mooring hole.

I had to revisit it.

A week after my return from the cruise of the *Candida,* I packed up my camera and my wife and we went up to the cape. A borrowed boat quickly took us out to the skerry and I set about measuring the mooring hole's distance above the water.

Mooring holes were usually cut at from four to five feet above high water. That height allowed plenty of room for higher storm tides occurring periodically and reasonably guaranteed that the hole would never be under water.

Today, the Follins Pond mooring hole is hewn in the rock at 51 inches above low water. The pond has a tide of about 20 inches. But the paper by Dr. Fairbridge has established that the water level of the Atlantic was two to three feet higher 1000 years ago than it is today.

Using the conservative figure in Dr. Fairbridge's estimate and assuming that the water level was but *two* feet higher in 1003, then two feet added to present low water in the pond would place the mooring hole only 27 inches above low water. Add 20 inches more for tide rise and the hole stands only 7 inches above high water. That leaves no margin for storm tides and would render the hold unusable at various times. If the water level were actually *three* feet more at the time of Leif's visit, then the hole would have been under water at each tidal rise. I don't think Leif's men would have made such an error.

And I don't think the Follins Pond "mooring hole" can be considered substantial evidence of Leif Ericsson's presence here.

While it can thus be inferred that the mooring holes in Follins Pond and along the Bass River were not cut by Leif, their very presence might still be admissible as evidence, but I feel that they were cut by a later expedition: that of Paul Knutson, who came to America in 1355. (His story is told in Chapter 17.) He was on an exploratory voyage and would have probed every river and lake he came upon because he was searching for the lost Vinland colony. At the time of his arrival, the Atlantic had begun to recede again, and the waters, during the fourteenth century, were about two feet *lower* than they are today.

Having retraced the last stage of Leif Ericsson's voyage to America, and determined that the mooring hole evidence could not be applied to him, I returned to Rocky Nook, this time with my nine-year-old son Christopher as my field assistant, and we prepared to comb the narrow strip of land where I thought Leif had landed. We were stopped with a jolt on the morning of the first day out.

In progress, at Rocky Nook, we found an archaeological dig sponsored by the Pilgrim John Howland Society. I had known nothing about it and stumbled into it quite by accident. When Christopher and I arrived on the scene, the dig was coming to a close, the excavations being filled. We engaged one of the archaeologists in conversation. He described the dig to us and told us what had come of it. We chatted for about an hour, and Chris was permitted to sieve a few handfuls of dirt from a site not yet covered, which investigation supplied him with a number of nails and buttons. As we were preparing to leave, the archaeologist made an observation which caused me to ask further questions about the site.

The expedition had, it seemed, discovered a substructure under the foundation of the house they believed to have been built by John Howland. All present at the time of its discovery were puzzled by it, and no explanation was forthcoming. The discovery of the substructure had occurred during a dig of the previous summer. In a report issued by the society in its publication *The Howland Quarterly*, James Deetz, who was in charge of the dig at Rocky Nook, refers to it thusly:

> There is actual architectural superimposition. The hearth of the later house (dated from about 1638) rests upon a wall, but is separated from

this wall by four inches of disturbed soil. This is indicative of reconstruction upon an earlier foundation.

The report containing the above information was dated January–April, 1960. A later report, issued in June 1960, indicates that the substructure was merely that of an earlier house built by Howland. That there is still some mystery apparent to Deetz is seen in his second report, summary, and conclusions:

> Additional excavation is planned . . . in the area surrounding the hearth of Structure 3, in an attempt to clarify further details of the relationship between Structures 3 and 2.

Structure No. 2 is the mysterious foundation.

I wonder.

The site of all of the foundations at Rocky Nook is on the rise overlooking the cove where I feel Leif Ericsson made his first landing in America. It represents a logical choice for a camp. Is it possible that this was the site of Leif's Shelters? And is it possible that John Howland, in the seventeenth century, investigating the land out on Rocky Nook, came upon their old foundations and utilized the stones and partially excavated cellar for himself?

It is not inconceivable at all.

As noted earlier in this volume, it is common in archaeology to find more than one human habitation on a single site, with great time lapses in between.

I believe it is entirely reasonable to enter into the conjecture that the Howland site, on Howland's Lane in Rocky Nook, in the town of Kingston, Massachusetts, may be the original site of Leif's Shelters. The two digs which have already taken place during the summers of 1959 and 1960 have contributed greatly to knowledge of the Howlands and, as Mr. Deetz declares, to the seventeenth century generally. In that event, I would think it beneficial to invite one of the members of the Danish Greenland expeditions which have been investigating the site of Eric the Red's settlement in that country to participate in the dig. The presence of an archaeologist familiar with Icelandic buildings would certainly go a long way toward determining whether there were any evidence of Leif Ericsson and his crew at Rocky Nook.

I have a suspicion that more than one person connected with the Pilgrim John Howland Society might have reflected upon the earlier origins of the Howland site. The society has reconstructed Howland House in Plymouth, and it is open to the public. It is a masterful reconstruction, fully furnished and overflowing with colonial charm and atmosphere. The pleasant ladies who serve as guides and hostesses are dressed in Pilgrim costumes and are most gracious in recounting the history of Howland House and its ancient occupants. All about are colonial implements and tools used by the Howlands, or people of their period.

There is one implement, however, which is hidden away, and can only be seen on request. And one must be specific in requesting the object if one should want to see it. One must ask for the "old Norse ax." To find something labeled—and considered as—an old Norse ax is indeed unusual in a museum with the colonial motif of the Howlands. Yet, there it is. An "old Norse ax," available to be seen only if one should ask to see it. I asked one of the charming ladies why the ax was kept in a closet, to which she replied:

"Well, it's a Norse ax, and we only display colonial things here."

A logical answer.

But several points disturb me. If it's a Norse ax, why is it kept at Howland House? Who, exactly, thinks it's a Norse ax, and is either so strongly convinced that it *is*, or is so undecided about its origin that it must be hidden away?

I may have some of the answers.

According to Mrs. W. Russell Greenwood, secretary-treasurer of the Pilgrim John Howland Society, the ax was dug from the site of John Howland's house at Rocky Nook, by Sidney Strickland in 1939. It is easy to label the ax an English broadax, since it came from the Howland house site. But the remarkable thing about the ax is that it is almost a twin of a medieval Norse ax found at Cole Harbour, in Nova Scotia. The greatest point of similarity between the two is in a series of semicircular markings on the faces of the axes which are thought to be either "secret" runes or perhaps some mark of ownership. The axes are indeed startlingly alike.

One was found in Nova Scotia and has been identified as Norse.

The other was found in Rocky Nook, at the site of the John Howland House. Is it Norse, or is it English? If it is English, why is it hidden away from public inspection? Obviously, the ax at Plymouth needs further examination. I would suggest a metallurgical test to determine the microstructure of the ax's metal, risking the circumstance which might put it beyond the NEBC Principle.

Unfortunately there is no test to verify my last piece of evidence suggesting that Leif Ericsson came to Rocky Nook and there built his house or Shelters. It is still under study, and I have submitted it to the people in the field whom I feel most qualified to render opinions. The opinions thus far are all unrevealing, and no conclusion can be reached. It will take time. The Roman head took twenty years for documentation.

The evidence lies in a small sandstone head, found in the town of Manomet, by twelve-year-old Joseph Notini, on May 14, 1959. The head is unfinished and is about eight inches high. The nose forms a straight bridge from forehead to lips, which latter are slightly reminiscent of old Danish heads, particularly those found on the famous Gundstrup Cauldron. At some point in the carver's endeavor, he dropped it and chipped a large chunk out of the upper forehead and temple. Deeming it spoiled, he threw it away, presumably to begin carving a new one.

When young Joseph found the rock, he picked it up because its cylindrical shape appealed to him. It was not until he got it home and cleaned the encrusted dirt from it that he discovered that it bore a head. Pleased and surprised, he showed it to his mother and father. They were puzzled, and thought it might be some kind of Indian effigy. They submitted a photograph of it to Mr. James Deetz, the archaeologist who supervised the dig at Howland House. Mr. Deetz's first reaction to the effigy was that it might be Norse. Mrs. Notini informs me since that he has retracted this statement.

A photograph of the head was then sent to the Smithsonian. Dr. Frank Roberts said that those who saw it at the Smithsonian agreed that it could not be Indian in origin. He then suggested that Mrs. Notini submit it to Peabody Museum at Harvard. It was sent, instead, to William Fowler, at the Bronson Museum in Attleboro, Massachusetts. He said it couldn't possibly have been made by the aboriginals of New England and thought it might have been imported from the South Seas by some ancient Plymouth sea captain.

Mrs. Notini sent me a photograph of the head in September of 1960 and asked whether I might know what it was. I had my suspicions, but preferred to ask those in the field what they thought it was.

At the American Museum, I received a flat "I don't know." One archaeologist there told me that the piece was finished; the carver would not have carried it any farther. My own background in art told me his opinion was incorrect. I next sent the head to Dr. Hugh Hencken, who told me he thought it was simply something carved by a resident of Plymouth.

It is still, as I have indicated, under study.

I think it was carved by some nameless Norseman.

While it was found in Manomet, later developments proved that it had actually come from the town of Plymouth, from a location about two miles from Rocky Nook. The head was scooped from a fill deposit off Route 44 and transported to Manomet, some ten miles to the south, where Joseph Notini found it.

The search for a prototype has seemingly proved fruitless, but there are a number of similarities which can be dwelt upon. The head has a decidedly Celtic look to it, and the Celtic influence was most profound upon Scandinavian art for many hundreds of years, including the time under discussion: A.D. 1000.

I have already noted its similarity to the head on the Gundstrup Cauldron, a resemblance which was also noted, independently, by the Notini family. It also looks remarkably like the small heads carved on the Oseberg Cart, a vehicle discovered aboard an ancient viking ship, dug from the blue clay deposits at Oseberg, along the Oslo Fjord. The Notini head shows that the carver intended to place a vikinglike helmet on the finished product, a helmet remarkably like that worn by the Oseberg head.

At the moment, I don't know, and can't say, what the Notini effigy really is. I do know one thing, however: considering the NEBC Principle, it may take quite some time to identify it with any hope of acceptance. The experts have said no Indian made it. They also decline to give any positive opinion. But it exists. And it was found in Manomet, Massachusetts, by a boy who liked to collect rocks. He thought it was Indian. The experts disagree.

In summary, it would appear that there is more than one piece of evidence pointing to Kingston, Massachusetts, and specifically the place called Rocky Nook Point as the site of Leif Ericsson's Shelters in America.

It can only be hoped that further excavations and more serious study of the area by qualified archaeologists will help determine whether the evidence is valid.

Leif's visit was brief, being of but one winter's duration. He returned to Greenland, but there dwelt within his breast the hope that he would one day return to Rocky Nook to live. That hope was never to be fulfilled. He remained in Greenland. But other vikings came to see this new land he had found.

The next one down from Greenland was his younger brother, Thorvald, who did stay, but not in the manner in which he had planned.

CHAPTER 11

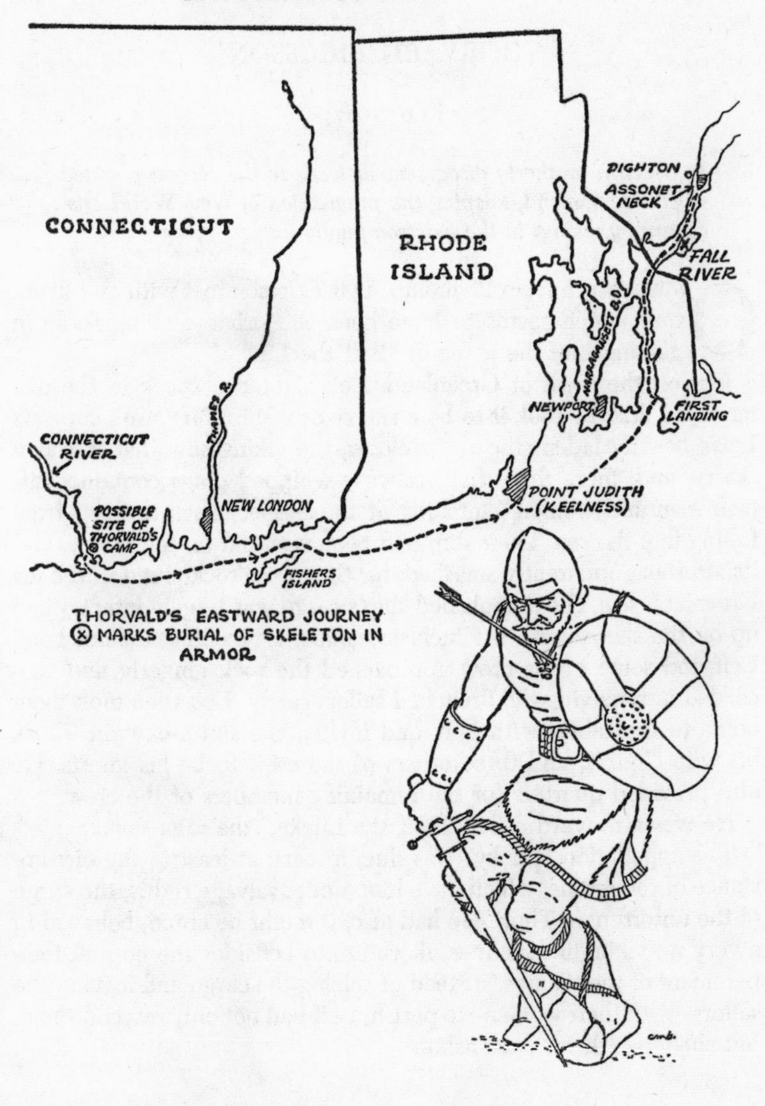
MASSACHUSETTS
CONNECTICUT
RHODE ISLAND
DIGHTON
ASSONET NECK
FALL RIVER
NARRAGANSETT B.
NEWPORT
FIRST LANDING
THAMES R.
CONNECTICUT RIVER
POSSIBLE SITE OF THORVALD'S CAMP
NEW LONDON
POINT JUDITH (KEELNESS)
FISHERS ISLAND
THORVALD'S EASTWARD JOURNEY
⊗ MARKS BURIAL OF SKELETON IN ARMOR
cmb.

Chapter 11

THORVALD ERICSSON

[A.D. 1007]

In which a brotherly disagreement leads to the second planned voyage to Vinland, keeping the progression of New World Discovery by vikings in the Ericsson family.

ON HIS return from Plymouth, Leif Ericsson met with an adventure which seems to have been the prime moving force in gaining him the name of "Leif the Lucky."

Just off the coast of Greenland, Leif sighted a speck in the distance. At first, he took it to be a skerry or a ship; he wasn't sure. As Leif's heavily laden ship drew closer, the viking saw that it was a skerry, and, more than that, its wave-whipped crags contained fifteen men and women, clutching at the slippery rock to keep from falling into the sea. Their ship had been wrecked on the skerry, and its afterboat apparently smashed, for they were rockbound in the icy Greenland sea. The demolished ship's cargo was largely intact, piled up on the skerry with the luckless sailors. Launching a small boat, Leif and some of his crew approached the rock gingerly and succeeded in removing the drenched sailors safely. Leif then took them home to Brattahlid with him, and invited the ship's captain Thori, his wife Gudrid, and three others of the crew to be his guests. He also provided quarters for the remaining members of the crew.

He was afterward called "Leif the Lucky," the saga states.

The appellation "Lucky" was due, in part, at least to the circumstance of the rescue, which gave him, under salvage rights, the cargo of the unfortunate Thori. He had also, it might be noted, behaved in a very un-vikinglike manner, if we are to consider the normal temperament of the vikings. Instead of seizing the cargo and leaving the sailors—with their women—to perish, Leif had not only rescued them, but sheltered them, once ashore.

The saga adds: "Leif had now goodly store both of property and honor."

The excitement of the discussions of Leif's new-found land swept through the tiny settlement, and it is evident, from later references in the sagas, that Leif was quietly making plans to return to Vinland the Good as soon as he could, to settle there. But his plans were never to come to fruition. Sickness came to the Greenland colony, and Thori and many of his crew died, casting gloom over the colony.

The greatest gloom, however, came on the death of Eric the Red. As the colony mourned, Leif realized that he would have to delay his return to Vinland, for now he must assume leadership of the Greenland settlement. As fate dictated, Leif never saw Vinland again.

The discussions on Vinland continued, and it appears that Leif was not the only one nurturing plans about the new land. His younger brother Thorvald had been engrossed with thoughts of his own, and, in the words of the saga:

". . . Thorvald held that the country had not been sufficiently explored."

With a possible hint of sibling rivalry, Thorvald's complaint may have been his way of minimizing the importance of his big brother's voyage. Thorvald, however, was right in his thought. Leif, admittedly, had not permitted his men to venture farther from the shelters than a distance from which they could return the same day. Probing of the new land had certainly been limited. In all probability, the two brothers discussed the idea of further exploration at great length, with Thorvald ultimately deciding that he must go to Vinland himself.

"If it be thy will, brother," Leif agreed, "thou mayest go to Vinland with my ship, but I wish the ship first to fetch the wood, which Thori had upon the skerry."

And so it was done.

Here is the saga of Thorvald Ericsson, brother of Leif, and his voyage of exploration to America in A.D. 1007—the second planned voyage to the New World:

Now Thorvald, with the advice of his brother, Leif, prepared to make this voyage with thirty men. They put their ship in order, and sailed out to sea; and there is no account of their voyage before their arrival at Leif's booths in Wineland. They laid up their ship there, and remained there quietly during the winter, supplying themselves with food by fishing. In the spring, however, Thorvald said that they should put their ship in order, and that a few men should take the afterboat, and proceed along the western coast, and explore [the region] thereabouts during the summer. They found it a fair, well-wooded country; it was but a short distance from the woods to the sea, and [there were] white sands, as well as great numbers of islands and shallows. They found neither dwelling of man nor lair of beast; but in one of the westerly islands, they found a wooden building for the shelter of grain. They found no other trace of human handiwork, and they turned back, and arrived at Leif's booths in the autumn. The following summer Thorvald set out toward the east with the ship, and along the northern coast. They were met by a high wind off a certain promontory, and were driven ashore there, and damaged the keel of their ship, and were compelled to remain there for a long time and repair the injury to their vessel. Then said Thorvald to his companions: 'I propose that we raise the keel upon this cape, and call it Keelness,' and so they did. Then they sailed away, to the eastward off the land, and into the mouth of the adjoining firth, and to a headland which projected into the sea there, and which was entirely covered with woods. They found an anchorage for their ship, and put out the gangway to land, and Thorvald and all of his companions went ashore. 'It is a fair region here,' said he, 'and here I should like to make my home. They then returned to the ship, and discovered on the sands, in beyond the headland, three mounds; they went up to these, and saw that they were three skin canoes, with three men under each. They thereupon divided their party, and succeeded in seizing all of the men but one, who escaped with his canoe. They killed the eight men, and then ascended the headland again, and looked about them, and discovered within the firth certain hillocks, which they concluded must be habitations. They were then so overpowered with sleep that they could not keep awake, and all fell into a [heavy] slumber, from which they were awakened by the sound of a cry uttered above them; and the words of the cry were these: 'Awake, Thorvald, thou and all thy company, if thou wouldst save thy life; and board thy ship with all thy men, and sail with all speed from the land!' A countless number of skin canoes then advanced toward them from the inner part of the firth, whereupon Thorvald exclaimed: 'We must put out the war-boards, on both sides of the ship, and defend ourselves to the best of our ability, but offer little attack.' This they did, and the Scraelings, [Indians] after they had shot at them for a time, fled precipitately, each as best he could. Thorvald then inquired of his men, whether any of them had been wounded, and they informed him that no one of them had received a wound. 'I have been wounded in my arm-pit' says he; 'an arrow flew in between the gunwale and the shield, below my arm. Here is the shaft, and it will bring me to my end! I counsel you now to retrace your way with the utmost speed. But me ye shall convey to that headland which seemed to me to offer so pleasant a dwelling-place; thus it may be fulfilled, that the truth sprang to my lips, when I expressed the wish to abide there for a time. Ye shall bury me there, and place a cross at my head, and another at my feet, and call it Crossness for ever after.' At that time Christianity had obtained in Greenland; Eric the Red died, however, before [the introduction of] Christianity. Thorvald died, and when they had carried out his injunctions, they took their departure, and rejoined their companions, and they told each other of the experiences which had befallen them. They remained there during the winter, and gathered grapes and wood with which to freight the ship. In the following spring they returned to Greenland, and arrived with their ship in Ericsfirth, where they were able to recount great tidings to Leif.

And that is how it was with Thorvald.

He died in the new land, after noting that his wish to abide there was being granted swiftly, and in most unforeseen manner. His death was the first of three tragedies visited upon Leif's two brothers and his half-sister. The capricious fate which doled grief to his siblings spared Leif; another demonstration that he was, indeed, "the Lucky." Or was he? Subsequent events demonstrate that neither Leif, nor any member of his family, or for that matter, *any* viking was to benefit greatly from the land which already held many Icelanders prisoner.

Speculation on the extent and specific regions of Thorvald's explorations has naturally received the same amount of application by scholars as that given Leif. Thorvald has been placed in the St. Lawrence, in Nova Scotia, the coast of southern New England, and other places. In offering still more speculation, I will join those who place the luckless viking in southern New England to start. From his base of operations there (and I don't believe he ever went to Leif's Shelters), he sent an exploring party west, and later made an extremely limited voyage east himself.

First, I must stress that this version of the Thorvald saga is that which appears in the *Flateybook*. A much briefer version appears in the *Hauk's Book* saga of Thorfinn Karlsefni. In the latter version, Thorvald is said to have accompanied Karlsefni on an expedition to find one Thorhall, missing from Karlsefni's party. While somewhere to the north of Karlsefni's base, Thorvald is shot by a Uniped, who escapes. As a result of the viking's death, the others conclude that they are near Unipedland. Since the circumstance of Thorvald's demise, and its insertion almost as an afterthought, seem inconsistent with the main thread of Karlsefni's story, I will take the liberty of assuming that the *Flateybook* version is the correct one. As many scholars have pointed out, it is substantial, whereas the Karlsefni insertion is not.

The *Flateybook* saga contains at least one glaring inconsistency in its reference to the death of Eric the Red *before* Christianity came to Greenland. In Leif's saga it states as clearly that Eric died on Leif's return. Since Leif brought Catholicism to Greenland in 1001, a contradiction exists. This, and other inconsistencies, existing among so many known facts as put forth in the sagas, serves again to illustrate the conjecture that the author of *Hauk's Book*, and the transcribers of Vellum 557 and the *Flateybook* used the same common, accurate source, drawing from them whatever they considered important—but confusing minor details in the process. To Hauk—and to the author of No. 557—Thorvald was not an important figure, being a Greenlander. He achieves much more importance in the *Flateybook*, because he *was* a Greenlander. There is another element to be found in the saga of Thorfinn Karlsefni which I feel strongly was borrowed from the original story of Thorvald, just as the reference to absence of snow in Leif's saga was probably borrowed from Karlsefni's saga. We will pursue this element in due course.

Returning to the explorations of Leif's explorer brother, we will consider first the "arrival at Leif's booths." Careful study of the explorations authorized by and pursued by Thorvald, and of the descriptives concerning these travels precludes the use of Leif's booths at Jones River as a base for Thorvald. I would place his camp in the Connecticut or Thames rivers, further analysis demonstrating why.

The saga tells us that Thorvald sent the afterboat on an exploring trip to the west. The men participating in this excursion found "neither dwelling of man nor lair of beast; but in one of the westerly islands, they found a wooden building for the shelter of grain." The designations "west" and "westerly" can only mean that the coast from which the journey departed was one which faced south. On this point I am in agreement with Gathorne-Hardy and with Pohl, but for different reasons. I am also in agreement on the incident of the "wooden barn," which can only have been an Indian corncrib. Gathorne-Hardy suggests that it might also have been a deserted wigwam. Hardly. Since they were on a journey of exploration and investigation, they undoubtedly inspected the structure carefully. The presence of corn is noted in the reference to "storing grain."

I must now, however, leave the two gentlemen noted above, and their excellent theories, while I propose still another; one which I sincerely trust, will offer a sounder interpretation of the explorations of Thorvald. Before I bid them adieu, I will quickly summarize their thoughts: Gathorne-Hardy would have Thorvald, after sending his afterboat to the west, sail east and north, sailing around Provincetown. On Cape Cod, the keel was damaged, and repaired, after which the ship sailed into the Pamet River, where Thorvald was killed. A bit weak, since the saga says that after the keel was repaired, they sailed "to the eastward off the land." To reach the Pamet River from any point on the forearm of Cape Cod they would have had to sail north, or south, or west. But not east. Pohl also places the shipwreck on Cape Cod, but has them sailing to Maine after the damage to the ship, despite the precision with which the saga states that they sailed eastward, and into the mouth of the *adjoining* firth (or fjord). Untenable.

Here is what I think happened:

Thorvald sailed down to the Cape Cod region, but continued on past it. He had no intention of founding his colony at the place where Leif had dwelled. When he had sailed for another day or so, he began to search for a suitable campsite. I am inclined to feel that he found it at the Connecticut River. Its many snug coves near its mouth would have made it a logical choice. The Thames offers similar advantages, but he may have missed it altogether had he skirted Fishers Island to the south. Assuming, then, a camp established somewhere along the Connecticut River, I will attempt to follow Thorvald's examination of Vinland.

First, he selected several crewmen and dispatched them to the west, in the afterboat. The "westerly islands" referred to are many, and dot the coast from the Thimbles, off Stony Creek in southern Connecticut, to the islands found in the western portion of Long Island Sound between Long Island proper and New York. Had they gone as far, for instance, as Rikers Island before turning back, it is logical to assume that they came back along the North Shore of Long Island, crossing the sound to their camp when they reached, and circumnavigated Plum Island. The voyage consumed the entire summer; they returned in the autumn. Nothing is said of the events of the following winter, but when summer came, Thorvald decided to lead the next expedition himself, and so it was decided that they would "sail toward the east with the ship, and along the northern coast. The direction "east," indicates where they were going; the descriptive "along the northern coast," again bears out the knowledge that they were sailing along a coast facing south.

Now we come to the most pertinent clue: the damaged ship blown onto a promontory, its repair, and how they sailed into an adjoining fjord. Once again, related geographical points must be established, as they had to in the maddening pursuit of Leif's "island to the north of the land" and its nearby river flowing down, from, or through a lake.

The vikings were compelled to remain on the promontory for a long time in order to repair their ship. When the ship had been fitted with a new keel, Thorvald proposed that they set the old one up, as a sort of memorial, and call the place "Keelness," or "Cape of the Keel."

And so they did.

Now ". . . they sailed away, to the eastward off the land, and into the mouth of the adjoining firth [fjord], and to a headland, which projected into the sea there, and which was entirely covered with woods."

Both Pohl and Gathorne-Hardy placed the scene of the damaged keel on Cape Cod, partially because Thorfinn Karlsefni, on a later expedition, is said to have found a keel upon a cape, and called the place "Keelness." I don't believe Karlsefni ever found a keel anywhere. I think the keel sequence in Thorfinn's saga is borrowed from Thorvald's saga, in that curious admixture of "interchangeable" incidents occurring in the sagas. Pohl then takes Thorvald's expedition all the way to Maine, to find their fjord on Mount Desert Island. But Thorvald's saga clearly states that they sailed into an *adjoining* fjord. Mount Desert Island is about 200 miles from Provincetown, on Cape Cod. Not too adjoining. Gathorne-Hardy has them sail into the Pamet River after repairing the damage, but, again as clearly, the saga states that they sailed "to the eastward off the land."

If the ship had been blown ashore on the east side of Cape Cod, they would have had to sail north and west and southeast to reach the Pamet. If the accident occurred on the west side of the cape, they would have had to sail south and then east. But the saga is specific. It says they sailed *eastward*.

Being unable to accept any of the theories concerning Thorvald, and excluding completely those which placed him in northerly regions such as Nova Scotia or the St. Lawrence, I set about finding a promontory which lay next to a fjord, and which would exist on the southern shore of New England. A bloc, similar to the one which delayed my finding Leif's mysterious island for so long, existed in my pursuit of the promontory and fjord. I was misled by the word *fjord*, again taking it in its literal meaning, as I had the word *sund*. Douglas W. Johnson's *The New England Acadian Shoreline*, a comprehensive geological study of the area in question, insists that only two true fjords exist on the Atlantic coast: the Hudson River region and Somes Sound, on Mount Desert Island. If that were true, then Pohl was right, but how could I reconcile the knowledge that Somes Sound and Provincetown are 200 miles apart? If I discarded Pohl's theory and settled for the Hudson as the fjord in question, it wouldn't make any better sense. If it had been the Hudson, then Thorvald's camp would have had to be to the west of it. Impossible, because the New Jersey coast, which abuts the mouth of the Hudson, extends *southward*, thus rendering *westward* exploration inconceivable.

It couldn't be either, but where was I going to find a fjord, if not in the Hudson, or at Mount Desert? A fjord is a sunken glacial trough created by the erosive action of ice occupying pre-existing river valleys. It is also considered to be a long arm of the sea, surrounded by high banks or cliffs. I began to wonder whether the vikings knew the geological definition of a fjord, or whether they might term any river surrounded by even relatively low banks a fjord, simply because it resembled a fjord. Since it was highly improbable that any of the vikings in Thorvald's party were geologists, I could rule out the submerged glacial valley definition. I would have to settle on finding a river, or delta, perhaps, that might cause a viking to call it a fjord, as opposed to merely a river. And I found it.

It was Narragansett Bay.

And the promontory was Point Judith.

Point Judith is the only point along the southern New England coast from which one can sail *eastward* into an adjoining body of water resembling a fjord. Thorvald, then, repaired his ship on Point Judith, and sailed to the east, skirting Beaver Neck and Aquidneck, and turning north into the Sakonnet River. The headland which ends at Sakonnet Point was that which attracted him. He landed at Church Point, High Hill or Fogland, where the waters are deep enough to permit a gangplank landing, as opposed to mooring and going ashore in the afterboat.

Once ashore, Thorvald was pleased with what he saw.

"It is a fair region here," said he, "and here I should like to make my home."

After some investigation of the headland, he returned to the ship and steered it farther into the Sakonnet River and north to Assonet Neck, which lies at the confluence of the Taunton and Assonet rivers. It was there that the vikings sighted the three skin canoes, each with three men under them, presumably asleep. For some unexplainable reason, Thorvald killed all but one, who escaped in his canoe. The seemingly unnecessary slaughter might be explained by surmising that the seized Indians put up a fight. Perhaps Thorvald intended only to attempt communication with them, and they resisted, which circumstance led to their untimely deaths. But we can only conjecture. The slaying of the Indians was, as later events prove, a regrettable act on Thorvald's part.

Now I must offer a most intriguing thought concerning events which followed. The saga relates that the vikings then ascended the headland above the sands where they found the men under the canoes. The passage states that "they ascended the headland again," implying that they returned to their first landing place. But Thorvald's dying instructions negate such a return; he instructed his men to take him back to the headland he had thought "so fair," to bury him. The passage can only mean they ascended a headland above the site of the killings. There they "discovered within the firth certain hillocks which they concluded must be habitations."

I detect here a trace of one of the mission outposts of Great Ireland. The habitations described are referred to as "hillocks," not as wooden buildings, or tents, or wooden dwellings, or houses. They are described as hillocks—implying that they might have been partially underground. It is entirely possible that Thorvald had stumbled into a mission peopled by Irish-Icelander-Indians. Thorvald's journey to the east took place in 1007. Twenty-two years had passed since the first Icelanders were added to the Irish colony at North Salem; twenty-one since the greater influx of castaway Greenlanders. There had been adequate time for not only the establishment of a mission as far south as Aquidneck, but also to produce a new, mixed generation. It is also entirely possible that the mission population knew of Thorvald's difficulty with his ship; perhaps they had even observed the repair of the vessel from a safe and undetectable distance. All of this was duly reported to the monks in charge of the outpost. The monks, now grown older, and mellower, and remembering that they had once assaulted peaceable vikings, decided to take no action until Thorvald's ship was once again afloat, at which time they would know whether he intended to sail near the colony, in which case he would have to be taken, or whether he would glide past the colony, presumably to return to Greenland. Perhaps the old Icelanders at the outpost had prevailed upon the monks to defer action. It is entirely conceivable that they had, on one of their spying sorties on Thorvald's Point Judith camp, learned his identity, or even recognized him, by noting a resemblance to Eric the Red.

I venture to re-create such a possibility because the next passage has within it all the elements of bafflement. The vikings were awakened by a shout from above them: "Awake, Thorvald, thou and all thy company, if thou wouldst save thy life; and board thy ship with all thy men, and sail with all speed from the land!"

Such a cry is a cry of warning more apt to be delivered by one not about to take part in the departure he is urging so strongly. A spectator, perhaps. An expatriate Icelander? Why not? Had the cry come from a sentry, he would doubtless have limited his cry to a single word, "Scraelings!" and forthwith joined the others in readying swords and shields for the battle. Following his single-word warning, he would have used the Greenland equivalent of "Let's go!" or "Now we're in for it!" or "To arms!" I doubt very seriously that a viking sentry would shout out a warning to flee. No right-minded viking ever ran from a potentially good fight. That is borne out in Thorvald's immediate reaction. He did not attempt to flee, but ordered his men to make ready a defense.

I think the voice of warning belonged to an Icelander, now indoctrinated in the ways of the monks, but still concerned enough about people of his own kind to try to warn them off. The saga says "*all* fell into a heavy slumber," indicating that the posted sentry was among the sleepers.

(William B. Goodwin, the gentleman from North Salem, was inclined to attribute the mysterious voice to an Icelander also. I am in concurrence, but, as in the cases of others who have delved into the viking puzzle, I disagree with Goodwin's placement of Leif and other vikings along the Penobscot River. The topography just doesn't fit.)

Thorvald sprang into action at once. He commanded that the warboards be put out and a defense offered against the great number of "skin canoes" advancing upon them from the inner firth, possibly the Assonet River. No description of the battle is proffered, nor any account of casualties inflicted upon the Indians. The viking crew escaped unharmed—all but their leader.

Thorvald had been mortally wounded.

With wry humor, he commanded his men to take him back to the headland he thought so fair, reflecting that the truth had, indeed, sprung from his lips when he expressed a desire to abide there for a time. And Thorvald died.

The vikings executed his command. They immediately rowed downriver until they came to the site where Fall River is located today. There, where the Taunton River pours into Mount Hope Bay, was the beginning of the headland which extended down to Sakonnet Point. At the very first suitable landing place, they took his body ashore and buried it, reasonably secure in the knowledge that the routed scraelings were distant enough to preclude another attack during the burial service. It is highly probable that some sort of Catholic burial service was read, or spoken, since Thorvald was a Catholic, and he had instructed that his burial place be marked by a cross at his head and at his feet. The saddened vikings, on marking the grave, then returned to their ship and sailed back to their camp on the Connecticut River.

And that is how Thorvald died, and was buried.

Now I will tell you about the circumstances relating to his disinterment, 824 years later, and how he was mistaken for an Indian wearing English ornaments, and how Carl Christian Rafn properly identified his body and was ridiculed for it.

In 1831, the skeleton of a man was dug up at the corner of what is now Fifth and Hartley Streets, in the town of Fall River. The remarkable aspect of this male skeleton was that it was adorned with metal ornaments, none of which were readily identifiable. Much speculation was offered by the newspapers of the day, and it was finally decided that the skeleton was that of a dead viking. Now discussion of the skeleton reached fever pitch, and inspired Henry Wadsworth Longfellow to write a poem titled "The Skeleton in Armor." A tale of love, the poem dwells on the viking in armor and recounts his amorous adventures with a beautiful lady, for whom he builds a "bower," in Newport. The "bower" is, of course, the Newport Tower, or Old Stone Mill, which we will examine in a later chapter. The poem created a sensation and did much to substantiate the idea that the skeleton was truly a viking.

But our astute historians knew full well that such a preposterous thought must not be permitted to shake the structure of our tightly knit colonial history. If one permitted the encroachment of a viking savage as a forerunner of the Pilgrims, who knew where it might lead? Further cause for alarm was precipitated when, in 1839, Carl Christian Rafn, the erudite archaeologist from Copenhagen, published the second edition of his *Antiquitates Americanae,* and stated that the skeleton was the body of Thorvald Ericsson, and that the Newport Tower had been built by one Eric Gnupsson, a bishop dispatched in the twelfth century to find, and minister to, the Lost Colony of Vinland. The public took to Rafn's pronouncements enthusiastically, but a lugubrious air hung over the historians. Something must be done to stop it. A most fortuitous circumstance provided hope for the historians in 1843. A great fire swept through the city of Fall River, where the wretched skeleton was housed, and it was destroyed. But the ornaments he wore were not. Some of them had been sent to the Royal Ethnological Museum in Copenhagen, some found a home at the Peabody Museum at Harvard, and, according to Miss Constance Winslow, curator of the Massachusetts Historical Society at Fall River, two little ¼ inch metal rings from the skeleton stayed in Fall River.

But the destruction of the skeleton and rapid dispersal of his personal possessions did not stop acceptance by the public that it was Norse. Then, about 1886, Dr. Samuel Kneeland wrote a paper in which he surmised that the brass tubes found with the remains of the skeleton were parts of a belt. The article was appropriated and republished, in part, in the Twentieth Annual Report of the Peabody Museum in 1887. Philip Means, in his *The Newport Tower*, refers to the intelligence noted above, and adds that in the Peabody report, it is revealed that the brassy character of the material proved it to be English. (Prior to this evaluation—apparently by some chemical means—the material was thought to be of bronze or iron, and therefore Norse.) With that pronouncement, the case was considered closed—the NEBC Principle unshaken.

No one had bothered to comment on the skeleton, since it had long since been destroyed, but the pronouncement of the deans of the Brass and Bronze Department at Peabody had concluded that the items were English. Finis. Means then adds that he had been assured by no less a distinguished anthropologist than Dr. C. C. Willoughby that the skeleton was that of a proto-historic Wampanoag Indian. Dr. Willoughby's identification was made in 1938. It had been 95 years since the skeleton was last seen. That provided a remarkably comfortable distance in time to identify a nonexistent skeleton.

When I encounter situations of this sort I become vaguely uneasy. By what, or whose, rules is our history laid down? What highly malleable law permits the evaluation of a nonexistent skeleton, vanished for 95 years, as a Wampanoag Indian? Is it the same law which permits the inspection of an *existent* artifact, say a Norse ax found in Minnesota, and then, incredibly, permits the denial of its authenticity? I am puzzled.

But let us return to the unfortunate skeleton for a moment. Even though the public leaned toward the viking explanation of the skeleton, the experts said it was an Indian. Ninety-five years after it had disappeared in smoke it was identified as a proto-historic Wampanoag Indian by an eminent anthropologist. (Is this truly science?) Such opinions would seem conclusive. And they were conclusive enough to cast a shadow over the findings of Rafn, and cause a general apathy toward his theories. The door was opened to attacks on Rafn, and they came in great numbers, being brought to ultimate perfection in the Delabarre book.

And now I am in a dilemma.

I can state my belief that Rafn's opinion was correct, and expose my naïveté. Or, I can cast intelligence aside and accept the opinion, offered by sober scientists, that this skeleton was that of an Indian. Great emotional stress overcomes me as I recall Dr. Hrdlicka's observation that Minnesota Man "looked like a Sioux Indian." Is that science's yardstick? If a pile of bones *looks* like a Sioux Indian, is it a Sioux Indian? I am also in despair when I recall the circumstance attendant upon the finding—in 1856—of the famed "Dusseldorf Man," known more popularly as the Neanderthal Man. C. W. Ceram, writing in *Gods, Graves and Scholars,* relates the opinions given on this extraordinary find when it first came to light:

> At the time, however, Professor Mayer, of Bonn, declared that the bones belonged to a Cossack killed in 1814. Wagner, of Gottingen, maintained that the skeleton was that of an old Hollander; and Pruner-Bey, of Paris, that of an old Celt. The great pathologist Virchow, whose too rashly applied authority retarded so many sciences, said that the skeleton was that of a gouty old man.

These opinions were stated—by some of the greatest scientific minds of the day—about an old skeleton found in Europe. Do we have here a similarity of pompous error linking Neanderthal and Thorvald? Or must we assume that America, in the year 1831, had produced anthropologists of such remarkable knowledge that they were able, with no qualifications, to identify a skeleton wearing metal ornaments as an Indian who had covered himself with English trade objects before he died? Were these anthropologists and paleontologists and morphologists who looked at the skeleton so far in advance of their European colleagues—whom they preceded by 25 years—that they could unerringly make such an identification?

I think not. Yet I am expected to accept the inalterable fact that the Skeleton in Armor was an Indian. I must accept it because a poet, inspired by the find, thought to immortalize it in verse. That in itself, I am told, is enough to show that there is no scientific basis for thinking the skeleton to be Thorvald. It is only the product of a romantic's vivid imagination. Apparently there *is* scientific basis for identifying the bones as those of an Indian 95 years after they had disappeared. But I must not forget that it had been identified earlier, in 1831, as an Indian. Or was it a Cossack—or a gouty old man?

Neanderthal Man, I might add, fared better than did Thorvald. There were champions to defend Neanderthal and ultimately establish his ancient age and importance. For Thorvald, no champions; merely oblivion via the NEBC Principle.

Simple research could have provided clues to follow in the case of the Skeleton in Armor. It is a known fact that viking graves in Norway, dating from the ninth century, have revealed Norse skeletons wearing Irish and Anglo-Saxon metalware. The authority for the above is Dr. Johannes Brøndsted, former director of the Royal Museum in Copenhagen, and probably the world's foremost authority on vikings, their times and lives (except, as you will see, when they are encountered in America).

But simple research was considered unnecessary. The skeleton was found in America, therefore it had to be an Indian. It was encased in metalware of brass, or bronze or iron, or whatever, so the metalware, quite naturally, had to be English. These deductions, arrived at after great deliberation by the scientists of the day, are based on two incontrovertible facts: 1. The NEBC Principle, 2. If metalware be found, it clearly had to be English. Not Dutch, not Spanish, not French, not Portuguese; not anything other than English. There is no other avenue of approach. It is evident that when following rule No. 2, based on the Law of our Heritage as begun by the Pilgrims, it would be entirely permissible to identify the skeleton of a Portuguese fisherman, buried with his net, as that of an Indian wearing English lace.

But I must return to the simple research. It is not only possible, but highly probable, that Thorvald Ericsson came to America wearing belts, bracteates, etc., obtained from England. The Greenlanders themselves made none of these things; they depended on import for their clothing and decoration. That they kept abreast of fashions in Europe is manifest in the clothing worn by fifteenth-century bodies dug out of Greenland's frozen soil. They were wearing fifteenth-century European fashions. A brisk trade was carried on among Greenland, Iceland, Norway, and England. It is not only highly probable, but rather a positive fact that Greenland vikings of the eleventh century would wear clothing and armor and decorative metalware obtained from other countries, including England.

But the skeleton was found in America.

It is an Indian.

It was wearing metal ornaments, or armor, or decoration, or whatever.

It was English.

That is the law.

We cannot amend it.

The objects in question are still obtainable for highly precise twentieth-century metallurgical testing. I don't think they will ever be put to such a test. What—and the thought is horrible to contemplate—if the metal should prove to be of Norse origin? No. It is better left alone, in its museum cases, to be viewed with a smile as a joke that was played on the people of Fall River, and America, by Henry Wadsworth Longfellow, in collusion with the newspapers.

Obviously, we can't call for a new morphological examination of the skeleton. It doesn't exist. We are safe. Our heritage is safe. And the viking "myth" is labeled so.

I think the Skeleton in Armor, found at the corner of Fifth and Hartley Streets, in the town (now city) of Fall River, Massachusetts, and clad in metalware of indeterminate nature, was the skeleton of Thorvald Ericsson. It is the unfortunate Thorvald, killed by Irish-Icelander-Indians, and buried in a Catholic ceremony with a cross at his head and at his feet.

Will some historian come forward to corroborate?

I think not.

But I must not become angry.

I will simply close by stating that the crewmen of Thorvald's ship returned to Greenland, there to bring great tidings to Leif. Obviously, the great tidings concerned the information they had gathered about the new land, and not the tidings of Thorvald's death.

And so ends the saga of Thorvald Ericsson, leader of the second planned voyage by a viking to the New World. Thorvald, the hapless brother to Leif, the maligned Skeleton in Armor, victim of the ill luck that dogged the Ericsson family, victim of the ill fortune that has, in almost every case, destroyed or clouded the evidence of pre-Columbian occupation of our country.

There is a pathetic footnote to the Saga of Thorvald, a footnote which again brings the haunting spirit of misfortune to the siblings of Leif Ericsson. The summer following the return of Thorvald's crew, the second Ericsson brother, Thorstein, set out to sail to Vinland, to find his brother's body. He was tossed about in stormy seas for many months, and eventually, disconsolately, returned to Greenland. Sickness again descended on the Greenlanders the following winter, and Thorstein died.

But talk of Vinland continued, and the next year there arrived in Greenland an Icelander named Thorfinn Karlsefni, a distinguished man of noble family. He married Thorstein's beautiful, accomplished widow, Gudrid, and then sailed to become the third viking discoverer of America.

CHAPTER 12

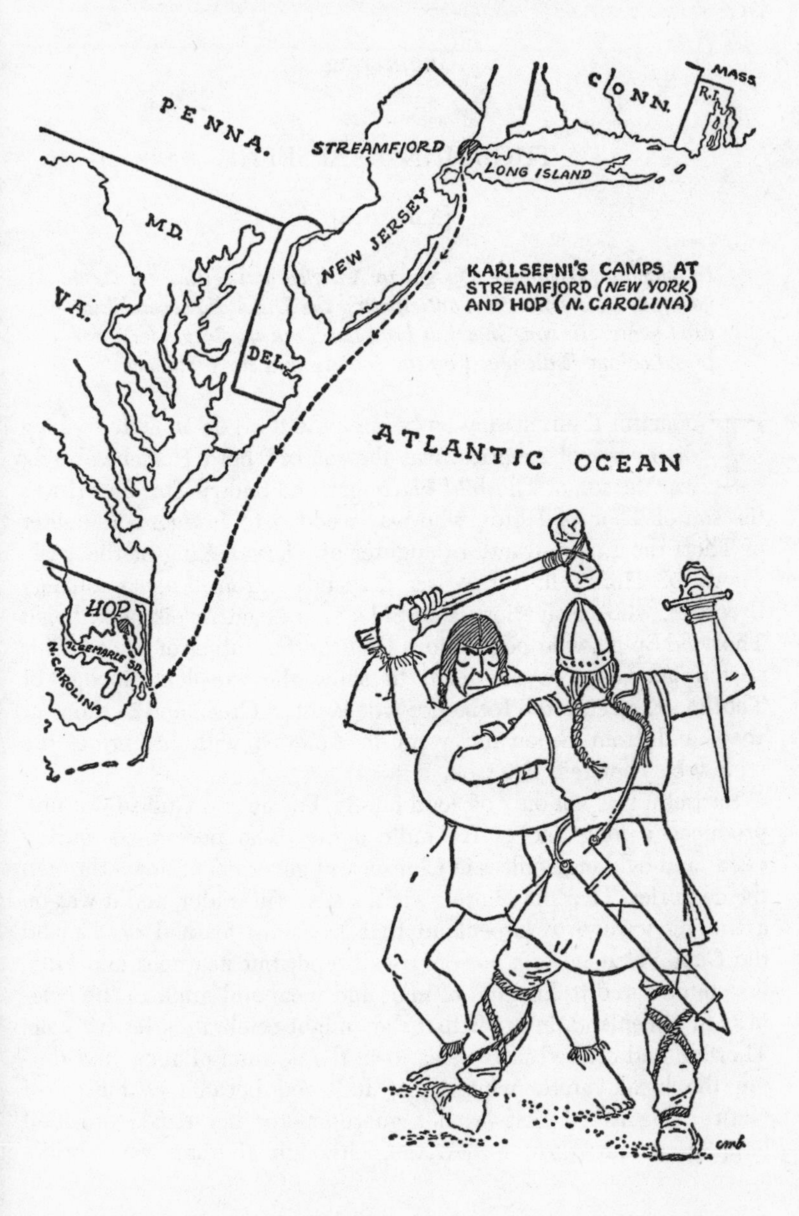

PENNA.
STREAMFJORD
CONN.
MASS.
R.I.
LONG ISLAND
MD.
NEW JERSEY
KARLSEFNI'S CAMPS AT
STREAMFJORD (NEW YORK)
AND HOP (N. CAROLINA)
VA.
DEL.
ATLANTIC OCEAN
HOP
ALBEMARLE SD.
N. CAROLINA
cmb

Chapter 12

THORFINN KARLSEFNI

[A.D. 1010]

In which an Icelander voyages to America and settles, for three years, in New York, thus anticipating the Dutch by several hundred years. His son, Snorri, is born here, but the Icelander's proposed colony is dissolved by the Indians and sex problems.

THORFINN KARLSEFNI, who became the third documented viking discoverer of America, was the son of Thord Horsehead, who was the son of Thorhild Ptarmigan and Snorri. This Snorri was the son of Thordof Hofdi, who was wedded to Fridgerd, daughter of Thori the Loiterer and a daughter of Kiarval, King of the Irish. Thord of Hofdi, in turn, was descended from Ragnar Shaggy Breeches, who begat Biorn Iron-Side, who begat Asleik, who begat Thorvald Spine, who begat Biorn Chestbutter, father of Thord. This partial genealogy is set forth to show the excellent lineage of Thorfinn Karlsefni, the Icelander who went to Greenland in the year 1009, and from Greenland went to America with his bride, the widow of Thorstein Ericsson.

Karlsefni was not only of good family, but he and Gudrid, in turn, produced a long line of Icelandic nobles who performed worthy deeds and held high offices in Church and government down through the centuries. Thorfinn himself was a successful trader, and it was on a trading voyage to Greenland that Karlsefni learned of Vinland the Good. That he was not only well-bred, but generous and kind, is demonstrated in his gifts of malt and meal and grain to the colonists in Greenland, in order that they might celebrate a festive yule. Thorfinn had arrived in Greenland in the autumn of 1009, and during the bleak, arctic winter that followed became enamored of Gudrid. He asked Leif—as her guardian—for her hand, and Leif happily consented to the marriage. Although Thorfinn was a bridegroom, he was not too high in the clouds of new love to listen to the talk about Vinland which he heard everywhere. It occurred to him that this New World might be good for a colony, and possibly for trade, once established. He gained information concerning Vinland from Leif, and from the crew of Thorvald's ship. The prospect seemed a pleasant one. He decided to strike out for Vinland. According to *Hauk's Book*, in the *Saga of Eric the Red*, here are the adventures of Thorfinn Karlsefni, first viking to attempt the establishment of a permanent colony in America:

About this time there began to be much talk at Brattahlid, to the effect that Wineland the Good should be explored, for, it was said, that country must be possessed of many goodly qualities. And so it came to pass, that Karlsefni and Snorri fitted out their ship, for the purpose of going in search of that country in the spring. Biarni and Thorhall joined the expedition with their ship, and the men who had borne them company. There was a man named Thorvard; he was wedded to Freydis, a natural daughter of Eric the Red. He also accompanied them, together with Thorvald, Eric's son, and Thorhall, who was called the Huntsman. He had been for a long time with Eric as his hunter and fisherman during the summer, and as his steward during the winter. Thorhall was stout and swarthy, and of giant stature; he was a man of few words, though given to abusive language, when he did speak, and he ever incited Eric to evil. He was a poor Christian; he had a wide knowledge of the unsettled regions. He was on the same ship with Thorvard and Thorvald. They had that ship which Thorbiorn had brought out. They had in all one hundred and sixty men, when they sailed to the Western Settlement, and thence to Bear Island. Thence they bore away to the southward two "doegr." Then they saw land, and launched a boat, and explored the land, and found there large flat stones [hellur], and many of these were twelve ells wide; there were many Arctic foxes there. They gave a name to the country, and called it Helluland [the land of flat stones]. Then they sailed with northerly winds two "doegr," and land then lay before them, and upon it was a great wood and many wild beasts; an island lay off the land to the south-east, and there they found a bear, and they called this Biarney [Bear Island], while the land where the wood was they called Markland [Forest-land]. Thence they sailed southward along the land for a long time, and came to a cape; the land lay upon the starboard; there were long strands and sandy banks there. They rowed to the land and found upon the cape there the keel of a ship, and they called it there Kialarnes [Keelness]; they also called the strands Furdustrandir [Wonder-strands], because they were so long to sail by. Then the country became indented with bays, and they steered their ships into a bay. It was when Leif was with King Olaf Tryggvason, and he bade him proclaim Christianity to Greenland, that the king gave him two Gaels; the man's name was Haki, and the woman's Haekia. The king advised Leif to have recourse to these people, if he should stand in need of fleetness, for they were swifter than deer. Eric and Leif had tendered Karlsefni the services of this couple. Now when they had sailed past Wonder-strands, they put the Gaels ashore, and directed them to run to the southward, and investigate the nature of the country, and return again before the end of the third half-day. They were each clad in a garment, which they called "kiafal," which was so fashioned, that it had a hood at the top, was open at the sides, was sleeveless, and was fastened between the legs with buttons and loops, while elsewhere they were naked. Karlsefni and his companions cast anchor, and lay there during their absence; and when they came again, one of them carried a bunch of grapes, and the other an ear of new-sown wheat. They went on board the ship, whereupon Karlsefni and his followers held on their way, until they came to where the coast was indented with bays. They stood into a bay with their ships. There was an island out at the mouth of the bay, about which there were strong currents, wherefore they called it Straumey [Stream Isle]. There were so many birds there, that it was scarcely possible to step between the eggs. They sailed through the firth, and called it Straumfiord [Streamfirth], and carried their cargoes ashore from the ships, and established themselves there. They had brought with them all kinds of live-stock. It was a fine country there. There were mountains thereabouts. They occupied themselves exclusively with the exploration of the country. They remained there during the winter, and they had taken no thought for this during the summer. The fishing began to fail, and they began to fall short of food. Then Thorhall the Huntsman disappeared. They had already prayed to God for food, but it did not come as promptly as their necessities seemed to demand. They searched for Thorhall for three half-days, and found him on a projecting crag. He was lying there, and looking up at the sky, with mouth and nostrils agape, and mumbling something. They asked him why he had gone thither; he replied, that this did not concern any one. They asked him then to go home with them, and he did so. Soon after this a whale appeared there, and they captured it, and flensed it, and no one could tell what manner of whale it was; and when the cooks had prepared it, they ate of it, and were all made ill by it. Then Thorhall, approaching them, says: "Did not the Red-beard prove more helpful than your Christ? This is my reward for the verses which I composed to Thor, the Trustworthy; seldom has he failed me." When the people heard this, they cast the whale down into the sea, and made their appeals to God. The weather then improved, and they could now row out to fish, and thenceforward they had no lack of provisions, for they could hunt game on the land, gather eggs on the island, and catch fish from the sea.

CONCERNING KARLSEFNI AND THORHALL

It is said, that Thorhall wished to sail to the northward beyond Wonder-strands, in search of Wineland, while Karlsefni desired to proceed to the southward, off the coast. Thorhall prepared for his voyage out below the island, having only nine men in his party, for all of the remainder of the company went with Karlsefni. And one day when Thorhall was carrying water aboard his ship, and was drinking, he recited this ditty:

When I came, these brave men told me,
  Here the best of drink I'd get,
Now with water-pail behold me,——
  Wine and I are strangers yet.
Stooping at the spring, I've tested
  All the wine this land affords;
Of its vaunted charms divested,
  Poor indeed are its rewards.

And when they were ready, they hoisted sail; whereupon Thorhall recited this ditty:

Comrades, let us now be faring
  Homeward to our own again!
Let us try the sea-steed's daring,
  Give the chafing courser rein.
Those who will may bide in quiet,
  Let them praise their chosen land,
Feasting on a whale-steak diet,
  In their home by Wonder-strand.

Then they sailed away to the northward past Wonder-strands and Keel-ness, intending to cruise to the westward around the cape. They encountered westerly gales, and were driven ashore in Ireland, where they were grievously maltreated and thrown into slavery. There Thorhall lost his life, according to that which traders have related.

It is now to be told of Karlsefni, that he cruised southward off the coast, with Snorri and Biarni, and their people. They sailed for a long time, and until they came at last to a river, which flowed down from the land into a lake, and so into the sea. There were great bars at the mouth of the river, so that it could only be entered at the height of the flood-tide. Karlsefni and his men sailed into the mouth of the river, and called it there Hop [a small land-locked bay]. They found self-sown wheat-fields on the land there, wherever there were hollows, and wherever there was hilly ground, there were vines. Every brook there was full of fish. They dug pits, on the shore where the tide rose highest, and when the tide fell, there were halibut in the pits. There were great numbers of wild animals of all kinds in the woods. They remained there half a month, and enjoyed themselves, and kept no watch. They had their live-stock with them. Now one morning early, when they looked about them, they saw a great number of skin canoes, and staves were brandished from the boats, with a noise like flails, and they were revolved in the same direction in which the sun moves. Then said Karlsefni: "What may this betoken?" Snorri, Thorbrand's son, answers him: "It may be, that this is a signal of peace, wherefore let us take a white shield and display it." And thus they did. Thereupon the strangers rowed toward them, and went upon the land, marvelling at those whom they saw before them. They were swarthy men, and ill-looking, and the hair of their heads was ugly. They had great eyes, and were broad of cheek. They tarried there for a time looking curiously at the people they saw before them, and then rowed away, and to the southward around the point.

Karlsefni and his followers had built their huts above the lake, some of their dwellings being near the lake, and others farther away. Now they remained there that winter. No snow came there, and all of their live-stock lived by grazing. And when spring opened, they discovered, early one morning, a great number of skin canoes, rowing from the south past the cape, so numerous, that it looked as if coals had been scattered broadcast out before the bay; and on every boat staves were waved. Thereupon Karlsefni and his people displayed their shields, and when they came together, they began to barter with each other. Especially did the strangers wish to buy red cloth, for which they offered in exchange peltries and quite gray skins. They also desired to buy swords and spears, but Karlsefni and Snorri forbade this. In exchange for perfect unsullied skins, the Skrellings would take red stuff a span in length, which they would bind around their heads. So their trade went on for a time, until Karlsefni and his people began to grow short of cloth when they divided it into such narrow pieces, that it was not more than a finger's breadth wide, but the Skrellings still continued to give just as much for this as before, or more.

It so happened, that a bull, which belonged to Karlsefni and his people, ran out from the woods, bellowing loudly. This so terrified the Skrellings, that they sped out to their canoes, and then rowed away to the southward along the coast. For three entire weeks nothing more was seen of them. At the end of this time, however, a great multitude of Skrelling boats was discovered approaching from the south, as if a stream were pouring down, and all of their staves were waved in a direction contrary to the course of the sun, and the Skrellings were all uttering loud cries. Thereupon Karlsefni and his men took red shields and displayed them. The Skrellings sprang from their boats, and they met them, and fought together. There was a fierce shower of missiles, for the Skrellings had war-slings. Karlsefni and Snorri observed, that the Skrellings raised up on a pole a great ball-shaped body, almost the size of a sheep's belly, and nearly black in color, and this they hurled from the pole up on the land above Karlsefni's followers, and it made a frightful noise, where it fell. Whereat a great fear seized upon Karlsefni, and all his men, so that they could think of nought but flight, and of making their escape up along the river bank, for it seemed to them that the troop of the Skrellings was rushing towards them from every side, and they did not pause, until they came to certain jutting crags, where they offered a stout resistance. Freydis came out, and seeing that Karlsefni and his men were fleeing, she cried: "Why do ye flee from these wretches, such worthy men as ye, when, meseems, ye might slaughter them like cattle. Had I but a weapon, methinks, I would fight better than any one of you!" They gave no heed to her words. Freydis sought to join them but lagged behind, for she was not hale [she was pregnant]; she followed them, however, into the forest, while the Skrellings pursued her; she found a dead man in front of her; this was Thorbrand, Snorri's son, his skull cleft by a flat stone; his naked sword lay beside him; she took it up, and prepared to defend herself with it. The Skrellings then approached her, whereupon she stripped down her shift, and slapped her breast with the naked sword. At this the Skrellings were terrified and ran down to their boats, and rowed away. Karlsefni and his companions, however, joined her and praised her valor. Two of Karlsefni's men had fallen, and a great number of the Skrellings. Karlsefni's party had been overpowered by dint of superior numbers. They now returned to their dwellings, and bound up their wounds, and weighed carefully what throng of men that could have been, which had seemed to descend upon them from the land; it now seemed to them, that there could have been but the one party, that which came from the boats, and that the other troop must have been an ocular delusion. The Skrellings, moreover, found a dead man, and an axe lay beside him. One of their number picked up the axe, and struck at a tree with it, and one after another [they tested it], and it seemed to them to be a treasure, and to cut well; then one of their number seized it, and hewed at a stone with it, so that the axe broke, whereat they concluded that it could be of no use since it would not withstand stone, and they cast it away.

It now seemed clear to Karlsefni and his people, that although the country thereabouts was attractive, their life would be one of constant dread and turmoil by reason of the [hostility of the] inhabitants of the country, so they forthwith prepared to leave, and determined to return to their own country. They sailed to the northward off the coast, and found five Skrellings, clad in skin-doublets, lying asleep near the sea. There were vessels beside them, containing animal marrow, mixed with blood. Karlsefni and his company concluded that they must have been banished from their own land. They put them to death. They afterwards found a cape, upon which there was a great number of animals, and this cape looked as if it were one cake of dung, by reason of the animals which lay there at night. They now arrived again at Streamfirth, where they found great abundance of all those things of which they stood in need. Some men say, that Biarni and Freydis remained behind there with a hundred men, and went no further; while Karlsefni and Snorri proceeded to the southward with forty men, tarrying at Hop barely two months, and returning again the same summer. Karlsefni then set out with one ship, in search of Thorhall the Huntsman, but the greater part of the company remained behind. They sailed to the northward around Keelness, and then bore to the westward, having land to the larboard. The country there was a wooded wilderness, as far as they could see, with scarcely an open space; and when they had journeyed a considerable distance, a river flowed down from the east toward the west. They sailed into the mouth of the river, and lay to by the southern bank.

THE SLAYING OF THORVALD, ERIC'S SON

It happened one morning, that Karlsefni and his companions discovered in an open space in the woods above them, a speck, which seemed to shine toward them, and they shouted at it: it stirred, and it was a Uniped, who skipped down to the bank of the river by which they were lying. Thorvald, a son of Eric the Red, was sitting at the helm, and the Uniped shot an arrow into his inwards. Thorvald drew out the arrow, and exclaimed: "There is fat around my paunch; we have hit upon a fruitful country, and yet we are not like to get much profit of it." Thorvald died soon after from this wound. Then the Uniped ran away back toward the north. Karlsefni and his men pursued him, and saw him from time to time. The last they saw of him, he ran down into a creek. Then they turned back; whereupon one of the men recited this ditty:

Eager, our men, up hill down dell,
Hunted a Uniped;
Hearken, Karlsefni, while they tell
How swift the quarry fled!

Then they sailed away back toward the north, and believed they had got sight of the land of the Unipeds; now were they disposed to risk the lives of their men any longer. They concluded that the mountains of Hop, and those which they had now found, formed one chain, and this appeared to be so because they were about an equal distance removed from Streamfirth, in either direction. They sailed back, and passed the third winter at Streamfirth. Then the men began to divide into factions, of which the women were the cause; and those who were without wives, endeavored to seize upon the wives of those who were married, whence the greatest trouble arose. Snorri, Karlsefni's son, was born the first autumn, and he was three winters old when they took their departure. When they sailed away from Wineland, they had a southerly wind, and so came upon Markland, where they found five Skrellings, one of whom was bearded, two were women, and two were children. Karlsefni and his people took the boys, but the other escaped, and these Skrellings sank down into the earth. They bore the lads away with them, and taught them to speak, and they were baptized. They said, that their mother's name was Vaetilldi, and their father's Uvaegi. They said, that kings governed the Skrellings, one of whom was called Avalldamon, and the other Valldidida. They stated, that there were no houses there, and that the people lived in caves or holes. They said, that there was a land on the other side over against their country, which was inhabited by people who wore white garments, and yelled loudly, and carried poles before them, to which rags were attached; and people believe that this must have been Hvitramanna-land (White-man's-land), or Ireland the Great. Now they arrived in Greenland, and remained during the winter with Eric the Red.

That Thorfinn's saga is replete with borrowed material has already been suggested; I will deal with these intrusions as they are examined.

The expedition, consisting of 160 people, men and women, also carried cattle for the sustenance of the proposed settlement. In this saga we also become acquainted, for the first time, with Freydis, monstrous extra-marital issue of Eric Raudi, and her effete husband Thorvard. Their full story is yet to be told, but an insight into Freydis' character is given in her strange behavior during the battle with the scraelings. Freydis was either completely without fear, or demented. I'm inclined toward the latter explanation, as will be aptly shown in the following chapter.

Although Thorvald is treated on in the saga, I must repeat that I consider that portion dealing with his death a borrowed, and mightily edited, version of the *Flateybook* saga of Thorvald. Gathorne-

Hardy points out that the dying speech of Thorvald, as recounted in Karlsefni's saga, is evidently borrowed from an utterance by another viking, Thormod Kolbrunarskald, who made the observation after the battle of Stiklestad. I will, therefore, pass by the Thorvald episode.

Also aboard was Thorhall the Hunter, who had plainly been to Vinland on one of the two earlier expeditions. Considering the unflattering picture portrayed of him in the saga, it is at once apparent that he was taken only because "he had a wide knowledge of the unsettled regions." Thorhall is important to the story in that he demonstrates conclusively that Thorfinn never arrived at Leif's Shelters in Plymouth, as the *Flateybook* version of this voyage would have it.

I will begin, now, at the beginning of Karlsefni's saga.

The first hint of borrowed material in this saga occurs in the sailing directions given in describing the start of the voyage. It is only at the beginning of the saga that any time periods of sailing are given. Nowhere else in the story are times noted. To me, this circumstance is notable in that it reveals the presence of extraneous material, copied from the saga of Leif Ericsson, and copied carelessly at that. They begin by sailing southward for two *doegr*, or two *days,* after having been to the Western Settlement (in Greenland) and visiting a place called Bear Island. The two-days' sail brought them to a land which they called *Helluland,* and which could only be Labrador-Newfoundland. Next they sail for two more days to a place they call Bear Island, then to a place they call *Markland.* Then the sailing times are dropped entirely, and Thorvald's Keelness is brought into the story.

Patently, both the sailing times, and the naming of the lands found are taken haphazardly from Leif Ericsson's saga. The carelessness of the copyist is evident in his transcription of the number of days sailed, and in the puzzling knowledge that he simply gives up at Markland and relies on generalities to describe distances covered. Regarding the sighting of the cape, and of their visit to it, upon which they find the keel of a ship, and name the place *Keelness,* little need be said. I think that Karlsefni did pass Cape Cod, and call its beaches *Wonderstrands,* "because they were so long to sail by;" I also think that Hauk took the incident of the keel and the naming of the cape out of Thorvald to add a mite of color. I think it is safe to assume then, that the early passages of this saga are worthless; we might, in fact, borrow the beginning of Thorvald's Saga to insert here: ". . . there is no account of their voyage before their arrival at Leif's booths in Vinland." In this case, we will amend it to read ". . . before their arrival at Furdustrands."

The statement that they sailed past Furdustrands, and on into a country indented with bays is proof that they had no desire to go to Leif's Shelters, which they obviously knew lay to the west of the cape and its wonderful beaches. Having talked at great length with Leif, and having been given his sailing directions, it is apparent that Thorfinn, like Thorvald, chose to settle in a new place. Such a choice would be extremely logical. In the *Flateybook* versions of these sagas, it is stated that Leif was asked to give his shelters to Thorfinn, and later to Freydis. In both cases, he replied that he would *lend* them, but not *give* them. With this implication that he intended one day to live in Vinland himself, it would naturally follow that Thorvald and Thorfinn would not encroach on Leif's property, but look elsewhere to start their own colonies.

Karlsefni, then, sailed past Cape Cod, and the island of Provincetown which lay to the north of it, and continued southward, rounding the cape and entering into a country indented with bays. They sailed into Buzzard's Bay, where they released the two Gaels with instructions to run southward along the land. Either shore of Buzzard's Bay would enable the slaves to run southward along the land. They returned, after two and one-half days, bearing a bunch of grapes and an ear of new-sown wheat. Then the ship moved on, this time to the western end of Long Island Sound, where they found an island at the mouth of a bay, surrounded by strong currents, and they called it Stream Isle. It may have been Governors Island. Then they sailed into a fjord, and called it Streamfjord, and there made camp.

Clearly they were in the vicinity of Manhattan. The strong currents were encountered from their entrance into the East River and into Upper New York Bay, where the currents are equally as strong. The fjord they sailed into could only be the Hudson River, flanked, as it is, by the Palisades and the mountains beyond. The saga states that "there were mountains thereabouts," and, since the camp at Streamfjord was occupied for three years, it would follow that they probed the Hudson for some distance, perhaps as far as Bear Mountain. Lest you ask why I am so positive that the fjord in question be the Hudson (particularly since I have already selected a "fjord-like" area in which to place Thorvald), I must point out that a later passage in the saga tells us that Thorfinn sailed southward off the coast to reach Hop. Had he been anywhere in New England, he would have had to sail west to reach Hop. The New Jersey coast, below New York Harbor, wends southward. Hop was far to the south of the present site of New York.

The episode dealing with the unwholesome Thorhall serves further to prove that Karlsefni was well below Leif's Shelters at Rocky Nook. Thorhall wanted to sail *northward beyond Wonderstrands* in search of Vinland, demonstrating that he had been there before, and knew it lay beyond Wonderstrands. The lament he voices concerning his inability to get a drink of wine also proves they were not in Vinland, but in a region where grapes did not grow wild. All of which narrows down to the region of the mouth of the Hudson River.

After Thorhall's departure in pursuit of the grape, and his ultimate, but at the time unsuspected death, Karlsefni elected to sail southward with an expeditionary force. He did, and came to a river which flowed down from the land, into a lake and thence to the sea. Great bars guarded the entrance to the river, and when they were able to ascend the river at high tide, they called the place *Hop*, a Norse term meaning "land-locked bay." They found the land good, and they built huts above and near the lake, and some others farther away. They remained there that winter and noted that there came no snow, and all of their livestock lived by grazing.

In order to determine the site of Hop, it is first necessary to separate the intermixed details. It would appear that the river flowing down through a lake and into the sea sounds suspiciously like Leif's river, but here we can grant a coincidence. We are told that great bars prevented easy access to the river, so that it could only be entered at floodtide. Once inside the bars, and having established themselves on, or relatively near the lake, they called the place Hop, determining its name by the character of the land, and its waters.

They "sailed for a long time" to reach Hop, and they sailed southward. Along the Atlantic coast to the south of the present site of New York City, there is only one area which matches the description given in the saga. It is the Pamlico Sound-Albemarle Sound area off the coast of North Carolina. Of the two, Albemarle Sound (the lake) would be the more enticing, and for the same reason it attracted the displaced Romans. It is smaller, and friendlier-looking to a seaman, and appears to offer better opportunity for shelter. Both sounds are almost totally landlocked, entrances into them being afforded only at the various inlets which break through the sandbars periodically along their enormous length, which stretches all the way from Princess Anne County in southeastern Virginia, snaking along the coast to Cape Fear, at the southern tip of North Carolina, a distance of nearly three hundred miles.

I think Karlsefni's Hop was in the Albemarle Sound.

No snow came there that winter, and their cattle were able to graze continually. Here, again, we have evidence of transferred material, but in this case it is transferred from the Karlsefni saga to the saga of Leif Ericsson. In Chapter 8, I pointed out that the reference to "no frost in winter," and the observation that cattle would need no fodder during the cold season, plus the note concerning the unwithered grass were not in keeping with Leif's location. For one thing, Leif brought no cattle with him, and the observation about the cattle is put on a speculative basis. It . . . "seemed . . . that cattle would need no fodder during the winter."

To reiterate, I think the snowless winter applied only to Karlsefni—in North Carolina—and turned up in Leif's saga for no reason except that known only to the copyist.

Karlsefni's camp at Hop, in the Albemarle Sound, was probably on the spit of land which juts down between the North River and Currituck Sound. That the houses which were built above the lake were in the vicinity of Powell Point is suggested by the route of the Indians who came first to satisfy their curiosity, next to trade and finally to battle bloodily. They invariably came from the south "around the point." It follows then, that a logical site for the camp was on the west shore of Powell Point—and that the Indians were coming from somewhere in Currituck Sound.

The incident of Freydis may be accepted *de facto*. That she was possibly mentally disturbed is also evident in her apparently fearless stand before the scraelings. Her action at this juncture is quite curious, and seemingly unfathomable. There is no counterpart for her action in any other culture, that is to say we have no mythology which deals with amazons indulging in mammary massage by naked sword in order to repel invading forces.

The battle with the Indians most certainly discouraged Karlsefni from his great plan for a colony. "Their life would be one of constant dread and turmoil by reason of the hostility of the inhabitants . . ." and so Karlsefni regretfully capitulated and elected to return to his own country.

Now they all left Hop and returned to Streamfjord, where the remainder of the company had stayed while Karlsefni sojourned in Hop. There is evidently some conflict in the exact details of the Hop excursion; the story indicates that ". . . some men say that Bjarni and Freydis remained behind there with a hundred men . . ." which, if true, would dispose of the Freydis incident in the battle with the Indians. Whatever the circumstance, it is clear that the voyage to Hop did take place—together with the battle—Freydis or no. I am inclined to feel that the above passage is not pertinent. It is preceded by the phrase: "Some men say . . ."

I find a hint of more borrowed material in the slaying of the five Indians found asleep on the beach. It is more than strongly reminiscent of the Indians slain by Thorvald, and does not warrant further comment.

Once rested, and events of the past winter discussed and compared, Karlsefni, worried about Thorhall, who might possibly be lying in an alcoholic stupor up on Rocky Nook, decided to go in search of the vagrant viking. Taking his departure from Streamfjord, he sailed to the northward around Keelness (Cape Cod), and then bore to the westward, having land to the larboard. After that they journeyed a considerable distance, "having land to the larboard." Ultimately they came to a river which flowed from the east to the west.

It is apparent that Karlsefni was steering back to where he knew Leif's Shelters to be, hoping to find Thorhall there, happily making wine. He sailed around Cape Cod, and then bore to the westward, which direction would take him directly to Plymouth, and thence to the Jones River. Failing to find the missing Thorhall there, Karlsefni then continued for a "considerable distance." From Plymouth, the only direction he could sail in for a great distance would be north and eastward along the New England coast. Surely he would not have retraced his course and sailed back toward Streamfjord. Thorfinn knew where Leif's Vinland was, as did Thorhall. When Thorfinn failed to find his quarry at Leif's Shelters, he simply continued north, combining his hunting trip with an exploratory voyage. The incident of the river which flows from east to west gives us the terminal point of the expedition. A map of the New England coast quickly demonstrates that there is little possibility of finding such a river, since all of New England's rivers empty into the Atlantic, thus requiring a flow from west to east. But Karlsefni's river flowed from east to west. When they left that river, they sailed *back* toward the *north*, meaning that they were now homeward bound.

These directions and descriptives take us to the west coast of Nova Scotia to find Karlsefni's river. The viking sailed north and east from Plymouth, and into the Bay of Fundy. He probed Chignecto Bay, then turned his course southwest and then east to investigate Minas Basin. Now he sailed southwest again, and came to the east-west river. There are a number of rivers on the west coast of Nova Scotia which fit the description. The Salmon River, flowing into Cobequid Bay, to the east of Minas Basin, could answer. So, loosely, could the Annapolis River, or the Salmon River below Cape St. Mary.

I think it was the Salmon River, below Cape St. Mary.

There seems to be evidence there.

Sometime prior to 1875—the exact date is unknown—a curious rock was found on the shore of the Bay of Fundy, opposite the town of Yarmouth, in Nova Scotia, about fifteen miles south of the Salmon River. It was discovered by a man named Fletcher, attracted to it because it bore a peculiar series of marks which appeared to be letters, although in a tongue unknown to Fletcher. Mr. Fletcher told others about it and periodic attempts were apparently made to determine the nature of the marks or letters. Copies of the inscription were made and sent to men of learning. None came forth with a translation, but more than one saw hints of a Semitic origin in the characters.

In 1875, a copy of the inscription was sent to Mr. Henry Phillips, Jr., then corresponding secretary of the Numismatic and Antiquarian Society of Philadelphia. Mr. Phillips, having satisfied himself that the "inscription is neither a modern fraud nor the work of the wayward playfulness of the leisure hours of the sportive redskin," attempted a translation.

He eventually concluded that the rock bore a runic inscription and that it read: "Harkussen Men Varu," or "Harko's son addressed the men." He then adds that research had produced the evidence that the crew of Thorfinn Karlsefni included a man named Harko and expressed his own surprise at the remarkable coincidence.

Mr. Phillips read a report on his findings to the Society and it was included in the Society's report of February 5, 1880. The report also includes mention of two other marked rocks, found near the mouth of the Tusket River, east of Yarmouth. The reference is from a letter forwarded by Mr. T. B. Flint of Yarmouth, who gives no further details on the nature of the inscriptions, and does not include copies of them.

I think that this is an authentic runic rock, but I must confess some hesitation in accepting Mr. Phillips' translation. Of the members of Karlsefni's crew, the one whose name most resembles "Harko," is *Haki*, the Irish slave. It is entirely possible that Mr. Phillips evolved a translation which confused the two names, making *Haki* "Harko," but, since the inscription, according to the translator, indicates that the speaker was Harko's *son*, there remains some doubt concerning Mr. Phillips' judgment of the identity of the speaker.

It is entirely possible, however, that Karlsefni did have a crewman named Harkussen, or "Harko's son" who, in scouting the surrounding territory, issued a report at Yarmouth, and the event was duly graven in the rock. Unhappily, there exist no transcriptions of the other two inscriptions from the Tusket River.

I sent a copy of this inscription to Vilhjalmur Bjarnar, curator of the Fiske Icelandic Collection at Cornell, and Mr. Bjarnar is inclined to believe that the characters might be Semitic. He offered several objections to the progressions and character of the runes, but prefaced his reply modestly by reminding me that he was not a runic scholar. His analysis of the inscription was certainly scholarly, and would seem to negate it as authentic runic.

With a bow to Mr. Bjarnar, and acting on the thought voiced in his preface, I enter a plea for someone to translate the markings on the rock, if it is at all possible. I must add that this inscription has been seen by other scholars. They offer no opinions (NEBC). The inscription is reproduced in Plate 23, and can be seen on the rock itself in the Yarmouth Public Library in Nova Scotia.

Having paused at the Salmon River, and perhaps having left evidence of his visit, Karlsefni then informed his crew that it was time to return to Streamfjord, gather the colonists together and return to Greenland. In sailing back to the north, the viking ship steered across to the Bay of Fundy toward Grand Manan Island, probably changing the course to southwest just below that island. In taking this short cut, Karlsefni avoided the slow coastal voyage which would have been necessary had he simply retraced his initial course.

In passing, it is noteworthy that the vikings observed the relationship of the mountains of New Brunswick to the mountains they had seen at Hop, concluding that they were of one chain, and that they were "an equal distance removed from Streamfjord, in either direction. It is apparent, as Frederick Pohl has noted, that they had established the general shape of the Appalachian chain. In placing Streamfjord at the Hudson River, I offer the observation that Albemarle Sound and the coast of Maine, south of Grand Manan Island, which is about where they would have noted the mountains, are nearly equidistant from the Hudson.

Now I should like to return to the Unipeds for a moment. I have already pointed out that the death of Thorvald was borrowed from the saga of that viking, and the circumstance of his death garbled by the copyist. If we read that Karlsefni saga up to the sentence which says: "They sailed into the mouth of the river, and lay to by the southern bank," and then delete the entire passage concerning Thorvald, we resume with the sentence which begins: "Then they sailed away back toward the north, and believed they had got sight of the land of the Unipeds."

Perhaps they had.

One of William Goodwin's suspected sites for a Celi Dei mission outpost was at South Windham, Maine. Goodwin also suggested that if Thorvald had been shot by a monk, his robe, concealing his legs, might well have given him the appearance of a Uniped. Could it be that the crew of Karlsefni's ship, somewhere off the coast near Portland, which lies to the south of South Windham, could have seen one or more of these monks, standing on the beach? Could they then have run from the sight of the striped sail, to make ready for battle, not knowing that they had been mistaken for Unipeds, thus frightening the vikings?

Why not?

Returning to Streamfjord, Karlsefni discovered dissension among the men, over the few women in the colony. This circumstance, plus the Indian problem, may well have decided, in Karlsefni's mind, that the colonists had better be taken back to Greenland.

And so Karlsefni sailed from the region which provided the later sites of New Amsterdam and New York, and steered for Greenland together with Gudrid and his infant son Snorri, first white child born in America. The last notable event in the saga is the taking of the five scraelings. Here is corroboration of the existence of Great Ireland, direct from a saga. Remarkably, one of the scraelings wore a beard, something no New England Indian ever wore. All escaped but the two boys, whom Karlsefni had baptized and taught to speak Icelandic. They learned from the boys that "there was a land on the other side over against their country, which was inhabited by people who wore white garments, and yelled loudly, and carried poles before them, to which rags were attached; and people believe that this must have been Hvitramanna-land (White Man's Land) or Ireland the Great.

The escapees "sank down into the earth." Or into earth-covered beehives, similar to the ones at Upton and other sites in New England? Where did the older scraeling get his beard? And what of the land "on the other side"? Since the capture of these boys took place in Markland, which is Nova Scotia, could that mean across the Bay of Fundy, in Maine? And the people who lived in caves or holes, and wore white garments, and yelled loudly, and carried poles before them? Could this be, as has been suggested by Goodwin and others, a description of a monkish processional, marked by chanting?

I think it could—and was.

I think the two captured boys were the product of assimilation between the monks and the Indians, and had wandered, with others like them, over to Nova Scotia. The bearded one need not have been an old man; he could have been a young man, even in his late teens. All of these could have been produced during the time period elapsing between the first settlement of Great Ireland by the Celi Dei, and the arrival of Thorfinn. Their names give us no clues. Any strange name would have lost its original spelling in its transferal to the written sagas, and we will never, of course, know how they were pronounced. The shadow still hovers above the clues that might further clarify the stories recounted herein.

Thorfinn's attempted colonization of the New World came to an end in the year 1013, and the sailing routes from Greenland to America were untrafficked until the following year, when Freydis, she of the sword-caressed breasts, returned to Vinland and reddened its sands with blood.

CHAPTER 13

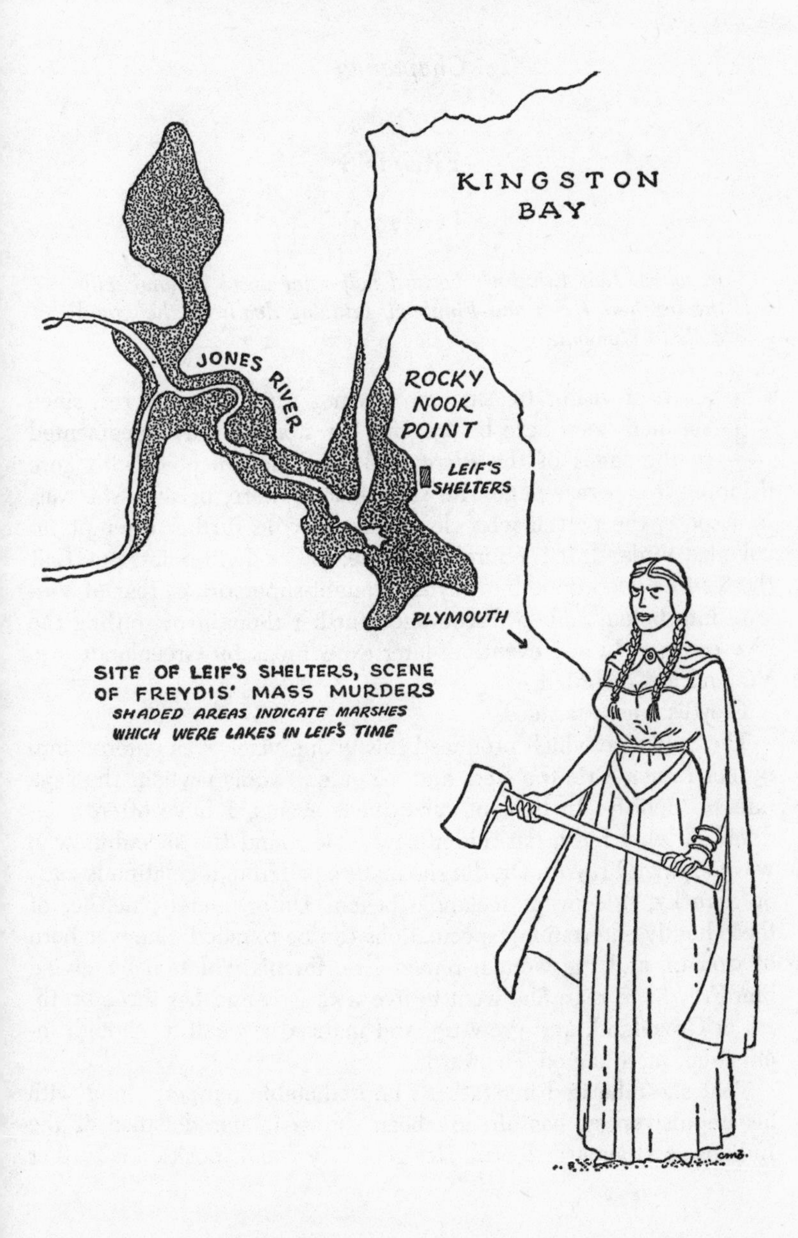

KINGSTON BAY
JONES RIVER
ROCKY NOOK POINT
LEIF'S SHELTERS
PLYMOUTH
SITE OF LEIF'S SHELTERS, SCENE OF FREYDIS' MASS MURDERS
SHADED AREAS INDICATE MARSHES WHICH WERE LAKES IN LEIF'S TIME

Chapter 13

FREYDIS

[A.D. 1014]

In which Leif Ericsson's bastard half-sister visits Vinland with the brothers Helgi and Finnbogi, bringing death on the grand scale to Plymouth.

THE next visitor to America was not truly a discoverer, since she had been here before, but her story is fully documented in the sagas of the *Flateybook*, and documented with gore dripping from every page. Her story belongs here, because she was, in a sense, the person who closed the door on further attempts to colonize Vinland. It is entirely possible, as Goodwin points out, that the terrible deed done by Freydis brought superstitious fear of Vinland into being, and so discouraged further thought of settling the new country. In any event, no later expeditions by Greenlanders to Vinland are recorded.

Freydis was a bastard.

The dalliance which produced this viking vixen was entered into by her father, Eric the Red, and a random woman whom the saga fails to identify. In light of subsequent events, I have often wondered in what fetid, bat-ridden cave Eric found the succubus who was to spawn Freydis. Or, did she materialize from a gelatinous mass on a rocky, tide-swept Icelandic beach? Unfortunately, neither of these highly entertaining speculations can be pursued. She was born of woman, and the woman repaid Eric for his violation by giving him Freydis to rear. She went to live with Eric and her three brothers in Greenland, and grew up, and married a wealthy, though ineffectual, man named Thorvard.

That she inherited her father's unpredictable temper, along with his impulsiveness, has already been shown in her defiance of the Indians at Albemarle Sound. Her generally vile disposition is further demonstrated in the vituperation she hurled upon the routed vikings prior to her victory.

Now we will see an even more monstrous side of this demented woman. Here is the way in which the *Flateybook* tells the story of Freydis and her voyage to America in the year 1014:

There was now much talk anew, about a Wineland-voyage, for this was reckoned both a profitable and an honorable enterprise. The same summer that Karlsefni arrived from Wineland, a ship from Norway arrived in Greenland. This ship was commanded by two brothers, Helgi and Finnbogi, who passed the winter in Greenland. They were descended from an Icelandic family of the East-firths. It is now to be added, that Freydis, Eric's daughter, set out from her home at Gradar, and waited upon the brothers, Helgi and Finnbogi, and invited them to sail with their vessel to Wineland, and to share with her equally all the good things which they might succeed in obtaining there. To this they agreed, and she departed thence to visit her brother, Leif, and ask him to give her the house which he had caused to be erected in Wineland, but he made her same answer [as that which he had given Karlsefni] saying, that he would lend his house, but not give it. It was stipulated between the brothers and Freydis, that each should have on ship-board thirty able-bodied men, besides the women; but Freydis immediately violated this compact, by concealing five men more [than this number], and this the brothers did not discover before they arrived in Wineland. They now put out to sea, having agreed beforehand, that they would sail in company, if possible, and although they were not far apart from each other, the brothers arrived somewhat in advance, and carried their belongings to Leif's house. Now when Freydis arrived, her ship was discharged, and the baggage carried up to the house, whereupon Freydis exclaimed:

"Why did you carry your baggage in here?"

"Since we believed," said they, "that all promises made to us would be kept."

"It was to me that Leif loaned the house," says she, "and not to you."

Whereupon Helgi exclaimed:

"We brothers cannot hope to rival thee in wrong-dealing."

They thereupon carried their baggage forth, and built a hut, above the sea, on the bank of the lake, and put all in order about it; while Freydis caused wood to be felled, with which to load her ship. The winter now set in, and the brothers suggested, that they should amuse themselves by playing games. This they did for a time, until the folk began to disagree, when dissensions arose between them, and the games came to an end, and the visits between the houses ceased; and thus it continued far into the winter.

One morning early, Freydis arose from her bed, and dressed herself, but did not put on her shoes and stockings. A heavy dew had fallen, and she took her husband's cloak, and wrapped it about her, and then walked to the brothers' house, and up to the door, which had been only partly closed by one of the men, who had gone out a short time before. She pushed the door open, and stood, silently, in the doorway for a time. Finnbogi, who was lying on the innermost side of the room, was awake, and said:

"What dost thou wish here, Freydis?"

She answers: "I wish thee to rise, and go out with me, for I would speak with thee."

He did so, and they walked to a tree, which lay close by the wall of the house, and seated themselves upon it.

"How art thou pleased here?" says she.

He answers: "I am well pleased with the fruitfulness of the land, but I am ill-content with the breach which has come between us, for, methinks, there has been no cause for it."

"It is even as thou sayest," says she, "and so it seems to me; but my errand to thee is, that I wish to exchange ships with you brothers, for that ye have a larger ship than I, and I wish to depart from here."

"To this I must accede," says he, "if it is thy pleasure."

Therewith they parted, and she returned home, and Finnbogi to his bed. She climbed up into bed, and awakened Thorvard with her cold feet, and he asked her why she was so cold and wet.

She answered, with great passion: "I have been to the brothers," says she, "to try to buy their ship, for I wished to have a larger vessel, but they received my overtures so ill, that they struck me, and handled me very roughly; what time thou, poor wretch, wilt neither avenge my shame nor thy own, and I find, perforce, that I am no longer in Greenland, moreover I shall part from thee, unless thou wreakest vengeance for this."

And now he could stand her taunts no longer, and ordered the men to rise at once, and take their weapons, and this they did, and they then proceeded directly to the house of the brothers, and entered it, while the folk were asleep, and seized and bound them, and led each one out, when he was bound; and as they came out, Freydis caused each one to be slain. In this wise all of the men were put to death, and only the women were left, and these no one would kill.

At this Freydis exclaimed: "Hand me an axe!"

This was done, and she fell upon the five women, and left them dead.

They returned home after this dreadful deed, and it was very evident that Freydis was well content with her work.

She addressed her companions, saying: "If it be ordained for us, to come again to Greenland, I shall contrive the death of any man who shall speak of these events. We must give it out, that we left them living here, when we came away."

Early in the spring, they equipped the ship, which had belonged to the brothers, and freighted it with all of the products of the land, which they could obtain, and which the ship would carry. Then they put out to sea, and, after a prosperous voyage, arrived with their ship in Ericsfirth, early in the summer.

Freydis now went to her home, since it had remained unharmed during her absence. She bestowed liberal gifts upon all of her companions, for she was anxious to screen her guilt. She now established herself at her home; but her companions were not all so close-mouthed, concerning their misdeeds and wickedness, that rumors did not get abroad at last. These finally reached her brother, Leif, and he thought it a most shameful story. He thereupon took three of the men, who had been of Freydis' party, and forced them, all at the same time, to a confession of the affair, and their stories entirely agreed.

"I have no heart," says Leif, "to punish my sister, Freydis, as she deserves, but this I predict of them, that there is little prosperity in store for their offspring."

Hence it came to pass, that no one from that time forward thought them worthy of aught but evil.

A most lamentable tale.

It is patent that Freydis had evil in her heart when she planned the voyage to Vinland. Going to visit Helgi and Finnbogi, she persuaded them to accompany her. With the glowing description of the fine qualities of the land, and Freydis' promise of equal shares in whatever wealth they might obtain, the brothers' decision to sail with her was natural.

Happily, Freydis went now to Leif and asked for the house he had built in Vinland. Leif, still harboring his dream of returning to Vinland himself, agreed to *lend,* but not give the dwelling.

Then the Greenland harpy evidenced further proof of her evil intent. Secretly, she placed five additional men aboard her ship. That assured her of numerical superiority in case of conflict; palpably, Freydis anticipated trouble. And with good reason. She was planning to create it herself.

Having consummated the bargain and put to sea, Freydis dwelled on her plan. That she took full command of the expedition is clear; on arrival at Leif's House, she expelled the bewildered brothers, who had arrived a short time before and had already placed their gear within. Thorvard, her timorous husband, had little, if anything to say in the matter.

Freydis then put her crew to work felling wood, and it follows that the brothers' crewmen were busy at the same task. When winter descended, Helgi and Finnbogi, in anticipation of a long, dreary winter, suggested that games be played. This sincere overture was accepted, but the gaming season was short-lived. Dissensions ended the contests, and it would not be difficult to deduce the cause of these dissensions.

The two camps remained isolated throughout the winter.

And when the brothers gratefully noted the approach of spring, they made plans to leave the oppressive atmosphere of Leif's Shelters and return to Greenland as quickly as possible.

But when spring came, death came with it.

Among the scholars who have commented on this incredible story of murder most foul, there is divided opinion. Some simply refuse to acknowledge that it happened at all, others accept it, with explanations. Samuel Laing, for example, in his *Heimskringla,* states a seemingly incontrovertible argument in favor of the greater value of the sagas as laid down in the *Flateybook* (which includes the saga of Freydis), insisting that they are decidedly more authentic than *Hauk's Book.* Then he performs a fascinating turnabout by dismissing the Freydis saga as too incredible to dignify by comment. Other writers seem hurt by it, and consider it such a reflection on the vikings that it must be discredited, or at worst, dismissed as a fabrication.

Of those who accept it, with deductive reasoning, the two best explanations of Freydis' actions are from Gathorne-Hardy and Pohl. The Englishman asserts that her act was that of a woman scorned. She failed in her bargaining, and was driven, in furious temper, to badger her husband into an act of carnage. Pohl speculates that she might have been having an affair with Finnbogi, and was fearful of gossip by the women in Finnbogi's party. Since the punishment for adultery in Iceland—and therefore Greenland—was death, she might have decided to eliminate witnesses to her infidelity before returning home.

I accept the saga of Freydis without question. It is so monstrous that it can't be a fabrication, and significantly, appears only in the *Flateybook*. That collection is considered to be a faithful documentary of events in the Greenland colony, and set down in more detail than their counterparts in *Hauk's Book,* for reasons already given.

I think it is simply the gruesome story of Freydis and what she did in Vinland, and nothing more.

I also think there is a much more credible explanation of her actions.

Freydis was insane. Thoroughly and incurably insane.

It would appear that she had more than a hint of schizoid in her makeup. She showed all the symptoms of a disturbed person when she thrust herself at the Indians, breasts bared, sword flailing. She demonstrated her moody extremes in the efficiency with which she planned the voyage to Vinland and in the glowing promises to the brothers, as opposed to her senseless expulsion of the latter from Leif's Shelters in Vinland at journey's end.

Her obvious state of paranoia was demonstrated in her concealment of five additional men in her ship before she left Greenland. Why would she so "insure" herself if she weren't planning murder? Perhaps she had hoped to accomplish the deed on arrival in Rocky Nook when she cast out the brothers, hoping such an act would so inflame them that she would be justified in demanding their deaths of Thorvard. I suspect that the dissensions which arose during the games were precipitated by her in another attempt to bring the holocaust into being. If so, she had failed twice; and by spring, it became apparent that she would have to act fast, before Helgi and Finnbogi took their departure from Vinland. I don't believe she ever bargained with Finnbogi. The tremendous differences in the two versions of what happened on the fateful morning negate that possibility. It must be remembered that the story of the alleged meeting with Finnbogi had to come from Freydis, and was retold only after the episode became a saga, and public property. The conversation with Thorvard on her "return" from the Finnbogi meeting, would, of course, have been corroborated by her husband.

We know, therefore, that she made accusations against the brothers to her husband, thereby coercing him into murdering not only the brothers, but their entire crew as well, excepting the women. We *don't* know that anything at all transpired between her and Finnbogi prior to her climbing back into bed with Thorvard. (She may have gotten her feet wet as she walked the forest, formulating her plot.) If, as she asserts, Finnbogi agreed to exchange ships, what reason would exist to trigger such a carnage? None. What, then, motivated the murders?

Gathorne-Hardy's premise that she was a woman scorned is not unreasonable, but how did she know she was going to be scorned when she took out her "five-man insurance policy" in Greenland?

Pohl's conclusion doesn't fit into the tone of the saga. She had shown her evil self to the brothers on two occasions after reaching Rocky Nook. I think it unlikely that either of the brothers would have been interested in an amorous excursion with her. It would have been neither desirous nor necessary. The brothers had ready access to the women in their party for biological research.

She murdered because she was insane.

Her derangement may have dated from her second year in Vinland with Karlsefni. At the time of her engagement with the Indians, she was pregnant. Her child was either stillborn, or she miscarried. The saga mentions nothing of the birth of a child to Freydis; it refers only to the birth of Snorri, son of Karlsefni and Gudrid.

It is entirely reasonable that Freydis may have been an unstable person basically. When, during the battle with the Indians, she realized that the vikings were fleeing, she may been overwrought to the point of attempting to rout the Indians herself. Fear of safety for her unborn child could easily have brought about such an otherwise insane performance.

If, as a result of that experience, she lost her child, and gradually crossed the line from schizoid into paranoiac, it might well be that she plotted the murder of the vikings as a punishment. Perhaps they symbolized the "cowardly" forces of Karlsefni to her; her words during the battle at Hop clearly reflect her contempt for those battered warriors.

Freydis must not be viewed with revulsion. She was mentally ill.

But she did cause a mass murder; and worse, she personally saw to the slaying of five women, a deed her own men could not bring themselves to commit. When she had done it, she probably piled the bodies in her own ship, and gave them a viking burial: she set the ship afire in Cape Cod Bay.

And she was punished. And Thorvard was punished.

At first blush, Leif's reaction to Freydis' crime seems surprisingly tolerant. It was not. Good, kind Leif could not punish his half-sister in the accepted legal manner, by banishment, as prescribed by Icelandic law, nor could he sentence her to death. But he did punish her—and Thorvard—by ostracism.

"Hence it came to pass," the saga mournfully relates, "that no one from that time forward thought them worthy of aught but evil."

In a colony as tiny as Greenland, such an opinion held by the populace could only result in slow death. Since none would deal with them, they were forced to live as recluses, and a more frightful existence is difficult to conceive. Day upon endless day they stared at each other, with no release from the plane of mutual hatred on which they were trapped. They hated—and waited.

And that is all there is to know of Freydis, and of Thorvard.

The Vinland House of Leif Ericsson fell into decay, crumbling gradually until only its foundation held together, the wood and sod of the walls and roof rotted and collapsed into the big room which, for one winter, housed a viking and his dream of the new land he planned to dwell in—a dream he was never to achieve. Leif was fated to continue as ruler of the Greenland colony until his death in 1025, when his son, Thorkel, succeeded him.

And the forest mulch continued to rise, layer upon layer, above the hole in the ground at Rocky Nook until John Howland found it and built himself a dwelling upon it. And blood was not spilled again in Plymouth colony until 1630, when John Billington, one of the Pilgrim Fathers, waylaid and shot one John Newcomin. Billington was hanged for his crime, and it would appear that fate had sent him to lift the shadow Freydis had cast over Vinland, for it was decided by the Plymouth Elders that "he ought to die, and the land be purged of blood."

Amen.

PLATE 17. *(left)* Brendan's Bay, on the Kerry seacoast in Ireland. It was from here that St. Brendan departed on his epic voyage to America in the sixth century.

ATE 18. *(right)* The in-
ibed viking rock, dating
m about the tenth century,
Aptuxcet Trading Post,
ırne, Massachusetts. The
tom line is runic; the top
e an Indian pictograph
obably carved at a later
e.

ATE 19. *(below)* The famed Dighton rock on Assonet Neck, Rhode Island, with
multitudinous, largely indecipherable inscriptions. This photograph, with the
vings whitened, was made in the nineteenth century.

PLATE 20. Two views of effigy found at Manomet, Massachusetts, by Josep
Notini. The head bears strong Norse characteristics. Did one of Leif Ericsson
vikings carve it?

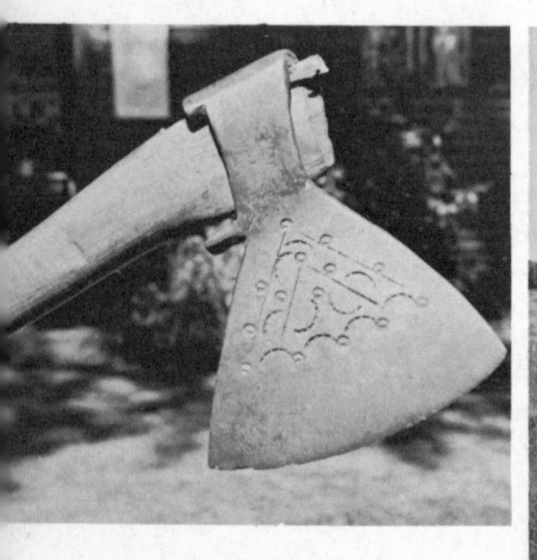

PLATE 21. Medieval ax excavated from Howland House site at Rocky Nook Point, Massachusetts, site of Leif Ericsson's camp. The ax is called the "old Norse axe" and is kept at Howland House.

PLATE 22. The marsh which now
ers the cove at Rocky Nook P
Massachusetts, where Leif Eric
landed 1000 years ago.

TE 23. *(above)* The Yarmouth,
a Scotia, runestone; possibly a
c of the eleventh-century Ameri-
expedition of Thorfinn Karlsefni.

PLATE 24. *(above)* Old Stone Tower at Newport, Rhode Island, the most tantalizing structure in America. Its architectural style dates to the twelfth century, yet historians insist it is colonial! The author believes it was built by an Icelandic bishop.

PLATE 25. *(left)* In examining this, and other aerial photographs of the Newport Tower, the author found a telltale discoloration in the grass north of the tower, indicated by arrow. It may cover a hidden foundation which could date the tower with some precision. The city of Newport refuses to permit a "dig."

ATE 26. *(below)* Facsimile of the Plowden Paper which dates the Newport
ver at 1632, or seven years before English settlers in the region.

26 By which and service of [illegible] and hope of gaine
grows of order and discipline and intelligence with the Savages b[illegible]
Virginia on the South New England on the North the entry
Plantation 60 miles on the west be had. /
So that 30 idle men as souldiers or gent be resident in a roun[illegible]
stone towre and by turnes to trade with the Savages and to keep the
ordinance and armes neate, so yt 300 one colony of [illegible]
so yt 100 of them be Negro slaves condemned men or apprentices
[illegible] all danger is a [illegible] for his [illegible] and

PLATE 27. The head in this Aztec vase seems remarkably viking-like.

PLATE 28. —and even more so wh the proper headdress is added.

PLATE 29. This is what the typical Aztec of the ninth century looked like.

PLATE 30. The head on this Az effigy cup is certainly not that o Middle-American Indian. T weary, bearded face belongs m properly to an eleventh-century I monk.

TE 31. Sand Island (the triangular islet in the foreground), in the Ohio River
Louisville, Kentucky. The island figured in a battle between twelfth-century
lshmen and Indians.

PLATE 32. *(left)* America's ol
historical document: the Kensing
Runestone, carved by vikings in
fourteenth century near Kensing
Minnesota. Discovered in 1898,
stone has had a stormy history.

PLATE 33. *(below)* The swo
and small piece of horse-harr
claimed to have been disc
near Beardmore, Ontario, in 1
1932*. (The footnote is suppli
the Royal Ontario Museum.
NEBC principle!)

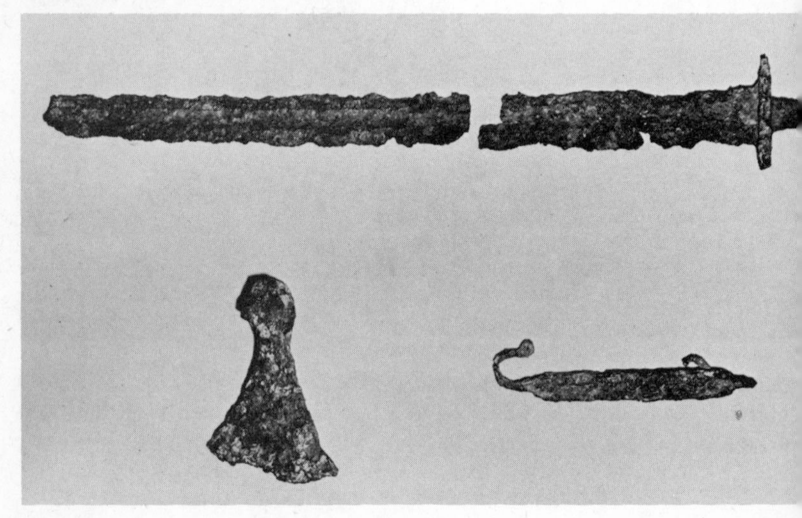

*In spite of protracted research on the part of the Royal Ontario Museum (which
owns the objects), it has not been possible to authenticate the story of the all
discovery nor even to prove that the objects are of undoubted viking origin. The B
more objects cannot, therefore, be used to demonstrate the presence of Norseme
the interior of America.

ATE 34. *(right)* The amazing
ight of Westford, Massachusetts.
e effigy, carved on a rock, holds a
ield bearing the crest of four-
enth-century Sinclairs, rulers of
e Orkney Islands.

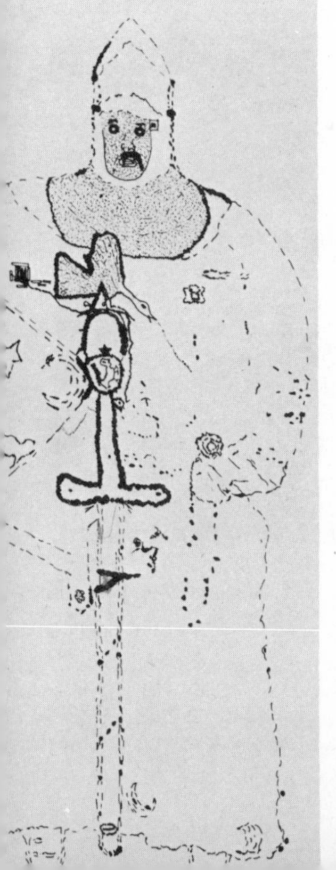

PLATE 35. *(left)* A drawing of the complete effigy, reconstructing areas now worn away.

PLATE 36. Mr. Albert Wheeler, holding a fragment of the suspected viking
found on his property in Massachusetts.

CHAPTER 14

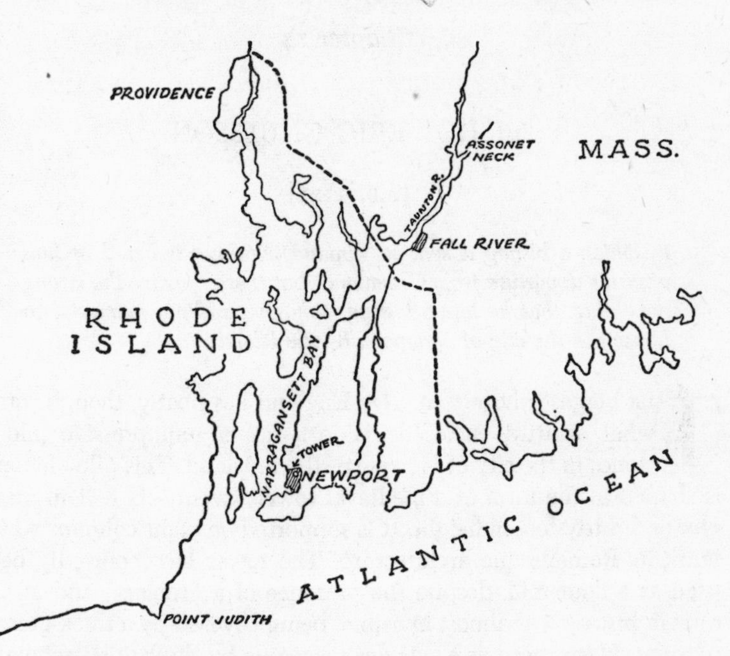

NARRAGANSETT BAY REGION

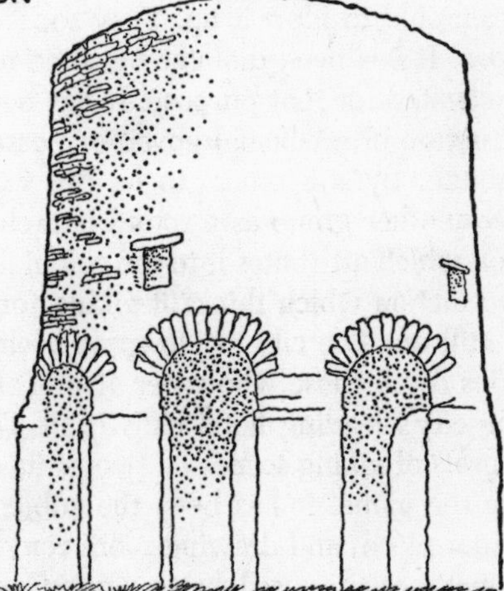

Chapter 14

BISHOP ERIC GNUPSSON

[A.D. 1121]

In which a bishop is sent to Vinland. Nothing is heard of him after his departure from Greenland, but there remains the strong possibility that he left a lasting, though puzzling, memorial to himself in the city of Newport, Rhode Island.

THE biggest mystery in New England lies neatly, though somewhat draftily, enclosed inside a rather unimpressive pile of stones in the city of Newport, Rhode Island. This pile of stones is shaped in the form of a medieval tower, twenty-six feet in diameter and thirty feet in height. It is supported on eight columns which mark its Romanesque architecture. The tower has reportedly been used as a flour mill, despite the presence of a fireplace, and at one time in history was almost invisible, being covered by a thick growth of vines. It was used as a powder magazine by the British, who also attempted to blow it up. They succeeded only in disintegrating the apex. It has been thought by some to harbor Spanish treasure, and excavated for that purpose. It has been thought by others to be the structure of a colonial governor possessed of great ego. It has been thought by still others to be the work of the Portuguese, and by yet another group as a round church built by the vikings. The faction which attributes it to the colonial governor has been at war with the faction which thinks it viking for many decades, and the battle is still on. The city of Newport itself is divided. Within its boundaries dwell those who sneer at un-colonial theories regarding it, yet the city's leading hotel calls itself The Viking, and boasts colorful murals of viking scenes on two of its dining-room walls to substantiate the name. It has been the subject of books and articles, newspaper pieces and drawing-room conversation as well as the center of sometimes furious debates among scholars of high standing. It appears on the official letterheads of the city government of Newport.

But nobody knows who built it.

I suspect an Icelandic bishop.

America's next discoverer was sent here by the Vatican, in the year 1121, when the country was still called Vinland. He was a bishop named Eric Gnupsson and, from the six entries in as many different annals of Iceland, he knew that Vinland existed, but wasn't quite sure just where it was.

"Bishop Eric sought Wineland" is the brief entry in the *Annales Reseniani,* and it occurs under events listed for the twelfth century, and more specifically, for the year 1121. Five other historians note the same excursion by the bishop, and all list it for the same year. Some, like the entry in the *Annales Regii,* identify him as the Bishop of Greenland, in addition to recording his journey to the New World. Unfortunately, that is the only information we have relating to Eric and Vinland. But other Icelandic documents tell us more of his background and life as a dignitary of the Church.

In the period following the Christianization of Iceland and Greenland, the Church in Rome examined the problems in these countries as closely as the wretched transportation and communication of the day permitted, and set about supplying the necessary churchmen to look after the flocks in those countries. Iceland was granted two bishoprics soon after the conversion of that country, but it wasn't until the second decade of the twelfth century that Greenland was so honored. The prelate chosen to guide the Church in Greenland was Eric Gnupsson, an Icelander of excellent family. In 1112, or 1113, the record is not quite clear, he was called before Pope Paschal II, and informed that he was to depart for Greenland as bishop.

We know, therefore, that Eric was indeed the Bishop of Greenland by the year 1112 or 1113. According to the entries in various collections of Icelandic annals, we know that later he went to Vinland. It can only be concluded that this chronology was in keeping with the natural progression of ministering to the members of the Catholic Church in remote places. It had taken Greenland many years to get its bishopric; the Church had quite obviously been busier with matters in Europe proper and had achieved a pile-up of detail yet to be disposed of in out-of-the-way places. By the twelfth century, however, the Church was organized with relative smoothness in Europe and the gap between appointing bishops to Greenland and Vinland was not nearly so great as it had been in the case of Iceland and Greenland. So it was that Eric, Bishop of Greenland, was sent to Vinland before he had completed a decade of service to the Church in Greenland.

The first thought that occurs when considering this most interesting appointment is: If Eric were being sent to Vinland, whom was he expected to serve as spiritual leader? Indians? Northmen? Or both?

An excellent question, and one which can only be answered in conjecture. Hjalmar Holand, in *Explorations in America Before Columbus,* suggests that while he might have been sent as a missionary to the Indians, or *Skraelings,* who were known to dwell in Vinland, it is more probable that there was in Rome a suspicion, at least, that a flourishing colony of Norse was settled here, and therefore warranted a bishop. Philip Ainsworth Means, in *The Newport Tower,* agrees with Holand's second suggestion, and offers an intriguing fragment of intelligence to support it.

In the eleventh century, Means states, a King of Norway named Harald the Severe took a fleet of ships across the North Atlantic, to a place where the sea was frozen over perpetually, and which proved so dangerous that Harald escaped with his life only through extreme good fortune. The authority for this knowledge is Adam of Bremen. Means then speculates that Harald might actually have sought for, and reached Vinland and set up a trading colony there. He kept it secret, in the manner of the Phoenicians, and it proved a steady source of revenue for the Norwegian Crown. This speculation is not as improbable as it would appear at first blush. The sagas tell us that Karlsefni and Gudrid went to Norway after they left Greenland in 1013. That they kept silent about their stay in Vinland is absolutely inconceivable. More probably, they recounted their exciting adventure over and over to new audiences; the tale was perhaps the main after-dinner topic in Norway for a long time. It is therefore reasonable to assume that Harald the Severe, on his accession to the throne in 1047, went in search of the land to the west, and set up a trading post, manned by a powerful guard to defend the traders from the Indians. It is also entirely possible that they maintained friendly relations with the natives, despite the evidence of the unpleasantness experienced by Karlsefni. These Northmen would be interested only in trading, and not land-grabbing. It was this later circumstance, aggressively pursued by the Pilgrims and Puritans which led to the bloody Indian wars of the seventeenth century.

I think that Holand and Means are quite correct in predicating Eric's mission to Vinland on an existing colony.

And I think Eric came here with a fleet of ships bearing more colonists, and cattle and, most importantly, a particular kind of highly skilled artisan. To Eric, the artisans, which may have numbered in the hundreds, were vital.

He needed them to build a church.

And when they arrived in Vinland and found the colony begun by Harald, he set them to the task. And they built it. It was a beautiful church, round and tall and stately, and it was supported on eight columns and covered with pure white plaster, and could be used as a signal tower for other Norse craft coming to the Vinland settlement.

It stood on what is now called Aquidneck, in Narragansett Bay, and its precise location was within what is now the city of Newport.

It is still there and is sometimes called the Old Mill, or The Old Stone Mill, or The Newport Tower. That it was actually built by Eric Gnupsson is, I must confess, a theory which I alone seem to hold today, although in the past it was held by such interested scholars as Carl Christian Rafn and Philip Ainsworth Means. Hjalmar Holand attributes it to the expedition sent here in 1355, led by Paul Knutson, and so forceful have his arguments been that Means began to be swayed by them even after he had written his masterful *The Newport Tower,* in which he stated the case for Eric Gnupsson so well.

Among contemporary writers probing into the viking problem, however, I stand, to the best of my knowledge, alone in postulating Eric as the builder of the tower. Among the others, and in that group I will include historians and archaeologists along with the writers, divers opinions are held, creating a never-ceasing battle over the identity of the tower's builder or builders.

To understand how this battle came to be, and why it is still raging today, it is necessary to learn of the two most prominent theories which have existed concerning the origin of the building, and how they came into being.

The first theory holds that the tower was built by Governor Benedict Arnold (not the traitor) who was presiding officer of the Newport colony from 1633 to 1677. According to the belief held by the Arnoldists, the governor built the tower to provide a windmill for the Newporters after a storm had boldly disposed of the mill owned by Peter Easton. Since Easton's mill was the only one in the settlement, the townspeople turned to Arnold to supply them with a new one. Arnold then caused a huge stone tower, built in the style of the twelfth century, to be built to grind flour for Newport. For this effort both Arnold and the good people of Newport must be given citations for bravery, serenity, persistence, and possibly for sheer idiocy. The year of the alleged erection of the tower by Arnold was 1675, a year of terror and pillage and destruction throughout New England, because of the Indian war engaged in by the natives, under King Philip, and the colonials. The war continued through 1676, with great fatalities on both sides.

Yet the Arnoldists would have us believe that in a time of such utter terror, the people of Newport contrived to build a tower which required the moving of a million pounds of stone, in order that they might have a windmill. Since their fields, along with their homes, had conceivably been burned by the rampaging red men, I find it difficult to imagine what they planned to mill in such a structure. Means asks where they would have obtained the labor. From among terrified colonists whose only thought was survival? Hardly. Holand remarks that such labor would have been understandable had they been building a fort; then he wonders why, if it were designed as such, did they put it on decorative columns leaving eight open arches for easy access by the Indians? I simply ask why they would build it at all—war or no war. It matches no known colonial building on this continent. And its architecture is Romanesque, a style which fell into disuse after the twelfth century.

In *The Newport Tower,* written in 1942, Philip Means delineated the history of the controversy over the tower in an erudite and thoroughly charming manner. He swung freely at the Arnoldists, chopping down their frail platform plank by plank, and documented—in a comprehensive assimilation of facts—the theory of the Northmen.

He examined all the theories, in every facet, and examined the architecture of the tower itself. He noted the beginnings of the Arnold theory, as it came from the pen of John Gorham Palfrey, who blasted the Norse theory to bits. After Palfrey's pronouncement in 1858, Means related, "The Arnold theory became robust, self-satisfied, and generally acceptable to almost everyone; the Norse theory became a furtive, skulking outcast—at least for a time."

I must note, here, that the Arnold theory was built upon three vague predications:

1. It was built by Arnold because he mentions it in his will, dated 1677, referring to it as "my stonebuilt windmiln."
2. It resembles a windmill standing in Chesterton, England, near the boyhood home of Arnold. In providing the colonists with a new mill, he was stricken with nostalgia and caused the new mill to be built on the same architectural scheme.
3. There is no mention of it in written records of Newport prior to 1677.

Means blasted these predications thoroughly. He proved, first, that there exists in Newport, a document mentioning the mill—or tower—in February of 1677, ten months prior to the Arnold will. It proves conclusively that the tower was near ground belonging to Nathaniel Dickens, who in turn deeded it to the Jewish congregation at Newport for a cemetery. The tower is referred to as "ye stone mill." Note that it is not referred to as "Governor Arnold's Stone Mill," a most logical designation had it been the case. While not conclusive proof that the mill is older than 1677, the earlier document casts much doubt on Arnold's authorship of the structure.

Next, Means proved that Arnold had *not* been born in Chesterton, and that the "mill" which the Arnoldists referred to was actually an observatory. Would it seem sensible that Arnold would pattern a windmill after an observatory?

Means also discovered that Governor William Coddington, who founded Newport in 1639, is said to have made inquiries of the Indians concerning its origin. Obviously, in order to inquire about it, the tower had to be standing in 1639, thirty-eight years before its mention in Arnold's will.

Unfortunately, Means, though straining through every page of his remarkable book, was able to come to no conclusion about the mill other than that which proved that Arnold did not build it. In his summary, he pled for excavation of the site, and added that in an attempt he himself made to obtain permission to dig there, he was met with flat refusal by the town fathers of Newport, based on the supposition that such excavations would ruin the old mill. He also noted the rugged treatment accorded a Virginian who arrived in Newport in 1941 to study the tower. It would seem that the town fathers at that time were assuring themselves that no pre-Columbian evidence was going to be brought to the surface while *they* were handling things. But Means's book apparently had some effect on the good burghers of Newport. They were forced to give permission for a "dig."

In 1949, William S. Godfrey, Jr., began to excavate under the tower. The report on his dig appears in *Archaeology,* Summer 1950. But the town fathers had exercised extreme caution in granting permission for the excavation. Godfrey was told to confine his investigation to the area enclosed by the fence surrounding the edifice. He was not permitted to go beyond it in any direction. Means had suggested that "trenching out" in radiating lines, as spokes from a hub, might produce evidence of other foundations since he suspected the structure to be an old round church. But Godfrey was not permitted to trench out. The application of such a prohibition could help keep safe the NEBC Principle. And so Godfrey dug at the base of the tower, and under one section of the walk surrounding it.

The Godfrey excavation produced nothing but colonial artifacts. He also noted that there had been no less than five previous excavations revealed as he dug down. He does not connect the colonial artifacts with these five previous excavations, however, but simply uses the objects to prove that the tower was colonial. There is no supposition that all Norse artifacts, if any, had been removed by earlier digs. Since he did not trench out, no attempt was made to determine the location of another circular foundation. His report contains inconsistencies with later reports on the dig. In the Autumn 1951 issue of *Archaeology,* Frederick Pohl commented on Mr. Godfrey's finds, shredding them somewhat. Mr. Godfrey then answered Mr. Pohl in the same vein. Hjalmar Holand entered into it a bit later, and in 1956, dissected Mr. Godfrey neatly. The battle still rages.

After the Godfrey dig, Pohl became acutely interested in the tower and eventually made three extremely valuable contributions to the debate. His arguments, unfortunately, do nothing more than discredit the Arnold theory with much more finality than did Means.

Pohl's contributions to the brouhaha were these:

1. He demonstrated that the tower was not built by an English linear measurement, and the measurement actually used was closest to the old Norse system.
2. Acting on a tip from two friends, Robert King of Merrick, Long Island, and Mrs. Geraldine Houston of Teaneck, New Jersey, he investigated a document concerning land grants to Sir Edmund Plowden in 1632, 7 years before the colonial settlement of Newport. They mention the tower.
3. He discovered an old map, made by one William Wood, who visited the area between 1629 and 1634. Wood listed the town of Plymouth, Massachusetts, in its correct position, but then listed another town, on Narragansett Bay, which he calls "*Old* Plymouth." The map is included in a volume titled *A Book of Old Maps,* by Fite and Freeman.

To the best of my knowledge, none of Pohl's additions to the problem have been received with scholarly acclaim. I have seen no further discussion of the linear measurements in any scientific publication, nor have I seen any comment on the Plowden Paper, which conclusively establishes the tower as being older than 1639, the year of settlement in Newport. I have seen nothing in any archaeological journal on William Wood's old map. In short, "if the scholarly gentlemen ignore Mr. Pohl's findings, perhaps they will go away."

To illustrate my point, I enjoyed the interesting experience of being shouted at by one of America's most distinguished archaeologists during a discussion of the Newport Tower. When I dared mention the Plowden Paper, he jolted me rather severely by literally yelling that "he would believe it when he saw it!" This remarkable behavior is even more remarkable when it is considered that Pohl wrote an article on that paper for the *New England Quarterly* in December 1945. I must needs add that that publication did not consider the article earth-shaking, and, rather than give it the prominence it deserved, they buried it in the back of the book under the umbrella of a department they called "Memoranda and Documents." Apparently they realized the importance of the paper, but tried as little as possible to jar the Arnoldists among their readers.

The most frightening aspect of my own conversation with the distinguished gentleman mentioned above is his declaration that he would believe only when he *saw* the document. Such a statement is clear implication of fraud on Pohl's part, and collusion on the part of the *New England Quarterly* for printing such fraudulent claims. Pohl gives his source for the document, and actually went to England, where it is kept, to examine it. He was extremely careful to check the phraseology of said paper, wishing to have no part of an inadvertent misquote. The attitude of the howling scholar is typical, unhappily, of many who are riveted to the NEBC Principle.

To establish the reality of the Plowden Paper, I have obtained, from the Public Records Office in London, England, located at Chancery Lane, W.C., 2, photostats of the document. Its title is: *The Commodities of the Island called Manati or Long Isle within the Continent of Virginia.* Since there are twenty-nine paragraphs to the paper, I reproduce, in Plate 26, only the segment which contains paragraphs 26 and 27. In paragraph 27 is the passage which refers to the Newport Tower. This document can also be found in the *Collections of the New York Historical Society for 1869,* vol. II, pages 217–18.

The paper was drawn, in 1632, by Sir Edmund Plowden, who had petitioned the Crown to settle some 500 inhabitants on "Long Isle," which is noted as an alternate name for "Isle Plowden." In addition, other isles and areas on the mainland were noted under the inclusive name, New Albion. Following custom and requirement, Sir Edmund listed twenty-nine *commodities,* or advantages through natural resources, etc., which could be found in the proposed colony. In great detail, the paper lists the excellence of fishing in the waters adjacent, the abundance of wild vines, deer, turkeys, the variety of trees, and many other enticing qualities, including water which was "as good as small beer." This last, no doubt, had a strong appeal.

In paragraph 27, a suggested garrison strength is noted, and the method of housing them duly recorded:

> 27: So that 30 idle men as souldiers or gent be resident in a rownd stone towre and by tornes to trade with the savages and to keep their ordinance and arms neate. . . .

Recalling that Sir Edmund's grant was to be on Long Island and the mainland to the north, the paramount question here is: Where is the "rownd stone towre" referred to in article 27? Clearly it is not a building standing on Long Island; there is not—nor has there ever been—any record of such. And, as Pohl has noted, if it were a "commodity" to be built in the future, it would not be listed in the twenty-nine paragraphs at all. These paragraphs listed only *existing* commodities—advantages which were to be had immediately on settling in New Albion. Nor does it seem sensible, if the building *were* a proposed structure, that it would be specified as "round" and "stone." Such an edifice would be a waste of time and effort for a trading-post palisade, and entirely out of keeping with colonial procedures. In every case of trading-post construction, the buildings were invariably built as stockade types, never as incongruities such as a round stone tower.

It can be safely assumed then, that the tower was standing in Newport when Sir Edmund Plowden—who had obviously investigated the area thoroughly if one considers the completeness of his list of commodities—went seeking settlers for New Albion. This evidence, in itself, absolutely negates the idea that the tower was built in 1677 by Benedict Arnold, and was, indeed, built by someone many years prior to 1632.

There is unquestionably a connection between the Plowden Paper and the map made by William Wood after he visited the area in the years from 1629 to 1634. The map, you will recall, lists Plymouth, Massachusetts, in its proper place, but calls it "New Plymouth." In the Narragansett Bay region, approximating the location of Newport, is another settlement, called "Old Plymouth." Obviously there was, in 1634, record of an earlier settlement in Rhode Island, which the map maker saw fit to call Old Plymouth, thus differentiating it from the later settlement, described by the word "New."

We also have the coincidence here of the "White Indians." In describing the natives of the Narragansett in 1524, a member of the Verrazano expedition, one Bernardo Carli, had this to say:

> . . . the most beautiful people and the most civilized in customs that we have found . . . they excel us in size; they are of bronze color, some inclined more to whiteness. . . .

It is more than coincidence, and certainly cannot be ascribed to error that Sir Edmund Plowden listed a "rownd stone towre" in his commodities, and that William Wood listed a colony at Newport which he called "Old Plymouth" . . . and that Bernardo Carli should note the whiteness of the inhabitants along with their "most civilized customs."

The Plowden Paper and William Wood's map speak for themselves; unfortunately neither one points directly to the Northmen, or more specifically, to Bishop Eric as the tower's builder, or builders.

In February 1960, however, there appeared a paper written by Edward Adams Richardson, an engineer. It was published in the *Journal of the Surveying and Mapping Division, Proceedings of the American Society of Civil Engineers.*

Mr. Richardson became interested in the tower after he noted the peculiar arrangement of its windows. A thought began to germinate, and, when he had completed his study of the tower, he concluded that it had been built sometime during or before the fourteenth century as a round church equipped for signaling purposes. According to Mr. Richardson, the second floor of the tower was designed to act as a signal-receiving station, and the first floor as a sending station. His paper is extremely technical and, for a layman, difficult to follow. It boils down, however, to this: The windows on the first floor are designed so that a fire in the tower's fireplace would be capable of sending light out to points in Narragansett Bay, concentrating on the areas to the east and south of the tower. The second-floor windows were designed to enable the sighting of approaching lights at night from the same directions.

Mr. Richardson's theories make sense. They help to explain the absence of windows to the north of the tower, a puzzling factor which has nearly always served to cloud the idea of a watchtower in connection with the structure. It would also explain the peculiar shape and size of the windows. Mr. Richardson also comments on the fireplace design, noting that it is of a style which was certainly obsolete by the seventeenth century, when Arnold is said to have built the tower.

I think that Mr. Richardson has hit on the proper function of the tower, apart from its initial conception as a church. Returning to Means's supposition of a colony begun here by Harald the Severe, it is reasonable to presume that Eric was sent here because the Vatican was aware of Harald's colony and meant to extract tithes from it. Harald, even if he had hoped to keep the colony secret, certainly could not protest such a move on the part of the Church. When Eric arrived, he set about building his round church, and, possibly at the request of the commander of the Narragansett Trading Post, incorporated in its design a signaling and receiving system. Since the windows are oriented for transmitting and receiving signals from the east and south, they naturally adhere to the prime requirement of such a structure placed in the position it occupies on Aquidneck Island.

That the tower is ancient is apparent to even an unpracticed eye. That there remains a stanch and determined group of people who are grimly resolved that this twelfth-century structure was built by an egomaniacal governor in colonial times is more than mildly surprising. It can only demonstrate a strange sense of "patriotism," or a deep and abiding desire to cling to a historical framework which, accepted unquestioningly, must be protected at all cost.

The only other reason for grown men, including scientists and historians, to pronounce such a structure colonial is stupidity.

In 1948, Dr. Johannes Brøndsted, then director of the National Museum of Denmark, was shown the tower, along with many other supposed Norse sites in North America. Dr. Brøndsted does not agree with supposed Norse origins of the tower, but, in his 1950 report, published in *Aarbog før Nordisk Oldkyndighed og Historie,* a journal published in Copenhagen, he makes this curious observation:

"Thus there remain as typically Romanesque architectural details the pillars, the arches and the double splay. These medievalisms are so conspicuous that, if the tower were in Europe, dating it to the Middle Ages would probably meet with no protest."

Unhappily, the tower is in the United States of America. And visitors to the United States, and in particular, New England, prior to 1492, are as unlikely as visitors from outer space.

Again the monumental reluctance of men of science to identify an object, or a structure, or an inscription as pre-Columbian, even though the evidence apparent in that object, structure, or inscription screams out its antiquity in anguish.

This odd reluctance is not confined purely to men of science. The American Heritage *Book of Great Historic Places,* published in 1957, a magnificent volume done in the usually excellent manner and taste of its parent publication, lists the Newport Tower as "more probably the ruin of a windmill built by Benedict Arnold's great-grandfather, the first Governor of Rhode Island." This despite the evidence in the

Plowden Paper and the Coddington inquiry . . . and all the other evidences.

There may yet be a way to determine the actual nature of the Newport Tower, and, in so doing arrive at a closer approximation of the date of its erection, if not the name of its builder. The chances for accomplishing this are, however, more than dim, as will be shown. In a discussion with Frank Glynn, during which we reviewed all the theories extant concerning the tower—and the one serious excavation made in modern times of its base—Glynn suggested that I study aerial photographs of it. Such photographs might show differences in the color of the grass surrounding the tower, possibly hinting at a buried foundation.

The aerial photography technique was widely used in Britain and produced evidences of Roman walls in many regions. Its principle is simple: where an ancient foundation remains in the ground, covered over with years of accumulation of grass or grain, the presence of the substructure can sometimes be determined by a difference in the color of the grass lying directly above it. For example, a lush growth of grass will reveal lighter patches where a foundation or object is buried because the grass in that immediate area is not rooted as nourishingly as the surrounding cover. The cover above the buried foundation, therefore, reflects the slightly less healthy state of the grass. By using this method underground walls and foundations of entire villages have been located.

Aerial photography has never been used by scientists and scholars studying the Newport Tower. The chances in favor of finding an additional foundation, now buried, in Touro Park seemed relatively good. Touro Park is essentially the same today as it was when Judah Touro bought the land on which the tower stands and deeded it to the city in 1854. It has not been built upon and the surface remains rather as it has always been. Most of those who regard the tower as pre-Columbian reason that it must have been a round church. Philip Means stated the strongest case for such thinking and showed 26 prototypical churches as the basis for his argument. If it were a round church of medieval construction, two additional structures probably were built coincident with the tower. The first would have been a round wooden ambulatory surrounding the tower, and the second a nave projecting from the tower and ambulatory, probably toward the north. In the round church, the rotunda was usually called the nave, but the small size of the Newport Tower would seem to call for additional space for services; thus, an additional nave.

What I hoped to find, then, in examining aerial photographs of the Newport Tower was a hint of foundations, now covered over—one presumably round, the other rectangular—and jutting from the church to the north. Finding the round foundation could be ruled out immediately; the tower is now surrounded by a circular sidewalk which covers the area to a point beyond that which would have been occupied by the ambulatory. The only hope would be in detecting evidences of the rectangular structure, long since vanished.

I succeeded in obtaining two sets of aerial photographs of the tower, some taken—at high altitudes—directly overhead and others slightly oblique. It becomes easier to evaluate the nature of an aerial photo if pictures taken from different perspectives, at the same altitudes, are used. Called "overlaps," they reveal dimension when placed on a stereopticon device. The first set of pictures came from Robinson Aerial Surveys and were taken in 1939. The second set was supplied by the Commodity Stabilization Service and were taken in 1951.

When I examined the Robinson pictures I received a shock. Extending northward from the tower, between the structure and Mill Street, a light rectangular area was plainly evident! It was limned out as two light lines going out from the building, with a darker stripe between. The dark stripe was the same color as the surrounding grass. It appeared to project from the circular crater of the tower about 40 feet. Excited, I quickly examined the CSS pictures made eleven years subsequent to Robinson's and they appeared to confirm the earlier photographs' revelations. The American Geographic Society extended me the courtesy of examining the pictures on their stereopticon, but this procedure revealed nothing more than was visible to the naked eye due to the flatness of the terrain in question.

I wrote immediately to the Mayor of Newport and asked permission to excavate a narrow trench between the tower and Mill Street, in order to determine whether a foundation might actually be there. I also stated that, as a matter of routine, the dig would be carefully executed, and the small section subject to the excavation returned to its natural state.

Permission was refused.

About two weeks after I had written to Mayor Maher, I received the following letter from Robert A. Shea, Deputy City Clerk of the City of Newport:

Jan. 16th, 1961

Mayor James L. Maher has entrusted me to reply to your letter of 3 January 1961.

The Council of the City of Newport, following the examination of the Newport Tower by Arlington H. Mallery, R.P.E., passed Resolution #220–55 dated November 9, 1955, as follows:

"RESOLVED: That no further permission shall be granted, at any time, to excavate the foundation of the Old Stone Mill located in Touro Park, Newport."

Very truly yours,
ROBERT A. SHEA
Deputy City Clerk

The above is highly reminiscent of the problem faced by Philip Means. He was refused permission to dig, simply on whim. Now the town fathers have strengthened their position. They've passed a resolution that no more digs will take place. The resolution includes only the *base* of the tower. I asked permission to dig to the *north* of the tower, between it and Mill Street.

Permission was still refused, based on Resolution #220–55.

I know not by what authority Mr. Mallery was invested with the power to recommend that further investigation of the tower cease. Nor do I know the identities of the members of the city council of November 9, 1955, who as self-appointed guardians of the NEBC Principle, determined, once and for all time, to prevent further probing of the Old Stone Mill. I don't know whether Mayor James L. Maher and Robert A. Shea are supporters of the resolution. It matters not.

The resolution is on the books, and it will be honored.

Any attempt to determine further the nature of the tower is forever blocked. The full delineation of America's past is therefore impossible. An important segment of your history is neatly enshrouded by a city council not proud of the ancient relics within the limits of its jurisdiction, but frightened to death of them.

It is at once apparent that none will ever find the secret of the Newport Tower. Eric Gnupsson left no documents behind for scholarly study. If he had, they would, in all probability, be disdained as evidence by the Arnoldists . . . as have the Plowden Paper and William Wood's map of Old Plymouth.

The NEBC Principle is now strengthened legally to shield the tower from barbarian archaeologists who would seek the truth. But I wonder why the tower has no plaque upon it. A stranger, seeing it for the first time, must inquire if he is to learn of its history. There is no marker to tell of it.

Thus the Newport Tower, possibly one of the most important pre-Columbian monuments in America stands in Touro Park, unmarked, unauthenticated, but certainly not unnoticed.

And if Newport's Guardians of Our Colonial Heritage have their way, it will continue to stand, silent, unmarked and unauthenticated until the end of time.

All hail, Resolution #220–55!

CHAPTER 15

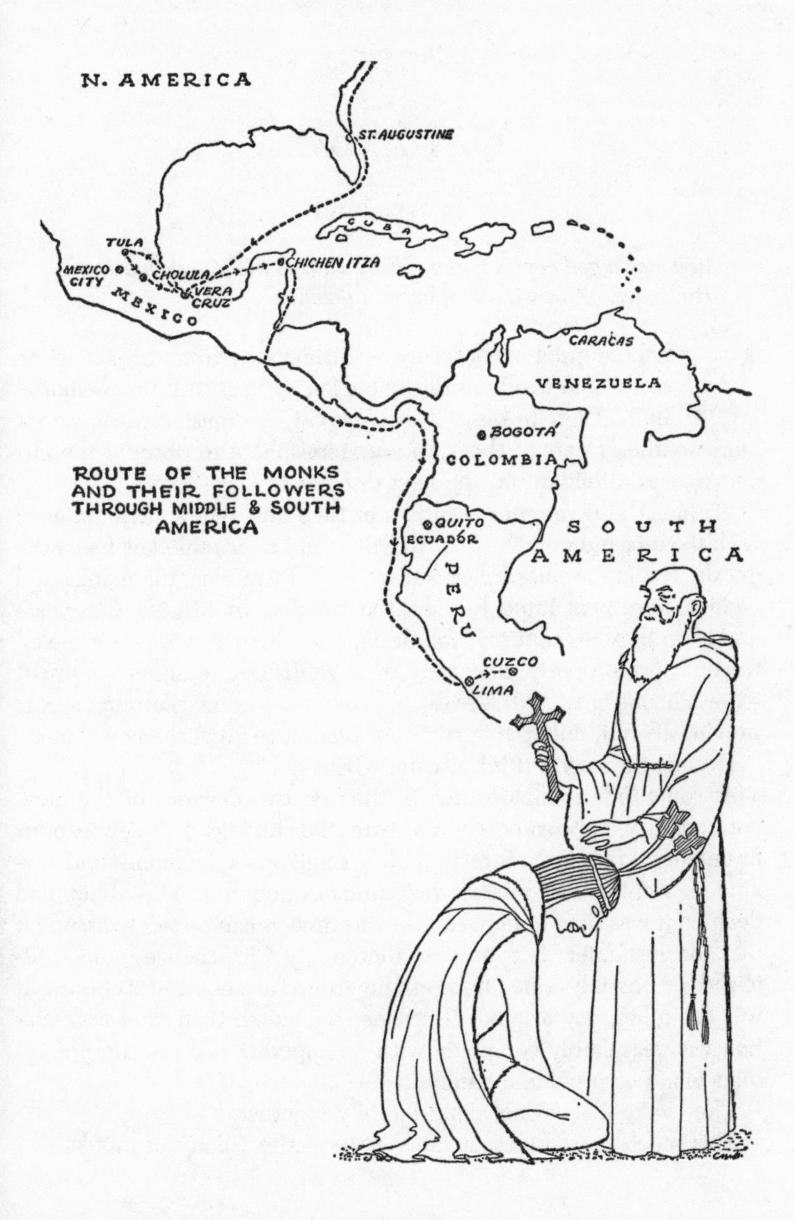

N. AMERICA
ST. AUGUSTINE
CUBA
TULA
MEXICO CITY
CHOLULA
VERA CRUZ
MEXICO
CHICHEN ITZA
CARACAS
VENEZUELA
BOGOTÁ
COLOMBIA
ROUTE OF THE MONKS AND THEIR FOLLOWERS THROUGH MIDDLE & SOUTH AMERICA
QUITO
ECUADÓR
SOUTH AMERICA
PERU
CUZCO
LIMA

Chapter 15

QUETZALCOATL

[A.D. C. 1010]

In which a god comes to the Aztecs, later to the Mayas and Inca. He leaves with each a prophecy of doom.

WITH the quiet evanescence of Bishop Eric from the American scene, and insidious decay beginning to assault the memorial he had left to himself at Newport, we must turn now to a more southerly part of the Western Hemisphere to observe the circumstances attendant on the next discovery.

We must also retreat a century in time and renew acquaintance with the intrepid monks of North Salem and their reluctant Icelandic guests. Having accomplished a discovery of America, the monks and vikings were next fated to view the wonders of Middle America—and from there to continue wandering and discover yet another continent. More properly, they went on to *re*-discover another continent—the Phoenicians had already discovered it one thousand years previously, but, unhappily, were not present to greet the newcomers.

Here is the way I think it came about:

At some indeterminate time in the first two decades of the eleventh century, approximately A.D. 1010, the stirrings of a new exodus undulated through the forests of New England as the monks and Icelanders were recalled from their mission outposts. The abbot had decided it was time to move on. At this time, it can be safely assumed that the Icelanders had become thoroughly Christianized and Celticized, or possibly, since both ethnic groups are notably stubborn, it was the other way around. It can be concluded, then, that assimilation was reasonably complete, with a tempering (?) injection of Indian blood to provide a catalyst.

They were all getting along happily together.

This much must be assumed, for the entire colony of monks and vikings disappeared, almost as suddenly as it came. And for good reason.

Leif Ericsson's visit in 1003–1004 had not been observed by the Celi Dei. That much is certain; the saga specifically notes that no contacts were established with natives in Vinland. Leif spent his entire stay on the banks of the Jones River at Rocky Nook, limiting exploration to as much as could be covered within the confines of a day, going and returning. He had arrived at Provincetown in the dark of night, sailing across Cape Cod Bay with the first glimmers of dawn. In that way he had been able to come to Vinland the Good without being detected. Assuming that he returned by the route which had taken him here, he would have passed the mouth of the Merrimack well out to sea, again drifting silently by the Celi Dei, unnoticed.

It was Karlsefni who precipitated the next flight of the Celi Dei, and in this hegira, they took the Icelanders with them.

Karlsefni's arrival, complete with women, cattle, and heaven only knows what else was recorded by the Celi Dei. It will be recalled that on leaving Markland (Nova Scotia), Karlsefni "coasted," that is, he sailed along the coast, steering south and west. Then he rounded Cape Cod and turned west to reach Streamfjord. In coasting, his itinerary would have taken him past the Merrimack, where he was sighted, and caused another alarm to go up. It had been a scant two decades since the great visitation of Greenland-bound Icelanders was thrust unceremoniously onto the Celi Dei, and now . . . well, now the entire unpleasantness seemed about to begin all over again.

Even though the monks thought these new Icelanders to be peaceable, the jig was clearly up. On reflection, they didn't really know whether these newcomers *were* Icelanders, and it certainly seemed that they were planning to stay. Palpably, the country wasn't big enough for the Irish-Icelanders and the new arrivals.

The old vikings were now put to supervising ship construction, recruiting their laborers from among themselves and the second generation product whose blood was mixed. Reasonable facsimiles of the old *langskips* were designed and built, and launched without ceremony. There was no fear now that the Icelanders would attempt to flee. They had children who were of the new breed, and by this time they had resigned themselves to life as proscribed by the meandering monks. What's more, they were vikings, and inherently as eager to sail off and discover new lands as the Celi Dei were to escape the new threat.

And so it was done.

The ships of the odyssey moved silently out of the Merrimack and sailed into the Atlantic. Orders were barked by the vikings, elated now by the feel of plank of deck beneath their feet. Crews were placed at their stations, women and children herded aft where tents could be raised, if necessary, to protect them from heavy seas or inclement weather. Of small talk there was none. The deep emotions of regret and loss must surely have touched all of them as they watched the land fall away. New England at its worst can only be described as beautiful. In winter its beauty achieves a majesty unique unto itself; in summer it is a magnificent conglomerate of all the things that typify the good life, a life based on communion with nature. Thoreau found his Walden in New England. I am inclined to think that his work would have shown a different value had his Walden been elsewhere.

We know not how many ships comprised this unhappy fleet. The population of the Irish colonies had swelled within itself since the first expatriates had set down in Iceland. Now it had added the castaway Icelanders and their families, and perhaps more than a few Indians. Among all, they had doubtless strengthened the complement by a large percentage. As the abbot sat in the fo'c'sle of the flagship and contemplated the odd flock he had gathered about him, it is possible that he wondered what had gone wrong. He, like those who had preceded him, and the monks who were now subordinate to him, had merely desired peace and solitude. All he had sought of life was the freedom to communicate with God, and the time to meditate and offer prayers. Somehow, the plan had gone awry. Here, in his own ship, were his own monks, Icelanders, Indians, and mixed offspring resulting from the unions forged among them. And now he was steering for yet a new land where only the good Lord knew what would be added to his homogenized following.

The fleet rounded Cape Ann and steered for Cape Cod, sailing past its *wunderstrands*, as had Karlsefni a short time before. Some of the monks had explored the southern New England coast and most probably had circumnavigated Long Island. The fleet's commander, then, a monk sharing navigational chores with one of the vikings, ordered the ships to sail north of the island and steer for the New Jersey coast.

They may even have left the wreck of one of their ships along that coast. In September 1960, immediately after Hurricane Donna, Albert and Salvatore Maraziti, two brothers resident in Manasquan, New Jersey, hauled ashore the soggy skeleton of an old ship. Both men have knowledge of ships and wrecks; both thought it different from other wrecks they had seen on the New Jersey sands. Obtaining a crane, they transported it to the home of Salvatore and built a plywood enclosure about it. I went to see the ship. I had to agree with the brothers Maraziti; it certainly *looked* old. I wasn't convinced that it was viking, however, since it showed traces of copper sheathing. Such precautions were rarely, if ever, taken by the vikings, and the ship's timbers seemed too big for a viking ship. They were reminiscent of the timbers described by Caesar in that portion of his diary which treats on the ships of the Venetii. It also seemed that it could have been one of the early seagoing vessels of the Phoenicians. It is reasonable to assume that the Phoenicians built their first oceangoing vessels much heavier than was necessary. Experience on the Atlantic over a protracted period would have shown them that 12-inch ribs were not essential. But this ship had 12-inch ribs. Early coastal vessels built in America sometimes had ribs as thick, because, as Francis Herreshoff has told me, they were "just too lazy to cut them down to the proper sizes." But this ship had a "feel" of ancient age to it.

Wood from the ship has, at this writing, been tested by the Humble Oil Company. Two readings have been obtained: one, that the ship is fifty years old; two, that it is one thousand years old. Further tests are in progress, but the laboratory is somewhat handicapped by the inordinate amount of extraneous organic material in the wood, a circumstance which greatly handicaps C-14 dating. Should this hoary craft prove to be one thousand years old, the chances are that it might have been one of the ships of the North Salem fleet, southward bound. The copper sheathing can readily be accounted for if the wrecked ship were Ari Marson's own, hauled up on blocks after its capture, instead of being destroyed. Ari, a trader, conceivably spent time in the Mediterranean, an area much frequented by tenth-century vikings. There he might have had the copper sheathing added as protection against the parasites found in warmer waters.

An equally intriguing theory occurs concerning the copper, and the iron and brass nails and pins found in the ship. The Icelanders knew how to work iron, and they were thoroughly familiar with bog iron, found in the Baltic area in great quantities. Is it unthinkable to consider that underneath the now reconstructed Saugus Iron works, at Saugus, Massachusetts, lies an even older bog-iron foundry, operated by Icelanders in America? I think it entirely possible. The pattern of archaeology shows that good locations for houses, mills, etc., were used over and over by new "discoverers" of such sites. I wonder whether the New Englanders of the 1640s might have stumbled upon evidence of an old ironworks and reconstructed it. The present reconstruction may well be the second. It would not be unusual to consider that the diggers at the site didn't go deep enough, or did not recognize older evidence if they encountered it. Remember Pattee's Caves, and the mysterious substructure at Rocky Nook.

Steering south along the New Jersey coast, the ships (less one, if they did, in truth, lose a vessel at Manasquan) continued down past Cape Hatteras and coasted to Florida. They may have tarried briefly in the Palmetto State in the manner of Brendan the Bold, but their stay there could not have been long and it is doubtful that descendants of the monks encountered by the navigator were there to greet them. The fugitives from North Salem were destined for much greater things, and a prodding fate, if they did tarry, sent them even farther to the south. This whimsical fate had decreed that they were to live among the Indians of Middle America, there to create a god-role for the abbot; a role which led to a legend—which in turn sped the conquering of Mexico by Cortez, and of Peru by Pizarro.

When the god-abbot left Mexico, he proceeded to South America, there to duplicate his earlier role and anticipate the voyage of the *Kon-Tiki* by some 800 years.

But I steal ahead of myself.

In the year 1010 or thereabouts, the Irish-Icelander-Indians, led by their unnamed abbot, landed somewhere near Veracruz and made their way inland to the ancient city of Tula. The selection of Tula as their destination was likely prompted by their desire to escape the steaming jungles around Veracruz and ascend to the highlands above. Tula, once thought to have been a mythical city, lies 8000 feet up on the Mexican Plateau, and offers a much more agreeable climate for such as Irish monks and Icelandic vikings. In myth and legend, it was called Tollan, and archaeologists simply thought it was a sort of Olympus of the Mixtec, the predecessors of the Aztec. Victor von Hagen in his *The Aztec: Man and Tribe,* notes that the "myth" of the city has been shattered by archaeological finds which apparently confirm its existence, although von Hagen himself is not thoroughly convinced. He notes the description of it as recorded by Bernardino de Sahagun, the Spanish historian, who described it as a beautiful city ". . . of rich palaces of green jade and white and red shell, where the ears of corn and pumpkin reached the size of a man, where cotton grew in the plant in all colors and the air was always filled with rare birds of precious feathers." Somewhat wryly, von Hagen adds: ". . . If this is Tollan, eight centuries have changed the land. It is now dry, parched, dust-filled, no 'precious bird' in its right avian mind would go there . . . and yet . . ."

Continuing finds, however, confirm the actuality of Tula as the cultural center of the Toltec, builders of gigantic temples, hewers of gigantic sculpture and creators of a culture which was later to reach southward to the Maya and contribute to the amazingly different art forms of the Totonac, a tribe still living in the Veracruz region.

Once in Tula, the abbot was astonished to find himself venerated as a god. He was given the name Quetzalcoatl, or the Plumed Serpent, and the perspiring band of refugees which accompanied him were called the *Nonoalca.*

At this juncture we find a blending of myth and fact, creating the problems rampant in any such admixture. The name "quetzalcoatl" did not apply to any single god in Mexico. It was used much as the Roman Emperors used the title Caesar. The first Quetzalcoatl is said to have sprung from a virgin birth. His mother swallowed a piece of jade, long after the violent death of her husband, and conception occurred forthwith. The result of this mineralized insemination produced Quetzalcoatl.

The mexicologists Robert Barlow and Wigberto Jiménez Moreno, who have delved deeply into the origins of the Mexican civilizations, have arrived at a reasonably precise redaction of the Quetzalcoatl legend, which in sum, reads thusly:

Quetzalcoatl was born *Ce Atl Topiltzin,* on the day *Ce Atl.* Reared by his grandparents, he was made a high priest of Quetzalcoatl because of his piety, and thereafter the name Quetzalcoatl was appended to his own.

Having reached that high station, he sought his murdered father's bones, found them, and removed them to the royal palace for burial befitting the sire of a high priest.

Then he visited an uncle, Ihuitimal, and went with him to the top of a pyramid. The uncle had killed Quetzalcoatl's father, Mixcoatl, and now Quetzalcoatl, precipitating an argument, returned the compliment, thus avenging his father's death. For this he was considered holy. He then renamed the hill Mixcoateptl, or Mixcoatl's Hill, and established a religious cult in his name, granting his father the character of a hunting god.

Next, the young priest assumed leadership of the Toltecs and moved the capital first to Tulancingo and later to Tula.

(It is at this point that I believe our legendary Quetzalcoatl and the wandering Ab of the Celi Dei become one.)

Now follows an extremely significant facet of the legend:

Quetzalcoatl came to Tula with people who were decidedly not Toltec. The Toltec called them *Nonoalca,* which, as Barlow puts it, means Deaf and Dumb People, *or* Those Who Cannot Speak Correctly! This descriptive was used, Barlow adds, because they probably spoke a *different, and therefore unintelligible language.* (My italics)

Then comes another pertinent circumstance: Quetzalcoatl was very friendly to these people *because they worshiped the same god that he did.* He also abolished human sacrifices and ordered that only tortillas, snakes, flowers, incense, and butterflies should be offered as sacrifice.

The Toltecs, quite naturally, were disturbed at such a heresy, fearing that their gods would become weak and that rains would fail. But, for the time, at least, Quetzalcoatl's ukases held. In spite of their unhappiness at his un-Toltec attitudes, the people liked the Plumed Serpent because he was indeed a pious man—celibate and given to meditating all day in a dark room.

He taught the people agricultural methods which greatly improved their crop growths and showed them how to grow variegated corn and cotton. He instructed them in the arts of silver-, gold- and copper-smithery, and taught them to make beautiful ornaments. Frederick Peterson, commenting on the above in his *Ancient Mex-*

ico, reasons that credit for these accomplishments should go to the Nonoalca; the Toltec thought that these People Who Could Not Speak Properly were capable of many miraculous things.

Life was peaceful in the Toltec country for many years under Quetzalcoatl, but seething among the more reactionary Indians was a desire to return to the old ways. Quetzalcoatl was firm in his determination to abolish, completely, human sacrifice, and the Toltecs eventually plotted to rid themselves of him.

There are several versions of Quetzalcoatl's hasty departure from Tula, one of which makes him the victim of a dastardly character blacking.

He was visited, it seems, by three evil deities, who invited him to dine with them. One of the wicked gods made a stew of tomatoes, onions, beans and corn, and, while it was brewing, mixed a batch of pulque, the lethal national drink of Mexico, said to have been invented by a woman. (If this is so, the woman could only have been an avowed misanthrope.) Armed with these delicacies, the three evil ones persuaded Quetzalcoatl to share their feast. He did, but showed reluctance to drink the pulque. Again their persuasions were effected and the Plumed Serpent succumbed. When he reached the singing stage, he called for his sister to join in the merriment. The evil ones summoned her, and left them. Quetzalcoatl soon blacked out, and when he awoke later, with a monumental hangover, he was shocked to find his sister beside him. He came to the realization that he had lost his priesthood by his drunken, unchaste, ungodly behavior.

And so he punished himself. He went into exile, wailing and weeping, with many of his followers. South to Cholula he wended his way, there to stay, as some would have it, for about twenty years.

When he left Cholula, sailing away to the east, he told the weeping throng assembled on the beach that he would return on an anniversary of his birth, when, at some time in the future, the year Ce Atl would recur in the Toltec cycle.

His prophecy was to have extraordinary repercussions. In the year 1519, the year Ce Atl on the Aztec calendar, Cortez appeared in Mexico City. Montezuma, vacillating because he wasn't sure whether this was Quetzalcoatl or not, delayed action against the Spaniards. This royal hesitation led to the conquering of all Mexico by the gold-hungry soldiers of the Spanish crown.

Barlow, Moreno, Peterson, von Hagen, and many other distinguished archaeologists have noted that fact and fancy is freely intermixed within the legend of Quetzalcoatl. I don't think it too difficult to perform a wheat and chaff operation upon its structure to determine the fact in the story.

I think that Topiltzin Quetzalcoatl did exist, and was given the name of the Plumed Serpent as were many before him, and—as history demonstrates—many who succeeded him. I think also that there is historical basis for his banishment, but the "banishment" was actually murder: he was killed for his heresy in wanting to abolish human sacrifice. In one of those awkward coincidences of history, there appeared in Tula, at the time of Topiltzin's murder, a strange white man who professed a horror at the thought of human sacrifice, and who was kind and gentle and pious, like Topiltzin. The plotting priests of the Toltec, who had disposed of Topiltzin, and explained his disappearance as an act of the gods, now were placed in an embarrassing position. Seemingly, a reincarnation of the dead one appeared in Tula, together with a strange band of people whose speech was unintelligible.

The citizens of Tula, learning of Topiltzin's disappearance, and noting the timing of these new arrivals, immediately identified their leader with the discarded priest-god. And so a puzzled Irish abbot found himself cast as a god, a sudden elevation which startled him so that he accepted the role and proceeded to act like one.

Like Topiltzin, he declared against human sacrifice and demonstrated saintly qualities. He set his people (the ones who worshiped the same god as he) to building temples and working with the Indians in various arts and crafts. It is more than reasonable to assume that he built temples in the style of the region with an eye to revealing them as Catholic churches at a time when he could effect a mass conversion of the people. Or, he may not have entered into temple building at all. His greatest task, it must be acknowledged, was in Catholicizing these heathens. And, from what we know of Aztec religion, he was well on his way to success when he was forced to leave the country. He seems to have achieved a similar success among the Mayas, whom he visited later, and among the Inca to the south. We shall examine the impress he wielded shortly.

How long the Plumed Serpent abbot lived in Tula is not known. The legend asserts that he was forced to flee to Cholula, where he dwelled twenty years, a figure which is open to speculation. It would seem that the Toltecs, having killed one Quetzalcoatl, took steps as soon as possible to banish this unexpected replacement and so effected his flight from the capital to the more southerly city. Nothing is known of the daily lives of the god and the Nonoalca in Cholula. All that is evident is that he left, with a vow to return in the year of his birth.

It is more than a coincidence (which condition seems to be ubiquitous throughout the tale of Quetzalcoatl) that at the time of the Plumed Serpent's embarkation from Cholula, there appeared, among the Maya, a new, powerful, beneficent god named Kukulcan. The same saintly attributes which had distinguished Quetzalcoatl were seen in the Mayan deity. The only reasonable conclusion one can reach in this remarkable coincidence is that Quetzalcoatl, on leaving Cholula, did, indeed, sail to the east, but his journey was short. He merely sailed across the Golfo de Campeche, the waters separating the east coast of Mexico from the peninsula of Yucatán. He landed, probably at the site of the present seacoast village of Progreso, and again undertook an inland trek. His destination this time: Chichén Itzá, capital city of the Mayas, the place of the wells of the Itzá.

According to the timetable which seems to be a proper one, Quetzalcoatl is said to have left Cholula after about twenty years, thus dating his departure at around 1030, allowing a margin of a few years on either side. The appearance of Kukulcan in the Maya country coincides loosely with that date.

The troubles which beset the abbot and his faithful band of Irish-Icelander-Indians, were centered about the abbot-god's horror of human sacrifice, and it is more than reasonable to imagine the same unpleasantness pursuing him while he held his position as deity to the Maya. I would be inclined to think that he remained among them for only about ten years, eventually being forced to flee, as he had been from Tula, and later Cholula.

That he did leave the Yucatán Peninsula and emerge around the middle of the eleventh century, incredibly enough as another god with yet another name is manifest in the legends of the Inca to the south. When he left Chichén Itzá, he again sailed to the east, promising a return. I think he simply rounded the peninsula and steered south, landing somewhere in the Golfo Duce, a small bay in Guatemala. Thence he went overland, reaching the Pacific. Ships were built again by the Nonoalca, the flock of Irish and Icelanders and Wampanoag Indians, re-enforced by a touch of Aztec and Maya. Now they sailed south and east, wearily deciding to land when they drew near the present city of Lima, or perhaps they went as far south as the Paracas Peninsula.

Ashore, they duplicated their overland journey from Veracruz. Leaving the dry lowlands along the coast, they made for the highlands. Again they were greeted by natives, this time the Inca (thought to have emerged as such about A.D. 1050) who had wandered up from the south and had penetrated the highlands. Again occurred a case of mistaken identity and the Inca looked upon this bearded, white stranger as their god, Viracocha, or Kon-Tiki Viracocha, to distinguish him from the eighth emperor of these proud Indians, who also bore the name Viracocha.

This time, the abbot's task began with the selection of a site for the building of a city. In the valley of Cuzco, he found the land to be fertile, the countryside agreeable. It seemed a good place to settle. And the wondrous city of Cuzco began to take shape. According to John Alden Mason, in *The Ancient Civilizations of Peru,* the Viracocha, once he had traveled about the country, instructing his people in matters theological, assumed the role of high dignitary, not completely worshiped as a god, but consulted frequently by the nobles in time of crisis.

His stay in Peru is not given us in time, either. He terminated it, however, by sailing into the west from Ecuador, possibly walking with his flock to Guayaquil Bay, from there to seek new places in the western sea. Again he promised he would return, and his prophecy again led to the identification of a conqueror with a god. When Pizarro invested the Inca empire in 1531 it was first thought that he was the returning Viracocha; his subsequent behavior, however, successfully corrected that misimpression of the Inca.

I think the identification of the Abbot of North Salem as Quetzalcoatl, Kukulcan and Kon-Tiki Viracocha is safe. The suggested dates of each of these gods' entrance into the lives of the three Indian nations coincides with an eerie exactness to the years in which it would have been mete for the monks and their followers to bid good-by to North Salem and its network of missions, an adieu thrust on them by a threat of wholesale viking invasion.

The evidences that such was the case are strong throughout Central and South America.

Quetzalcoatl, Kukulcan, and Kon-Tiki Viracocha is each described in the various legends which honor him as an aged, bearded white man. (Beards were quite rare among the "hairless" Amerinds.) The Aztecs noted that he wore a cross around his neck and paintings of priests in all three nations show men wearing long, black, cassocklike robes, strikingly similar to those worn by Catholic priests, ancient and modern.

The Aztec god brought to Tula a people who "could not speak correctly," and particular note is made of the fact that the god favored these people because "they worshipped the same god as he did."

It would be well, here, to note the amazing similarities between Aztec religious ceremonies and those of the Catholic Church, as set down by William Hickling Prescott, nineteenth-century historian. The same similarities are seen, to a lesser degree, in likening the religion of the Inca and the Christians. The three Indian nations with which we are concerned possessed stories of a deluge. The Aztec Noah, Coxcox, was saved from watery death by building a large boat; a dove brought him the first intimation that the waters were receding. The Michuacan, a neighboring tribe to the Inca, preserve the same tradition, except that a hummingbird serves as a dove.

The Aztec goddess, Cioacoatl, was called "our lady and mother," "the first goddess who brought forth," "who bequeathed the sufferings of childbirth to women," "as the tribute of death," "by whom sin came into the world." Usually represented with a serpent nearby, her name actually meant "serpent-woman." Is this the biblical *Eve*?

With some awe himself, Prescott tells of the surprise of Spanish soldiers on witnessing a communion ceremony. In it, a flour of maize was mixed with blood, and, after consecration, distributed to the worshipers, who ate it "with signs of humiliation and sorrow, declaring it was the flesh of the deity!"

The Spaniards also recorded the rites of the Aztec baptism. This paralleled the Catholic baptism closely, the child being touched on head and lips with water, and a name given it. The presiding priest then implored Cioacoatl "that the sin, which was given to us before the beginning of the world, might not visit the child, but that, cleansed by these waters, it might live and be born anew." Clearly a duplication of Catholic ceremony, complete with its symbolic cleansing of original sin.

The Inca observed a communion ceremony also, theirs consisting of a distribution of bread and wine. Inca and Aztec priests alike administered confession and absolution. With the flexibility of heathens retaining once-practiced Christian rites, the Aztecs of Cortez's day had added a fillip or two of their own to the ancient ceremony. A sin repeated, if once atoned for, was deemed inexpiable, and confession was required only once in a man's life. Thus it was usually deferred until relatively late, presumably after the subject had sinned himself out. Priestly absolution could be substituted for punishment in the case of criminal offenders, and could result in acquittal. Certificates of confession were issued, showing the holder to be pure, and the naïve sixteenth-century Mexican frequently produced it in attempts to escape punishment from the Spaniards for various infractions.

The Incaic "Virgins of the Sun" were very like convents, the young maidens of the order being instructed rigorously in religious duties. It was the mass rape of these Virgins by the Spaniards, while they were en route to Cuzco, that probably revealed to the Inca the ungodlike nature of the pillaging legions briefly thought to be the returning flock of Viracocha.

I must tell you, also, of the crosses.

In 1518, Juan de Grijalva, a nephew of Velasquez, Spanish governor of Cuba and jealous superior of Cortez, landed at Yucatán, the country of the Maya. He was astonished to find large stone crosses scattered about the country. Their presence so reminded him of his own country that he called the country New Spain. In 1519, Cortez himself, preparing for his advance on Mexico City, landed on the tiny island of Cozumel. In the court of one of the houses there he came upon a cross, ten palms high, made of stone and lime. The Spaniards were puzzled on seeing the cross used in services in the temples of Anahuac, and a bas-relief in the Mayan city of Palenque contains a sculptured cross, while, as Prescott relates ". . . a figure bearing some resemblance to that of a child is held up to it, as if in adoration."

These crosses were noted by the Spaniards and reported by them. Their own priests, following them into the conquered countries, were as amazed at them as the soldiers had been, but were inclined to attribute them to Satan, who had patently put them there in some obscene travesty on the religion of the Old World. It was completely inconceivable to these friars that a pre-Spanish, Christian penetration of these regions could have occurred.

Only the cultural influences left by the monks and their flocks remains to be examined. I give you simply the photograph of an Aztec head, adorning a plumbate vase (Plate 27). Is it an Aztec, or is it a sculptured likeness of an Icelandic viking? Compare it with the retouched photograph; same head, viking headdress (Plate 28). I say it's an Icelander, complete with beard. But let me refer you to the *pièce de résistance,* Plate 30. Study carefully the features of this tired old man. It's the face of a thousand ancient Irish monks, weary of their peregrinations and longing for a small peek at a sod they never once have seen.

That these "gods," whom I have considered to be one and the same man, once lived is difficult to deny. That their prophecies were fulfilled, bringing doom to the Indians of Middle and South America is historical fact. Montezuma, Emperor of the mighty Aztec, and Atahualpa, proud ruler of the Inca, both thought they were welcoming returning gods when the Spaniards appeared on their shores. Instead, they were greeting avaricious *conquistadores* who brought them the ultimate gift: the end of time.

John Alden Mason, in *The Ancient Civilizations of Peru,* writes: "In these days, when anthropologists are giving more credence than formerly to the probability of pre-Columbian trans-Pacific influences and voyages, these old American traditions of culture heroes might well be accorded new appraisals." He then adds the information that the Inca name *Viracocha* "seems to have been equivalent to 'Lord'; the semantic analogy with both uses of the English term is obvious."

Victor von Hagen, in *Realm of the Incas,* says simply: "This is a persistent legend throughout the Americas about ships returning over the ocean sea, and *must somewhere have substance.*"

The case rests.

There remains but one question to be answered concerning Quetzalcoatl-Kukulcan-Kon-Tiki Viracocha: Where did he lead his flock when he sailed from Ecuador?

The answer is quite simple.

In the manner of Thor Heyerdahl's latter-day voyage to Polynesia, the Ab-god sailed his people to the Polynesian Islands. There he dropped the appendage "Viracocha" and entered into the legends of the Polynesians as the "white god who brought their ancestors from a land to the east; a god who taught them architecture and agriculture and gave them their manners and customs."

The Ab, known throughout Polynesia as Kon-Tiki, left many descendants resembling him and his people. The stories of white-skinned inhabitants of the beautiful South Sea Islands are many and have been recounted by explorer and historian alike. I offer but one sample, from Thor Heyerdahl's *Kon-Tiki:*

"Now it happened that, when the Europeans came to the Pacific Islands, they were quite astonished to find that many of the natives had almost white skins and were bearded. On many of the islands there were whole families conspicuous for their remarkably pale skins, hair varying from reddish to blonde, blue-gray eyes, and almost Semitic, hook-nosed faces."

The story of the South Sea Islanders and their white god Kon-Tiki is, of course, not to be told in this volume. I have strayed too far into the Pacific.

We will return to the Atlantic and observe a Welshman of noble birth. He came to America in the twelfth century. He liked it here and hurried back to Wales to enlist colonists for the new land.

Returning to America, he settled first in Kentucky.

Let us proceed, then, to Louisville.

CHAPTER 16

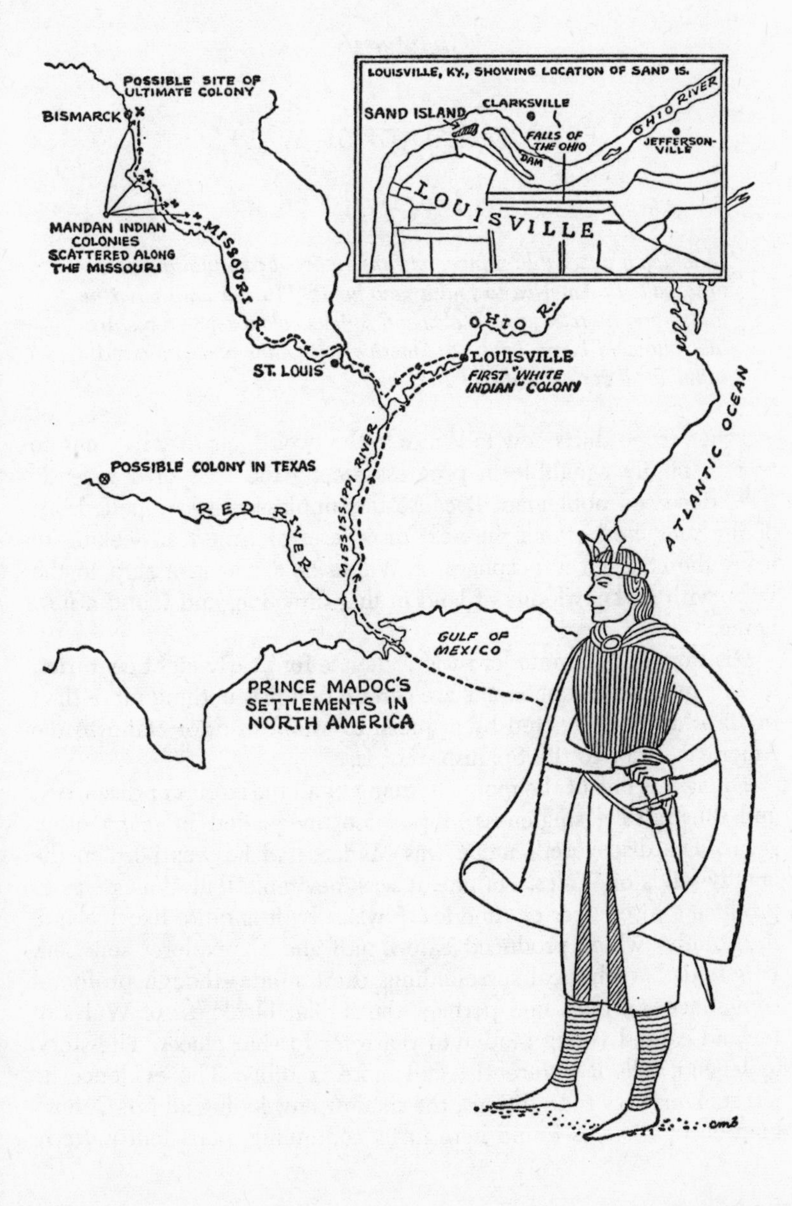

LOUISVILLE, KY., SHOWING LOCATION OF SAND IS.
SAND ISLAND
CLARKSVILLE
FALLS OF THE OHIO
DAM
OHIO RIVER
JEFFERSON-VILLE
LOUISVILLE
POSSIBLE SITE OF ULTIMATE COLONY
BISMARCK
MANDAN INDIAN COLONIES SCATTERED ALONG THE MISSOURI
MISSOURI R.
ST. LOUIS
OHIO R.
LOUISVILLE
FIRST "WHITE INDIAN" COLONY
ATLANTIC OCEAN
POSSIBLE COLONY IN TEXAS
RED RIVER
MISSISSIPPI RIVER
GULF OF MEXICO
PRINCE MADOC'S SETTLEMENTS IN NORTH AMERICA

Chapter 16

PRINCE MADOC OF WALES

[A.D. 1171]

In which a peaceable prince, wishing to avoid family unpleasantness, sails to America to find a new home. Pleased with what he finds here, he returns to Wales and solicits colonists. In ten ships, his followers come back to America with him and profoundly influence a certain tribe of Indians.

THE scene shifts now to Wales in the twelfth century . . . and to a family squabble in progress among the sons of a recently deceased nobleman. Because this unpleasantness repelled one of the sons, he became the next discoverer of America. Seeking to leave the charged atmosphere of Wales, he sailed in a ship to the west, with no knowledge of land in that direction, and found a new home.

His story has been under furious debate for nearly eight centuries, and its most rabid opponents are certain that it is nothing more than myth or a lie—concocted by a queen to establish prior claim to the Americas. Prior to the Spanish, that is.

To me it is one of the more charming of all the stories of discovery, and illustrates a singleness of purpose unequalled in many other sagas. The discoverer's name was Madoc, and he was born in the craggy wilds of Wales. Perhaps it was inevitable that Wales was to produce a discoverer of America. Physically, it is quite like Iceland, the country which produced Eric Raudi and his explorer son Leif. It is said that physical surroundings exert subtle—though profound—influences on men, and perhaps the similar bleakness of Wales to Iceland caused young Madoc to yearn for foreign places. The story, or legend, tells it differently, and more credibly. The evidence he left remains only in traditions; the shadow enveloping all pre-Columbian occupations is found here in its continuing, persistent pattern.

The one area in which the truth of Madoc's voyage might have been unearthed disappeared overnight, but that is a later paragraph in my story.

The story, or legend, or myth of Prince Madoc begins with the death of a parent and ensuing squabble among his sons over right of possession, a theme which recurs with dismal frequency in the saga of man. The dead parent was one Owen Gwynedd, and on his demise, the sons "fell at debate" over who was to take rule of the father's holdings. Owen Gwynedd had lived in a castle at Harlech, and we can assume that his holdings were extensive. At least they could have been, although the definition of a castle in times past was not always the popular one held today of great, ramparted structures complete with moats and armored guards. The "debate" apparently grew to awkward proportions, and Madoc sought solace on the high seas, eventually becoming a discoverer of America. The story of Madoc's voyage first appeared in a book of Hakluyt's in 1582. Hakluyt is thought to have learned it from one Gutton Owen, a Welsh bard who seems to have run across it in the records of the Abbey of Conway in North Wales. It was also said to have been recorded at the Abbey of Strata Florida in South Wales. Welsh custom caused reports of all events considered important to be preserved in the abbeys of the land, and thus it may be stated that the story of Madoc is founded in truth. We can, I believe, rely on Gutton Owen as being an honest man, not given to falsifying. His reputation seems to have been of the best, for he was commissioned by Henry VII to search that monarch's family tree, presumably because Henry needed some background to justify his ascent to the throne of England. Through the conjunction of records in abbeys and a bard with spotless, or nearly so, reputation, we have the authority for the story as quoted and recounted by the eminent Hakluyt, scrivener of voyages of exploration and deeds of derring-do.

Many writers have delved into the Madoc story, most treating it as though it were a pleasant enough legend, but nothing more. I think the voyage was entirely possible, and that it did take place. Here is Hakluyt's report on the voyage of Madoc:

> After the death of Owen Gwynedd, his sonnes fell at debate who should inherit after him, for the eldest sonne born in Matrimony Edward or Jorwerth Drwidion [Drwyndwn] was counted unmeet to govern because of the maime upon his face, and Howel that took upon him the rule, was a

base sonne, begotten upon an Irish woman. Therefore, David, another Sonne, gathered all the power he could and came against Howel, and fighting with him, slew him and afterwards enjoyed quietly the whole land of North Wales until his brother Jorwerth's Sonne came to age.

Madoc, another of Owen Gwyneth's Sonnes, left the land in contentions betwixt his brethren and prepared certain ships with men and munition and sought adventures by seas, sailing west and leaving the coast of Ireland so farre north, that he came to a land unknown, where he saw many strange things.

This land must needs be some parts of the Country, of which the Spanyards affirm themselves to be the first Finders since Hanno's Time; whereupon it is manifest that the country was by Britons discovered long before Columbus led any Spanyards thither.

Of the voyage and return of this Madoc, there be many fables framed, as the common people do use in distance of place and length of time, rather to augment than to diminish, but sure it is, there he was. And after he had returned home, and declared the pleasant and fruitful countries, that he had seen without inhabitants; and upon the contrary, for what barren and wild ground his brothers and nephews did murther one another, he prepared a number of ships and got with him such Men and Women as were desirous to live in quietness, and taking leave of his friends, took his journey thitherwards again.

Therefore, it is supposed that he and his people inhabited part of those countries, for it appeareth by Francis Lopez de Comara that in Acuzamil, and other places, the people honoured the Cross. Whereby it may be gathered that Christians had been there before the coming of the Spanyards but because this people were not many, they followed the manner of the land which they came to, and the language they found there.

This Madoc arriving in that western country, unto the which he came in the year 1170, left most of his people there, and returning back for more of his own nation, acquaintance and friends to inhabit that fair land and large country, went thither again with Ten Sailles, as I find noted by Gutton Owen. I am of the opinion that the land whereunto he came was some part of the West Indies.

And that is the story of Madoc. A simple little tale, but one containing food for controversy. At least that was the attitude the distinguished Jeremy Belknap took to it. Belknap, who lived in the eighteenth century, devoted a good part of his life to the study of America's history, and while he tells of the vikings and their arrival with some positiveness, he hesitates greatly while telling the story of Madoc, and even tells it apologetically. He gets off to a clouded start immediately in the title of his piece on Madoc: *Madoc, Prince of Wales—His supposed discovery of America—An Account of his voyage Examined—The Improbability of His Supposed Discovery Shown.* Right at that point the reader is guided away from Madoc as fact and urged to regard him as fancy. He then proceeds to recount the Hakluyt story, and adds the opinions of that writer concerning the probability of Madoc's landing in America. In the last sentence of Belknap's version, Hakluyt is said to have stated that in his opinion Madoc's arrival was in Mexico, as opposed to the West Indies—indicated in the above version. Hakluyt then continues, in the Belknap version:

1. The common report of the inhabitants of that country, which affirm that their rulers descended from a strange nation, that came thither from a far country; which thing is confessed by Mutezuma, king of that country, in an oration made for quieting of his people at his submission to the King of Castile; Hernando Cortez being then present, which is laid down in the Spanish chronicles of the conquest of the West Indies.

2. The British words and names of places used in that country even to this day do argue the same; as when they talk together they use the word GWRANDO, which is "hearken," or "listen." Also they have a certain bird with a white head, which they call penguin, that is, *white head.* But the island of COOROESO, the river of GUYNDOR, and the white rock of PENGUYN, which be all British or Welsh words, do manifestly show that it was that country which Madoc and his people inhabited."

In a slight voice of complaint, Belknap then informs his readers that in this extract from Hakluyt "is contained all the original information which I have been able to find respecting the supposed discovery of America by the Welsh." He also states that the account itself is confused and contradictory. Despite Jeremy Belknap's disbelief, and his prejudicial attitude toward the Welsh, I shall later pit his arguments against those of Mr. Reuben F. Durrett, who was truly a professional when it came to excavating the facts. We shall then see whether the incredulousness of Mr. Belknap or the research of Mr. Durrett shall prevail.

Yet Belknap's criticisms, on the whole, are well taken. He criticizes Hakluyt for comparing the words Penguin and Penguyn, and declares that the "white-headed" bird that he refers to actually has a black head. Correct. He also complains that Madoc could not possibly have been driven to America's shores since the current would have carried him to Nova Scotia. That statement would have been difficult to transmit convincingly to Bjarni Herjulfsson. He then mentions a book written recently which attempts to ascertain the truth of Madoc's voyage. The writer, Dr. John Williams, disappoints Dr. Belknap: "no new facts have been adduced," he remarks. But he does make a slight concession, and puts forth arguments in favor of the Nova Scotia theory. He is reminded of some of the native words (in the Indian language) of Nova Scotia which bear a resemblance to Madoc's name. According to Belknap, a sachem of the Penobscot tribe who lived in the seventeenth and eighteenth centuries bore the name Madokawanda. A village on the Penobscot, he asserts, was called Madawankee. He cites Medoctack and Medocscenacasis as further examples of Indian names bearing seeming Welsh influences. He then sides with the critical reviewers of the incident in that "if Madoc left Wales and discovered any other country, it must always remain uncertain where that country is." Apparently feeling that this statement needs fuller qualification, he quotes historian Dr. Robertson to the effect that "if he made any discovery at all, it might be Madeira, or one of the Azores."

But he saves the *coup de grâce* for last. "The book of Hakluyt," he avers, "in which the original story is preserved, was written in the reign of Queen Elizabeth, and in the time of her controversy with Spain. The design of his bringing forward the voyage of Madoc appears, from what he says of Columbus, to have been the asserting of a discovery prior to his, and consequently the right of the Crown of England to the sovereignty of America, a point at that time warmly contested between the two nations. The remarks which the same author makes on several other voyages evidently tend to the establishment of that claim. But, if the story of Bjarni [Herjulfsson] be true, which [though Hakluyt has said nothing of it] is better authenticated than this of Madoc the right of the Crown of Denmark is, on the principle of prior discovery, superior to either of them.

"Perhaps the whole mystery may be unveiled if we advert to this one circumstance; the time when Hakluyt's book was first published, national prejudice might prevail even with so honest a writer, to convert a Welsh fable into a political argument, against a powerful rival, the claim of his sovereign to the dominion of this continent."

Intriguing. Dr. Belknap advances an excellent argument for the falsity of the story of Madoc which he calls "fable." But it must also be borne in mind that Dr. Belknap lived during the American Revolution and perhaps could not resist a dig at the expense of a British queen. And so Belknap disposed of Madoc. But a true discoverer is not to be disposed of so easily. And, in keeping with the theme of this volume, I shall endeavor to present forceful, if mystifying, evidence that Good Prince Madoc did indeed come to America, return to his homeland, and, in the manner of Eric the Red, come back to our fair land with ten shiploads of colonists.

In 1908, a man named Reuben F. Durrett wrote a disquisition called *Traditions of the Earliest Visits of Foreigners to North America.* It was written for and published by the Filson Club of Louisville, Kentucky, a group of people interested in, as their charter states, "the purpose of collecting, preserving and publishing the history of Kentucky and adjacent states, and cultivating a taste for historic inquiry and study among its members." The Filson Club, to 1908, had published no less than 23 volumes of a similar nature, well written and professionally published.

Durrett, assigned to cover the adventures of Madoc, performed a well-done research job and his book was offered to the members as part of the club's responsibility. Durrett, like Belknap, was not able to resist taking a broadside at the British, although in his day the Revolution had long been over. His sympathies obviously lay toward Wales. He tells of the circumstances surrounding the acquisition of the first Prince of Wales by Madoc's homeland.

He relates that Edward the First, who conquered Wales (and a difficult task it must have been), disposed of the Princes David and Llewellyn, who were popular rulers, and set about putting his own heir in charge of Wales. The Welsh set up an ungrateful howl at this news and complained bitterly that they would have no part of a foreigner to rule them. But Edward was a crafty individual, and operated purely within the law. He sent his *enciente* wife to Caernarvon Castle, in Wales, there to produce her child. In due time she brought forth a son. Edward then announced to his subjects that "here was a native, who doesn't speak a word of English and whose life no one can stain." With that he proclaimed the infant the first Prince of Wales. It's small wonder the individualist Madoc fled the country in the face of such chicanery.

Having chided the British for their evil ways, Durrett presses into the story of Madoc. The reason for the selection of Madoc as a subject for the Filson Club, an organization located in the unlikely city of Louisville, was based on the persistent traditions that were heard concerning a storied band of "White Indians" once populous in the area. According to Durrett, the story was accepted unequivocally by Kentuckians from the seventeenth century on.

Tradition had it that Madoc and his band of pioneers came up the Ohio in the twelfth century and settled at the Falls of the Ohio. There they lived peaceably for a time, but eventually friction developed between them and the Indians, culminating in a great battle fought at the Falls. Great numbers of the whites were slain and the bedraggled remnants fled northward, up the Mississippi and into the Missouri. It was said that the slain ones had been bottled up on an islet in the river, Sand Island, and there killed in such numbers that their bodies lay stacked. Time and the silt of the river eventually covered them over, and apparently no one has ever dug for them. The tradition of the Indians then living in Kentucky indicated that the victorious group were Red Indians, the vanquished ones white. And so we have a tradition of White Indians, which easily become Welsh Indians. And I mean not to be flippant. The White Indians were real enough, and there is great evidence to prove that they spoke fluent Welsh.

To continue with the traditions, Durrett states that some skeletons were dug up at an unnamed time in the area, and they wore brass-plated shields which bore the mermaid and harp, indicative of the Welsh coat of arms. A tombstone was also said to have been found, or a fragment thereof, bearing the date 1186. It was carried away by a person or persons unknown and has since disappeared completely.

Durrett, in a great surge of understatement, has two comments to make about the above noted traditions. In re the tombstone, he says: "Whose tombstone could it have been but that of a Welshman, since we have no record of any but the Welsh being at the falls in 1186?"

Concerning the tradition of the battle, and the acknowledged presence of the Welsh by the pioneers, he has this to say:

"There were a few Welshmen among the pioneers, and they spurred the tradition. Nonetheless, the tradition was there, with or without the Welshmen, and was much talked of in newspapers, magazines, and books. The old settlers admired Madoc's courage in leaving his country to come to America, and while they were not sure exactly where he landed, they knew he had lived along the banks of the beautiful Ohio, and even thought, perhaps, that he had built the numerous mounds which lie scattered about the vicinity, now known to be the work of prehistoric Indians and their descendants right down to modern times."

But let us examine the legend itself for a moment and attempt to determine its pattern.

Owen Gwynedd, father of Madoc and his nine siblings, was real enough. His home at Harlech Castle has been established, and there is little doubt that he produced Madoc and others, and under various circumstances, while in residence there. His eldest son Edward, an unfortunate one, was counted out of the game from the start. The "maime upon his face" seems to have been a broken nose suffered in some unrecorded brawl, perhaps with a fellow Welshman, but since the incidence of a broken nose doesn't seem strong enough to warrant the others casting him out, there was possibly some other kind of disfigurement involved. As for the unhappy Howel, "base sonne begotten upon an Irish woman," I strongly suspect that if Hakluyt were guilty of the enforced chauvinism thrust upon him by the queen, that sentence probably was added for color. That doesn't necessarily make it so, however; there was no noticeable affection among the Irish and Welsh or the English and Irish shown at that time.

The one possible area for doubt lies in the statement that David gathered all the power he could and came against Howel, fought with him and slew him. David then was able to settle back and enjoy his holdings "until his brother Jorwerth's sonne came of age." Somehow, I don't see the other brothers, with the exception of Madoc, sitting back and accepting David's behavior. However, David could well have been a fearsome creature who caused the blood in his brothers to run cold, and he must have been indeed an unusual person, to take his father's holdings and protect them for his rejected brother's son. The ways of the Middle Ages were curious, and not everyone was as savage as depicted, although the Welsh were said to have been fierce people, given to fighting among themselves, and promiscuous with one another and with strangers.

We get a hint of "contentions" between the brothers which indicate that perhaps David was not experiencing as much joy from his holdings as the bard's tale would have us believe. It was because of these contentions that Madoc prepared certain ships and men and munitions and "sought adventures by seas." Now he sailed west, and left the coast of Ireland "farre north" and came to a strange land where he saw many strange things.

This is an important area in the bard's tale. It fits completely with records of other ships which were driven south by the trade winds, and it is entirely possible that Madoc made landfall somewhere on the coast of Florida, skirted it and eventually came to the mouth of the Mississippi. By that time he knew that this was where he wanted to settle, and accordingly returned home for more colonists.

But here the suspicions of Belknap are seemingly confirmed. "The land," says Hakluyt, "must needs be some part of the country, of which the Spaniards affirm themselves to be the first finders since Hanno's time, whereupon it is manifest that the country was by Britons discovered long before Columbus led any Spanyards thither."

Whereas Belknap has his doubts raised on that paragraph, I do not. First, I am intrigued with the matter-of-fact way in which Hakluyt acknowledges the discovery of America by the Carthaginians. Did Hakluyt know something that later historians discarded, or refused to acknowledge, treating it, also as legend? Perhaps. Its presence in the argument is significant. And if he referred to Hanno, why not Bjarni? I think the answer is clear. It could well have been a religious issue. Hakluyt was writing in 1582, many years subsequent to the discard of the Catholic Church in England, and possibly felt that if any earlier voyage were to be recorded, it was safe to record one of a pagan.

One of the arguments set forth by the anti-Madoc faction centers about the phrase "[the country] that he had seen without inhabitants." A trifling detail. We already have evidence that Leif Ericsson spent a year on our shores without ever encountering a native, and his countryman, Karlsefni, spent three years here, the first of which was without any contact with the Indians.

Hakluyt then refers to the writings of Francisco López de Gómara for verification of the fact that there was evidence of Christian occupation, or, at least Christian visits, of long duration prior to the arrival of the Spanish. That is so, but I must contest Hakluyt's reference and subsequent conclusions. The evidence is there, but it was not created by Madoc, as shall be shown in a later chapter. No,

Madoc went north from the Gulf of Mexico and left his evidence there.

And so it would seem that Madoc, journeying back to Wales from his new-found land in 1171, did convince a great many others that the new land was one where they could live in peace. In all, ten shiploads of colonists accompanied him on his return.

The question might be raised here, as it inevitably is when the discussion arises about early discoverers: Why did he sail west?

My reply is only that to the west there was vast open space, and Madoc was a courageous man, unafraid of the mysteries of the deeps, and willing to see what lay beyond the horizon which historians seem to think acted as a permanent barrier to men until that magical day that Columbus landed in the Indies. Hakluyt's reference to Madoc's landing in the Indies is, of course, pure conjecture. In addition, Madoc may have known of Brendan's voyage.

But now we must seek further confirmation for the presence of Madoc in America. The locale seems fairly well established. Despite those who sneer at "tradition," that condition is nonetheless important in establishing certain details of any story which has basis in fact, but which time has twisted and distorted to a point beyond acceptability by modern standards.

I see no reason to doubt the existence of the tombstone, any more than I do the excavation of the shield-bearing corpses along the Ohio. I have stated it before, and I will state it again, the better to enforce the idea. We will never know how much priceless material—how many priceless artifacts—have been destroyed unintentionally or no in this country, due to the ignorance of our early settlers. They looked at everything about them as "Indian" even to such exotic items as shields with coats of arms, and no effort was made to preserve such finds. The fascination of a piece of rock bearing the date 1186 was naturally what caused its finder to take it, examine it, then store it away in an attic to be burned later by the Indians, hopefully to be dug up at some later date. We must accept the fact that many of our treasures of these periods have been utterly and irretrievably lost.

The tradition of the Red and White Indians is not hard to accept. Durrett, in his typical understatement, says that the early pioneers knew about—and kept alive—the tradition of Madoc and, as if to reenforce these ideas, the occasional appearance of a Welsh Indian among them only furthered the idea. When Durrett speaks of the Welsh Indian, he does not bother to put the descriptive in quotes. The Indian was Welsh, and that's all there was to it.

In examining these "mythical" reports of Welsh Indians, we leave tradition for a moment and stare at some hard, cold facts. Let us turn to the adventures of Morgan Jones. Morgan Jones wrote an account of his travels in the Kentucky area many years ago, and saw fit to comment on what he considered an unusual circumstance. Now it must be remembered that Morgan Jones was a man of the cloth and doubtless of good character. There could be no possible reason for Morgan Jones to fabricate this particular section of his journal. Particularly since we will shortly find other corroboration for the Jones story.

Morgan Jones was a parson who lived in Virginia in 1660. In that year he was sent out from that region as chaplain to an expedition journeying to South Carolina, in command of a Major General Bennet. On arrival in South Carolina, Parson Jones was sent inland to a place called Oyster Point, there to serve as minister to a colony newly begun. The assignment apparently left much to be desired, for Jones complains that he stayed there eight months, being largely "starved for provisions" during that period. Eventually, he and five others decided to leave that most inhospitable post and return to Virginia. En route, the little party was captured by Tuscarora Indians and imprisoned in their town. The tribal council, after debating the disposition of the six, decided to put them to death.

On hearing this calamitous news, Parson Jones became "very much dejected" and, speaking aloud "in the British [Welsh] tongue," did bemoan the fate which dictated that he must now "be knocked on the head like a Dog." His plaint overheard by an Indian, he was approached by the brave, who spoke to him in Welsh. It was then decided that the men of Jones's party would be spared on payment of ransom. Apparently Jones was able to meet the ransom, although this bit of legerdemain is not clarified, for the white men then were made welcome to the Tuscaroran town and resided there for four months. During that time, Jones preached to the Indians three times a week, in Welsh, and the savages came to him for counsel on matters difficult.

This intelligence was published in the *Gentlemen's Magazine,* in London, in 1740, although the original journal from which it was taken was written in 1685. In closing, Jones showed an apparent desire to revisit the scene of his brief incarceration, for he stated that he stood ready "to conduct any Welshmen, or others to the country."

In itself, the foregoing isn't too exciting. Morgan Jones was a Welshman, and the language he spoke, though he refers to it as British, was Welsh. It is plain, however, that he and the Indians understood each other very well.

But let us consider the adventures of Captain Isaac Stewart, a dashing officer of the Provincial Cavalry of South Carolina. Captain Stewart, in an article published in the *American Museum* for July 1787, relates that he experienced the awkward circumstance of being taken prisoner by Indians about 50 miles westward of Fort Pitt, and carried from there to the banks of the Wabash, in company with many others. The incident had occurred about 1771. Unhappily, his companions were executed with "circumstances of horrid barbarity," but the dashing captain, by virtue of the intercession of a tribal maiden was spared. The gentleman was not for burning since the maiden produced a horse as his ransom.

Stewart was, however, held as a captive for two years, until the arrival of a Spaniard who succeeded in ransoming him and a luckless Welshman named John Davey. The three left and traveled westward until they came to the Red River, whereupon they went north for 700 miles. They came eventually to an Indian nation which was indeed unusual. These Indians, Stewart wrote, were "remarkably white" and all, or nearly all, boasted "hair . . . of a reddish color. They are a bold, hardy, intrepid people, very warlike, and the women beautiful when compared with other Indians."

They were friendly to the newly arrived trio and John Davey announced, on the morning after their arrival, that he planned to stay among them, chiefly because they spoke Welsh!

The Indians possessed parchment scrolls which Stewart could not decipher, and unfortunately, Davey, being unlettered, could not identify them as Welsh. They told the three that their forefathers had come from a foreign country, apparently to the east.

Captain Stewart's remarkable Indians were probably those of the Paducah tribe, who, at that time were resident in northwestern Texas.

But we have evidence of a tribe which supposedly possessed a Welsh Bible, if we are to believe the account given by Benjamin

Sutton in 1776. Mr. Sutton had lived among various Indian nations for many years, and was most impressed by an Indian nation which dwelled a great distance above New Orleans. These aboriginals were of different complexions from other Indians he had known . . . they were "not so tawny as . . . other Indians . . . *and spoke Welsh.*" The Indians had a Bible, which Sutton presumed to be Welsh; they kept it carefully wrapped in some sort of skin. Since neither the Indians nor Sutton could read it, there is no further light on its origin, other than to associate it with the knowledge that the untawny redskins spoke Welsh.

There is another account of a Welsh-speaking Indian nation far up the Missouri which comes to us from Captain Abraham Chaplain, a Kentucky gentleman whose veracity was unquestionable. He learned of this nation from two Welsh Indians whom he had met at his garrison at Kaskasky. But his account pales when cited together with that of one Lieutenant Joseph Roberts, a Welshman born and reared in Wales, who encountered a Welsh-speaking Indian in the dining room of a hotel in Washington. The account of his meeting with the aboriginal was carried in *The Public Advertiser,* a newspaper published in Louisville, Kentucky, on May 15, 1819, according to Durrett.

The lieutenant, it seems, was being served by a young waiter who was also a Welshman. On bringing the officer a glass of brandy and water which had turned warm, the waiter was jocosely berated, in Welsh. At the moment of utterance, an Indian chief, who happened to be in the room hurried to Roberts' table and inquired, in Welsh, if that language were the tongue of the officer. On being assured that it was, the Indian stated that it was also his, and the two entered into conversation.

The curious officer asked the chief whether his tribe retained traditions of where his forefathers had come from, to which the Indian replied that "they had come from a far distant country, very far in the east and from over the great waters." The savage also told Roberts that all the tribe's children were taught only Welsh until they reached the age of twelve, at which time they were free to learn and speak other languages. In some awe, the officer stated that the Indian spoke Welsh better than he, Roberts, did.

Durrett also cites the instance of an encounter with White Indians as told by the Honorable Harry Toulmin, Secretary of State under

Governor Garrard, of Kentucky, in the early nineteenth century. Toulmin published the story, concerning one Maurice Griffiths, in a letter to *The Palladium*, a Frankfort, Kentucky, newspaper. Griffiths, as Toulmin described it, had been taken prisoner by the Shawnees about 1764, and stayed with them some two or three years. While on a hunting and exploring trip with five of the young braves of the tribe, he ascended the Missouri River for many days, ultimately coming to an Indian nation which was white, or of light complexion, and spoke Welsh. Griffiths and his companions first became aware of these odd Indians when they encountered three men whom they took to be white men in Indian dress. Griffiths was further startled when he discovered that they spoke Welsh.

The Griffiths party then accompanied the Welsh Indians to their town and saw that the entire populace was of light skin. On their arrival, a council was held and it was decided to put the travelers to death. Griffiths then put forth an eloquent plea, in Welsh, for their lives and all were spared by the startled, comprehending Indians. Griffiths related that the ancestors of this tribe had "come up the river from a very distant country," but he was unable to learn more of their history or traditions.

It is at once apparent from the locales given in each of the foregoing accounts (with the exception of the north Texas Indians) that all of these references are to the Mandan Indians. These Indians were encountered by many parties of white explorers before their total decimation in 1838. All the adventurers commented on the color of the Indians and some expressed wonder concerning their origins.

The most comprehensive study of the Mandans was made by the brilliant artist-historian, George Catlin, who lived among them and recorded all facets of their daily lives, customs and traditions. Catlin was born in Wilkes-Barre, Pennsylvania, on June 26, 1796, and began his professional life as a lawyer. Law bored him, however, and he soon turned to portraits and then to serious study of the American Indian. In 1832 he went west to begin learning about them. When he published his first works, he was branded a liar by anthropologists and historians who asserted that his writings were patent falsifications. Many years were to pass before others were to observe the things Catlin had in the Indian country to the west and corroborate his writings. As a small boy, I read Catlin's books avidly, identifying with him readily since I was born in Wilkes-Barre and spent most of the first fifteen years of my life in Swoyerville, about five miles north of Wilkes-Barre. By my tenth birthday, I had decided to go west and study the Indians as Catlin had, but encountered some difficulty in executing my plan from a highly unsympathetic father.

In 1857, Catlin published his *The Manners, Customs and Conditions of the North American Indians*, a prodigious two-volume work which carried more than 300 engravings made from his paintings. In this work he treated extensively on the Mandans and their origins, being convinced that they were the descendants of Prince Madoc and his colonists. In Appendix "A," Part Two, which is contained in all editions of the work, Catlin dwells on their similarities to the Welsh, and on the route he thinks they followed to arrive at the camps on the upper Missouri. I have taken the most pertinent excerpts from his lengthy descriptive:

THE WELSH COLONY,

Which I barely spoke of in page 319, which sailed under the direction of Prince Madoc, or Madawc, from North Wales, in the latter part of the Twelfth century in ten ships, according to numerous and accredited authors, and never returned to their own country, have been supposed to have landed somewhere on the coast of North or South America; and from the best authorities (which I will suppose everybody had read rather than quote them at this time) I believe it has been pretty clearly proved that they landed either on the coast of Florida or about the mouth of the Mississippi, and according to the history and poetry of their country, settled somewhere in the interior of North America, where they are yet remaining, intermixed with some of the savage tribes.

In my letter just referred to, I barely suggested, that the Mandans whom I found with so many peculiarities in looks and customs, which I have already described, might possibly be the remains of this lost colony amalgamated with a tribe, or part of a tribe of natives which would account for the unusual appearances of this tribe of Indians and also for the changed character and customs of the Welsh colonists, provided these be the remains of them.

Since these notes were written as will have been seen by my subsequent letters, I have descended the Missouri river from the Mandan village, to St. Louis, a distance of eighteen hundred miles, and have taken pains to examine its shores; and from the repeated remains of the ancient location of the Mandans, which I met with on the banks of that river, I am fully convinced that I have traced them down nearly to the mouth of the Ohio River, and from exactly similar appearances, which I recollect to have seen several years since in several places in the interior of the state of Ohio, I am fully convinced that they have formerly occupied that part of the country, and have, from some cause or other, been put in motion, and continued to make their repeated moves until they arrived at the place of their residence at the time of their extinction, on the Upper Missouri.

Now, I am inclined to believe that the ten ships of Madoc, or a part of them at least, entered the Mississippi River at the Balize, and made their way up the Mississippi, or that they landed somewhere on the Florida coast, and that their brave and persevering colonists made their way through the interior to a position on the Ohio River, where they cultivated their fields, and established in one of the finest countries on earth, a flourishing colony; but were at length set upon by the savages, whom, perhaps, they provoked to warfare, being trespassers on their hunting-grounds, and by whom, in overpowering hordes, they were besieged, until it was necessary to erect there fortifications for their defense, into which they were at last driven by a confederacy of tribes, and there held till their ammunition and provisions gave out, and they in the end had all perished except perhaps that portion of them who might have formed alliance by marriage with the Indians, and their offspring, who would have been half-breeds, and of course attached to the Indians' side; whose lives have been spared in the general massacre; and at length, being despised, as all half-breeds of enemies are, have gathered themselves into a band, and severing from their parent tribe, have moved off, and increased in numbers and strength, as they have advanced up the Missouri river to the place where they have been known for many years by the name of Mandans, a corruption or abbreviation, perhaps, of "Madawgwys," the name applied by the Welsh to the followers of Madawc.

The Mandan canoes which are altogether different from those of all other tribes, are exactly the Welsh caracle, made of raw hides, the skins of buffaloes, stretched underneath a frame made of willow or other boughs and shaped nearly round, like a tub; which the woman carries on her head from her wigwam to the water's edge, and having stepped into it, stands in front, and propels it by dipping her paddle forward and drawing it to her instead of paddling by the side.

How far these extraordinary facts may go in the estimation of the reader, with numerous others I have mentioned in volume 1, whilst speaking of Mandans, of their various complexions, colors of hair, and blue and grey eyes, towards establishing my opinion as a sound theory, I cannot say; but this much I can safely aver, that at the moment I first saw these people, I was so struck with the peculiarity of their appearance, that I was under the instant conviction that they were an amalgam of a native with some civilized race; and from what I have seen of them, and of the remains on the Missouri and Ohio rivers, I feel fully convinced that these people have emigrated from the latter stream; and that they have, in the manner that I have already stated, with many of their customs, been preserved from the almost total destruction of the bold colonists of Madawc, who, I believe, settled upon and occupied for a century or so, the rich and fertile banks of the Ohio."

It would seem, then, that such a distinguished person as Catlin was more than a little convinced of the descent of the Mandans from Prince Madoc, and his suggested route confirms the tradition of a Welsh colony along the Ohio.

The clues are few, the evidence nearly nonexistent, except in traditions. I have already mentioned the tombstone bearing the date 1186, and the skeletons bearing Welsh coats of arms. To attempt to offer them as evidence today would be naïve. The Welsh colonials are gone, and their descendants, the Mandan, decimated. They perished, to a man, within a two-month period in 1838, after a river boat brought them a white man's gift: smallpox.

In attempting to determine whether modern-day searches for evidence of the vanished Welshmen had ever occurred in the Louisville area, I asked Mrs. Dorothy Thomas Cullen, curator and librarian of the Filson Club to locate papers by archaeologists concerning digs in that region. Mrs. Cullen forwarded an excerpt from *Reports in Archaeology and Anthropology*, Vol. II, a publication of the University of Kentucky, dated September 1932. The paper is jointly written by W. D. Funkhouser and W. S. Webb and deals with the archaeology of Jefferson County, Kentucky. In it, the writers describe the region and then dwell for a time on the incidence of the battle between the Red and White Indians at the Falls of the Ohio:

Whatever archaeological sites Jefferson County may have had, have long since been obliterated by the progress of civilization. This is particularly true since the more important of these sites would probably have been along the Ohio River, and a large area of the river front is now occupied by the city of Louisville and its suburbs. This part of the river is of course associated with the well known and oft repeated tradition of the "White Indians" and the famous battle at the "Falls of the Ohio" at which the supposed white race was wiped out of existence. This tradition is reviewed by Young with considerable dramatic effect in his *Prehistoric Men of Kentucky* in which he presents the evidence to show that

> "the primitive inhabitants of this State had perished in a war of extermination waged against them by the Indians; that the last great battle was fought at the Falls of the Ohio; and that the Indians succeeded in driving the aborigines into a small island below the Rapids where the whole of them were cut to pieces"

and repeats the story of the Indian Chief Cornstalk that

> "Kentucky had once been settled by a white people who were familiar with arts of which the Indians knew nothing; that these whites after a series of bloody contests with the Indians, had been exterminated; that the old burial places were the graves of an unknown people; and that the old forts had not been built by the Indians, but had come down from 'a very long ago' people, who were of white complexion and skilled in the arts."

Whether or not there is any basis of fact for these ancient traditions, it is certain that there is little evidence now to substantiate them. It is very likely, however, that this part of the Ohio River Valley may have been extensively occupied by the aborigines since the same factors would have influenced them which induced the first white settlers to establish themselves at this place.

On learning that Jefferson County's archaeological sites "have long since been obliterated by the progress of civilization," it became apparent that another archaeological locale had been forever erased by modern encroachment. I visualized Sand Island, the one site which I felt might be productive of any ancient Welsh remains, as being built up edge to edge with buildings. I asked Mrs. Cullen to obtain an aerial photograph of the island for me so that I might illustrate the destruction of another of our precious archaeological sites. To my surprise, the island is seen today as a pristine, woodland covered bar in the river, seemingly as virgin today as it was in the time of Madoc.

Again, with the oppressive monotony which marks the reluctance of archaeologists, amateur and professional, to excavate sites which might produce pre-Columbian evidence and thereby demand hastily concocted stories of why these pre-Columbian items are colonial, we see one more instance of scientific neglect.

If there is one place where evidence might be found, it is probably on Sand Island. Yet no one has seriously dug for the silted skeletons of the White Indians, or for the armor and crests they might have worn. In Louisville, the NEBC Principle, though rejected by many of its citizens, is stanchly upheld by its social scientists.

Madoc was a great man, and his Welsh blood was strong enough to perpetuate his existence and the existence of his colonists for nearly seven hundred years through the blood of the Mandan. That nothing can be found to verify the reports of his visit is regrettable.

But there is hope.

Sand Island still rises from the bed of the Ohio, its wooded acres amenable to a dig, should any be interested. Chance may yet resurrect the Welshmen who fell in the bloody slaughter of Sand Island.

But the Men of Wales continue to slumber in their eternal resting place on the islet in the Ohio. We must proceed now to the narrative of the next discoverer, and learn how his men left a memento of their visit which has provided discomfort for many scholars for sixty years.

CHAPTER 17

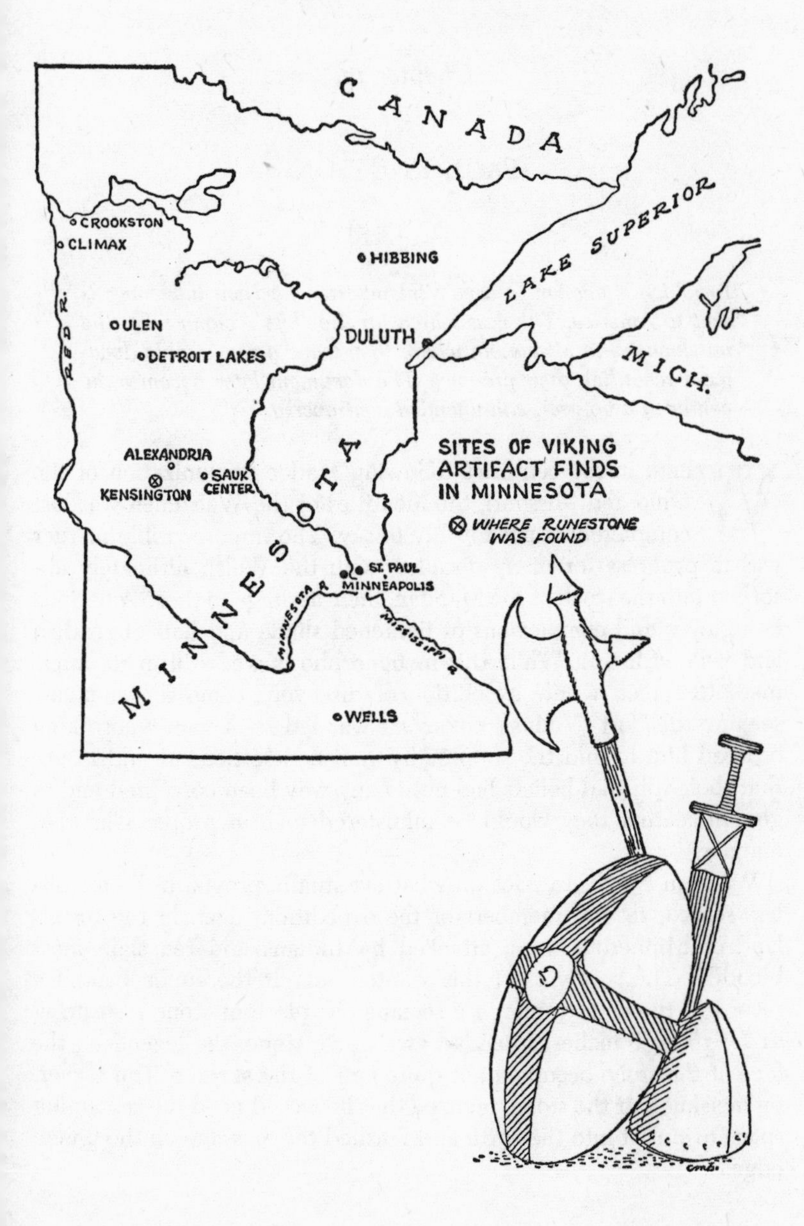
CANADA
LAKE SUPERIOR
MICH.
CROOKSTON
CLIMAX
HIBBING
RED R.
ULEN
DETROIT LAKES
DULUTH
ALEXANDRIA
SAUK CENTER
KENSINGTON
SITES OF VIKING ARTIFACT FINDS IN MINNESOTA
WHERE RUNESTONE WAS FOUND
MINNESOTA
ST. PAUL
MINNEAPOLIS
MINNESOTA R.
MISSISSIPPI R.
WELLS

Chapter 17

PAUL KNUTSON

[A.D. 1355]

In which a mission to save Vinland from heathen influences is sent to America. The vast search for the "lost" colony takes the missionaries to Minnesota where they leave a remarkable document recording their presence. The document later becomes the center of a 60-year, still-unended controversy.

WHEN, in the centuries following Madoc's colonization of the Ohio and Missouri, the identities of the Welshmen was lost completely is not for any to say. The imperceptible merger was in progress for many decades, with the Welsh ultimately absorbed into the stock of the Mandan, their heritage to those Amerinds being eyes and complexions of lightened shade and hair of reddish and yellowish tint. While this metamorphosis was still in its intermediate stages a new expedition of discovery came to America—seeking the "lost" Vinland colony. It was led by a man whose king ordered him to find the supposedly vanished settlement and insure that their spiritual beliefs had not in any way been corrupted and to guarantee that they would be ministered to in a proper Christian manner.

While in North America on what eventually proved to be a fruitless search, several members of the expedition, deep in the forestland of Minnesota, were attacked by Indians and ten slain most bloodily. The survivors of this wanton assault thereupon carved a record of the catastrophe in a rectangular piece of stone measuring 31 by 16 by 6 inches. Intended as a grave stone, the legend on the face of the stone occupied not quite half of the surface. The carver, on incising half the stone, realized that he would need the remaining space to sink it into the earth and finished the message on the 6-inch edge.

Whether or not the stone was ever put to its intended use must forever remain a mystery. When it was discovered some six hundred years after it had been carved, it was clutched in the roots of an aspen tree, which roots had conformed to the shape of the stone. Its discoverer, a farmer, recognized the scratches on its surface as man-made, and a curious friend sought to determine specifically what they were. With that first inquiry regarding the stone, made at the close of the nineteenth century, there began a still-unended battle over the authenticity of the stone which is truly a tragedy in one sense . . . and an exposition of scholarly petulance in another. That the stone is authentic has been undeniably established. But attacks upon it continue, from belligerent philologists whose puzzling attitudes will be examined in more detail as we unravel the mystery of the stone. Grief, shame and uncomprehending shock came to the innocent man who found it through the ruthlessness of these attacks, and unwarranted abuse to the man who has done most to authenticate it; their plights will also be examined. First, however, we must establish the appearance of what is now called the "Kensington Stone" on the American scene in 1362.

In the year 1354, restless King Magnus Erikson of Norway found himself in a peculiar position. Fired with the desire to bring the word of Christianity to all who were heathen and fell within his reach, he was planning a punitive expedition into Russia, there to bring the word, even at pain of death. The peculiar position he found himself in was because of an overflowing treasury—more than enough to invest Russia, and the coincidence of the plague in that country, which rendered it inadvisable to brave the steppes. Since his anticipated expedition had to be shelved, he turned his thoughts to Greenland. It appeared that the Greenland colony had vanished some years before, and it could mean that they had gone farther west. He also harbored the suspicion that these loyal subjects of his were falling away from the Church, and so it would be a capital idea to send an expedition to restore them to the faith. He therefore authorized an excursion to find his lost sheep; addressed to one Paul Knutson (Holand translation):

Magnus, by the grace of God, King of Norway, Sweden and Skaane, sends to all men who see or hear this letter [his wishes for their] good health and happiness.

We desire to make known to you that you are to select the men who shall go in the Knorr [the royal trading vessel] . . . from among my bodyguard and also from the retainers of other men whom you may wish to take on the voyage, and that Paul Knutson the commandant shall have full authority to select such men whom he thinks are best qualified to accompany him, whether as officers or men. We ask that you accept this our command with a right good will for the cause, inasmuch as we do it for the honor of God and for our predecessors, who in Greenland established Christianity and have maintained it until this time, and *we will not let it perish in our days.* Know this for truth, that whoever defies this our command shall meet with our serious displeasure and receive full punishment.

Executed in Bergen, Monday after Simon and Judah's Day in the six and xxx year of our rule [1354]. By Orm Ostenson, our regent, sealed.

The original of the above letter was burned in the great fire which ravaged Copenhagen in 1728. A photostatic reproduction of the only copy of the letter appears in the Smithsonian Miscellaneous Collections, vol. 116, no. 3, in William Thalbitzer's article, *Two Runic Stones from Greenland and Minnesota.*

Professor Gustav Storm first called attention to this letter in *Studier over Vinlandsreiserne,* in 1888, and it remained simply a curious document until Hjalmar Holand came upon it. When he realized that there was a specific connection between this letter and the Kensington Stone, he pursued it until he had pieced together evidence showing the route he believed the Knutson expedition followed in America. All of the research in this area has been performed by Holand; beyond the letter noted above, no other information is forthcoming from Norwegian historical sources other than the possible date of the return of the expedition: 1363 or 1364.

While Holand connects the expedition with the Kensington Stone, and rightly so, I do not agree entirely with the route he outlines for the travelers. I do agree, and most heartily, with his authentication of the Kensington Stone, and it is primarily that remarkable piece of pre-Columbian evidence that we shall be concerned with here.

On November 8, 1898, a Minnesota farmer named Olaf Ohman was engaged in clearing timber from a piece of woodland he owned, preparatory to planting. The undulating terrain on which he was working was, in times past, a lake, and Ohman was clearing the wood on the slope of a knoll which had once been an island within the lake. Long since vanished, the lake now remained only as a shallow depression surrounded by a grassy marsh. It is located in Solem Township, Douglas County, Minnesota, about three miles from the town of Kensington.

At some point during his labor, Ohman uncovered a rectangular stone, clutched in the roots of an aspen tree. The tree itself seemed to be about sixty, perhaps seventy years old, although Ohman was not concerned so much with the age of the tree as he was in getting it out, and removing the stone—which was only six inches below the surface—enmeshed in the roots. In a few minutes the tree was down, the stump pried loose, and the stone pulled from its bed. The stone was set on the ground until it, along with the many others which had been excavated, could be hauled away or piled away from the site of the intended planting area.

Helping Ohman in his task were his two sons, Olaf, Jr., aged twelve, and Edward, aged ten, and Nils Flaaten, a neighbor who owned the adjoining land.

When the time came to place the odd, rectangular stone in a pile with the others which they had amassed, Ohman noticed, on turning it over, that it seemed to be covered with strange writing, or carving of some kind. Closer examination and study proved the mysterious incisions to be runes. Being Swedish, Ohman knew what runes looked like. He possessed, in fact, a book called *The Well-Informed Schoolmaster,* which contained a sample runic alphabet. Thumbing through it, the identification was certain. The markings on the stone were runes. Had Ohman known at that time the grief that mere possession of the little book was to cause him, he would have destroyed it, and returned the stone to the ground whence it came.

Now excited about his strange discovery, Ohman called in neighbors to see it, and there was much discussion of the stone. It stood, for a time, in a shop window in Kensington, displayed as a curiosity. But no one knew what it said. Then around New Year's, a friend of Ohman's, J. P. Hedberg, wrote to the editor of the *Svenska-Amerikanska Posten,* a Swedish language newspaper in Minneapolis. In his note, Hedberg indicated that he thought the editor might have means of determining what the stone said, and in that light, enclosed a pencil copy of the inscription as exact as Ohman could transcribe it.

The paper published Hedberg's letter, together with the copy of the inscription, but the publisher, Swan Turnblad, intrigued with the possibilities of such an inscription, sent it on to Professor O. J. Breda, a teacher of Scandinavian languages at the University of Minnesota, and Norwegian-born. Breda, though not a runologist, was able to provide a fair translation of the inscription, even though he was totally unable to decipher the numerals and had to leave blanks for several words. But Breda was not convinced that the stone was anything but a fraud. Despite his being unable to obtain the full message from the stone's symbols, he told the press, in an interview in the *Minneapolis Journal* for February 22, 1899, that the stone was a fake because it seemed to contain a mixture of modern Swedish, Norwegian, and English.

Here is what the stone seemed to say:

> *. . . . Swedes and . . . . Norwegians on a*
> *journey from Vinland west . . . . We camped*
> *one day's journey north from this stone.*
> *We fished one day. After we came home we*
> *found . . . . man red with blood and dead.*
> *AVM save from . . . . Have . . . . men at the*
> *sea to look after our ships . . . . day's*
> *journey from this island. Year . . . .*

Obviously, the stone had to be a fraud. It implied that a party of Swedes and Norwegians had camped nearby and had engaged in battle, presumably with Indians. But the most sensational revelation was that they were on a journey from Vinland. Impossible! Many of the Scandinavians in the area had a slight acquaintance with the sagas which told of Vinland, but everybody thought that the old vikings had stayed close to the eastern coast of the United States. Here was a document which told of a journey from Vinland to Minnesota. The speculation was wonderful. But Breda knew better. He, a scholar, knew that such an event could not have happened. Even the sagas said nothing about journeys inland, and . . . well, the whole thing was ridiculous.

The stone went next to Professor George O. Curme at Northwestern University. Curme was a Germanic philologist. Apparently the stone made no sense to Curme, who, though unable to make a pronouncement on the translation, decided that the stone was doubtful because it didn't *look* old.

On April 16, 1899, Breda broke into print again, this time with proof positive. He released to the press a cablegram from Oslo, Norway, and signed by such notables as Gustav Storm and Oluf Rygh, professors at the university in that city. They had been sent copies of the inscription and now handed down their verdict: It was, they said ". . . a grand fraud perpetrated by a Swede with a chisel and a slight knowledge of runic characters and English."

The matter, it would seem, was closed. Truth had triumphed.

And Ohman was under suspicion. Since the stone had come to light through him, he was the prime suspect in the stated fraudulency of the stone. Disgusted, embarrassed, hurt, Ohman tossed the stone down at the entrance to his granary and used it as a stepping-stone.

And there the matter should have rested.

Ohman should have continued to live his life as though the stone had never appeared, shut up on his farm to nurse the wounds brought by it while the scholars, with smiles of amusement, discussed the charming little story of the Minnesota farmer and his "rune stone." Another hoax, they could proudly tell themselves, had been properly exposed, and again we have saved our thread of history from being knotted in the wrong place.

But the stone was not meant to lie unnoticed, subject to the indignity of being trod upon by a farmer and his family.

In 1907, Hjalmar Holand, then thirty-five years of age, went to see Ohman. He had heard of the alleged rune stone and wanted to see this curiosity himself. A historian, Holand was gathering material for a history he planned to write on the Norwegian settlement in Minnesota.

Holand looked at the stone with awe. He examined it carefully. He felt . . . he knew . . . it must be genuine, despite the pronouncement of Breda and the others in Norway. He asked Ohman to give him the stone. Ohman, glad to be rid of the stone which had so impinged upon his character, happily turned it over to Holand.

Then began a long, tireless, frustrating, but nonetheless unceasing effort on Holand's part to establish the authenticity of the stone. Begun in 1907, the effort is still being pursued, more than half a century later.

First, Holand, having a knowledge of runes, worked out a new translation, which was essentially the same as that provided by Breda, but Holand was able to supply the missing words and numerals, thus proving himself, an amateur, a better student of runes than his critics in America or Norway. His translation, it might be added, still stands, numerals and all. No scholar has been able to prove him in error.

The Holand translation now becomes even more sensational:

> *We are 8 Goths* (Swedes) *and 22 Norwegians on*
> (an) *exploration journey from*
> *Vinland round about the West. We*
> *had camp by* (a lake with) *2 skerries one*
> *day's journey north from this stone*
> *We were* (out) *and fished one day After*
> *we came home* (we) *found 10* (of our) *men red*
> *with blood and dead* AV(E) *M*(ARIA)
> *save* (us) *from evil*

This, the main text was on the face of the stone.

On the 6-inch edge, were these lines:

> (We) *have 10 of* (our party) *by the sea to look*
> *after our ships* (ship) *14 days-journeys*
> *from this island* (in the) *year* (of our Lord) *1362.*

Holand's translation was greeted with enthusiasm, for he had cleared up several errors in its transcription by another runologist who had misread portions of it, and deciphered some, but not all of the numerals. The date, 1362, had emerged as *1462* on the earlier translation.

It was now that Holand, through research, encountered Storm's evidence of the Paul Knutson expedition. He wrote reports for the Minnesota Historical Society, gave lectures on the stone, and wrote articles about it.

In 1910, the first in a seemingly never-ending series of senseless attacks on Holand, the Kensington Stone, Ohman, and anyone who came near the scene began.

A newspaper editor, Rasmus B. Anderson, in Madison, Wisconsin, published a long article in which he stated, by implication, that the stone was the work of Ohman, a defrocked minister named Reverend Fogelblad, and one Andrew Anderson, a worker on a dump operated by a railroad. In the course of the article, Anderson (Rasmus) identified Anderson (Andrew) as a former student at the University of Upsala, in Sweden, and the owner of a "nice farm" in Minnesota. Rasmus asserted that Andrew could quote Swedish poetry and words in Latin and Greek with absolute accuracy. Andrew was also, it seemed, a brother-in-law to Ohman. According to Andrew, he (Andrew), Ohman, and Fogelblad were wont to spend long winter evenings discussing and writing runes, which the learned Fogelblad would comment on for the company present. Fogelblad, it was stated, had written a book called *The Age of Reason* and owned a book on runes written by Fryxell.

From the conversation with Andrew, Rasmus concluded that all three of these nefarious characters could have perpetrated the runestone "hoax."

"From a runic, linguistic and historical standpoint the Kensington Stone is a fraud on the face of it," the erudite editor proclaimed.

He closed his article by indicating that Andrew had not actually admitted to the hoax, but had given him (Rasmus) some "significant winks" as they parted in the small hours of the morning, "the best of friends."

He delivers the *coup de grâce* by asking the gentle reader to draw his own conclusions.

Because of the space limitations here, I cannot hope to proffer a thorough analysis of the hundreds of thousands of words which have been written *pro* and *con* the Kensington Stone. I offer the above little gem because it was the first in a long series of excursions into idiocy indulged in by those who considered that they had the inside story, or knew patently more than those who considered the stone genuine. Rasmus Anderson was gullible; that much we will concede. His great offense was in printing what he had no substantiation for—in the devious way he did.

The facts:

> Anderson (Andrew) never attended the University at Upsala, did not own a "nice farm in Minnesota."
>
> Anderson and Ohman were not brothers-in-law.

Andrew *could* recite Swedish poetry, knew no Latin or Greek.

Fogelblad had never written a book called *Age of Reason.*

Ohman, Andrew, and Fogelblad did not pass their time together discussing runes.

Fogelblad did not own a book by Fryxell.

The above refutations come from letters written by Andrew Anderson himself, and Olaf Ohman, at the request of Professor N. H. Winchell, who, though an unbeliever in the stone's authenticity at the time, nevertheless, attempted to track down the truth of Rasmus Anderson's story.

That there were elements of jealousy present in Rasmus Anderson's unwarranted attack on Holand are evident. He himself had written a paper on the vikings and their voyages in 1874, coming to no worthwhile conclusions except that they had been here, somewhere.

The attacks continued, and Holand ignored most of them, publishing, at last, a book called *The Kensington Stone,* in 1932. Concurrent with the attacks came corroboration from such interested scholars as Dr. William Thalbitzer, a Danish authority on runes, who, surprisingly, had declared against the stone, but later reversed himself, and decided that the stone was genuine, its apparent anachronisms serving, as he put it, "to inspire us with confidence on the genuineness of the inscription."

Corroboration of the stone's authenticity has come from eight recognized scholars and philologists, according to Holand's own count. They are Hjalmar Lindroth, Andrew Fossum, Knut Soderwall, O. E. Hagen, William Thalbitzer, Gustav Indrebo, F. S. Cawley, and S. N. Hagen, whose treatise on the stone will be examined later.

Attacks on the stone have issued from G. T. Flom, Marius Hoegstad, Harry Andersen, Erik Moltke, Karl Martin Neilsen, Sven B. F. Jansson, Erik Wahlgren, and many others. We will examine some of these attacks, particularly those by Moltke and Wahlgren.

Despite the numerous attacks, ethnologists at the Smithsonian Institution felt it was genuine enough to display at that museum for a year in 1948–49. In 1951, the city of Alexandria, Minnesota, the Douglas County seat for Kensington, created a Runestone Memorial

Park, which features a huge replica of the famous and much maligned stone.

It was in 1949, however, that the biggest bomb was dropped on the stone, and may have had some influence in its later removal from the Smithsonian.

The year before, Dr. Johannes Brøndsted, director of the Royal Museum of Denmark, and its chief archaeologist, had been invited to America to inspect supposed viking sites and artifacts. His trip was financed by the American-Scandinavian Foundation. He covered much territory, and saw many sites and objects, some of which are dealt with elsewhere in this volume. While he was in America, Dr. Brøndsted expressed amazement that so much material had been found. He had not, it appeared, suspected the existence of so much evidence of viking visits. When he returned to Denmark, however, he wrote negative reports on most of the finds, and revealed some confusion on the others. He made no personal evaluation of the Kensington Stone other than to say that he was not too convinced of its authenticity. He then stated that he would rather leave an evaluation of the inscription to the philologists. Accordingly, he called in three eminent men of Denmark: Erik Moltke, a runologist, and Harry Andersen and Karl Martin Neilsen, both linguists. Their opinions were reproduced in his report, first issued on his return, later in Brøndsted's *Problemet om Nordboer I Nordamerika før Columbus.*

All three unequivocally damned the stone.

Brøndsted summarizes Neilsen's report in his own treatise, with brief mentions of the corroboration of the stone's fraudulency by Moltke and Andersen.

In order to acquaint you better with these attacks, it might be well to offer, simultaneously, the evaluation by Dr. S. N. Hagen.

First, I will tell you how Dr. Hagen became involved with the Kensington Stone.

In 1950, the distinguished Dr. Vilhjalmur Stefansson, in an effort to settle the whole matter for all time, requested the equally distinguished philologist, S. N. Hagen, to present a thorough analysis of the stone, and make pronouncement on it, one way or the other. Dr. Hagen had no great knowledge of the stone and its background, and he attacked the problem with enthusiasm.

After a lengthy study of the stone, he came to the conclusion that it was genuine. His report, published in *Speculum,* for July 1950, further enraged the stone's antagonists. Hagen, a philologist, had the colossal effrontery to acclaim Holand, a rank amateur, for the scholarly conclusions he had reached on the stone, and proceeded to deflate the attackers with a magnificently gentle humor. Rather than settle the question, as it should have, attackers rallied.

We will now examine the reports of Neilsen (con) and Hagen (pro) and perhaps learn why the anti-stonites were caused to stamp their collective feet and scream.

In his summarized report, reaching us through Brøndsted, Neilsen begins by asserting that the "Kensington Stone . . . is considered by many investigators to be a falsification, made towards the end of the nineteenth century."

Having set us straight on that count, he then proceeds to note that the words, *from, rise,* and *ded,* appearing in translation from the runes, are unexplainable, unless they be considered intrusions of English words, meaning, of course, that the stone's creator, either through lack of knowledge, or as part of his quiet hoax, thrust three English words into the text on the stone.

Continuing under the paragraph headed "Orthography and Phonetics," Neilsen criticizes the use of the letter *j* in the word *Skjar,* adding that it is an anachronism on the basis that *j* did not appear in the Swedish language until the sixteenth or seventeenth century, he's not sure which.

In acting on the assumption that the word *ded,* for example, was English—or reflected lack of knowledge on the carver's part (and the same arguments can be used for the other two words cited), Neilsen merely showed his own ignorance of his own science. Apparently he had not probed into the intricacies of the philology of runes and Old Swedish to know that there were two obvious explanations of the usage of the word. Holand, in defending the comments on the word, produced a manuscript of the fourteenth century, a letter from Queen Margaret, in which she refers to the death of a friend's husband: ". . . Effther the henne husbonde her Jens Herne ded er . . ." or: ". . . because her husband, Sir Jense Herne, is *dead.*" Yet Neilsen says, in his report: "The spelling forms *rise* and *ded* are unknown in Swedish."

Hagen, however, adds another thought to the meaning of the word. In a forceful genealogy of the word itself, he shows that all the scholars, including Holand, were probably wrong in its meaning.

The antis, in their superlative ignorance, claim that it is a misspelling of the English word *dead*. Holand translates it, accurately, as meaning "dead" in Old Swedish. Hagen reminds both parties that it probably derives from Old Icelandic, and means "tortured," or "tormented." This explanation makes sense, since the victims noted in the stone's inscription were, in all probability, scalped, which also partially accounts for their being "red with blood."

In the case of *rise*, Hagen demonstrates that it is a form quite pertinent to its use on the stone, and clearly means what it is intended to mean: *journey*.

From is considered by Neilsen to be English, and another critic, Gjessing, questions *fro*. In addition to blasting the use of these words, the question is raised by other critics: Why do the two versions exist in the same inscription? Hagen disposes of the *from-fro* protest neatly, then answers the question of their two forms. He cites Chaucer, using two forms of the word "from" in the Prologue to the *Canterbury Tales*, lines 404 and 408. Hagen then wonders why nobody questions Chaucer's variations (or denounces the manuscript as a fraud).

Under "Syntax," Neilsen protests that the phrase "*10 mans* gen. sing. after a numeral" is unknown in Swedish and is more probably an English plural form. *10 man*, singular after a numeral does not occur until modern Swedish.

This merely serves to show that Neilsen knew little about English, also, since he considers *mans* a plural English form. Holand cites examples of the use of the word *mans* both in modern Icelandic (apparently Neilsen's study of philology did not include Icelandic) and in Old Icelandic, referring to a ms. in the *Flateybook* from c. 1380. Hagen answers all the accusations of fraud based on plurals and "modern" verb forms by chiding the *anti* scholars gently:

"It has been argued," he writes, "that the Kensington inscription is a forgery because its verb forms are 'modern.' The answer to this is that insofar as some Scandinavian dialects used singular verbs with plural subjects they were 'modern' already around 1300."

Neilsen says the word *opdagelsefard* is out of place in a Middle Ages inscription.

Hagen and Holand both show that it is in perfect keeping.

And on and on and on and on it goes.

The most serious charge was that two rune forms used on the stone were not invented until after 1500: the *ö* and the *j*. Hagen offers a plausible explanation of the use of the *ö*, but Holand manages an even better counterargument. He shows evidence that the *ö* was in use as a matter of form by the Hanseatic League, which cast such a great influence over the northern countries in the 1300s. But then he delivers his coup. Neilsen states that the *j* was not invented until after 1500. Holand produces an article by another of the stone's critics, Adolf Noreen, which treats on the wide use of *j* as a consonant in the fourteenth and fifteenth centuries. It appeared in *Nordisk Familjebok*, Vol. 12, pages 1123–24. The critics, apparently, suffered from faulty communications with one another.

Hagen's masterful, erudite, humorous philological analysis of the stone should have closed the matter once and for all. But it didn't. Having had virtually all of their philological arguments against the stone shattered, there was only one way for the antis to go.

The attack must be continued by other and more indirect methods.

In 1951, Moltke was right back in the fray with gloves laced tight. In the Danish journal *Danske Studier*, 1949–50 edition, he had first let go his broadside. After Hagen's paper appeared, Moltke wrote an article for the June 1951, issue of *Antiquity*, which he later sent to the Massachusetts Archaeological Society. He wanted no bases untouched. It appeared in the Massachusetts *Bulletin* for July 1952.

Chafing from the wounds inflicted by Hagen, Moltke resorts to every attack he can muster to discredit the stone, realizing that his philological arguments are not strong enough to stand. He begins his piece by referring to the stone as a "blatant forgery" (of what?). He then calls it "despised," as he refers contemptuously to its degradation as a steppingstone on Ohman's farm. He then quotes Professor Winchell, who agrees with Moltke. Now he adds the names of runologists and philologists Sophus Bugge, Magnus Olsen, and Adolf Noreen, (the professor with the embarrassing *j*) as additional foes of the stone, and later piles Ossa on Pelion by adding still more.

Then he states that two younger runologists, himself and Sven B. F. Jansson, have questioned the authenticity of the stone. By including himself in the distinguished company noted above, he firmly impresses the reader with the fact that this is the end-all paper on the wretched stone. In a grudging five-line mention, he notes that Dr. William Thalbitzer upholds the stone's authenticity. Moltke seems hurt in having to make the admission. Now he makes use of the out-of-context quote. He notes that S. N. Hagen has written a paper on the stone and quotes a paragraph from Hagen's article:

"As far as I know, no linguist or runologist has come forward with the reconsideration suggested by Einarsson [disagreeing with Holand who is deficient in certain elementary fundamentals]. While we are awaiting a study of the inscription by a competent scholar, I offer a few observations. . . ."

Moltke uses Hagen's own modest appraisal of himself as certain indication that he (Hagen) is incompetent. In parentheses, he adds, speaking of Einarsson, that the latter disagrees with Holand, who is *deficient in certain elementary fundamentals.* Here is exactly what Einarsson has to say of Holand; as quoted by Hagen in *The Speculum:*

> In spite of his [Holand's] handicap, he has actually succeeded in producing some linguistic material not easily refuted in support of the inscription; as for instance, parallels to show that the singular of verbs could be used for the plural, or that the old dative plural was supplanted by the accusative.
>
> In view of this circumstance and of many other facts speaking for the genuineness of the stone—the well-documented story of its origin and its weathered appearance—it is my conviction that linguists and runologists would do well to take the matter under new consideration before rending their final verdict.

Perhaps Professor Moltke failed to read Einarsson's statement correctly . . . or fully.

Then he quotes one of Hagen's observations, plainly placing it where he does in the article to show that Hagen was not a scientific person, but a romanticist who would have us believe the stone authentic because of sentimental reasons:

> This inscription should be a perfect joy to the linguist because it is such a delightfully honest and unsophisticated record of its author's own speech. A forger would have tried to imitate a language other than his own. It is clear that this author tried to imitate no language but his own. In branding this beautiful inscription as a forgery, scholars have thrown away not only an important historical document but also a faithful record of medieval Scandinavian speech.

Thus having established Hagen's incompetency, and proving it by a romanticist paragraph from that scholar, and having noted Holand's deficiencies as asserted by Einarsson, but somehow having neglected to include Einarsson's true evaluation of Holand and the stone, Moltke performs even more incredibly.

He complains that Professor Richard Hennig of Düsseldorf, in spite of having read Jansson's and his (Moltke's) pronouncements on the stone, has the audacity to declare it genuine! But his complaint regarding Hennig's failure to recognize Moltke and Jansson as the final authorities on the rock is not enough. Read, if you will, the following quote from Moltke's article:

". . . and although he knows both Jansson's and my article, *he concludes his statement with the following pompous words, reminiscent of the runologists of the Hitler period:* 'The authenticity of the Kensington Stone has been proved and thereby the presence of Scandinavians in America fully 130 years before Columbus is no longer in doubt.'"

The italics, are, of course, mine, and no further comment on Hitler or pomposity is necessary.

He directs his fire at Hagen from time to time, but is extremely careful to avoid the *from, rise, ded,* brouhaha, except to refer to *ded* out of context, without stating Hagen's case for it.

He also quotes a particularly offensive paragraph from Professor Jon Helgason, professor in Icelandic at the University of Copenhagen. In it, Helgason, who speaks, as Moltke puts it, for *every* Scandinavian scholar, indicates that ". . . no philologist with any self-respect could in any decency write about it [the inscription] . . ."

Forgetting that the Kensington Stone was carved as a grave stone for the 10 men "red with blood and tortured," Moltke then draws himself up to his full height and, in support of his theory that the runes could not possibly have been carved on the stone in 1362, states, with full authority: "Runes ceased to be used in Denmark and Norway about 1300, but they survived in Sweden on grave stones and household goods, not to mention the runic calendars which continued up to the 1700s."

Next he asserts that the carver of the Kensington Stone probably copied the runes from a Swedish calendar of the nineteenth century. The carver, he states, also invented new symbols. (Or symbols which Professor Moltke's studies of the old alphabets had not revealed?)

Then, he brings his tract to a conclusion: "But it [the stone] has not yet received the *coup de grâce*. Here it comes."

Expecting to find some startling new orthographic or phonetic evidence, the reader is somewhat let down when Moltke drags out the tired old *ö* and *j* characters, forgetting that Noreen has already betrayed him in an earlier article which Moltke is presumably not familiar with.

Following the *coup de grâce*, he offers further proof in stating that Professor Brøndsted has proved that an initial, "H," carved on the stone by Holand forty years before has taken on a certain patina. That's all he says about it. It has taken on a certain patina. No explanations other than to note that the stone has been sheltered through these years. That's all. Then he delivers Moltke's farewell address to the stone:

"Farewell, Kensington Stone of 1362, farewell Paul Knutson expedition which perhaps never even started and which very likely never got to America; at any rate farewell to all the fruitless labors of scholars of nearly every branch of learning."

I can only murmur that I am happy the above paragraph did not appear in Professor Moltke's thesis. But it does show improvement in his literary style.

But he's not through yet.

In a garrison finish, he proves conclusively that the copy of the inscription sent to Swan Turnblad was not a copy, but the original draft of the inscription, from which the forger worked. I am too weak to comment on this charge. I leave Professor Moltke to his mutterings and take up with the latest, and equally petulant critic of the Kensington Stone.

He is Erik Wahlgren, and he is professor of Scandinavian languages at the University of California at Los Angeles. He wrote a book in 1958 called *The Kensington Stone: A Mystery Solved*, published by the University of Wisconsin Press. In April 1959, an article, based on the book, appeared in *American Heritage*. Proceeding on the not unreasonable supposition that more people read the article in *American Heritage* than those who might buy or read his book, I will direct my attention to the article.

I will not go into it in detail, other than to demonstrate that the weakening of the arguments against the stone has forced its critics, as in Moltke's case, to resort to *argumentum ad hominem* with more readily apparent de-emphasis on the content of the stone, which has not yet been successfully discredited.

So, to meet Professor Wahlgren.

Wahlgren shows some originality in his attack, I must confess, although it gets off to a slow start. He begins by telling the story of the finding of the stone and its examination by Turnblad, and how that editor sent the copied inscription on to Professor Breda. He then reproduces the translation *in full*, neglecting to tell his readers that Breda was unable to decipher the *entire* inscription. He also reproduces an editorial comment on Breda's report, which is written thusly:

"Perhaps further development will decide whether this find is to be ranked with the Rosetta Stone or with the Cardiff Giant."

Having thus implanted doubt, Wahlgren continues the story of the peregrinations of the stone, and concludes the first part of his article by writing: "The Kensington Stone was a clumsy forgery, its author a Swede with some scanty grasp of runic letters and of English. History might resume its normal course. The runic bubble had burst."

Now he begins on Holand. He asserts that Holand went to see Ohman, the stone's owner, and "what passed between the two men may never be known." (I can be of some help, Professor Wahlgren. Ohman gave the stone to Holand, glad to be rid of it. He made the statement himself in an affidavit, witnessed and signed in 1909. The official, or notary public, who presided at the occasion was R. J. Rasmusson, of Douglas County, Minnesota, and a man of unimpeachable reputation. Ohman gave Holand the stone in August 1907. The exact transcript of their conversation is not known to me, but I'm sure Mr. Holand would supply it, if requested.)

Then he attacks Holand for trying to raise money on the stone. Holand, he states, attempted to sell the stone to the Minnesota Historical Society for $5000 for, as Wahlgren puts it, "a compensation for my contribution to American history." In 1911, Holand was burning with the desire to go abroad for further study. He wanted to learn more of these vikings, if possible. The only thing to do was to go to Norway and there search records, and engage in whatever research he could accomplish. He had no money. The stone belonged to him. He tried to use it to raise money. A natural reaction for one desirous of furthering his education in an area he was so desperately determined to investigate. Knowing Holand, I can guess that if there were anything he wanted to part with, the last thing would have been the stone. To him it was more than a stone. It was a link in America's missing pre-Columbian history. I think the abuse he has weathered through the years is quite enough to reveal his feeling about it.

Now Wahlgren wades into the source of reports published about the Kensington Stone in favorable light, by the Minnesota Historical Society. To his shock, he discovered that they were all authored by Holand! Truly shocking. The society accepted them, as written by Holand. I can't conceive of Holand writing an unfavorable report on the stone he has risked his reputation on, any more than I can conceive of a Wahlgren writing a favorable report on it. These reports, says Wahlgren, were created by a committee within the Minnesota Historical Society. "No one," he asserts, "on the committee had the slightest familiarity with Scandinavian linguistics, let alone runological problems . . ." I think the same can safely be said for many of the scholarly critics of the stone, after reading Hagen's report.

Wahlgren is plainly hurt by Holand's tirelessness. He complains that Holand's production of articles, interviews, lectures, and books have enabled him to "Pilot his runic tablet through critical shoals to the high seas of international fame." And in the last quote I think I detect the embryo of Wahlgren's attitudes on the stone.

The next irrelevant injection centers about a lawsuit instituted after the stone was returned to Minnesota from the Smithsonian. In his comments on this suit, Wahlgren implies some sort of skulduggery on Holand's part. He states that the lawsuit was instituted to determine ownership of the stone, leaving a strong impression with the reader that the suit was directed against Holand. He notes that Holand received $2500, assertedly as purchase money for the stone. He also comments on the fact that Olaf Ohman had never received any money for the stone—understandable, since he gave it to Holand. Wahlgren then explains that the suit was mysteriously dropped.

Here is the story of the suit, as explained to me in a letter from Hjalmar Holand, on November 9th, 1960.

The "lawsuit" mentioned by Mr. Wahlgren had nothing to do with the merits of the Kensington Stone. Here are the facts:

Some time after the Minn. His. Society published its report on the Kensington Stone [1911], I had a letter from a lawyer in Alexandria, Minn. He wrote that he and nine other men were ready to give me $2500 for research in Europe providing I would give the stone to Douglas County. This offer was accepted and the stone was sent to Alexandria. About twelve years ago the stone was tentatively sent to the Smithsonian Institution, but was returned to Alexandria in 1949 to be exhibited in the principal festivities marking the centennial celebration of the state. It was the original intention to return the stone to the Smithsonian, but this did not meet with general approval. A suit was started by the descendants of the ten men who subscribed the $2500 I received that the stone belonged to sons and heirs of these men. I was called as a witness and testified that I did not sell the stone to anybody, but agreed to give it to Douglas County on condition that I be given a stipend of $2500 for research abroad.

The complaining heirs of the ten men did not further press their suit.

Sincerely,
H. R. HOLAND

I think no further comment is necessary.

Next, Wahlgren attacks the circumstances under which the stone was found, a hoary device frequently used when an artifact is not fully accepted. It enables the opposition to divert attention from the object itself and cloud the issue. And only a small cloud is necessary to prevent authentication in such a case.

Wahlgren also notes that Ohman, the stone's finder, possessed a book mentioned earlier, *The Well-Informed Schoolmaster*, which contained a runic alphabet of 16 letters. Then he would have you believe that this farmer was able to take such an alphabet and concoct from it a runic inscription which was translatable. He also states that some of the characters on the stone are "very weird," and indicates that others are probably "humorous adaptations" of Phoenician and archaic Greek alphabets. This latter is truly a compliment to a man not schooled in languages. And if he copied the runes from a book, from what source did he obtain the Phoenician and Greek letters which he caricatured so successfully that they were translatable as runes? The record showeth not that Ohman possessed such source books. Olaf Ohman was indeed a remarkable man. I doubt that the distinguished Professor Wahlgren himself could accomplish such "humorous adaptations" of old Phoenician, and achieve these amusing deviations with a skill that could make them readable in Swedish—old or modern.

There is one area of attack, however, in which Wahlgren may be right. He takes violent issue with the route of Paul Knutson's expedition into Minnesota as laid down by Holand. The defender of the Kensington Stone believes that Knutson sailed into the Hudson Bay, and into the Nelson River. From there he came down through Lake Winnipeg and into the Red River whence he entered the Buffalo River and proceeded down a now-vanished waterway which took him and his party into the vicinity of Kensington.

The inscription on the stone proclaims that the vikings had "10 men by the sea to look after our ship, [or ships] 14 days journey from this island." The distance from Hudson's Bay to Kensington, Minnesota, is admittedly greater than that which could be accomplished in 14 days' journey. Holand himself, since first postulating this theory, has qualified it, but Wahlgren, in the manner of a cross-examiner, nails him to it, with no concession that perhaps a different route could have been followed.

I would be inclined to believe that Lake Superior was the "sea" referred to on the stone, rather than Hudson's Bay. Holand says such a condition is not possible, because the runic word on the stone translates into *hawet*, meaning a *salt* sea, thereby ruling out Lake Superior. I can't agree with this reasoning. There is no evidence that these vikings were familiar with great inland fresh water bodies, and to them, this greatest of great lakes was simply a "sea." They certainly would not have called it a "lake," salt or no salt; it bore no resemblance to even the largest lakes in Norway or Sweden. And Kensington, Minnesota, about 170 miles from the western extremity of Lake Superior was easily within the "10 days' journey" from the place where the stone was found.

I suspect Knutson's expedition might have sailed into Hudson's Bay but turned into the Albany River and thence down the Kenogami until they were forced to abandon their ship and go overland. It is possible that they found an old Indian trail from James Bay to Lake Nipigon, and at that lake built another ship which took them into Lake Superior. They coasted the lake westward until they were forced east by its conformation at Duluth. They returned to Duluth and again struck out overland, meeting disaster at Kensington, 14 days from the lake.

My own speculation is based largely on the find of a viking sword, an ax and a flat, unidentifiable band of iron at Beardmore, Ontario, about seven miles from Lake Nipigon. Dr. Brøndsted saw these artifacts and thought they were medieval, but refrained from authenticating them because of a cloud of suspicion cast upon them by two men. One of the men later admitted that his doubts were ill founded, the other refuses to view the objects to affirm or deny his suspicions. During a luncheon with Dr. Brøndsted on October 19, 1960, he told me that he felt that the Beardmore find was undoubtedly genuine; in his report he did not feel that he could state as much conclusively because of the still-lacking retraction from the second doubter mentioned above. He also told me that he thought much of the evidence he saw here in America was genuine; he simply didn't feel there was enough to proffer a conclusive theory.

Again, respectfully, I must disagree with Dr. Brøndsted. I think there *is* enough. The Kensington Stone and the Beardmore sword and ax are only two finds of viking artifacts in the area. Holand lists a catalogue of nine others in *Explorations in America Before Columbus.* They consist of three firesteels, three halberds, two more axes, and a boathook. Holand also offers a trail of mooring stones through the central part of Minnesota. These holes are perhaps not the best evidence, but could be indicative of the presence of vikings.

The artifacts seem to present a pattern, which is what archaeologists look for in drawing their conclusions. The pattern, to me, seems to indicate an ever-westward journey from Lake Superior. It is even possible, perhaps, to determine the ultimate point of their journey. In central North Dakota, on the bank of the Missouri River, a strange, marked stone was discovered in 1738 by Pierre Gaultier de Varennes, Sieur de La Vérendrye. It was covered with strange writing on both sides. Unable to decipher it, he kept it, and took it with him to Quebec when he returned east in 1743. There he showed it to Jesuit scholars, who admittedly were stumped by it, but decided that the strange letters looked very much like the writings of the Tatars. (Runic and Tataric alphabets are quite similar.) The stone was eventually sent to Paris, where it has since vanished.

Now I will recount a most curious observation, by the distinguished Erik Wahlgren, professor at the University of California. After closing his case against the Kensington Stone, and pronouncing it a hoax for the readers of *American Heritage,* he adds a footnote:

"This does not," he notes, "preclude the possibility that evidence of early Norse exploration of Minnesota exists. In 1738, for example, a French explorer, the Sieur de La Vérendrye, discovered an inscribed stone west of Lake Superior which he took to Montreal. The Jesuits there thought the writing was "Tataric"—which looks much like runic. The stone was sent to France, and has since disappeared."

If I were to dig deeply for a better example of inconsistent reasoning, I should find it difficult to produce. Wahlgren vents his wrath on a "hoax" which he has yet to discredit successfully, and which was found in the center of a complex of other medieval finds and which is considered by such erudite philologists as S. N. Hagen to be authentic. Then, in an incredibly naïve footnote, he cites a nonexistent stone as possible proof that the vikings actually *did* penetrate Minnesota.

But such reasoning is neither going to damage the Kensington Stone permanently, nor will it prevent its rightful inclusion in our history books. A cheerful parallel which gives hope for the acceptance of the rune stone is seen in the incident of the Painted Cave of Altamira. As Geoffrey Bibby relates it in *Testimony of the Spade*, the breathtaking paleolithic paintings in the cave were discovered by a little girl, Maria de Sautuola, at play in the dark recesses of the cavern while her father probed its floor for artifacts. Her sire, Don Marcelino Santiago Tomás Sanz de Sautuola, a Spanish don of excellent reputation, on verifying what his small daughter had seen, prepared a paper on the discovery entitled *An Account of Certain Prehistoric Discoveries in the Province of Santander*. In it, he documented the paintings and other archaeological finds in the cave. It appeared in 1880. The don was pleased with himself as was his friend, Don Juan Vilanova y Piera, a geologist who had declared the paintings paleolithic in origin. But de Sautuola was soon to be struck down by critics and scoffers who heaped scorn and ridicule on the don and his "alleged" paintings. Cartailhac of the University of Toulouse denounced the don as a fraud, and would not trouble himself to travel the hundred or so miles to the cave to see the paintings. Paleontologist Eduard Harle discovered that the don had hired an itinerant, down-at-the-heels artist to make the drawings for his published paper. The artist had since disappeared, and Harle jumped to an erring conclusion: The don had hired the artist to paint the cave! Brokenhearted that his integrity should be questioned, the don withdrew from the world, but Vilanova pressed the fight.

Today the Cave at Altamira is considered the finest example of paleolithic cave painting in the world. But twenty-two years passed before the clouds were scattered above it. In 1902 Cartailhac, who, by his action proved himself a truly great man, published an apology for his pronouncement of 1880 for the world to see. Beyond that, since Don Marcelino and Vilanova were now dead, he journeyed to see the daughter of the old don, now a married woman. To her, he apologized for the wrong he had done her father.

The battle to gain acceptance of the Altamira Cave for what it was took twenty-two years. Holand's battle has been in progress for more than fifty. Eventually his battle will be won, totally.

It seems to me that direct action by the highest authority we can muster is necessary to brush away the flies and establish the Kensington Stone, for all time, as the genuine record of fourteenth-century exploration of America that it is. The Smithsonian Institution has acknowledged its authenticity. By the time this volume reaches publication, the United States will have gained a new President, known to be extremely knowledgeable in the history of his country. I think it not at all improper to enter a plea that President Kennedy put an end to the discordance that keeps the stone in partial eclipse. I respectfully submit that he could, with little time consumed, empower a committee from the Smithsonian to acknowledge this Kensington Stone publicly, and to recommend that historians begin placing it in history books from the time of its official recognition. Any announcement, should, of course, be released on a national basis, and not confined to some obscure archaeological journal.

If fortune smiles, perhaps we, in this generation, will see the validating of what Professor Hagen once called "an important historical document . . . a faithful record of medieval Scandinavian speech."

CHAPTER 18

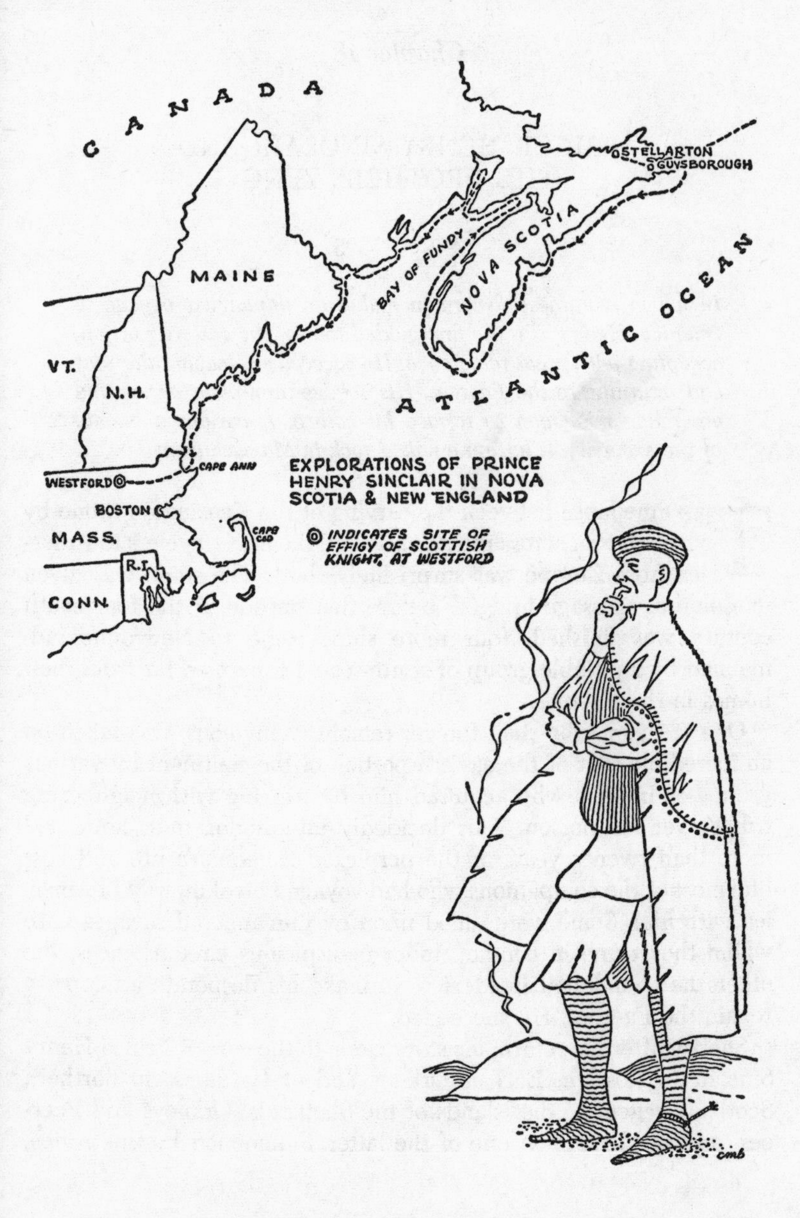
CANADA
MAINE
VT.
N.H.
MASS.
R.I.
CONN.
WESTFORD
BOSTON
CAPE ANN
CAPE COD
BAY OF FUNDY
NOVA SCOTIA
STELLARTON
GUYSBOROUGH
ATLANTIC OCEAN
EXPLORATIONS OF PRINCE HENRY SINCLAIR IN NOVA SCOTIA & NEW ENGLAND
© INDICATES SITE OF EFFIGY OF SCOTTISH KNIGHT, AT WESTFORD
cmb

Chapter 18

PRINCE HENRY SINCLAIR AND THE BROTHERS ZENO

[A.D. C. 1395]

In which a Faroese fisherman makes an unplanned voyage to America. He is given the first guided tour of the eastern portion, accepting with great reluctance. He succeeds in leaving the tour and returning to the Faeroes. His voyage prompts a prince and an Italian nobleman to retrace his course. A curious memento of the excursion is left on a naked rock in Massachusetts.

THE time lapse between the carving of the Kensington Stone by visitors from across the Atlantic and the next travelers to America from Europe was surprisingly short. The stone was given its dolorous message in 1362; before that decade of the fourteenth century was finished, four more ships came to Newfoundland, manned by a pitiable group of storm-tossed fishermen far from their homes in the Faeroes.

One of them, who shall forever remain anonymous, was taken on an incredible tour of the eastern portion of the continent by various groups of Indians who acquired him by warring with neighboring tribes over his person. This decidedly unorthodox tour consumed more than twenty years of the perplexed fisherman's life and cost him most of the companions who had voyaged involuntarily to America with him. Some were dined upon by ill-mannered savages with whom they came in contact under inauspicious circumstances, the others he abandoned in Mexico, to make his desperate attempt to regain the Faeroes. He succeeded.

Shortly after his return, his story came to the ears of Prince Henry Sinclair of Rosslyn, Earl of Orkney and of Caithness in northern Scotland, regent of the islands of the Shetlands, Orkneys and Faeroes—and resident upon one of the latter. Summoned by the prince, the fisherman told his remarkable story to that dignitary, who immediately decided to visit the strange lands described by his much-traveled subject.

But I am too hasty. The chronicle of the Faroese fisherman and the anxious prince really begins aboard a Venetian caravel captained by a young Italian noble stricken with the wanderlust.

About 1390, an adventuresome young Venetian named Niccolò Zeno, indulging himself in a compelling desire to see the world, outfitted a ship and set sail to the west from Venice, steering toward the majestic Pillars of Hercules. From there he steered north, planning to visit England and Flanders. Fair weather held for a few days, but suddenly his ship was caught in a fierce storm which buffeted him about cruelly, and drove him far north of his first objective, ultimately wrecking him on the bleak, rocky shore of one of the Faeroe Islands. He and his crew were able to save themselves, and get most of their cargo ashore. But their security was threatened almost immediately by the arrival of a villainous band of islanders intent upon appropriating the ship's goods and assassinating the unfortunate Niccolò and his battered sailors. The Italians, stunned by the sudden appearance of the bloodthirsty Faroese, and certainly in no condition to defend themselves, presumably shrugged and awaited their fate. It was one of the more violent customs of that era to sack a wrecked ship; execution of the survivors followed as a matter of form. But the islanders were thwarted of their evil intent by the unexpected appearance of Prince Henry Sinclair, accompanied by a full complement of knights in armor. A few well-aimed lance thrusts quickly dispersed his loyal subjects, and Niccolò and his crew were saved again. The prince was much impressed when he learned of Niccolò's rank and family—the Venetian was known as "The Chevalier" and came from a long line of Italian nobles—and invited him to be his guest. A strong friendship sprang up between the two, and Henry was by far the gainer in his new association, for he learned much from the Italian concerning naval warfare. Henry was then involved in bringing all of the Faeroes under his rule and kept a fleet of 13 ships busily engaged in the operation. Niccolò's great knowledge of nautical offensive proved invaluable to the Earl of Orkney, and Niccolò apparently thrived on the life he was leading in the earl's service. He did not return to Venice, but sent such glowing accounts of his adventures to a brother, Antonio, that the latter joined him in 1391. The brothers Zeno were now both in the service of the earl, and extremely happy. Niccolò was made captain of Sinclair's fleet and, with his brother, engaged in many punitive expeditions for the prince. After one of these forays, Niccolò decided to embark on a voyage of discovery. He succeeded in reaching Greenland and there saw many wondrous things which were later recounted in the book containing his and Antonio's adventures, published by a descendant in the sixteenth century. The Greenland climate, however, did not agree with Niccolò. He became ill and returned to the Faeroes, where he died in 1396 shortly after his arrival.

The grieving Antonio apparently decided now that he had had enough of life with Sinclair, and expressed the wish to return to his native Venice. But Sinclair turned a deaf ear to Antonio's pleadings and prevailed upon him to stay and assist in future conquests. Paramount on the agenda was a voyage of exploration to the west to investigate the lands seen by the old fisherman. According to the well-traveled sailor, the lands were populated and, in Henry's mind, ripe for conquest and colonization.

The old fisherman's story would indeed have intrigued a much less adventuresome mind than Henry's. Twenty-six years before, (as Antonio Zeno related it) he had been caught in a tempest, together with three other fishing boats and, after many days of wandering upon the sea they came to an island called *Estotiland.* One of their boats was wrecked there, the fisherman and five companions seized by the natives and taken to their "beautiful and largely populated city." The king of these people summoned interpreters to converse with them, and found one, a fisherman like themselves, who had been blown to the land in a similar storm many years before. This man spoke Latin, and was therefore able to communicate with the new arrivals. The king, on learning the details of their involuntary visit, decreed that they would remain with him. With no alternative, they stayed, living on the island of Estotiland for five years.

The fisherman told Prince Henry that the island was "rich, and abundant in all the good things of this world . . . rather smaller than Iceland, but more fertile. . . ." The inhabitants, he asserted, were quick-witted and possessed of all the arts known in the Faeroes. He also suspected that the people of Estotiland must have had traffic with Europe at some time in the past; he had seen Latin books in the king's library, but none on the island could read them. They had a distinct language, and could write, and obtained metals from the earth, including gold. They traded with Greenland, "whence they receive furs, and sulphur and pitch." They also sowed grain and made beer, which "the Northern people use as [Italians] do wine." They knew how to build small ships but had no lodestone.

The fisherman's compass beguiled the king and caused the ruler to hold his guests in much esteem. Thus far, the fisherman had lived a rather sedentary life, but his troubles began when the king decided, for some unexplained reason, to send him south to a country called *Drogio*, with twelve small ships. In Drogio, the fleet was wrecked and most of the luckless fisherman's companions were captured and consumed by these less-civilized natives.

Our protagonist, however, saved his own life by showing the chief of the cannibals how to make nets and thereby gather great quantities of fish. This facility so impressed the chief, and word of his magic spread so wide, that a neighboring chief declared war on the fisherman's host in order to gain the services of the net maker. For the next thirteen years, the unhappy fisherman was fought for and exchanged as spoils of war no less than twenty-five times.

His peregrinations took him farther and farther south until he arrived in a country where the climate was more temperate and the inhabitants lived in cities and worshiped idols. They also sacrificed, and ate, men. Inferring that Estotiland was Nova Scotia, and Drogio the New England mainland and below, the last stages of his journey, if the description is accepted, took the fisherman to Mexico. From that country he was fortunate enough to make his escape and eventually reach Drogio, leaving behind the few surviving companions who had made the journey southward with him. From Drogio he succeeded in returning to Estotiland, where he lived long enough to become rich and build a vessel in which he could return to the Faeroes.

It was not long after his arrival that he told his story to Prince Henry, and on that account, the prince could scarcely contain himself until he could set sail for this strange land. Antonio Zeno was made a member of the party when, at last, Sinclair was ready to depart, but was disappointed in that he was not made captain. Sinclair himself elected to lead the expedition. Preparations being made, all was ready when an evil omen struck. The old fisherman, who had agreed to go back to Estotiland with Sinclair, sickened and died. Undaunted, Sinclair engaged some of the sailors who had come with the deceased from Estotiland, and the excursion was underway. The time, summer 1395.

The expedition got off to a good start, with the fleet sailing together and fair weather prevailing. Steering west, the fleet skirted some islands subject to Prince Henry and arrived at an island named Ledovo, where all laid up seven days to rest and complete the provisioning and equipping of the ships. On the first of July, they arrived at another island, Ilofe, but sailed on past it since the wind was in their favor. Into the deepest ocean they sailed but were soon set upon by a storm which buffeted them for eight days and cost them a large number of ships of the fleet. When the storms abated, they sailed with a good wind and discovered land in the west.

This was not the land they sought, but an island said to be called "Icarus," where the inhabitants were most hostile. They succeeded in making a secret landing on the island to obtain wood and water, but were soon set upon by the discourteous islanders who attacked them with "weapons and arrows" and killed several of the fleet's sailors. Fleeing in haste, the remainder gained their ships and eventually resumed the voyage.

Now they sailed westward for six days and then, with a southwest wind, four days more, and sighted land. This new land was a most appealing place and forthwith the fleet put in to a good harbor. In the distance, they saw a great mountain which cast forth smoke, and this raised the hope that they might find inhabitants. Sinclair then despatched "a hundred good soldiers" to reconnoiter the country and report what kind of people inhabited it. Meanwhile, the fleet replenished its dwindled store of victuals with fishes, seafowl, and birds' eggs.

The climate of the country was more temperate than one could express and all suspected that the island must be uninhabited, until the good soldiers returned. From the scouting party, Sinclair learned that the smoke had come from the foot of the great mountain; a great fire burned there which produced a certain matter like pitch, which ran into the sea. The inhabitants, the scouts reported, were many—and half-savage. They sheltered themselves in caves, were of small stature and inherently timid. They had fled into their caves at the sight of the soldiers.

Sinclair digested the report, then reviewed his own impressions of the place. The country was healthy and of pure climate, and its many peculiar advantages—coupled with its very good soil and rivers—caused him to think that he might make his dwelling there, and build a city.

But the prince's enthusiasm for the new country was not completely shared by his followers. They began to rebel, and asserted that they wanted to return to the Faeroes, stating that winter was approaching and further delay would mean remaining until the following summer. Henry, surprisingly enough, was sympathetic to their complaints, and sent the entire fleet back to the Faeroes, retaining only the small rowing boats, and those of his company who chose to stay at his side.

Antonio Zeno was sent back with the fleet, against his wishes. Now in command, he sailed twenty days to the east without seeing land. He then changed his course and sailed southeast for five days and sighted an island which he knew to be east of Iceland. Taking time to put in new provisions, he sailed again for three days and reached the Faeroes, where the expedition was received with much joy.

The above account was first contained in letters from Antonio Zeno to his brother, Carlo, in Venice. Carlo saved all these communications from his absent brother and placed them in a trunk in an unused room or wing of the family mansion in Venice. Early in the sixteenth century, a great-great-great grandson of Antonio, bearing the name of Niccolò, found the letters when, as a small boy, he happened upon them in their dusty receptacle. He examined them, and then tore them up, leaving them where he found them. Years later, when the thrill of discovery was titillating Europe, Niccolò remembered the letters . . . and their contents. He retrieved them and painfully pieced them back together again. He himself was surprised at the story they told; it could be nothing more than a voyage to America, undertaken by his ancestor . . . and a hundred years before Columbus at that! He thereupon published the letters, with added editorial comment of his own, in 1558.

The volume containing the adventures of the Zeno brothers, in the service of Prince Henry Sinclair of the Orkneys, was accepted as a factual document for many years, but eventually doubt crept in to question it. Before the sixteenth century had faded from sight, Arngrim Jones, the noted Icelandic historian, began attacks on the tale, scoffing at what he termed "non-existent islands" mentioned in the narrative. He also derided the descriptions of Greenland by Niccolò. The French geographer, Michel Antoine Baudrand, in his *Geographical Dictionary,* published in 1681, expressed similar doubts and drew the fury of Padre Dottore Vitale Terra Rosa, who came forth with a vigorous defense of the narrative, and of Venetian nobility in general.

Atlases, globes, and divers maps appeared showing the locations of the Zeno islands, and others appeared which did not. Torfaeus, another Icelandic historian, rejected the tale, but Louis Moreri, in his *Le Grand Dictionnaire Historique,* in 1674, said the tale was true. The Lutheran missionary, Hans Egede, who rediscovered Greenland in 1741, was extremely doubtful, but Peter Kalm, the Swedish naturalist, thought the islands might have existed once and were submerged.

A vigorous champion of the Zeno narrative was found in Dr. John Reinhold Forster, who, in a history published in 1786, put forth a substantial argument in favor of the authenticity of the story. Forster was the first to deduce the identity of Sinclair, who is referred to in the narrative as "Zichmni." American historian Washington Irving thought the whole tale ridiculous, but German historian Baron Humboldt voted for the accuracy of the story with a firm "yea."

One of the most damaging attacks upon it came from Admiral C. C. Zarhtmann, hydrographer to the Royal Danish Navy, who blew the story nearly to bits, in 1833, in a paper published by the Society of Northern Antiquaries at Copenhagen. But Zarhtmann, in turn, was shredded by R. H. Major, of the British Museum, who wrote *The Voyages of the Brothers Zeno for the Hakluyt Society* in 1873. Major's arguments in favor of the tale's validity were so powerful that American historian John Fiske included the story in his brilliant *The Discovery of America,* one of our finest histories, in 1892. Fiske accepted the Major disquisition without question, and devoted much space to it. Justin Windsor, an equally distinguished American historian, referred to it but cast doubt upon its reliability.

The most profound attack upon it came in 1898, when an Englishman, Fred W. Lucas, dissected it in most scholarly manner and demonstrated almost unequivocally that the adventures of the Zeno brothers could never have happened . . . and that the identification of *Zichmni* as Sinclair was preposterous. His lengthy and well-written book bore the ponderous title: *The Annals of the Voyages of the Brothers Niccolò and Antonio Zeno in the North Atlantic about the End of the Fourteenth Century and the Claim founded thereon to a Venetian Discovery of America.*

Of those who felt that the narrative was true, a few attempted to determine where in America Sinclair and the Zenos might have come. The detection invariably was of vague nature, since the sailing directions are almost hopeless. But the stalwart defenders of the story agreed that the Sinclair landfall must have been in Newfoundland or close to it. During the 1940s, some attention to the problem was given by Dr. William H. Hobbs, one-time professor of geology at the University of Michigan. Hobbs had approached the problem from a different angle, seeking to find a location in America which would fit the description of Antonio Zeno. His biggest clue was the "great mountain which cast forth smoke." Dr. Hobbs suspected that this smoking mountain was possibly the source of a pitch deposit, and such deposits have been known to burn naturally, giving off great clouds of dense smoke. After much research, he determined that the Western Hemisphere contained four natural pitch deposits which might fit. They were in Venezuela, Trinidad, Los Angeles, and Stellarton, Nova Scotia. Since the consensus of those giving credence to the Zeno narrative placed the site of Sinclair's landing generally in the latter area, it could only be Nova Scotia. Hobbs satisfied himself that he had the proper location, and delivered a number of lectures on the subject. One of his most interested listeners at a lecture he delivered in 1950 was Frederick Pohl, who, on hearing this seemingly positive identification, went to Nova Scotia to find the smoking mountain.

In *The Lost Discovery,* Pohl relates that he found exposed seams of bituminous near Stellarton which were known to have burned naturally within recent times. In 1832, one of the seams burned for nearly a year. The waters of the East River had to be turned into it to extinguish it. He also learned of Micmac Indian traditions which told of smoking holes in the ground in that area. Nearby, he also found caves which fit the account of the timid natives by Sinclair's "hundred good soldiers." Using the time spent by the soldiers in reaching and returning from the smoking mountain, as his guide, Pohl determined that Sinclair's good harbor could have been Guysborough.

It is reasonable to conclude that Pohl's findings are correct. The geography of the Stellarton section of Nova Scotia and its relation to Guysborough Harbour fit the geography of the Zeno narrative admirably. Pohl has since scoured the region looking for further clues, none of which has produced more tangible evidence that Sinclair did indeed inhabit—for a time—the peninsula of Nova Scotia.

But all the while Pohl and others who were interested in cracking the secret of Sinclair's landfall in America were busily scouring Nova Scotia, the most sensational clue to the prince's wanderings in America lay unnoticed on a rock near Westford, Massachusetts. The Zeno narrative, unhappily, concludes with the return of Antonio and the rebellious voyagers to the Faeroes. Nothing is told of the length of Sinclair's stay in America. As Pohl notes, he had to return sometime before 1404, for that is the year in which he died —in the Orkney Islands.

But unanswered questions remain: How long did he stay here? Did he make any attempt at exploration during his stay? Or, did he simply settle for a time in Nova Scotia? And how did he get back? Did some of his followers return for him? Or did he build a ship here to take him home? (Antonio apparently never returned to America; the record shows that he went back to Venice at some time before 1406.)

The only one of the above questions which can be answered with any certainty is the second. Without doubt, Sinclair wandered south at least as far as Westford, Massachusetts. The silent rock speaks eloquently, if wordlessly, of his presence. The original evidence on the rock was thought to be a picture, graven in the stone by Indians. It was what appeared to be the drawing of a sword, but people in the vicinity regarded it not as a sword, but as a smallish drawing of an actual Indian. It was first brought to light by William Goodwin, who ran two pictures of it in one of his books, without any caption. Goodwin didn't profess to know what it was, nor did anyone else who saw the photographs. Frank Glynn pondered over it for a long time, and leaned toward the idea that it might be viking. The hilt of the sword was plainly visible as such, but not much more of its character was revealed.

On a hunch, Glynn sent a copy of the book, with the pictures specially noted, to Thomas Lethbridge, then curator of the Museum of Archaeology and Ethnology at Cambridge University in England.

He hoped Lethbridge could either confirm his suspicions that the sword was viking, or offer some concrete opinion on its origin. A few weeks later Lethbridge wrote Glynn that the sword was of fourteenth-century origin, and would Glynn please get more details on it? Lethbridge was excited over the find. With this encouragement, Glynn set out for Westford and found the rock with the sword upon it. As he studied it, he felt there was more engraving in the rock, but since the upper portion of it was overgrown with bushes, he couldn't be sure.

He went to work with a sickle and ax and cleared away the growth obscuring the remainder of the rock. Then he carefully washed its surface down. When he had finished, he gazed upon a six-foot portrait of a knight in full armor, complete with shield bearing heraldry!

Because the faintness of the figure prevented a good photograph, he made a drawing of the outline and sent it off immediately to Lethbridge. Back came a special from the Britisher telling Glynn that it was the heraldry of the Sinclairs of Orkney!

Up to this writing, that is the story of the discovery of America in the fourteenth century by Prince Henry Sinclair, accompanied by the Venetian noble, Antonio Zeno.

There has been no wild acclaim either of Pohl's specific identification of the Stellarton site—but, more ominously, there has been almost complete apathy toward the knight in armor on the Westford rock. The NEBC Principle has here held firmly; there is no academic recognition of Glynn's verification that the figure on the rock is a knight, or that it is—amazingly—a figure that could only have been carved by someone familiar with the Sinclair heraldry. The rock, with its carving, was there when the area was settled. People thought it was Indian. Thomas Lethbridge identified it as Scottish in origin, specifically of the fourteenth century. And the news has been greeted by those who write history with remarkable restraint. Thus NEBC.

To illustrate the widespread adherence to the NEBC Principle, lest it be suspected that I do protest too much, let me offer a piece written for the *Massachusetts Archaeological Society Bulletin*, for January 1960, Vol. 21, No. 2. It appeared nearly five years after Glynn uncovered the full portrait of the knight, and was written by William Fowler, curator of the society's Bronson Museum and editor of the *Bulletin*. Mr. Fowler made a trip to see the rock and declared it

Indian. He then published his opinion in the *Bulletin,* in an article entitled "The Westford Indian Rock." There is no question in Mr. Fowler's mind that the rock is Indian. He uses the word "Indian" in the title of his piece, and sets out to prove—unquestionably—that what Glynn saw as a knight, six feet in length, holding a shield, a sword, and dressed in knightish costume, is an *Indian tomahawk* . . . about fifteen inches long. *Vive la NEBC!*

In April 1960, I went to see the rock, with Glynn and Frederick Pohl. I examined it, studied it, photographed it and marveled at it. It is, without any doubt whatever, the figure of a Scottish knight. The entire portrait has been pecked, rather than engraved, in the rock, so that it is seen as a series of small dots rather than a linear carving. I had no trouble in ascertaining it to be a knight. I saw the sword—it's there. I saw the shield—it's there. I saw no tomahawks. By no stretch of the imagination could I find a tomahawk. In Plates 35 and 36 are photographs of the carving and a line drawing showing it in more clarity. The line drawing is an accurate rendering of what is on the rock in Westford.

But Mr. Fowler says it is a tomahawk fifteen inches long.

Go to the rock yourself. It is, as I have noted, located near the town of Westford, Massachusetts, about ten miles above Concord, a few miles north of Route 25. Most people in Westford know where the rock is. When you look at it, simply ask yourself: Is it a knight in armor—or a tomahawk (fifteen inches long)?

With a bow to Mr. Fowler, but continuing firm in the conviction that the portrait on the Westford Rock is that of a Scottish knight bearing the heraldry of the Earl of Orkney, the prime question now confronts us: Why was it carved on a Massachusetts rock?

The answer can only lie in that it is a memorial—a grave marker. It also demonstrates that Prince Henry ranged far and wide in his exploration of the New World. Apparently he was on an inland journey of investigation when death overtook one of his knights, either through the homicidal intent of an Indian, or from natural causes. The knight was buried beside the rock. His portrait was carved in the rock to mark his resting place.

Now the shadow falls again.

Glynn has excavated as much of the area to the west of the rock as would be logical, without results. But he can't ever excavate the east side of the rock.

The asphalt road beside which the rock lies nearly touches the rock itself. If the ill-fortune which pursues all pre-Columbian evidence holds good here, then it is safe to conjecture that the dead knight lies peacefully and eternally under the macadam of the roadway. Unless the town extends permission to tear up the road, a costly project at best, we will never know with certainty. An interested philanthropist is needed in the Case of the Apshalt-Covered Knight: someone willing to underwrite the cost of tearing up a section of highway—and replacing it. And with no guarantee that the evidence is still there. Purely a game of chance.

There is no doubt whatever that the voyage of Prince Henry Sinclair and Antonio Zeno did take place. Between Pohl's identification of the smoking mountain and Westford's graven knight, the circumstantial evidence is clear. While I have seen no attacks on Pohl's findings, I have seen no acclaim, either. I suppose either condition can be properly attributed to the location of the smoking mountain in Nova Scotia. For those who write America's history, the distance is comfortably away from Plymouth. But the application of NEBC is seen in its most valiant strength in Mr. Fowler's paper, issued in time to dispose of another threat to our carefully plotted history.

There must be many evidences of Sinclair's route down along the New England coast. I have traveled its littoral many times in search of clues, but have met with a singular unsuccess in the effort. I am, however, positive that it lies hidden somewhere along the Middle Atlantic shore. Again we must acknowledge that such evidence, if it is or was present, has been destroyed, or mistaken for something colonial. Sinclair must have touched at dozens of places along the coast and made inland journeys as well, as the Westford Rock testifies. And in Nova Scotia, it might even be possible to find the site where he built a ship. It is evident that he did build a ship; he would not have attempted a long coastal exploration in small boats, and there is still the mystery of how he returned to the Faeroes. I think he cut the pine and oak trees of Nova Scotia and built himself a fine ship with a single mast and turreted fore- and aft-decks, and perhaps even a swan's head thrust from its stem. It certainly carried a coarse flag bearing Henry's colors and crest. In it he sailed first along the North American coast, his terminal point forever unknown, and then sailed back to Estotiland and crossed to the Faeroes. When more evidence is added to that already known, we may one day learn the full story of America's Scottish discoverer.

So endeth the tale of the brothers Zeno and their valiant commander, Prince Henry, Earl of Orkney, and discoverer of America in the fourteenth century. Only one other recorded discoverer came after Henry and before the gentleman from Genoa. He was a Portuguese, and he, too, came in from the north.

In the next chapter, then, I give you João Vaz Cortereal.

CHAPTER 19

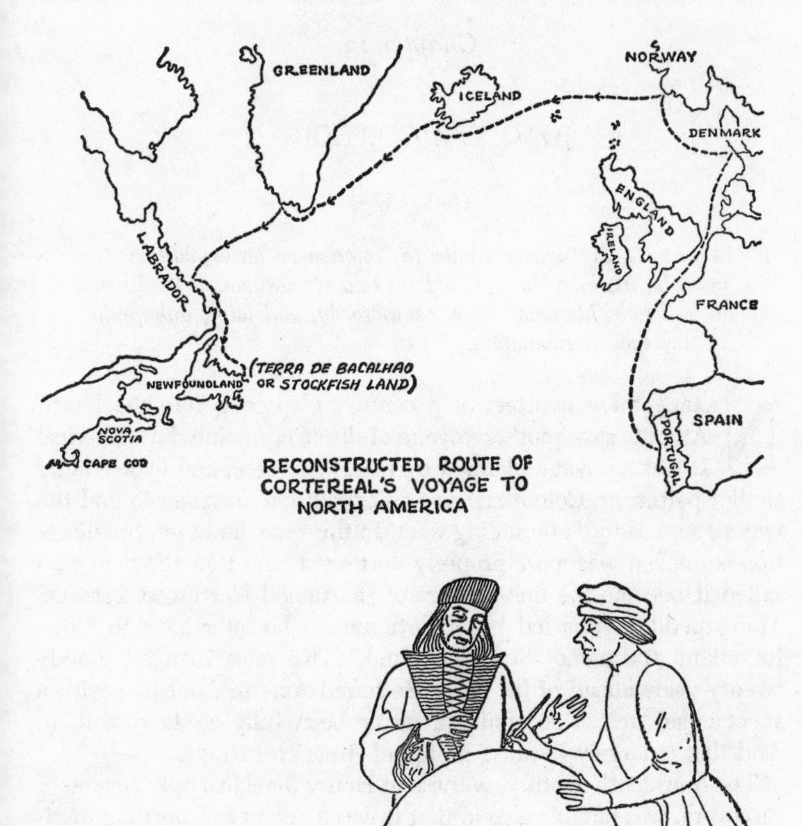
GREENLAND
NORWAY
ICELAND
DENMARK
ENGLAND
IRELAND
LABRADOR
FRANCE
(TERRA DE BACALHAO
OR STOCKFISH LAND)
NEWFOUNDLAND
SPAIN
PORTUGAL
NOVA
SCOTIA
CAPE COD
RECONSTRUCTED ROUTE OF
CORTEREAL'S VOYAGE TO
NORTH AMERICA

Chapter 19

JOÃO VAZ CORTEREAL

[A.D. 1472]

In which a Portuguese comes to America on an expedition decreed by his king, but piloted by two Norwegians. The Portuguese leaves his name here, temporarily, and later, unhappily, his two sons, permanently.

NEARLY three quarters of a century elapsed before the North Atlantic saw another voyage of discovery pointed at America. It was a voyage planned by the Portuguese, and in strikingly similar pattern to Columbus' was an expedition designed to find the water route to India by sailing west. In this case, however, the direction employed was more properly northwest, and thus the men who sailed it became the first seekers of the famed Northwest Passage. The expedition was led by a Portuguese who later gave to Newfoundland the name "Stockfish Land." This man voyaged exactly twenty years ahead of his time. He found America, but has, with a spectacular lack of recognition, never been fully credited with it. And that is largely because he found America in 1472.

The fourteenth century, witness to Henry Sinclair's epic voyage of discovery, was notable also in that it was a century of bustling maritime activity for the Portuguese, who were quietly seeking fortune in the waters of the Atlantic. In 1341, a Portuguese expedition landed in the Canary Islands and while the voyage is recorded presumably as a "first" landing, I suspect that the seafaring Portuguese knew of these islands for many years prior to the first documented date of their arrival. The Canaries had been discovered and rediscovered for centuries, doubtless going back to the years of Carthaginian sea domination. During the fifteenth century, when the Spanish Crown took possession of the islands, it was noted that a certain percentage of the population was semitic.

The Portuguese, as noted in Chapter 5, were tireless seekers of the Fortunate Isle, and, being a maritime people, it is inconceivable that they should not have come upon the Americas long before the sailor from Genoa. Their efforts directed at Atlantic investigation took them to the Azores well before the middle of the fourteenth century, and until the archives in Lisbon are properly studied, it can only be guessed that they wandered up and down the Atlantic charting and evaluating the islands they encountered, and on more than one occasion reached all the way across the Atlantic to observe the wonders of the New World.

That no real knowledge of any of these expeditions exists is due to a characteristic of the Portuguese which hearkens back to the Carthaginians. When the Portuguese began to burgeon as a seafaring, trading nation, they sought new, unknown, undeveloped sources for tradable items. They engaged, therefore, in widespread sea voyaging with an eye toward finding these suspected sources. But, in the manner of the Carthaginians, they frequently filed information gained from such explorations under the Portuguese equivalent of "top-secret," conceivably planning to assimilate all the information at some indefinite time in the future, when the atmosphere seemed right to capitalize upon it. But hints of their travels seeped out from time to time, even though the knowledge made public might have been puzzling to their contemporaries.

In 1448, for example, the Venetian, Andrea Biancho, produced a map which showed a large "island" lying in the Atlantic to the southwest of Cape Verde. Its position is startlingly near to that occupied by South America, and carries more than a slight suggestion that the Portuguese had visited that continent at some unknown time before 1448. When considering the extensive voyages undertaken by the Portuguese under Henry the Navigator, the idea is not incredible at all. Prince Henry sought to achieve the circumnavigation of Africa, and sent many expeditions down its western coast to find the extremity of the Dark Continent. While his attempts were constantly thwarted by his sailors' fear of the "unbearable, life-taking heat" which increased as one sailed south, he did succeed in sending his caravels to nearly all of the islands in the Atlantic, and occupied some. I would suspect that during the course of some of these African expeditions, the same winds and currents which were used so successfully by the Spaniards to get to South America were discovered by the Portuguese. The only terminal point of a voyage dependent on these forces would be South America or the West Indies.

Even before the all-out efforts of Prince Henry, the island journeys of the Portuguese must have brought them in contact with the Americas. In 1382, a voyage to Gran Canaria is recorded by an expedition under Francesco López. (The intriguing thought here is that gentle hints of the Portuguese peregrinations are derived from a paltry few recorded voyages. We know not how many were effected which never found public appraisal.) Additional islands in the Azores were noted and charted by Diego de Tieve and Pedro Vasquez in 1452. It is known that they were caught in a storm as they left the islands and blown northward. Their report exposes the possibility that they reached Newfoundland before returning to Portugal. The Basques, those mysterious people who live in the north of Spain and in southern France, are thought to have used the Grand Banks as fishing grounds long before Columbus. Did they obtain their knowledge of Newfoundland and its location from the Portuguese? And the Bretons, who are said to have used the same fishing grounds . . . were they receivers of Portuguese information also? It seems more than probable.

The prime motivating force behind the Portuguese excursion into foreign waters seems to have been the desire to find the water route to India, an almost universal desire in the fourteenth and fifteenth centuries, and one which the practical Portuguese took all steps possible to achieve. The multitudinous expeditions of Prince Henry failed to find the way to Asia by circumnavigating Africa, but Portuguese efforts in that direction continued long after the Good Prince's death in 1460. They confined themselves not simply to the rounding of Africa—which they eventually accomplished through Vasco da Gama—but looked speculatively toward the north, as had Henry. As a result of this latter circumstance, a warm, though unusual, relationship between the Portuguese and the Danes, begun by Henry, was carefully sustained when he died.

Henry's method in establishing friendship with a nation so far to the north was not in the least mad; he wanted to probe the arctic waters which possibly offered a route to Asia. He reasoned that Portugal would need the help of a people such as the Danes, who were familiar with arctic sailing. Psychology also played an important part in the reasoning. Henry had observed the fear displayed by his sailors when they began to encounter the fierce heat off the coast of Africa; that fear had posed the major obstacle in the search for a southern passage to Asia. The same condition, in reverse, might well thwart an expedition to the north: fear of the deadly cold. What better way to overcome such a superstition than by soliciting the aid of a maritime people thoroughly experienced in arctic sailing? The Danes, as rulers of Iceland, knew well the problems of cold-climate voyaging. And so they became the logical choice of the Portuguese as sailing partners.

Our next discoverer of America reached that distinction because of the liaison between Portugal and Denmark. His name was João Vaz Cortereal, and he came to America in 1472. The documentation of Cortereal's voyage is set forth with remarkable clarity in a short volume entitled *The Discovery of North America, Twenty Years before Columbus,* by distinguished Dr. Sofus Larsen, who, at the time of his book's publication in 1925, was chief librarian of the University of Copenhagen and a member of the Royal Northern Antiquarian Society in Denmark. He sifted through hundreds of papers, references, and royal documents to bring to light the story of a Portuguese expedition to America, authorized by King Alfonso V of Portugal and executed by two Norwegian captains, Didrik Pining and Hans Pothorst. The expedition carried João Vaz Cortereal as observer, representative of the King of Portugal, and—though neither Larsen nor others who have commented on the expedition make it clear—presumably the commander of the expedition.

The first hint of any rapport between the Danish and Portuguese kingdoms is apparent in the presence of a Dane in Portugal in 1448, and the record of his arrival and subsequent actions is found in the work of Gomez Eannes de Azurara, a noted Portuguese historian. He recounts that one Vallarte, a Dane, came to the court of the Infante, Prince Henry, at Sagres, and was commissioned as leader of an expedition to Cape Verde. This expedition was designed to seek the person and help of the king of that area in Africa, and to enlist his aid in Portugal's war against the Moors. This Negro king, Boor, was thought by Prince Henry to be a Christian, and by that token, would presumably be agreeable to assisting him in the contest with the heathen Moors. The expedition came to a sorry end. Vallarte and several others were captured, through a ruse on the part of the natives, and were never seen again. The ship which took them to Cape Verde returned to bring Henry news of this most unhappy circumstance. About 1452, Henry took some prisoners from among the inhabitants of that region and from them learned of four white men who were thought to be of the captured Vallarte party.

The foregoing episode is referred to in order to emphasize a puzzle which Larsen dwells upon at some length. In the Azurara history, he states that the Danish nobleman, Vallarte, came to the Portuguese with letters of introduction. He then wonders whether it was the news of the many Portuguese expeditions under Henry the Navigator which attracted notice in the Scandinavian countries which began the cordial relationship between Portugal and Denmark, rather than the overtures of the Infante. In any event, it is obvious that Henry's plan to cultivate the Scandinavians began at about the time of Vallarte's appearance.

The next notation of a northern visitor to the Court of Portugal is seen in a letter from Alfonso V, dated in the year after Henry's death, in which he extends a hearty commendation for one Laaland, a Dane who showed true valor in fighting the Moors in behalf of Portugal. The tone of the letter shows that happy relations with Denmark had been a continuing condition. Henry's death, then, did not halt further contacts between the nations, but only spurred Alfonso V to continue the Infante's planned search for a northwest passage.

King Alfonso eventually decided to finance an expedition to be led, physically, by the Danes, in hope of finding a northern water route to Asia and the Indies. Despite its chronicle in the history of Gomez Eannes de Azurara, no documentary proof of the voyage was known until the publication of a letter from one Carsten Grip, the Burgomaster of Kiel, to King Christian III of Denmark. The letter's owner, Dr. Louis Bobé, made it public in 1909, when he reproduced it in *Danske Magazin*, in Copenhagen. The letter was written on March 3, 1551, and states that the writer, Carsten Grip, has seen a map of Iceland, which bore a description of the strange things to be seen in that country. He then states that the map carried the information that His Majesty's grandfather, Christian I, had sent an expedition, at the request of the King of Portugal, to the new islands and the continent in the north. Holand remarks that the only islands lying beyond Greenland which had been discovered up to that time were Vinland, Markland, and Helluland, as recorded in the sagas. The continent could have referred to America, or to Asia: Christian I had once claimed that the Scandinavian Peninsula was close to, or connected with China. Since Christian I, grandfather of the letter's recipient, was regent of Denmark from 1448 to 1481, the only voyage this letter could have referred to was that of Cortereal.

The chronicle of the voyage of João Vaz Cortereal to America is necessarily a brief one, because of the previously noted reluctance of the Portuguese to publicize their finds. The beginnings of this discovery in 1472 were founded in Alfonso V's desire to continue the project his late uncle, Prince Henry the Navigator, had been so interested in: the finding of a northwest passage to India. In 1472, therefore, he sent a request to King Christian I of Denmark to supply him with ships and crews to sail the arctic waters which would presumably lead the caravan to India. The Danish king was also to supply a pilot for the expedition, one who knew the waters about Iceland and who was familiar with arctic sailing conditions. The king did more than that. He supplied two: Didrik Pining and Hans Pothorst. Pining was a freebooter who had sailed under his own and the British flag, and who had held some important offices in Denmark. He ultimately became Governor of Iceland, possibly as a reward for his participation in the Cortereal expedition. Pothorst was also a pirate, and a close friend of Pining's. That he was also possessed of some vanity is apparent in that he caused his escutcheon and portrait to be painted on one of the vaults in the Maria Church at Elsinore. For a man who pirated, and also fought pirates, for his king, a noble memorial.

The point of departure of the expedition is not known, although it is reasonable to assume that it started from Norway or Denmark, and proceeded to Iceland. From there it went to Greenland, and then to America. In the absence of a log or descriptive left to us by a historian, tracing the course of Cortereal must be accomplished through later evidences, scattered, but capable of telling the story once collated. These evidences, though few in number, establish conclusively the presence of Cortereal in America in 1472.

The most remarkable of these evidences lie in the cartography on the globe made by Martin Behaim, in 1492. It presents a delineation of the Scandinavian countries, but also shows land to the west of Iceland which bears a remarkable resemblance to Nova Scotia, Newfoundland, and the Gulf of St. Lawrence. Since no one had attempted a globe of this kind prior to Behaim, the question arises: Where did he get his information? The answer is not only simple, but verifies the voyage of João Vaz Cortereal. Martin Behaim, a famous astronomer and cartographer, was wed to Johanna de Mando in 1486. The beautiful bride was the sister of João Vaz Cortereal's son-in-law, Jobst de Utra, and, the newlyweds took up residence on the island of Terceira, which was then governed by old João. Behaim lived there for four years, or until 1490. His globe was produced in 1492. In the four years of his residence as a neighbor to the elder Cortereal, he doubtless spent many long hours with the governor, learning of the lands he had visited in 1472. Holand points out that the outline of the lands noted above are amazingly detailed, and it can be seen—if one compares this globe to the later map of the same region by John Cabot—that Behaim's is superior in some ways. It is logical to conclude, therefore, that the accuracy of the Behaim globe can only be attributed to knowledge gained from João Vaz Cortereal. It is also logical to conclude that the globe may have been seen by Columbus shortly before he sailed to America in the year of the globe's appearance.

The next proofs are seen in place names on a map of Labrador published in Kunstmann's Atlas in 1571. The map was apparently taken from an earlier version published in 1534 and bears markings for a point of land and a bay, called, respectively, *teso de João Vaz*, and *baia de João Vaz*.

Next, we find no less than five mentions of the expedition, which speak of Hans Pothorst, although the reference is by another name: Johannes Skolp, or Scolus. (There was much confusion for many years over the puzzling references to this "Scolus," until it was determined that he was one and the same with Hans Pothorst.) The references are found in an English State Paper dating from about 1575, a history by Dutch historian Cornelius Wytfleit, written in 1597, a globe made by Gemma Frisius and Gerhard Mercator in 1537, the *Historia general de las Indias*, written in 1533 by Francisco López Gómara and on a map made by Resen in 1605. In the Wytfleit reference, the name *Labrador* is used as a point of arrival, as is *Estotiland*, reminiscent of the Sinclair saga.

Finally, we have a passage in *Historia Insula* by the Portuguese historian P. Antonio Cordeyro, in which he touches upon events subsequent to Cortereal's return from America:

As the viceroy-ship of Terceyra was thus vacant on account of the death of the first vice-roy, Jacome De Bruges, thereupon there landed at Terceyra two noblemen who came from the land of stockfishes (terra de bacalhao, or Newfoundland) which they had gone out to discover by order of the Portuguese King. One called himself João Vaz Cortereal and the other Alvaro Martins Homem. Now, as soon as they had procured information about the island, it pleased them so much that they returned to Portugal and petitioned that they might have it i.e. the government of it as a reward for their services, and as our Infante Dom Henrique had already died then and had been succeeded as Governor of the Order of Christ by the Infante Dom Fernando whose widow the Infante D. Brites was still alive and as such was the guardian of her son the Duke, Dom Diego, who was a minor, this infanta rewarded the two noblemen who applied for the viceroy-ship of Terceyra by dividing it between them both, in two viceroy-ships of which one comprised Angra, the other Praya, just as that of Madeyra was divided in two: Funchal and Machico. Therefore the deed of gift of the viceroy-ship of Praya, made out to Alvaro Martins Homem, must be among the archives of the castle at Praya. The deed of gift to João Vaz Cortereal is extant; I have seen it in an old register in the archives of the castle of Angra on page 243. . . .

The quote above is from a document inspected by Cordeyro and bears the date 1474. It also contains an error in that Alvaro Homem did not accompany Cortereal on his voyage of discovery; he was doubtless included mistakenly as having come from "Stockfish Land" because of the coincidence of their receiving viceroyships at approximately the same time.

The Cortereal story is a melancholy tale. Because he was forced to undertake his voyage in such a shroud of secrecy, his discovery was never made known. Europe, in 1472, was just as ready to receive word of new lands to the west as it was in 1492. Had the news of Cortereal's voyage been proclaimed, as it should have been, it is likely that we would be, in America today, paying homage to him as we do Columbus. Of all the discoverers I have here documented, he is the one who made his discovery at a time when its revelation would have had an effect similar to that of Columbus'. That its news seeped out despite the ukase of the Portuguese Government that it be kept secret is manifest, it would seem, in the attempts made by Bristol merchants, from about 1480, to find land across the Atlantic. The most notable of these efforts was made by Thomas Lloyd, who, in 1480, scurried about the Atlantic for more than two months. Finding no land, he returned, unhappily, to Bristol. But other ships and fleets were dispatched from that famous British port for many years in attempts to find America. I cannot help but reason that these suddenly interested merchants of Bristol must have predicated their searches on the vague details they had gleaned of Cortereal's voyage.

In asserting, earlier, that Cortereal was the actual commander of the voyage, I am in conflict with the opinions of the few writers and historians who have commented upon this notable event. My colleagues—to a man—give joint command of the expedition to Pining and Pothorst, and place Cortereal aboard purely as an observer. I see no reason to view the excursion in this light. The facts decree otherwise. The map makers honored Cortereal, not Pining nor Pothorst, as a result of the voyage.

The expedition was "requested" by King Alfonso V of Portugal. The request was made of a Danish king, Christian I, who complied readily. Since Christian I was under no obligation whatever to Alfonso, the use of the word "request" is, in itself, misleading. Christian had no real reason for extending a favor to Alfonso. It is obvious, therefore, that the expedition was financed by Alfonso and put in charge of João Vaz Cortereal. The Danish king simply hired out one or more ships in command of two of his best skippers and they took their orders from Cortereal.

One puzzling aspect of the voyage is in a treaty between Portugal and Denmark which gave Christian I rights to all the lands discovered on the search. It is possible that the Portuguese king, having failed to produce India as a result of the expedition, considered the lands worthless. If that were the case, the climate changed overnight when news of Columbus' voyage was made known. The Portuguese Crown apparently thought the matter over and took a new look at this New World. After 1494, the king twice extended sole rights to Gaspar and Miguel Cortereal, sons of João, to the "islands and continent" discovered by their father.

Such grants could only mean that Portugal was abrogating the treaty, and would fight for its new lands if necessary. On May 12, 1500, King Manuel signed a grant wherein Gaspar Cortereal and his heirs were given extended rights in the lands which he "at his own expense and risk, intended to rediscover or search for." Note the use of the word "rediscover"—certainly an indication that old João had found land and that Gaspar intended to find it again and claim it for Portugal.

On his third voyage, in 1501, Gaspar was lost at sea. In 1502, his brother Miguel went searching for him, and for the land that Gaspar had found on his earlier voyages. Before he sailed, King Manuel granted him similiar rights, designating that half the lands found by his brother would be Miguel's; if proof were produced that Gaspar had indeed perished, then Miguel would receive all the lands, plus any additional lands he might discover himself. The melancholy theme of the Cortereals is climaxed here. Miguel Cortereal was never heard from again.

The voyages undertaken by the Cortereal brothers were, in every instance, financed by themselves. It was probably João's dream that his sons would inherit the lands he had seen, but which were apparently deemed worthless until the Columbus voyage created excitement over North America throughout Europe. Their fortunes were consumed, and the lands João had seen never came into the possession of his sons. Gaspar, however, did take his place in the annals of discovery, and the family name was perpetuated. The luckless Miguel, thought by Delabarre to be the inscriber of the Dighton Rock, simply vanished from the scene, his identity forgotten.

Again the shadow of misfortune manifests itself over a pre-Columbian discovery. The discoverer in this case, João Vaz Cortereal, has never received his full due for the voyage he achieved, the greater attention being paid to the Norwegians, Pining and Pothorst. The discoverer's sons met untimely deaths in the new land they hoped to bring them fortune.

But it is more than probable that João Vaz Cortereal fired Columbus with the desire to sail out across the Atlantic—thus to gain the acclaim the Portuguese never received.

Let us go now to meet Columbus and mark the close of the era that is called pre-Columbian. At the same time we will be able to judge whether or not the Genoese made his discovery by accident, or design.

CHAPTER 20

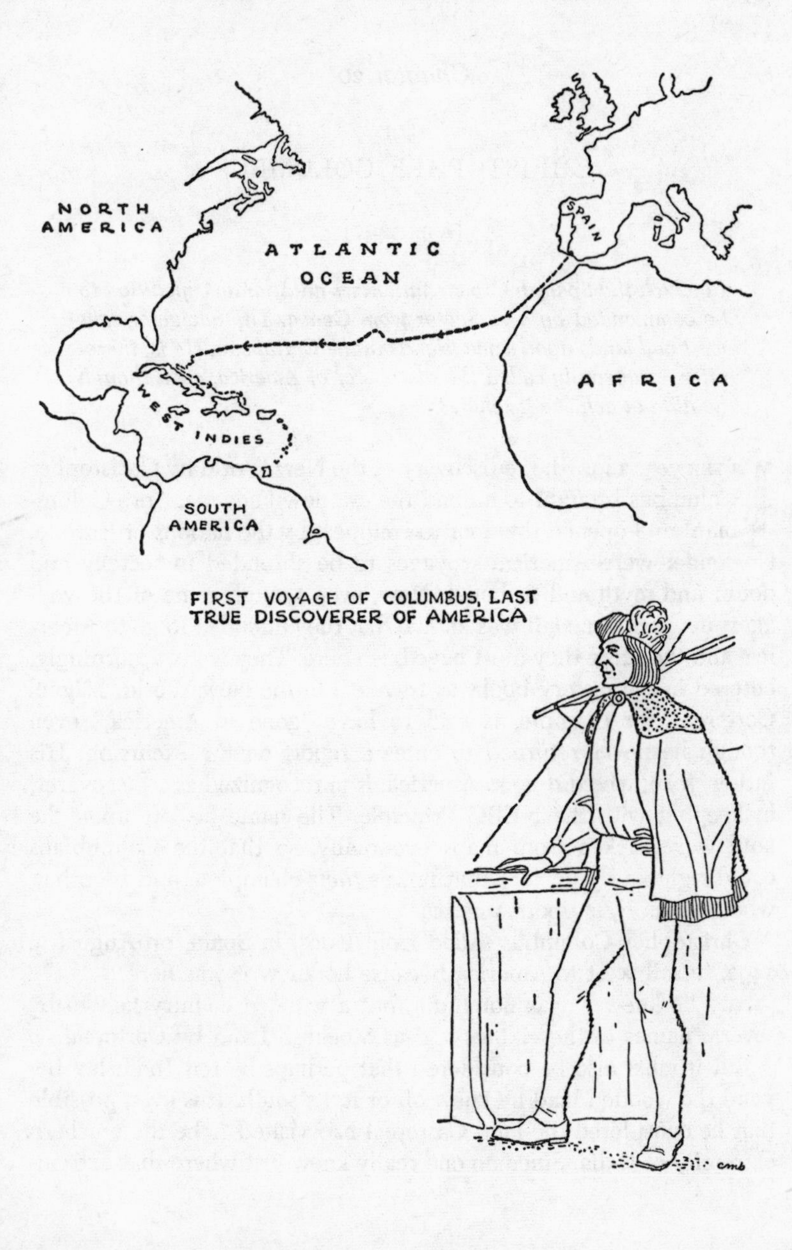

FIRST VOYAGE OF COLUMBUS, LAST TRUE DISCOVERER OF AMERICA

Chapter 20

CHRISTOPHER COLUMBUS

[A.D. 1492]

In which the Spanish Crown authorizes an Atlantic expedition to be commanded by a navigator from Genoa. The navigator sails west and lands upon some islands in the Caribbean. He is, thereafter, erroneously called the discoverer of America, even though he did not achieve its shores.

IN THE year 1492, the rediscovery of the New World by Christopher Columbus brought to an end the era now known as "pre-Columbian" and opened the door to conquest by the nations of Europe. No longer were American voyages to be shrouded in secrecy and doubt and myth and disbelief. Now, even though some of the voyagers never returned, it was known that they *intended* to go to America, and therefore they must have been here. They were, accordingly, entered in the history books as travelers to the New World. Miguel Cortereal, for example, is said to have "gone to America," even though he never returned to enter a report on the excursion. His father, João, who *did* go to America, is unrecognized as a discoverer, in keeping with the NEBC Principle. The name he left upon the land was stricken from maps eventually, so that the Columbians could righteously declare that it was *their* champion, and no other, who first set eyes upon America.

Christopher Columbus sailed from Palos, in Spain, on August 3, 1492, to sail west to America because he knew it was here.

And he knew it was not India, but a wooded country known by several names to the vikings and as Stockfish Land by Cortereal.

But it must also be considered that perhaps he felt India lay beyond the wooded land he knew of, or to its south. It is even possible that he considered the land Cortereal had visited to be the northern extremity of India. Since no one really knew just where that extremity lay, it could have been conceivable that Stockfish Land was the northern, relatively uninhabited portion of the rich, spice- and gold-producing country which was known to be warm of climate.

But I do not presume, in this volume, to dwell on the Italian navigator. His story has been told countless times by countless people. It has also been told with a variety of conflicting detail. Perhaps the best biographies of Columbus are those of Samuel Eliot Morison, but even Morison is loathe to allow Columbus any prior knowledge of America. Morison, in fact, praises Columbus for his courage in attempting to sail out over the unknown waters of the Atlantic. Respectfully, I submit such praise to be so much balderdash. The Atlantic crossing performed by Columbus was a calculated voyage, and one which he knew would bring him to land long before he reached India.

While in Galway, Columbus saw two corpses floating in an open boat. Because of their odd appearance, the Irish thought they must be Chinese. Morison hazards the guess that they were probably Finns. I suspect that they were American Indians, reminiscent of the Indians washed ashore in Germany and presented to the proconsul, Q. Metelus Celler. Columbus had seen the bamboo and "seabeans" which were cast ashore with some frequency on the islands of the Azores and Madeiras. He had also seen a map by Paolo Toscanelli which demonstrated that China and Japan were but a relatively short sail due west from Portugal.

But these are insignificant evidences that Columbus knew about land to the west. The incidents producing the most profound influences upon his decision to sail west were doubtless his visits to the Azores . . . and to Iceland.

It is hardly conceivable that Columbus, while in the Azores, did not learn of the earlier voyage of Terceira's governor, João Vaz Cortereal. Larsen seems to feel that the secrecy surrounding Cortereal's voyage was due, in part, to the old mariner himself in a desire to "save" the lands for his sons. But I can't agree completely. Had that been so, he would have helped finance Gaspar's voyage to the New World long before 1492. It was only when the news of Columbus' successful venture got abroad that the Cortereals hurried to claim the lands their father had seen and stood upon.

Meanwhile, during his governorship of the island of Terceira, and prior to the "discovery" in 1492, Cortereal surely must have talked about his own voyage of 1472. Few sailors can resist the temptation to talk about adventures which set them apart from their fellow mariners. It is certain that Cortereal talked to Behaim; his globe reflects it. But the Genoese needn't have gone to the Azores to receive intelligence of the Cortereal expedition. Sailors being what they are, the news undoubtedly penetrated the Madeiras, where Columbus went to live for a time with his new bride in 1482 or thereabouts.

His voyage to Iceland in 1477, as related in a biography by his son, wielded another profound influence. In Reykjavik, he would not only have heard about the Vinland voyages of the old vikings, but also of Cortereal, told now from the northern viewpoint and casting Pining and Pothorst as its heroes. But he would have learned one more bit of intelligence, and one which made him safe in the knowledge that he could sail to whatever it was across the Atlantic . . . and get back!

Familiar with the Madeiras and Canaries, he knew about the prevailing winds and currents which blew and flowed to the west in those regions. These, he reasoned, would take him across the Atlantic to some sort of landfall. While in Iceland, learning of sailing conditions from Vinland, it became clear that he would only have to sail north after finding land to catch the westerly winds which could carry him back to Spain. In short, Columbus was relatively sure that he could cross the Atlantic, find land, and sail back home by a northerly route.

The task he set for himself was difficult to achieve. He was turned down by Portugal and had to wait many years before the Spanish Crown would agree to finance his voyage. And even then he came close to a rejection by Queen Isabella. She did, in fact, turn him down, but was convinced, by her finance minister, after Columbus' departure from the court, that it would be wise to send this brash sailor out across the Atlantic.

The man of persuasive tongue who was directly responsible for Columbus' rediscovery of America was one Luis de Santangel, watchful guardian of the exchequer for King Ferdinand and Queen Isabella. The fable of the "pawned jewels" grew from this incident. The queen, excited by de Santangel's convincing logic, offered her jewels as bond to help finance the expedition, but Santangel asserted that he could arrange the financing himself. The beautiful queen, doubtless relieved, was permitted to keep her precious gems.

And so Columbus sailed from Palos in 1492.

It has not been the intent of this volume to detract in any way from the achievement of Columbus. I have told the stories of those who preceded him in an humble effort to gain a little recognition, and little understanding for them . . . and above all, a little dignity. They were every bit as courageous, adventuresome, romantic, determined, visionary, and practical as was the Italian sent by Spain.

But the divinity that shapes our ends has—thus far—decreed they are to be regarded by history as but "test launchings"—it was only Christopher Columbus who reached the moon.

APPENDIX

In bringing you the stories of my multitudinous pre-Columbian explorers, I have dispensed with the ubiquitous footnotes which so frequently distract the reader. There remain, however, a few random notes which should be appended for your further information.

In Chapter 2, I have reported the reluctance of Brazilian authorities to comment upon the Phoenician inscriptions found in that country. But I must acknowledge letters from Drs. Luiz de Castro Faria and Mario Ypiranga Monteiro, who sent me suggestions for further research resources, even though they would offer nothing in regard to the inscriptions personally. Dr. Faria is the distinguished head of the department of anthropology at Brazil's Museu Nacional and Dr. Monteiro is the equally distinguished President of The Academia Amazonense de Letras in Manaus. Neither of the two apparently attach any importance to the inscriptions; Dr. Faria notes that "our [in Brazil] modern archaeologists are not interested in the subject." Thus NEBC.

To the material in Chapter 3 I must add two other significant finds which hint at the presence of Romans but are seemingly not connected with the Howe Iron sites. The first, an amulet of indeterminate origin but bearing striking Roman characteristics was found in York County, Pennsylvania, near the Strong sites. I have not seen this amulet, but have examined photographs of it lent to me by Mrs. Strong, of Mechanicsburg. It certainly bears further study by archaeologists.

Second, in the Winter 1951, issue of *Archaeology,* Neil M. Judd of the Smithsonian Institution writes of three "cicada" whistles found in Missouri, Virginia, and North Carolina. They are of a type similar to insect effigy whistles sometimes made by early Romans. Mr. Judd comes to no conclusions about them and even wonders whether they might have been premiums made by a breakfast food company. His facetiousness simply serves to sharpen the mystery of their presence here in America. They were made by a mold process, but apparently a mold of such primitive nature that there are variations amongst the three despite the mass-production method used in their manufacture. Mr. Judd rejects the idea that they are Indian.

In that segment of Chapter 8 which treats on Delabarre, I have noted only a few inscribed rocks in New England. Delabarre's own book lists eighteen more, all of which he disposes of as the work of Indians or colonials. In straining for explanations of these rocks he sometimes achieves extremely amusing reasoning. Writing of a rock called the Arnold's Point Cupstone, which bears a series of six holes chiseled in the rock and connected by a shallow channel, he blandly attributed the holes to children at play. The holes are from 2½ to 2¾ inches in depth, cut in the living rock. Other rocks listed and discarded by Delabarre are those at Mount Hope, Newport, Tiverton, Portsmouth, Fogland Ferry, Middletown, Warwick, West Wrentham, and Dennison—all in Rhode Island. In Massachusetts, he notes one at Mattapoisett; one at Orient Point, Long Island; Scaticook, Connecticut; Bellows Falls, Vermont; and Machias Bay, Maine.

All bear inscriptions or strange markings; since Delabarre has clouded the picture concerning them it is impossible to obtain professional comment upon them.

Strandwold describes and translates inscriptions from stones found at Deer Lake, Ontario, a runic inscription found inside the Newport Tower, a stone on Popham Beach, Maine, a cliff inscription at Manana Island, Maine, and two stones from Ellsworth and Sebec, in Maine. He also treats on the Braxton-Wilson Tablet and the Grave Creek Tablet, both found in Virginia. These latter stones have both been pronounced forgeries and are completely ignored by scholars.

In Chapters 10, 11, 12, and 13 I have dwelt upon most of the various artifacts or other evidences left by the vikings, but there are a few more which bear mention here. In addition to the artifacts noted in the text, there are two axes reported by Frederick Pohl—both Norse—one found at East Orleans, on Cape Cod, in 1914, and another dug up at Saunderstown, Rhode Island, in 1899. Neither is in evidence today, to the best of my knowledge. Pohl also reports an intriguing circumstance at Lyons, New York. In 1838, a large tree was felled there and proved to contain ax marks made at its center. Since the tree was 460 years old, it was determined that the marks, made originally on the tree's bark, and later enveloped by the tree's growth, were made sometime in the fourteenth century by a metal implement of un-Indian origin.

Edgar Rowe Snow, in *A Pilgrim Returns to Cape Cod,* tells of a mysterious wall—or foundation—in Provincetown, thought to be Norse. It was first uncovered in 1853, on Chapel Hill. Its discoverers were amazed to find that it was mortared and showed traces of fire-blacking. The wall eventually became part of a house foundation. About 1900, some scientists from Harvard journeyed to see it and were granted permission to dig around it provided they replaced it as it had been originally. The great effort involved in such an operation discouraged them and they left without examining it. Shortly after that, a cement floor was laid in the cellar of the house and the wall forever placed beyond investigation. The house, with its hidden Norse wall, still stands in Provincetown.

Dr. Johannes Brøndsted, the Danish archaeologist, suggested, in his report on supposed viking remains in America, that a group of suspicious stone barrows near Sheepscott, Maine, be excavated in hope of producing Norse evidence. His report was issued in 1950; as of this writing in 1961, no effort has been made by the Maine Archaeological Society—or anyone—to investigate these barrows. This intelligence was supplied to me by Wendell S. Hadlock, director of the Farnsworth Museum at Rockland, Maine.

A truly amazing bit of evidence of viking penetrations of North America can be seen in the German city of Schleswig. Some twenty-odd years ago, a cathedral undergoing remodeling proved to contain a frieze adorned by no less than eight unmistakable American turkeys! Since archaeologists have dated the frieze at c. A.D. 1280, this remarkable frieze can only have resulted from the artist's reference to sketches made by American explorers of that date, or earlier. During the thirteenth century, Schleswig was a Danish City.

I am certain that much evidence remains to be uncovered in the Plymouth-Kingston area in Massachusetts, and I am continuing my own investigations of that region. I have been extremely fortunate in gaining the acquaintance of Mr. and Mrs. Robert E. Donovan of Kingston, who have extended themselves in my behalf and helped me in tracking clues. Among their efforts, the Donovans introduced me to Mr. Albert Douglas, also of Kingston, a rabid amateur archaeologist and possessed of an excellent collection of Indian artifacts. His collection also contains some other mysterious items which I cannot comment upon now. Mr. Douglas took me on several field trips to see strange evidence in and around Kingston, and on which I have formed no conclusions at this time.

While on a visit to Mr. Richard H. Bent of Plymouth to see an ax which unhappily proved to be Indian, I learned of the plight of Mr. Albert Wheeler of Pocasset, Massachusetts. Archaeologically, Mr. Wheeler is possibly the most frustrated individual in America. His frustration stems from the blustery day in 1958 when he pulled some fragments of an old ship from a pile of peat recently excavated from a bog on his own property. The fragments were identified as those of a ship—possibly old enough to be viking—by an old shipwright living in the town. On the identification of the timbers, Mr. Wheeler began to wonder about a series of odd mounds on his place—mounds which could be ancient foundations. He also wondered about an accumulation of worked iron and a pig, unrusted, which he had dug from what appeared to be an old forge site. He had generally considered his mounds and iron to be colonial. Reasoning that he might be possessed of a valuable archaeological site, much older than colonial, Mr. Wheeler wrote an extremely comprehensive and scholarly report on his finds and sent it to the Smithsonian. Then began an agonizing correspondence with the Smithsonian, the Peabody Museum, the Massachusetts Archaeological Society and others. Mr. Wheeler wanted someone to come look at his site. All of the august bodies he contacted succeeded magnificently in shunting him off to others. Those who were shuntees demonstrated remarkable agility in avoiding a visit to the site. Mr. Wheeler begged various sources for a Carbon-14 test on the ship's timbers. No results. After a great, long time, the Massachusetts Archaeological Society sent an observer to inspect the site. He inspected and left. Nothing further came of the inspection. I happened upon the frustrated gentleman last summer and spent a pleasant afternoon going over the property and examining the various artifacts, along with the ship's timbers, that Mr. Wheeler had excavated. On returning to New Canaan, I talked with Dr. Edward S. Deevey, of Yale's Geochronometric Laboratory, and told him of Mr. Wheeler's ancient ship. Dr. Deevey will make a C-14 test later this year. I have great hope that it will be revealing. I feel strongly that Mr. Wheeler's site is valuable.

The question of mooring holes has been, at best, moot since their introduction as proofs in the viking explorations of North America. In Chapter 17, I have not dwelled upon them, despite their seemingly powerful argumentation for the case of the Northmen. This apparent reluctance on my part to recognize them stems only from the conviction that they are not as powerful as are other proofs of viking visits. I do not discount them completely, but rather view them with mixed feelings; similar holes have been carved for hundreds of years by farmers, fishermen, and members of U. S. Geodetic Survey teams engaged in coastal survey. But minimizing the importance of the mooring holes in Minnesota, for instance, in no way weakens the case for the Kensington Stone. It is there, and it speaks for itself. It is truly America's oldest authenticated inscription.

SELECTED BIBLIOGRAPHY

CHAPTER ONE

BIBBY, GEOFFREY, *Testimony of the Spade,* Knopf, New York, 1956.

BIRD, JUNIUS B., *Handbook of South American Indians,* Bureau American Ethnology, Bulletin 143, 1946.

BRENNAN, LOUIS A., *No Stone Unturned,* Random House, New York, 1959.

BRYAN, KIRK, and RAY, LOUIS L., *Geologic Antiquity of the Lindermeirer Site in Colorado,* Smithsonian Misc. Collections, Volume 99, No. 2, 1949.

COVARRUBIAS, MIGUEL, *The Eagle, the Jaguar and the Serpent,* Knopf, New York, 1954.

GLADWIN, HAROLD S., *Men Out of Asia,* McGraw-Hill, New York, 1947.

HEYERDAHL, THOR, *Kon-Tiki,* Rand McNally, Chicago, 1950.

HOEBEL, E. ADAMSON, *Man in the Primitive World,* McGraw-Hill, New York, 1958.

HOOTON, EARNEST ALBERT, *Up from the Ape,* Macmillan, New York, 1931.

HOWELLS, WILLIAM, *Mankind So Far,* Doubleday, New York, 1949.

HRDLICKA, ALES, *The Genesis of the American Indian,* Proceedings of the 19th International Congress of Americanists, 1917.

———, *Exploration of the Aleutian and Commander Islands,* Exploration and Field Work, Smithsonian Institution, 1939.

———, *Exploration of the Aleutian and Commander Islands,* Exploration and Field Work, Smithsonian Institution, 1940.

JENKS, A. E., *Minnesota's Brown Valley Man and Associated Burial Artifacts,* American Antiquity Memoirs, Number 49, 1937.

PRESCOTT, WILLIAM HICKLING, *History of the Conquest of Mexico and History of the Conquest of Peru,* Modern Library, New York, 1936.

ROMER, ALFRED SHERWOOD, *Man and the Vertebrates,* University of Chicago, Chicago, 1941.

SAHAGUN, FRAY BERNARDINO DE, *Historia General de las Cosas de Nueva España, Edic. Robledo,* Mexico, 1938.

STEFANSSON, EVELYN, *Here Is the Far North,* Scribners, New York, 1957.
———, *Within the Circle,* Scribners, New York, 1945.
WENDT, HERBERT, *In Search of Adam,* Houghton Mifflin, Boston, 1956.

CHAPTER TWO

ARISTOTLE, *Politics,* Jowett and Weldon translations, 1892.
AYOOB, JOSEPH C., *Were the Phoenicians the First to Discover America?* the Compiler, Aliquippa, Pennsylvania, 1950.
CHILDE, VERE GORDON, *What Happened in History,* Parrish, London, 1960.
CHURCH, A., *Carthage, or the Empire of Africa,* New York, 1886.
DAVIS, N., *Carthage and Her Remains,* London, 1861.
FREUCHEN, PETER, *Book of the Seven Seas,* Messner, New York, 1957.
GLYNN, FRANK, *Report on Excavations at North Salem,* Eastern States Archeological Federation Report, 1959.
GOODWIN, WILLIAM B., *The Ruins of Great Ireland in New England,* Meador, Boston, 1946.
HENNIG, RICHARD, *Terra Incognitae,* Leiden, 1956.
HERRMANN, PAUL, *Conquest by Man,* Harper, New York, 1954.
HOBLEY, L. F., *Early Explorers,* Roy, New York, no date.
HOWELLS, WILLIAM, *Mankind So Far,* Doubleday, New York, 1949.
NANSEN, FRITJOF, *In Northern Mists,* Stokes, 1911.
NETTO, LADISLAUS, *La vérité sur l'inscription de la Parahyba avec facsimile des caractères phéniciens et la traduction en hébreu et français. Lettre à Monsieur Ernest Renan à propos de l'inscription phénicienne apocryphe soumise en 1872 à l'Institut historique géographique et ethnographique du Brésil.* Rio de Janeiro, 1885.
PEAK, HAROLD, and HERBERT, JOHN FLEURE, *Merchant Venturers in Bronze,* Yale University Press, New Haven, 1931.
PETERSON, MENDEL L., *History Under the Sea,* Smithsonian Institution Publication Number 4174, 1954.
RADAN, GEORGE, *Ancient Anchors and Their Special Uses,* Maritime Museum, Haifa, 1958.
———, *Helmet Found Near Ascalon,* Israel Exp. Journal, 1958.
RAMOS, BERNARDO DA SILVA, R., *Inscripcões e tradicões do América pré-histórica, especialmente do Brasil,* Imprensa Nacional, Rio de Janeiro, 1930–1939.
SCHLOTTMAN, *Janare Literaturzeitung,* No. 30, pp. 459–461, 1874.
SMITH, R. B., *Carthage and the Carthaginians,* London, 1887.

STEFANSSON, VILHJALMUR, *Great Adventures and Explorations,* Dial, New York, 1947.
———, *Northwest to Fortune,* Duell, New York, 1958.

CHAPTER THREE

CARTER, J. B., *Religious Life in Ancient Rome,* Boston, 1911.
CASSON, LIONEL, *The Ancient Mariners,* Macmillan, New York, 1959.
DRURY, VICTOR, *History of Rome and of the Roman People,* Ripley-Clarke translation, Boston, 1883–1886.
GLOVER, T. R., *The Ancient World,* Pelican, Middlesex, England, 1944.
HAYNES, E. S. P., *Religious Persecution, a Study in Political Psychology,* Duckworth, London, 1904.
HENDERSON, BERN. W., *The Life and Principate of Nero,* Methuen, London, 1903.
HODGES, GEORGE, *The Early Church,* Houghton Mifflin, Boston, 1915.
HOWE, JAMES V., Report Read to Eastern States Archaeological Federation, American Museum of Natural History, October 13, 1949.
———, Report Read to Archaeological Society of Virginia, November 11, 1949.
MC CREADY, L. S., CAPT., *The Epic Voyage and Shipwreck of St. Paul,* Publication of U.S. Merchant Marine Academy, Kings Point, New York.
TACITUS, P. C., *Church-Brodribb Translation,* Encyclopedia Britannica, Chicago, 1952.
WAGNER, EMIL F., *North American Wrought-Iron Pre-Columbian?,* Publication of the Gisholt Machine Company, Madison, Wisconsin.

CHAPTER FOUR

BEAZLEY, SIR CHARLES RAYMOND, *The Dawn of Modern Geography,* Oxford, 1897–1906.
CARRINGTON, GOODRICH L., *A Short History of the Chinese People,* New York, 1943.
COLLIER, JOHN, *Indians of the Americas,* New American Library, New York, 1959.
DONNELLY, IVON ARTHUR, *Chinese Junks,* Keeley and Walsh, London, 1920.
EKHOLM, GORDON, *Is American Indian Culture Asiatic?* Natural History Magazine, October 1950.

———, *Significant Parallels in the Symbolic Arts of Southern Asia and Middle America* (with Robert Heine-Geldern).

———, *In Tax: The Civilization of Ancient America Volume I, Proceedings of the 20th Congress of Americanists,* University of Chicago Press, Chicago, 1951.

———, *A Possible Focus of Asiatic Influences in the Late Classic Cultures of Mesoamerica,* Memoirs of the Society of American Archaeology, No. 9, 72–79, 1953.

———, *The New Orientation Toward Problems of Asiatic-American Relationships,* 75th Anniversary Volume of the Anthropological Society of Washington, 95–109, 1955.

———, *Aspects of Primitive Art,* 70–88, Museum of Primitive Art (University Publishers), New York, 1959.

GILES, H. A., *The Travels of Fa-Hsein,* Cambridge, 1923.

HORNELL, JAMES, *Junks, Sampans and Sea Rafts,* Nautical Magazine, Volume 128, 148–154, London, 1932.

LELAND, CHARLES, *Fusang,* New York, 1875.

PAN-AMERICAN UNION, *The Mayas,* Washington, 1959.

———, *The Aztecs,* Washington, 1959.

———, *The Incas,* Washington, 1959.

———, *The Auracanians,* Washington, 1959.

QUERININCUS, *The Junks of China,* Yachting Monthly, Volume 27, London, 1919.

RIVET, PAUL, *Maya Cities,* Putnam, New York, 1960.

SHARP, ANDREW, *Ancient Voyagers in the Pacific,* Pelican, Baltimore, 1957.

SMITH, MARIAN W., Editor, Asia and North America: Transpacific Contacts, Society for American Archaeology, Salt Lake City, 1953.

STEFANSSON, VILHJALMUR, *Great Adventures and Explorations,* Dial, New York, 1952.

THOMPSON, J. ERIC S., *The Civilization of the Mayas,* Chicago Natural History Museum Press, Chicago, 1958.

VAILLANT, G. C., *The Aztecs of Mexico,* Pelican, Baltimore, 1956.

VINING, EDWARD P., *An Inglorious Columbus,* Appleton-Century-Crofts, New York, 1885.

VON HAGEN, VICTOR W., *The Aztec: Man and Tribe,* New American Library, New York, 1958.

WILLETTS, WILLIAM, *Chinese Art* (two volumes) Penguin, Baltimore, 1958.

CHAPTER FIVE

BENEDICT, ROBERT D., *The Hereford Map and the Legend of St. Brendan,* Bulletin of the American Geo. Society, Volume XXIV, Number 3, 1892.

DE ROO, P., *History of America Before Columbus,* Lippincott, Philadelphia, 1900.

FAIRBANKS, CHARLES H., *Southeast Archaeology* (notes and news) American Antiquity, Volume 25, Number 2, 1959.

GOGGIN, JOHN M., *Underwater Archaeology,* American Antiquity, January 1960.

LITTLE, GEORGE A., *Brendan the Navigator,* Gill and Son, Dublin, 1946.

MOULD, D. D. C. POCHIN, *Ireland of the Saints,* Batsford, London, 1953.

O'DONOGHUE, REV. DENIS, *Brendaniana,* Dublin, 1893.

WATERS, E. G. R., Editor, *The Anglo-Norman Voyage of St. Brendan by Benedict,* Clarendon, London, 1928.

———, Editor, *An Old Italian Version of the Navigatio Sancti Brendani,* Oxford University Press, London, 1931.

WILLIAMSON, MARY MARJORIE, *Some Observations on the Legend of St. Brendan,* University of Chicago Press, Chicago, 1932.

WRIGHT, THOMAS, *St. Brendan, a Legend of the Sea,* in *Early English Poetry, Ballads and Literature of the Middle Ages,* Percy Society, London, 1884.

CHAPTER SIX

AYRES, HARRAL, *The Great Trail of New England,* Meador, Boston, 1940.

GILBERT, EDGAR, *History of Salem, New Hampshire,* Rumford, Concord, New Hampshire, 1907.

GOODWIN, WILLIAM B., *The Ruins of Great Ireland in New England,* Meador, Boston, 1940.

GWYNN, STEPHEN, *History of Ireland,* Macmillan, New York, 1923.

HENCKEN, HUGH, *The "Irish Monastery" at North Salem, New Hampshire,* New England Quarterly, Volume 12, Number 3, September 1939.

KENDRICK, T. D., *The Druids,* British Museum, Coleman, New York, 1927.

MACALLISTER, R. A. S., *The Archaeology of Ireland,* Coleman, New York, 1927.

MAC BAIN, ALEXANDER, *Celtic Mythology and Religion,* Mackay, Scotland, 1917.

MOVIUS, JR., HALLAM L., *The Irish Stone Age*, Cambridge, England, 1942.

PERRY, CLAY, *Underground New England*, Daye, Vermont, 1923.

SCOTT, ARCHIBALD B., *History of the Pictish Nation, Its People and Its Church*, Fouliso, London, 1917.

VIGFUSSON-POWELL, *Origines Islandicae*, Clarendon, 1905.

WILLOUGHBY, CHARLES C., *Antiquities of the New England Indians*, Harvard University Press, Cambridge, 1935.

CHAPTER EIGHT

BRØNDSTED, JOHANNES N., *Problemet Om Nordboer I Nordamerika før Columbus*, Aarbog for Nordisk Oldkyndighed og Historie, Copenhagen, 1951.

DELABARRE, EDMUND BURKE, *The Dighton Rock*, Neale, New York, 1928.

GOODWIN, WILLIAM B., *The Ruins of Great Ireland in New England*, Meador, Boston, 1946.

HOLAND, HJALMAR R., *Explorations in America Before Columbus*, Twayne, New York, 1956.

RAFN, CARL CHRISTIAN, *Antiquitates Americanae*, Copenhagen, 1837.

REEVES, A. M., *The Finding of Wineland the Good*, London, 1895.

STRANDWOLD, OLAF, *Norse Inscriptions on American Stones*, Bjorndal, 1948.

CHAPTER NINE

DU CHAILLU, PAUL, *The Viking Age*, (two volumes), Scribners, New York, 1889.

GATHORNE-HARDY, G. M., *The Norse Discoverers of America*, Clarendon, 1921.

POHL, FREDERICK, *The Lost Discovery*, Norton, New York, 1952.

STORM, GUSTAV, *Studier Over Vinlandsreiserne*, Aarbog for Nordisk Oldkyndighed og Historie, Copenhagen, 1887.

CHAPTER TEN

ANDERSON, RASMUS B., *The Norse Discoverers of America*, Norroena Society, New York, 1907.

BJORNBO, A. A., *Adam of Bremens Nordensopfattelse*, Aarbogr for Nordisk Oldkyndighed og Historie, Series 2, XXIV, 120–244.

BOLAND, CHARLES MICHAEL, *Iceland and Greenland,* American Geo. Society, New York.

BRØNDSTED, JOHANNES N., *Problemet Om Nordboer I Nordamerika før Columbus,* Aarbog for Nordisk Oldkyndighed og Historie, Copenhagen, 1951.

———, *The Vikings,* Penguin, Baltimore, 1960.

BURE, KRISTJAN, *Greenland,* Bogtrykkeri, Copenhagen.

DEETZ, JAMES, *Excavations at the Joseph Howland Site, Rocky Nook, Kingston, Mass., 1959: A Preliminary Report,* the Howland Quarterly, January–April, 1960.

———, *The Howlands at Rocky Nook,* the Howland Quarterly, July 1960.

DIESERUD, JUUL, *Norse Discoveries in America,* American Geog. Society, New York, 1901.

DU CHAILLU, PAUL, *The Viking Age,* (two volumes) Scribners, New York, 1889.

EINARSSON, STEFAN, *History of Icelandic Literature,* Hopkins, New York, 1957.

FAIRBRIDGE, RHODES W., *Recent World-Wide Sea Level Changes,* Bulletin of the Massachusetts Archaeology Society, April–July, 1960.

FERNALD, M. L., *Notes on the Plants of Wineland the Good,* Rhodora, Volume 12, Number 134, February 1910.

FISKE, JOHN, *The Discovery of America,* (two volumes) Houghton Mifflin, New York, 1892.

FLATEYBOOK, THE, Norroena Society, New York, 1906.

GATHORNE-HARDY, G. M., *The Norse Discoverers of America,* Clarendon, 1921.

HERMANNSSON, HALLDOR, *The Problem of Wineland,* Cornell, Ithaca, New York, 1936.

HOLAND, HJALMAR R., *Explorations in America Before Columbus,* Twayne, New York, 1956.

HORSFORD, EBEN NORTON, *The Landfall of Leif Erikson, A.D. 1000,* Boston, 1892.

HOVGAARD, WILLIAM, *The Norsemen in Greenland,* Geo. Review, Volume XV, Number 4, October 1925.

KOHL, J. G., *Discovery of America,* (two volumes) Chapman Hall, London, 1862.

LAING, SAMUEL, *Translation: Heimskringla,* London, 1844.

MAC LEAN, J. F., *Critical Examination: Norse Discovery of America,* American Antiquarian Office, Chicago, 1892.

MALMBERG-BRIEM, *Iceland,* Nordisk Rotogravyr, Stockholm.

MITCHELL, P. M., *History of Danish Literature,* American Scandinavian Foundation, New York, 1958.

OLD ICELANDIC DICTIONARY, Oxford Press, 1926.

OLSEN-BOURNE, Editors, *The Northmen, Columbus and Cabot*, Scribners, New York, 1906.

PIGGOTT, DANIEL, *Ancient British Art*, Cambridge, London, 1951.

POHL, FREDERICK, *The Lost Discovery*, Norton, New York, 1952.

REEVES, A. M., *The Finding of Wineland the Good*, London, 1895.

REMAN, EDWARD, *The Norse Discoveries and Explorations in America*, University of California, Berkeley, 1949.

ROBBINS, ROLAND W., and JONES, EVAN, *Hidden America*, Knopf, New York, 1959.

SAUNDERS, FREDERICK, *The Story of the Discovery of the New World*, Whittaker, New York, 1892.

SJØVOLD, THORLIEF, *The Oseberg Find*, Universitetes Oldsaksamling, Oslo, 1957.

SMITH, JOSHUA TOULMIN, *The Northmen in New England*, Hilliard Grey, Boston, 1839.

STEENSBY, H. P., *The Norsemen's Route*, Forlag, Denmark, 1918.

STEFANSSON, VILHJALMUR, *Iceland: The First American Republic*, Doubleday, Doran, New York, 1939.

STEWART, GEORGE R., *Names on the Land*, Random House, New York, 1945.

CHAPTER ELEVEN

BRØNDSTED, JOHANNES N., *The Vikings*, Penguin, Baltimore, 1960.

CERAM, C. W., *Gods, Graves and Scholars*, Knopf, New York, 1951.

FLATEYBOOK, THE, Norroena Society, New York, 1906.

GATHORNE-HARDY, G. M., *The Norse Discoverers of America*, Clarendon, 1921.

JOHNSON, DOUGLAS W., *The New England Acadian Shoreline*, Wiley, New York, 1925.

KNEELAND, SAMUEL, Twentieth Annual Report of the Peabody Museum, Volume III, Number 7, pp. 543–546, British Museum, Coleman, New York, 1927.

MEANS, PHILIP AINSWORTH, *The Newport Tower*, Holt, New York, 1942.

OLD ICELANDIC DICTIONARY, Oxford Press, 1926.

POHL, FREDERICK, *The Lost Discovery*, Norton, New York, 1952.

REEVES, A. M., *The Finding of Wineland the Good*, London, 1895.

CHAPTER TWELVE

FLATEYBOOK, THE, Norroena Society, New York, 1906.

GOODWIN, WILLIAM B., *The Ruins of Great Ireland in New England,* Meador, Boston, 1946.

OLD ICELANDIC DICTIONARY, Oxford Press, 1926.

PHILLIPS, HENRY, JR., Report to the Antiquarian Society of Philadelphia, February 5, 1880.

POHL, FREDERICK, *The Lost Discovery,* Norton, New York, 1952.

REEVES, A. M., *The Finding of Wineland the Good,* London, 1895.

CHAPTER THIRTEEN

BRADFORD, WILLIAM, *History of the Plymouth Settlement* (Paget process), Dutton, New York, 1909.

FLATEYBOOK, THE, Norroena Society, New York, 1906.

GATHORNE-HARDY, G. M., *The Norse Discoverers of America,* Clarendon, 1921.

LAING, SAMUEL, *Translation: Heimskringla,* London, 1844.

OLD ICELANDIC DICTIONARY, Oxford Press, 1926.

POHL, FREDERICK, *The Lost Discovery,* Norton, New York, 1952.

REEVES, A. M., *The Finding of Wineland the Good,* London, 1895.

CHAPTER FOURTEEN

AMERICAN HERITAGE, *Book of Great Historic Places,* Simon and Schuster, New York, 1957.

BRØNDSTED, JOHANNES N., *Problemet Om Nordboer I Nordamerika før Columbus,* Aarbog for Nordisk Oldkyndighed og Historie, Copenhagen, 1951.

CARLI, BERNARDO, Letter: New York State Local History Source Leaflets, University of the State of New York, 1916.

FITE-FREEMAN, *A Book of Old Maps,* Cambridge, Mass., 1926.

GODFREY, WILLIAM S., *The Newport Tower II,* Archaeology, Summer 1950.

HOLAND, HJALMAR R., *Explorations in America Before Columbus,* Twayne, New York, 1956.

MEANS, PHILIP AINSWORTH, *The Newport Tower,* Holt, New York, 1942.

NEW YORK HISTORICAL SOCIETY, Collections, Volume II, pp. 217–218, 1869.

POHL, FREDERICK, *The Newport Tower: An Answer to Mr. Godfrey*, Archaeology, Autumn 1951.

———, *Was the Newport Tower Standing in 1632?*, New England Quarterly, Volume 13, Number 4, December 1945.

———, *The Lost Discovery*, Norton, New York, 1952.

RICHARDSON, EDWARD ADAMS, *The Builder of the Newport Tower*, Journal of the Surveying and Mapping division, Proceedings of the American Society of Civil Engineers, February 1960.

CHAPTER FIFTEEN

BARLOW, ROBERT H., *The Extent of the Empire of the Culhua Mexica*, Ibero-American Series Number 28, Berkeley and Los Angeles, University of California Press, 1949.

HEYERDAHL, THOR, *Kon-Tiki*, Rand McNally, Chicago, 1950.

MASON, JOHN ALDEN, *The Ancient Civilizations of Peru*, Penguin, Baltimore, 1957.

PETERSON, FREDERICK A., *Ancient Mexico*, Putnam, New York, 1959.

PRESCOTT, WILLIAM HICKLING, *History of the Conquest of Mexico* and *History of the Conquest of Peru*, Modern Library, New York, 1936.

VON HAGEN, VICTOR W., *The Aztec: Man and Tribe*, New American Library, New York, 1958.

———, *Realm of the Incas*, New American Library, New York, 1957.

CHAPTER SIXTEEN

BELKNAP, JEREMY, *Belknap's Biographies of the Early Discoveries of America*, New York, 1798.

CATLIN, GEORGE, *O-Kee-Pa*, Trunner, London, 1867.

———, *The Manners, Customs and Conditions of the North American Indians*, Hengbohn, London, 1857.

DURRETT, REUBEN F., *Traditions of the Earliest Visits of Foreigners to North America*, Filson Club, Louisville, 1908.

FUNKHOUSER, WILLIAM D., and WEBB, W. S., Reports in Archaeology and Anthropology, Volume II, University of Kentucky, September 1932.

HAKLUYT, *Voyages*, London, 1582.

CHAPTER SEVENTEEN

ANDERSON, RASMUS B., Editorial: *Draw Your Own Conclusions,* Amerika, Madison, Wisconsin, May 27, 1910.

BIBBY, GEOFFREY, *Testimony of the Spade,* Knopf, New York, 1956.

BRØNDSTED, JOHANNES N., *Problemet Om Nordboer I Nordamerika før Columbus,* Aarbog for Nordisk Oldkyndighed og Historie, Copenhagen, 1951.

CURRELLY, C. T., *Viking Weapons Found Near Beardmore,* Ontario, Canadian Historical Review, 1919.

DE LAND, CHARLES E., *Vérendrye's Journey to the Mandans,* South Dakota Historical Collections, Volume 7.

EINARSSON, STEFAN, *The Kensington Stone,* Speculum Medieval Academy of America, Cambridge, Mass., 1933.

HAGEN, S. N., *The Kensington Runic Inscription,* The Medieval Academy of America, Speculum Volume XXV, Number 3, July 1950.

HOLAND, HJALMAR R., *The Kensington Stone,* Holand, Ephraim, Wisconsin, 1932.

———, *America: 1355–1364,* Duell, New York, 1946.

———, *Westward from Vinland,* Duell, New York, 1940.

———, *Explorations in America Before Columbus,* Twayne, New York, 1956.

MOLTKE, ERIK, *The Kensington Stone,* Mass. Archeo. Soc. Bulletin, July 1952.

STORM, GUSTAV, *Studier over Vinlandsreiserne,* Aarbog for Nordisk Oldkyndighed og Historie, Copenhagen, 1887.

THALBITZER, WILLIAM, *Two Runic Stones from Greenland and Minnesota,* Smithsonian Misc. Collections, Volume 116, Number 3.

WAHLGREN, ERIK, *The Kensington Stone: A Mystery Solved,* University of Wisconsin Press, Madison, Wisconsin, 1958.

WINCHELL, N. H., Article: *The Norwegian American,* Northfield, Minnesota, June 6, 1910.

CHAPTER EIGHTEEN

FISKE, JOHN, *The Discovery of America* (two volumes), Houghton Mifflin, New York, 1892.

FOWLER, WILLIAM, *The Westford Indian Rock,* Bulletin of the Mass. Archeo. Society, January 1960.

LUCAS, FRED W., *Annals of the Brothers Niccolò and Antonio Zeno,* London, 1898.

POHL, FREDERICK, *The Lost Discovery,* Norton, New York, 1952.

WINSOR, JUSTIN, *Narrative and Critical History,* Volume I, Houghton Mifflin, Boston, 1889.

CHAPTER NINETEEN

BEAZLEY, SIR CHARLES RAYMOND, *Prince Henry the Navigator,* New York and London, 1895.

BJØRNBO, A. A., *Johannes Scolvus,* Berlingske Tidende, July 7, 1909.

DAAE, LUDWIG, *Didrik Pining,* Norsk KistTidsskrift, Series 2, Volume 3, Oslo, 1882.

DE AZURARA, GOMEZ EANNES, *The Chronicle of the Discovery and Conquest of Guinea,* Hakluyt Society, London, 1896–1899.

HARRISSE, HENRY, *The Discovery of America,* New York, 1892.

———, *Les Corte-Reals et leur Voyages au Nouveau-Monde,* Paris, 1883.

HOLAND, HJALMAR R., *Explorations in America Before Columbus,* Twayne, New York, 1956.

LARSEN, SOFUS, *The Discovery of North America, 20 years Before Columbus,* Levin and Munksgaard, Copenhagen, 1925.

MARKHAM, CLEMENT R., *The Journal of C. Columbus and Docs. relating to the Voyages of John Cabot and Gaspar Cortereal,* London, 1893.

MARTINS, J. P. OLIVIERA, *The Golden Age of Prince Henry the Navigator,* Abraham-Reynolds Translation, London, 1914.

CHAPTER TWENTY

COLON, FERDINAND, *Life of Colon,* London, 1812.

MORISON, SAMUEL ELIOT, *Admiral of the Ocean Sea,* Little, Brown, Boston, 1942.

———, *Christopher Columbus,* Mentor, New York, 1956.

OLSEN-BOURNE, Editors, *The Northmen, Columbus and Cabot,* Scribners, New York, 1906.

APPENDIX

SNOW, EDGAR ROWE, *A Pilgrim Returns to Cape Cod,* Yankee, Boston, 1946.

INDEX